PLACES THAT COUNT

Heritage Resources Management Series

Series editor Don Fowler, University of Nevada, Reno

Sponsored by the Heritage Resources Management Program
Division of Continuing Education, University of Nevada, Reno

Books in this series are practical guides designed to help those who work in cultural resources management, environmental management, heritage preservation, and related subjects. Based on a series of successful workshops sponsored by the University of Nevada, Reno, the books are designed to be "workshops between book covers" on important strategic, legal, and practical issues faced by those who work in this field. Books are replete with examples, checklists, worksheets, and worldly advice offered by experienced practitioners in the field. Future titles in this series will deal with assessing historical significance, management of archaeological sites, working with native communities, and other topics.

Volumes in the series:

1. *Cultural Resource Laws and Practice: An Introductory Guide*, Thomas F. King (1998)

2. *Federal Planning and Historic Places: The Section 106 Process*, Thomas F. King (2000)

3. *Assessing Site Significance: A Guide for Archaeologists and Historians*, Donald L. Hardesty and Barbara J. Little (2000)

4. *Tribal Cultural Resource Management: The Full Circle to Stewardship*, Darby C. Stapp and Michael S. Burney (2002)

5. *Thinking about Cultural Resource Management: Essays from the Edge*, Thomas F. King (2002)

6. *Places That Count: Traditional Cultural Properties in Cultural Resource Management*, Thomas F. King (2003)

PLACES THAT COUNT

Traditional Cultural Properties in Cultural Resource Management

Thomas F. King

ALTAMIRA
PRESS

A Division of
ROWMAN & LITTLEFIELD PUBLISHERS, INC.
Walnut Creek • Lanham • New York • Oxford

All author's royalties from sale of this book are donated to Cultural Survival, Inc., an organization that works to help beleaguered societies the world over retain their cultures, languages, special places, and lives in the face of development and change. For information on Cultural Survival, see www.cs.org.

AltaMira Press
A Division of Rowman & Littlefield Publishers, Inc.
1630 North Main Street, #367
Walnut Creek, CA 94596
www.altamirapress.com

Rowman & Littlefield Publishers, Inc.
A Member of the Rowman & Littlefield Publishing Group
4501 Forbes Boulevard, Suite 200
Lanham, MD 20706

PO Box 317
Oxford
OX2 9RU, UK

British Library Cataloguing-in-Publication Information Available

Library of Congress Cataloging-in-Publication Data
King, Thomas F.
  Places that count : traditional cultural properties in cultural resource management / Thomas F. King.
    p. cm. — (Heritage resource management series ; v. 6)
  Includes bibliographical references and index.
  ISBN 0-7591-0070-5 (alk. paper)—ISBN 0-7591-0071-3 (pbk.: alk. paper)
  1. Historic sites—Conservation and restoration—United States. 2. Cultural property—Protection—United States. 3. Historic Preservation—United States. 4. United States—Cultural policy. 5. United States—Antiquities. I. Title. II. Series.

E159.K567 2003
363.6'9'0973—dc21
                                                    2003002716

Printed in the United States of America

♾ The paper used in this publication meets the minimum requirements of American National Standard for Information Sciences—Permanence of Paper for Printed Library Materials, ANSI/NISO Z39.48–1992.

For Pat, whether she likes it or not.

Contents

Foreword

HERITAGE preservation in the United States, and in most other nation-states, is long on practice and process and short on philosophy. In the United States, this is principally because heritage preservation is mandated by a plethora of laws and regulations based on the declaration ("Congress finds and declares . . .") that preserving the places and things of the past is a public good, is "in the public interest." But the "why" assumptions underlying the declaration are usually taken-for-granted truisms, not philosophically examined arguments. They assume that "places of association" mean *primarily* places *(qua* properties in the real estate sense) associated with "great" events important to the dominant society or with said-to-be-important dead white males. As Tom King points out in the present work, the laws and regulations were written by individuals who thought principally in these terms. They did, however, include some language recognizing that the country is a pluralistic, multiethnic, multi-cultural society. Within this mix, groups of every ethnic, social, and cultural persuasion are deeply concerned with the preservation and protection of an enormous range of places *other than* those associated with great events or reputedly great dead white males. The concerns exist in a multiplicity of senses for an enormous number of deeply understood, but often not publicly defined or, in some instances, even publicly discussable, reasons.

To try to help members of the heritage industry—individuals who earn their living "doing" historic preservation, cultural resource management (CRM), or heritage preservation—as well as all interested others recognize and understand places and the multiplicity of meanings attached thereto, King and his spouse and colleague, Patricia Parker, wrote *Guidelines for Evaluating and Documenting Traditional Cultural Properties* (TCPs), published in 1990 as Bulletin 38 of the National Register of Historic Places. The present work is an exegesis of the *Guidelines* and how they have been used to date in conjunction with other preservation laws and regulations, coupled with King's philosophical ruminations about how they might have been, and might yet be, better used in the interests of everyone concerned with the preservation of traditional places in all their kaleidoscopic and culturally variegated forms.

Both the exegesis and ruminations are elegantly and eloquently presented. King knows preservation laws and regulations perhaps better than any one in the country, and he is keenly aware that, in the end, both are matters of (often contested) interpretation. He also has delved deeply into, and thought deeply about, the best of past and present writings on "place" and "sense of place"—for example, the profoundly insightful works of Keith Basso and Eugene Anderson. King has two main themes: (1) What does a place *mean* to the group, or groups, that value it for one or many different reasons, and how might the place, its ambience and its meanings, best be preserved and protected from on-going change? (2) What is the best way, or ways, for all parties concerned with a traditional place and its integrity and continuity to see to its preservation?

King's answer to both is essentially to adhere to Socrates' Court of Reason. Socrates was concerned with two very human issues, reason and the moral basis for decision making and action. He recognized the importance of "keeping the talk going," and *keeping it going in terms that did not discriminate, in principle, between any and all parties to any issue.* "Reasoning together" in a context of humanistic sympathy and fairness for all the thoughts and positions of all sides constitutes the Court of Reason. In the Renaissance, those who achieved *humanitas*, in Michel de Montaigne's or Giannozzo Manetti's sense of the term, were said to conduct themselves in this manner. King urges that discussions and decisions about TCPs would best be conducted in this framework. But, then, discussions and decisions in the framework of much else in heritage resource management, and beyond, would be better served if those involved acted in this way. Tom King's *humanitas* is deeply felt and cogently expressed. We would do well, in the interests of heritage preservation in general and TCPs in particular, to listen to—and act upon—what he has to tell us.

Don Fowler

Acknowledgments

FOR several reasons, in writing this book I have not consulted my National Register Bulletin 38 coauthor Patricia Parker—Pat has complete deniability when it comes to the opinions and interpretations offered here. But among those whose help, advice, inspiration, and direction I acknowledge here, I have to give her primacy of place. Without her inspiration, guidance, and fellowship, I might or might not have stumbled by myself into involvement with traditional cultural properties, but I suspect that the stumbling would have been a lot less interesting and perhaps enlightened than it's been in her company.

I'm also especially in debt to the Agua Caliente Band of Cahuilla Indians for putting my feet on the TCP path back in 1971. Pat Patencio, Richard Milanovitch, and particularly Tony Andreas had a lot to do with setting my direction, though they bear no blame for the ways I've wandered.

Other communities whose efforts to protect their special places have inspired and influenced me, and taught me important lessons, include the Mahilkaune Pomo; the Fallon Paiute-Shoshone Tribe; the people of Poletown in Detroit and Stiltsville in Biscayne Bay; the elders and leaders of villages in Yap, Palau, Pohnpei, Saipan, Chuuk, and Kosrae; the Protect Kaho'olawe Ohana; the defenders of Yellow Thunder Camp; the Pamunkey, Mattaponi, and Upper Mattaponi Tribes of Virginia; the Hualapai Tribe; the Tlingit people of Sitka; the people of Iras and Mechchitiw Villages; the Quechan Tribe; and the Bad River, Red Cliff, and Mole Lake Bands of Great Lakes Ojibwe. I'm especially grateful to Fred Ackley, Vic April, Floyd Buckskin, Yolanda Chavez, Adeline Fredin, Reba Fuller, David Grignon, Jan Hammil, Johnson Holyrock, Deb Hutt, Ikefai of Satawal, Kelly Jackson, Loretta Jackson, Teddy John, Vicki Kanai, Andrew Kugfas, Bill Kuenen, Pensile Lawrence, Al Lizama, Donna McFadden, Nathan Napoka, Camillo Noket, Mao Pialug, Kealoha Pisciotta, Lorri Planas, Moses Sam, Fran Van Zile, Robert Van Zile, Bill Tallbull, Jeff Van Pelt, and Mati Waiya.

I'm grateful to all the people—friends, acquaintances, enemies, and people whose works I've only read—who've struggled with TCP studies and things like them. Special thanks are due John Anfinson, Scott Anfinson, Roger Anyon, Mike Backsh, Lowell Bean, Richard Begay, Judy Brunson Hadley, Julia Costello, Dave Cushman, Sherrie Deaver, Mike Evans, Nancy Farrell, T. J. Ferguson, Kay Fowler, Harris Francis, Will Gilmore, Sally

Greiser, Sissel Johannesen, Klara Kelley, Larry Nesper, Alexa Roberts, Darby Stapp, Richard Stoffle, Dotty Theodoratus, Gail Thompson, Sylvia Vane, Edrie Vincent, Anna Willow, Robert Winthrop, and Clyde Woods.

Although no one but me is responsible for this book's errors, omissions, and peculiarities, a number of people have helped me write it. Carol Legard and Alan Stanfill have kept me straight on a number of Section 106 cases, and Alan Downer, Alexa Roberts, and Klara Kelley have advised me about some Navajo cases. Sandy Zelmer kindly shared with me her comprehensive review of "sacred sites" case law long before its publication, and Ellen Prendergast shared her master's thesis on *Chelhtenem*. Lisa Duwall introduced me to the work of Randolph Hester. Bob Jeske read and critiqued chapter 8, Marrilie Gunnier did the same for chapters 1 and 9, and Jack Elliot suffered through chapter 5. Darby Stapp, Don Fowler, and Deborah Morse-Kahn read the whole thing and gave me a great deal of helpful advice. Larry Nesper put me on to Marshall Sahlins's thoughts about the invention of tradition. Sherrie Deaver introduced me to ethnohabitats; it's only a shame I couldn't do more with the concept.

Others whose influences I've felt in preparing for and writing this book—some teachers, some critics, some supporters, some questioners and challengers, and all broadeners of perspective—include Sherman Banker, Michelle Berditschevsky, Elaine Blender, Michael Bond, Sarah Bridges, Michael Burney, Anita Canovas, Dave Carmichael, Charles Carroll, Jim Carucci, Duane Christian, Jamie Cleland, Courtney Coyle, Richard Davis, Bill Dodge, Dwight Duetschke, Rob Edwards, Jack Elliott, Carl Fleishhauer, Fran Gale, Bob Garvey, Tom Gates, Mike Gawel, Ric Gillespie, Ward Good-enough, Cynthia Grassby-Baker, J. T. Griffin, Lydia Grimm, Andy Guilliford, Sean Hagerty, Brian Haley, Fr. Fran Hezel, Shauna Holmes, Lea Hong, Nancy Howard, Jane Hubert, Mary Hufford, Alan Jabbour, Russ Kaldenberg, Hans Kreutzberg, Dale Lanzone, Rodney Little, Ron May, Toby McLeod, Tim McKeown, Charles Miller, Mike Moratto, Dave Morris, Reid Nelson, Loretta Neumann, Steve Newman, Claudia Nissley, Michael Nixon, Peter Noyes, Dave Phillips, Fred Plog, Nichol Price, Daniel Pratt, James Reap, Deldi Reyes, Mike Roberts, Glenn Reynolds, Dave Rotenstein, Scott Russell, Kurt Russo, Lynne Sebastian, Tim Smith, John Snyder, George Somerville, Sam Stokes, Dean Suagee, Nina Swidler, Sonia Tamez, Ken Tapman, Al Tonetti, Joe Trnka, John Welch, Larry Wilcoxon, Frank Winchell, Bob Yohe, and innumerable participants in my classes and in discussions on ACRA-L.

Finally, as always I'm grateful to Mitch Allen and his hardworking colleagues at AltaMira Press for their patience, encouragement, useful critiques, and understanding, to say nothing of simply making this book possible.

And if I weren't dedicating this book to Pat Parker, I'd do so in respectful memory to two of the profoundest influences on us both, her late Chuukese parents Katin and Nesema, who more than anyone else taught me to respect the cultural landscape.

Chapter One

Getting Started with TCPs

> [Among] the most basic dimensions of human experience [is] that
> close association of heart and mind, often subdued yet potentially
> overwhelming, that is known as *sense of place.*
> —anthropologist Keith Basso (1996:106)

What's This Book About?

IN 1990, in a publication of the U.S. National Register of Historic Places[1] widely if obscurely referred to as "National Register Bulletin 38,"[2] Patricia Parker and I coined the term *traditional cultural property* (TCP). We used these innocent words to refer to places that communities think are important, because they—the places—embody or sustain values, character, or cultural coherence. A fancy way of saying places that *count* to ordinary people, are held dear by them, whatever significance they may have for professional scholars. The bulletin's purpose was to clarify how such places could be eligible for the National Register and hence be accorded a degree of protection by federal law.[3]

Our made-up term and its acronym *TCP* have come to be used familiarly by practitioners of historic preservation[4] and cultural resource management (CRM)[5] in the United States, though there is argument about their meaning and proper use. How to deal with TCPs has been hotly discussed from time to time, at one point even generating a threat of legislation forbidding their identification and management. Not a very credible threat, but enough to panic a federal official or two.

A rising concern for places to which communities ascribe value is by no means limited to the United States. It's worldwide, passing under different names in different countries, regions, and academic milieus. It's one expression of the ferment over loss of cultural diversity and local autonomy to spreading

1

globalism. In the context of what's variously called cultural resource management, heritage protection, and historic preservation, it also reflects the perception that programs for the protection of cultural resources have been co-opted—or dominated from their inception—by disciplinary experts, to the detriment of ordinary people.

This book is about traditional cultural properties—or places, as some prefer[6]—in the United States, though I hope that it will have some relevance to people in other countries and at the same time help people in the United States put TCPs in an extranational context. It responds to calls from cultural resource practitioners for guidance about how such places should be addressed under U.S. environmental protection and cultural resource law and policy.

I have no official brief whatever to provide such guidance; thankfully, I am no longer with the federal government. But I hope that the thoughts of one who has considered TCP issues in some depth will have value and be considered by those who for better or worse inevitably *will* produce official direction.

I'll begin with a brief account of how the U.S. government came to issue guidance about TCPs and how the term came to be. Next I'll try to put U.S. practice in larger geographic and theoretical contexts. I'll then look at what I think we've learned in over a dozen years of explicit work with such properties. Based on this experience, and what can be adduced from the experience and writings of others, I'll end by trying to offer some recommendations.

Who Should Read This Book?

I've written this book for people who are struggling with TCP issues in their work as agency officials, state officials, members or employees of Indian tribes and other indigenous groups, consultants, members of community organizations, or simply concerned private citizens. Reading it may be good preparation for a class like those I teach for the National Preservation Institute,[7] a good follow-up to taking one, or—if you must—a way to avoid taking one. It may have utility in academic CRM courses and in related classes in anthropology, history, geography, and historic preservation.

It may also have some relevance to readers outside the United States. Communities all over the world value places associated with their traditional beliefs, values, and practices, and scholars all over the world are involved in studying such places and the belief systems within which they're important. Some examples are provided in chapters 3 and 4. The legal systems of some countries provide for protecting some such places, while others do not.[8] International organizations such as UNESCO, the European Union (EU), and the World Bank[9] encourage attention to them, along with other aspects of the cultural environment.

But *TCP,* as acronym for *traditional cultural property* (or *place*), is an artifact of the strange and not-so-wonderful world of cultural resource management in the United States, and TCPs are what this book is about. Necessarily, then, many of the specifics discussed in these pages will seem obscure to people who live or work in other countries.

Visualizing Traditional Cultural Properties

But what *is* a TCP? In National Register Bulletin 38 we said:

> A traditional cultural property . . . can be defined generally as one that is eligible for inclusion in the National Register because of its association with cultural practices or beliefs of a living community that (a) are rooted in that community's history, and (b) are important in maintaining the continuing cultural identity of the community.[10]

We'll make more of that definition later, but for the moment let's set aside particulars—including the "National Register"—and try an exercise. Stop reading for a moment; sit back, close your eyes, and think about a place that's dear to you. I don't care *why* it's dear; just make it someplace that has personal value to you, that's redolent with emotional significance. I don't care whether it still exists or not. Maybe it doesn't matter whether it *ever* existed, but let's not pursue that right now. Just think about a place you hold—or have held—dear.

Got it? OK, in the context of your own internal, personal life, your own individual "community," that's your TCP. Nothing more complicated than that—a place that lives in your emotions, that's important to you as a person. Keep it in mind, because we'll return to your place from time to time.

Now let me tell you about one of my places. It creeps into my memory whenever I smell eucalyptus trees. A sun-dappled hillside, horehound, dry grass, scrub oak. The rattling roar of wind in the high gum trees that lined the base of the hill, behind the chicken houses. The Hill at Kings X Ranch, my boyhood home, a chicken ranch in Petaluma, California, was where I'd go to work through my adolescent angst or just to feel grounded in the throb and pulse of nature. Gone now, swallowed up by the expensive homes lining—of all named things!—Kingswood Court, but warm in my memory. Still a place I go in imagination, and find calming, a place to focus.

Each of us has places like The Hill and like Your Place, whatever and wherever it is or was. Maybe a few, maybe a lot—places that are linked somehow with who we are, how we go in the world. Or maybe some people don't have such places, but if such people exist, I wonder if they're not poorer for it, crabbed somehow.

Figure 1.1. The Hill, King's X Ranch, Petaluma, California, circa 1979. Photo by the author.

Many of us leave our special places behind, perhaps connecting to other places as we move through life. Many of us lose our places as physical realities—as I've lost The Hill. This is as it must be. We grow, we go on, things change. We're a little sad, maybe a lot sad, but it's necessary, proper.

But sometimes the association between person and place grows deeper roots, through generations, and spreads beyond the individual to infect, as it were, a community of some kind—a tribe, a family, a neighborhood, a social group. My lost hillside lies at one end of a spectrum, at the other end of which lie Mount Sinai, Galilee, Mecca, the Ganges. In between lie innumerable places that for one reason or another groups of people associate with their cultural values and beliefs. When this happens, the place becomes something that government and change agents can ignore only at their peril, regardless of what "objective" qualities of significance the places may have. Mount Sinai is not a terribly exciting geological feature, and the Ganges doesn't hold the world's hydrologists in thrall, but that's not relevant to their significance. What's relevant is how they're perceived by the communities that hold them dear. In the same way, a gravel parking lot in New Mexico may have no interest to an archaeologist, historian, or architectural historian other than as a place to sip a cold Corona purchased in the adjacent cantina, but the opinions of the professionals don't matter a bit to the people of El

Rancho, to whom it's the site where the Matachines dance is performed—a treasured embodiment of El Rancho's cultural roots.

Whose TCPs Ought to Be "Protected"?

I put *protected* in quotation marks because the legal requirements that come into play (sometimes) when a TCP or any other kind of place is recognized as important don't necessarily "protect" such places in the sense of guaranteeing their survival. But the laws do require that government agencies consider what they can do to manage such places and to avoid, reduce, or somehow make up for damage they do to them. That, I think, is about as close to "protection" as a society with competing values and needs can get. But if everybody can have TCPs, we surely can't extend even that kind of "protection" to all of them. It is surely silly, for example, to think that the Petaluma Planning Commission, in approving the subdivision and development of Kings X Ranch, should have considered protecting The Hill because of its cultural value to an aging and by then long-relocated adolescent. But, as we'll see in chapter 7, it was *not* regarded as silly for government to consider and try to remedy the impacts of an electrification project on the Matachines Dance Site. What's the difference between that parking lot in New Mexico and my hill in California?

One difference is numbers, of course; there are a lot more El Rancheros than there are of me. We'll return to the sticky question of numbers in chapter 6.

Another distinction lies in the *kinds* of people who value a place. There's a widespread assumption among U.S. CRM practitioners (and especially among Indian tribes) that only tribal or Native Hawaiian TCPs merit consideration, and that's certainly not true. Witness the Hispanic people of El Rancho. But does that mean that *everybody's* TCPs ought to be afforded the "protections" of law? On balance, I'd say yes, though that doesn't mean that everybody's TCPs ought to be given the same *level* of consideration. There are populations who need more help from the legal system in protecting their TCPs than others do.

Among these populations are Indian tribes, Native Hawaiian groups, and other ethnic minorities, because their cultural interests (to say nothing of their social, economic, and other interests) are easily bowled over by the interests of the majority society. But there are groups ethnically indistinguishable from mainstream America whose cultural values are at risk in the contemporary world, too, and they're not all easily defined, charismatic communities like the Amish. Mary Hufford, then of the American Folklife Center, neatly described a member of one such group who can stand as representative of all. Ed Hazelton, a "Piney" of the New Jersey Pinelands,

> is not Native American or Pennsylvania Dutch. Nor is he a refugee from
> Central America or Indochina. Though some people might call him a

Piney, he is also a Middle American citizen with a South Jersey accent. His family has lived along Barnegat Bay for generations. . . . His way of life is perhaps most endangered because it is hard to see except when cast into relief by cultural change. Contrast makes it visible, contrast between the old way of doing things and the modern way, and contrast between the way newcomers think things should be done and the ways that "the natives" are used to.[11]

Communities made up of Ed Hazeltons aren't always easy to recognize, but they, along with Native Americans, Amish, refugees, and a host of other more readily identifiable groups, have cultural values, including those attached to place, that are often ignored by mainstream society—or if not exactly ignored, just lost in the shuffle because there's no well-understood way to consider them in decision making about change.

Don Fowler and Marian Salter, writing on archaeological ethics, have followed the Organization of African Unity in calling such groups "self-defined peoples."[12] That may be as good a term as any, though it doesn't quite satisfy. If I got together with several other people and we defined ourselves as "The Hill People," should that have forced Petaluma to pay more attention to The Hill when it considered plans for the subdivision and development of Kings X Ranch?

I don't have an answer to that question, to which we'll return in chapter 6. For now, let's just understand that while everybody and anybody can have TCPs, in writing Bulletin 38 we were primarily concerned about people outside the American cultural, ethnic, and economic mainstream. We wanted such people to have access to the protections of environmental and historic preservation law for the places they hold dear.

TCPs and "Sacred Sites"

The kind of TCP that's gotten the most attention in the media and among public officials in recent years is what's commonly and rather loosely referred to as the "Native American sacred site."[13] Such sites comprise only one type, or subtype, of TCP. National Register Bulletin 38 gives examples of several places that, while traditional, and cultural, and places, are not definable as "sacred" and are not associated with "Native Americans."

Indigenous people—Indian tribes, Pacific islanders, and in their own lands Africans, Aboriginal Australians, Chinese, and Laplanders—may have *more* TCPs than other people do and may feel more intimate associations with them, but every community, if not every individual, ascribes traditional cultural value to places. And not every place ascribed traditional cultural value by a community is thought to be inhabited by spirits. The place where folks gather mushrooms or hunt ducks may not have any supernatural connotations at all, but its function in the community may very well make it a TCP.

Even where places *are* ascribed some sort of spiritual qualities, *are* sanctified by practice or belief, I've become wary of calling them "sacred." The term carries a great deal of semantic freight in Western culture that may be counterproductive to load on a place—even one to which supernatural power is ascribed.

In 1978, in negotiating about a project on Mount Tonaachaw, a very important mountain in the traditional beliefs of the people of Chuuk,[14] I referred to the mountain as "sacred" and was promptly taken to task by my good friend Fran Hezel. Fr. Francis Hezel, S.J., is one of Micronesia's preeminent historians as well as being a respected Jesuit priest, a dedicated educator, a prolific writer, and a famously aggressive player of pickup basketball. The mountain is important in traditional history, Fran acknowledged, and therefore of great sensitivity to the Chuukese people. In the spirit-laden *itang* traditions of Chuuk, it is associated with mystic creatures and fantastic events, but, said Fran, it is not strictly *sacred* as theologians understand the term.

Jesuitical hairsplitting, I thought, but it wasn't long before I was confronted with the fruits of my sloppy thinking. Parker and I were trying to help make sure that the concerns of the two villages at the foot of the mountain were considered and accommodated as an airport was planned there. Among the concerns the villagers voiced—quietly, because to speak incorrectly of such things was to invite spiritual injury—was about impacts on the "sacred" mountain. But then in a meeting one evening some of the village leaders opined that maybe such impacts would be acceptable if the government would pay them, say, $25,000.

I was appalled. All the way back to Parker's proper ethnographer's shack in an adjacent village I railed about the sale of birthrights for messes of pottage. Parker listened politely and then pointed out that I didn't understand beans about Chuukese culture, in which it is perfectly acceptable to offer and accept compensation for all kinds of damages, even the murder of relatives. My error, I realized in the hot clear light of the next tropical morning, was that when the Chuukese said the mountain was "sacred" I had assumed they meant that it was "sacred" in the way I, and I imagine Fr. Hezel, understand the term.

I understand something sacred to be something you really don't mess with. But to the Chuukese, *sacred* was simply the only English word they could find to label the spiritually energetic character of the mountain. That character was not necessarily something that had to be kept inviolate or whose integrity could not be somehow assuaged through financial compensation.

I continued to use the word pretty indiscriminately, however, until a while after the publication of Bulletin 38, when a couple of elderly women in a couple of different Indian tribes quietly reminded me of the same thing I'd failed to learn fully back in Chuuk. There's a spiritual aspect to everything, they said, and we need to respect it. But you can't squeeze it all into specific places, and "respect" doesn't necessarily mean "make inviolable." In many cases, "violation" of a place, in the sense of changing it somehow, is not a problem at all if the proper things are done—words said, tobacco offered, pipe smoked. *Sacred* is far too loaded a word for such places.

But a place is not culturally unimportant, even in spiritual terms, simply because it is not regarded as sacrosanct. If we were to limit our attention to those places that *are* thought of as sacrosanct—truly sacred, if you will—we would fail to consider a tremendous number of other places that are important to people.

The discomfort I feel for calling things "sacred" is not unique to me. Writing of Australia, Howard Creamer notes:

> There is . . . an increasing tendency throughout Australia to ascribe the quality of "sacred" to sites about which there is no recent tradition of them being so. . . . As with their traditional counterparts, the sacredness of these sites is rarely open to negotiation with the Aboriginal consultants. This is something which anthropologists and the public have to some extent brought about by their interest in, and emphasis on, the importance of the "sacred" life in Aboriginal culture. Aborigines are then left with the impression that Europeans will only take notice of something if it is "sacred."[15]

This is one thing that makes me uncomfortable with the rising tide (at this writing) of sentiment for "sacred site protection." Most people who call for such protection aren't very explicit about it, but when you pin them down, what they say they want is to protect "sacred sites" from all impact—to place their preservation above all other public interests. Even if one agrees that this is a proper system of priorities, it seems to me that it raises a lot of practical questions. If "sacred site" is taken to mean everything that indigenous groups tell us has spiritual power or meaning, it's going to embrace a very expansive territory, very severely constraining all kinds of things the government does, assists, or permits in the public interest. If our concern is to protect such "sacred sites" not only from physical damage but also from relevant visual, auditory, and other less direct impacts—as it certainly should be, because such impacts can be devastating—then we're talking about constraining use of even more territory. To avoid this clearly impractical (and probably unconstitutional[16]) situation, lawmakers and courts are inevitably going to define "sacred sites" very narrowly, and they'll probably do the same with regard to impacts. The result, I'm afraid, will be that a very few, tightly defined "sacred sites" will be absolutely protected from physical destruction, while a tremendous number of places that aren't amenable to narrow definition aren't protected at all, and effects other than direct physical damage aren't considered even on "sacred sites."

So, *in the interests of "sacred site" protection itself*, I think we should be careful about what we call "sacred," recognizing the implication that each such place should be sacrosanct, its protection placed above all other values. We should use the term very sparingly and have other ways to refer to the many places that are thought to have spiritual power but about whose management we can exercise some flexibility. I was encouraged by the wise and diplomatic elders to use a term like "spiritual place" for such locations and to be skeptical of using "sacred site" at all.

Unfortunately, I was enlightened on this subject only shortly before President Bill Clinton, at the behest of tribes and their attorneys, issued Executive Order 13007 on "Indian Sacred Sites," which includes a definition of the term that manages, remarkably, to be both quite restrictive and too loose to be very helpful.[17] The executive order notwithstanding, I'll stick with *spiritual places* to refer to places that people invest, or believe are invested, with spiritual energy. Some of these places doubtless ought to be kept inviolate, and those perhaps we *should* call "sacred sites," but I wouldn't want to give a place that name without thinking thoroughly about its implications.

There's one more thing I should say about sacred sites. Throughout this book I write about the significance of traditional cultural places lying in the heads of those who value them. With reference to sacred sites, Christopher Peters of the Seventh Generation Fund recently expressed a precisely opposite opinion:

> In the native belief system sacred places are not sacred because native people believe they are sacred. They have sacredness in and of themselves. Even if we all die off, they will continue to be sacred.[18]

That is certainly an accurate characterization of the belief system of many indigenous groups, in North America and around the world. It may, for all I know, even be a true statement about the nature of the universe. But I don't think it can possibly be a basis for policy in a secular democracy, and I also don't think it's something that federal government officials ought to get into arguments with communities about. The mind boggles at the idea that government could somehow define what is "really" sacred, independent of what people *think* is sacred. However true Peters's statement may be as an expression of indigenous belief or even as a description of reality, I don't see any way to operationalize it through government policy. We can't ask agency decision makers to respect those places that *really are* sacred. We can, and should, ask them to respect those places that people honestly *think* are sacred—or otherwise of traditional cultural value to them. So whether sacred sites have objective external existence or not, the only values we can be sure adhere to such sites, and to other traditional cultural properties, are those that *do* lie in people's heads.

Managing Impacts on TCPs

If TCPs aren't all sacred and aren't necessarily inviolable, what are they? For an example that may be clarifying, let's consider the Sea of Galilee.

No one—not even someone violently opposed to or oppressed by those who profess it—would dispute the fact that Christianity ascribes cultural and spiritual value to the Sea of Galilee. Miracles are said to have happened there, and the very religion that gives it honor was born on its shores. Is it "sacred"? Some would say so. Others would say that only of specific places around the Sea—the outcropping where Jesus is reported to have called Peter the rock, or the place where the loaves and fishes are said to have been multiplied. But there's no question that the sea, as a water body and its environs, is of traditional cultural importance to Christians, among others.

Galilee is also quite a big place, however, and lots of people live around it. The water that flows into it and out—down the Jordan—is the lifeblood of modern states. The sea lies in the shadow of the strategic Golan Heights. Whatever its cultural and spiritual significance, it cannot be set aside as a shrine, any more than my hillside could have been held inviolate against the power of the California real estate market. Choices have to be made, balances struck, in managing places dear to our individual and collective hearts.

In the United States, as in most countries, there are laws that more or less provide for the thinking that's needed to strike such balances. None of our laws are directed specifically toward TCPs, and there may be little need for such specificity. Places of cultural significance can be (in theory) and are (sometimes) effectively considered along with other aspects of the environment during general impact management planning. In fact, such places often *are* other aspects of the environment. Galilee is a big natural lake, an ecosystem, an economic resource. Mecca contains important Islamic architecture. In the United States, laws like the National Environmental Policy Act (NEPA) and the National Historic Preservation Act (NHPA)—along with local planning and zoning laws, state environmental and historic preservation laws, and laws dealing with specific locations or resource types—should provide the tools needed to make sure that we think about special places and whether we can preserve them, before we do things that muck them up.[19]

The laws don't always do that, however—often because such places aren't identified by the people doing the analyses the law requires. Or because nobody in authority can quite understand that such places can be important for reasons that have little or nothing to do with economy or fine architecture or the health of their resident species. Or because the people who value the places aren't consulted, or aren't consulted effectively, or aren't listened to. Or because having identified them, and the problems that their management present, we can't figure out what to do about them and so try to avoid thinking about them. We sweep them under the rug; we find some way to define them out of existence. I think this is sad, and wrong.

But this does not mean giving TCP protection priority over everything else. When I hear—as I did from a U.S. congressional aide recently—that we really need to "lock up" some kind of TCP, I shudder. We can't preserve everything that's emotionally important to everybody, or even to every community whose population exceeds some specified size, or to every group that, like an Indian tribe, has a special legal status. And if we were to "lock up" places important to one community, how would we justify not "locking up" places important to another? Who's to decide? And managing impacts on a place doesn't necessarily *mean* "locking it up." There are myriad ways to manage TCPs and impacts on them—ranging from absolute protection to unmitigated destruction, with lots of permutations in between. We ought to consider them all, and reach decisions that reflect such consideration, whatever those decisions are.

There was a time in the 1980s when cultural resource managers in the United States were sweeping TCPs under the rug with fastidious vigor. This was what led to the "invention" of TCPs as a named type of "historic property." In chapter 2 we'll look at how this happened, but first, some historical background.

What Is "CRM" in the United States?

There's no agreement about what "cultural resource management" is. The word *management* isn't a problem—everybody understands that this means managing something. *Cultural resources,* however, are something else again. Some of us use the term broadly to refer to all elements of the physical and social environment that are thought by anybody—a community, a tribe, an interest group—to have cultural value. For example:

> In [one Indian tribe's] world-view, cultural resources include: themselves, their treaty rights, religious beliefs, communities, and way of life; Indian elders, due to their unique information regarding personal and tribal histories; clean air; clean water for the salmon and other varieties of fish, eels, and riverine resources; and the root grounds and berry patches, especially huckleberries.[20]

When the term is thus broadly defined—which I believe is consistent with the total body of federal law—then cultural resource management means managing such resources—particularly managing their interactions with the rest of the world.

It's possible to imagine all manner of interactions between cultural resources, writ large, and other aspects of the world around us. However, we who call ourselves cultural resource managers are typically involved in managing the *impacts* of the modern world on cultural resources—what happens to some cultural aspect of the environment when a change takes place.

Others define *cultural resources* much more narrowly—though the definition is often only implicit and not uncommonly denied. *Cultural resource* is taken by such people to mean a place that's eligible for the National Register of Historic Places or even just an archaeological site.[21] This is unfortunate, because it makes it easy for government to ignore cultural resources that *aren't* archaeological sites or don't appeal to the keeper of the National Register and her staff and hence to allow their damage or loss without considering the feelings of those who value them.[22]

NEPA and Cultural Resources

Whatever the term is understood to mean, under the National Environmental Policy Act (NEPA), cultural resources are supposed to be considered by federal agencies when analyzing the environmental impacts of actions they are thinking of doing, or assisting, or permitting.[23] The responsible agency is supposed to decide about the action only after fully and objectively considering its environmental impacts, including those on cultural resources. The agency doesn't have to *avoid* damaging cultural resources, but it needs to take a hard look at alternatives that won't do such damage, and it has to explain itself to the interested public.

Section 106 Review

The regulations[24] implementing Section 106 of the National Historic Preservation Act (NHPA) provide much more specific direction to agencies with regard to those cultural resources that qualify as "historic properties"—that is, "districts, sites, buildings, structures, and objects included in or eligible for the National Register of Historic Places."[25] Importantly, agencies are required to *consult* with state and tribal historic preservation officers (SHPOs and THPOs), Indian tribes, local governments, and other concerned parties about how to identify such properties, how to assess impacts on them and what to do about impacts that are adverse. As under NEPA, the agency is not forbidden to damage a historic property—even if in the end the Advisory Council on Historic Preservation[26] recommends against such damage—but in the vast majority of cases, the consultation required under Section 106 leads to negotiated agreement about how damage will be avoided or mitigated.

Other Legal Requirements

A number of other federal legal requirements—to say nothing of state, tribal, and local laws—deal with particular kinds of cultural resources. The American Indian Religious Freedom Act, the Religious Freedom Restoration Act, the Native American Graves Protection and Repatriation Act, the Archaeological Resources Protection Act, and Executive Orders 12898, 13006, and 13007[27] do not necessarily result in the kind of detailed impact analysis prescribed by NEPA or in the consult-to-agreement process that is carried out under Section 106,[28] but they need to be considered as such analyses and consultations are carried out.

National Register Eligibility

If a place is eligible for inclusion in the National Register of Historic Places, then under Section 106 an agency must consider ways to avoid or mitigate the impacts its actions may have on it. It must do so in consultation with concerned parties, including but not limited to the SHPO or THPO and concerned Indian tribes. It must try to reach agreement about how impacts will be dealt with.

Eligibility for the register is established by agencies, in consultation with SHPOs and others, by applying the "National Register Criteria" published in federal regulation[29] by the National Park Service. If the agency and SHPO agree that the criteria are met, then the property is regarded as eligible; if they agree that they're not met, then the property is regarded as not eligible, and the agency has no further responsibilities under Section 106. It may have responsibilities under NEPA and other laws, but the property loses the protections afforded by Section 106's consultative process. If the agency and SHPO can't agree, or if the Advisory Council or the keeper of the National Register so request, then the agency goes to the keeper for a final, formal determination.[30]

The National Register criteria say that a property is eligible—that is, significant in American history, archaeology, architecture, engineering, or culture—if it has "integrity" (i.e., isn't too badly mucked up) and

- is associated with significant events or patterns of events in history;
- is associated with significant people in history;

- reflects an important style or school of architecture, the work of a master, or high artistic qualities, or is part of a larger significant entity; or

- has produced or may produce important information about history or prehistory.

Since a property that meets the criteria gets considered under Section 106, and one that does not, does not, the ways the criteria are interpreted determine in any given case whether impacts on a place will or will not be subjected to Section 106 consultation. So interpretation of the criteria is pretty important. To help agencies and others figure out how to interpret the criteria (among other purposes), the National Register publishes "National Register Bulletins." As of 2002 there were over forty such bulletins, one of which, of course, is Bulletin 38—*Identification and Documentation of Traditional Cultural Properties.*

Theories of Significance in U.S. Historic Preservation

The National Register criteria were developed in the late 1960s and early 1970s, as one part of the "system"[31] put in place by the National Park Service and Advisory Council to implement the newly enacted National Historic Preservation Act. This system is designed, in theory, to ensure the fair, systematic consideration—and, where feasible, the preservation and enhancement—of places regarded as historically significant.[32] One thing that makes this system rather unsystematic, I think, is that it tries to accommodate at least six distinct "theories of significance"—that is, six quite different worldviews within which people evaluate the significance of old places. This is not necessarily a bad thing; indeed it reflects a hurly-burly sort of creative ferment. What *is* a problem is that most people adhere to one or two such theories only and have trouble understanding that there may be others or that other theories may be legitimate. This lack of understanding is exacerbated by the fact that the theories have never—until now—been explicitly categorized.

Perhaps the most venerable is the *commemoration and illustration* theory, which holds that places are historic when they commemorate or illustrate some important historical event, process, or theme. This theory undergirds the National Historic Landmark (NHL) program created by the National Park Service in response to the Historic Sites Act of 1935.[33] Within this theoretical frame, significance is judged based on the strength of a property's association with an event (e.g., a battle), a significant historical process (e.g., industrialization), or a specific "theme" or interpretive construct (e.g., "Man in Space"), together with the importance of the event or theme itself and the property's ability to "convey" this association to a viewer. The commemoration and illustration theory is pedagogical; it seeks to use historic places to inform the public about that which is worthy of being commemorated or illustrated.

Closely related to commemoration and illustration is the *uniqueness-representativeness* school, which espouses the seemingly contradictory notions that places are significant if they are either one-of-a-kind, last-ditch survivors or representatives of a type (or both). Uniqueness-representativeness practitioners are usually architectural historians, landscape historians, historians of engineering, or military historians. Their school of thought, like commemoration and illustration, was embedded in the nation's perception of historic preservation by the 1935 Historic Sites Act. The 1935 act not only resulted in the NHL program with commemoration and illustration at its core; it also made permanent the Historic American Buildings Survey (HABS)[34] and led to creation of the Historic American Engineering Record (HAER).[35] These documentation programs are all about recording the unique and the representative among works of architecture and engineering.

Competing with commemoration and illustration and uniqueness-representativeness in the venerability department is the *scholarly value* school of thought, which holds that a place is significant if it can be studied to learn something important about the past. The scholarly value school arguably goes back to before the 1906 Antiquities Act,[36] when the Smithsonian Institution's Bureau of American Ethnology conducted government-sponsored archaeological research in the Mississippi Valley, the Southwest, and elsewhere.[37] Like commemoration and illustration, the scholarly value school seeks to inform, but where advocates of commemoration and illustration value what can inform the public of what *it* does not know but scholars *do,* scholarly value practitioners attribute significance to places that can inform scholars about what *they* do not know. Scholarly value also overlaps with uniqueness-representativeness, but where uniqueness-representativeness is usually the province of various history subdisciplines, scholarly value tends to be practiced by archaeologists—who in the United States are (or at least are supposed to be) anthropologists. Moreover, the scholarly value theory seeks to tease information out of places, while uniqueness-representativeness is often satisfied simply to record and preserve them.

A fourth and newer theoretical approach may be thought of as the *ambience retention* school. Ambience retention adherents recognize that certain places—often urban neighborhoods or commercial districts, but also rural landscapes, agricultural areas, and the like—convey a distinct and valuable sense of place that is recognizable and valued by most people—notably people who do not necessarily live in the places thus valued. Many historic districts have been established because of their ambience, and it is often a major challenge to retain that ambience in rehabilitating and adapting historic districts to a changing world.

A related but nonetheless distinct school of thought is the *kitsch* school, which holds that a place is significant if it reflects some perhaps obscure but interesting or amusing aspect of popular history and culture. Practitioners of the kitsch school value places like drive-ins and motels along old Route 66.

Finally, there is what I think can best be called the *community value* school, which sees a place as significant if it is valued by a living community. Such value may be ascribed to something because community members feel it contributes to the community's sense of its identity, its cultural integrity, or its relationships with the biophysical—and sometimes spiritual—environment. TCPs are obviously significant primarily within this school of thought, which, I'll suggest in the next chapter, found its legislative expression in 1966 in the National Historic Preservation Act.

Of course, any given structure or piece of ground can reflect all six kinds of significance; they are not mutually exclusive, and some are quite closely related to one another. However, the people who subscribe to the six schools of thought tend to break down into distinct categories, and each looks at significance through its own lens. The significance of TCPs looks reasonable through some lenses, but not through others, and those used to looking at significance through lenses other than that of community value often need to do some deliberate restructuring of perspective in order to deal effectively with TCPs. National Register Bulletin 38 was designed to encourage and facilitate such restructuring, and this book has a similar purpose.

Notes

1. A list of formally evaluated historic places maintained by the National Park Service in the Department of the Interior; also the division of the Park Service that maintains the list, headed by the "Keeper of the National Register." Despite its location in the Park Service, the National Register has nothing to do with national parks. Registered and register-eligible places can be found anywhere, and the fact that a place is registered does not mean that it's ever going to be a park.

2. National Register, *Guidelines for Evaluating and Documenting Traditional Cultural Properties* (National Park Service, Washington, D.C.) (sometimes [accurately] dated 1990):38. With fine consideration for historians and bibliographers, the National Register has never consistently given dates to its bulletins (though it has done so occasionally). The National Register has now stopped assigning numbers to its bulletins, too, which will further complicate the lives of writers on historic preservation topics.

3. Under Section 106 and other provisions of the National Historic Preservation Act. For details, see Thomas F. King, *Cultural Resource Laws and Practice: An Introductory Guide* (AltaMira, Walnut Creek, CA, 1998a), and Thomas F. King, Stupid TCP

Tricks, in *Thinking about Cultural Resource Management: Essays from the Edge* (AltaMira, Walnut Creek, CA, 2002), for details.

4. Generally, the identification, management, documentation, and care of old buildings, archeological sites, and other "historic properties"; see this chapter and King, *Cultural Resource Laws and Practice.*

5. A term that means different things to different people; to me it means managing the cultural aspects of the environment generally and the effects of change on such aspects; see this chapter and King, *Cultural Resource Laws and Practice.*

6. We called them "properties" in Bulletin 38 because the National Historic Preservation Act talks about "historic properties." Some have objected to "properties" because to them it implies commodities that can be bought and sold; some such critics prefer "places." I see the argument as hairsplitting and use the words interchangeably.

7. See www.npi.org.

8. Most, in fact, do not, even when they have laws ostensibly protecting cultural heritage. See Thomas F. King and Samuel Struelson, Historic Preservation Laws, in *Encyclopedia of Life Support Systems* (EOLSS Publishers for UNESCO, Geneva, 2002).

9. See UNESCO, *Recommendation Concerning the Safeguarding of the Beauty and Character of Landscapes and Sites,* adopted by the General Conference at its twelfth session, Paris, December 11, 1962; UNESCO, *Recommendation Concerning the Protection, at National Level, of the Cultural and Natural Heritage,* adopted by the General Conference at its seventeenth session, Paris, November 16, 1972; UNESCO, *Recommendation Concerning the Safeguarding and Contemporary Role of Historic Areas,* adopted by the General Conference, November 26, 1976; EU, *Treaty on European Union* (The Maastricht Treaty) as amended, 1993: Article 151, point 4; World Bank, Policies, procedures, and operational directions for environmental assessment, http://wbln0018.worldbank.org/essd/essd.nsf/EnvironmentalAssessment/Overview, 2000. Also see Ismail Serageldin, Ephim Shluger, and Joan Martin-Brown (eds.), *Historic Cities and Sacred Sites: Cultural Roots for Urban Futures* (World Bank, Washington, D.C., 2001).

10. National Register n.d.: 38:1.

11. Mary Hufford (ed.), *Conserving Culture: A New Discourse on Heritage* (University of Illinois Press, Urbana, 1994), 7.

12. Don D. Fowler and Marion W. Salter, "Archaeological Ethics in Context and Practice," in Christopher Chippendale and Herbert Maschner (eds.), *Handbook of Archaeological Theories* (AltaMira, Walnut Creek, CA, forthcoming); Organization of African Unity, *African Charter on Human and Peoples' Rights,* www.umn.edu/humanrts/instree/zlafchar.html, 1981.

13. See, for example, Executive Order 13007; Christopher McLeod (producer/director), *In the Light of Reverence,* videotape, Sacred Lands Film Project (Earth Image Films, La Honda, CA, 2000); Jake Page (ed.), *Sacred Lands of Indian America* (Abrams, New York, 2001).

14. Formerly "Truk." Chuuk is a state of the Federated States of Micronesia. In the 1970s, it was administered by the United States as part of the Trust Territory of the Pacific Islands.

15. Howard Creamer, Contacting Aboriginal Communities, chap. 2 in Graham Connah (ed.), *Australian Field Archaeology: A Guide to Techniques* (Australian Institute of Aboriginal Studies, Canberra, 1983), 15.

16. In *Lyng v. Northwest Indian Cemetery Protective Association*, the Supreme Court made note of this issue, commenting, "No disrespect for these [tribal religious] practices is implied when one notes that such beliefs could easily require *de facto* beneficial ownership of some rather spacious tracts of public property."

17. "'Sacred site' means any specific, discrete, narrowly delineated location on Federal land that is identified by an Indian tribe or Indian individual determined to be an appropriately authoritative representative of an Indian religion, as sacred by virtue of its established religious significance to, or ceremonial use by, an Indian religion, provided that the tribe or appropriately authoritative representative of an Indian religion has informed the agency of the existence of such a site."

18. Quoted in Page, *Sacred Lands of Indian America*, 131.

19. See King, *Cultural Resource Laws and Practice: An Introductory Guide*, for more discussion of these laws than most normal people could possibly need.

20. Albert Abee, Forest Management Plan, Umatilla Indian Reservation, Oregon, ms., Bureau of Indian Affairs, Umatilla Indian Agency, Mission, OR, 1982:3, 9, quoted in Michael S. Burney, Jeff Van Pelt, and Paul L. Minthorn, Palàyniwaash: A Traditional Cultural Property of the Imatalamláma, Weyíiletpuu, Walúulapam, and Niimíipuu of the Southern Columbia Plateau of the Pacific Northwest, in M. S. Burney and Jeff Van Pelt (eds.), *It's about Time, It's about Them, It's about Us, Journal of Northwest Anthropology,* Memoir No. 6 (Moscow, Idaho, 2002), 45 (original 1993).

21. A classic expression of this unfortunate worldview is Thomas W. Neumann and Robert M. Sanford, *Practicing Archaeology: A Training Manual for Cultural Resources Archaeology* (AltaMira, Walnut Creek, CA, 2001).

22. "Cultural resources" are among the factors to be considered in judging the intensity of environmental impacts under NEPA (see 40 CFR 1508.27[b][2] and [b][8]). If the term is defined narrowly, only those phenomena that fall within the narrow definition are considered. See Thomas F. King, How the Archaeologists Stole Culture: A Gap in American Environmental Impact Assessment and What to Do about It, *Environmental Impact Assessment Review* 18(2) (1998b):117–34, for discussion.

23. See 40 CFR 1508.27(b)(2) and (b)(8).

24. 36 CFR 800.

25. NHPA Sections 106 and 301(5).

26. The small independent federal agency that oversees Section 106 review.

27. For discussion, see King, *Cultural Resource Laws and Practice,* 149–218.

28. The NAGPRA regulations (43 CFR 10) do provide extensively for consultation and agreements, but only in rather narrowly defined contexts.

29. 36 CFR 60.4.

30. All this is laid out in the Advisory Council's regulations at 36 CFR 800. Properties are also formally nominated to the National Register outside the context of Section 106 review.

31. I put *system* in quotation marks because it's really far too chaotic to justify the name; I just don't have an alternative.

32. The law and regulations speak of "districts, sites, buildings, structures, and objects" important in American "history, archaeology, architecture, engineering, and culture" at the "national, state, and local" levels of significance.

33. Until 1966 the central legal basis for historic preservation in the U.S. government, the 1935 act directed NPS to identify, designate, and record places of importance in the commemoration and illustration of the nation's history, and to maintain records of such places.

34. Originally a Depression-era "make work" program, HABS became a permanent part of NPS by virtue of the 1935 act's direction to the secretary of the interior to document historic properties.

35. HAER was created by NPS as a sister to HABS in the 1970s. The Historic American Landscape Survey (HALS) has recently been added.

36. This act allows the president to designate national monuments and prohibits excavation of antiquities on federal and Indian land without a permit.

37. It may be, however, that enactment of the Antiquities Act was motivated more by nationalistic chauvinism than by scholarship—Congress's ire was raised by the fact that a Scandinavian expedition had excavated and exported artifacts from the Southwest.

Chapter Two

How did *TCPs* Come into Our Vernacular?

A Personal Perspective

Before the gods existed, the woods were sacred, and the gods came to
dwell in these sacred woods.
—Gaston Bachelard, *The Poetics of Space*
(trans. Maria Jolas, 1994:186)

The Prehistory of Bulletin 38

WITH the preceding chapter as background, let's look at how and why Bulletin 38 came to be. In retrospect, I think that the problem the bulletin was designed to address resulted from the interplay among politics, the various historic preservation-related academic disciplines, and the "theories of significance" outlined in the last chapter. I think that a concern for TCPs was fundamental to the creation of the National Historic Preservation Act but became submerged by contrary theories of significance as programs created by the act evolved.

Attitudes toward Significance in the Early History of Modern American Historic Preservation

Modern American historic preservation has its roots in the late 1950s and early 1960s, when Americans began to rebel against the unfettered forces of change that were transforming their center cities (through urban renewal) and their countryside (through interstate highways). I had firsthand experience with this rebellion as it played out in San Francisco, where as a college undergraduate I joined my fellow neighbors of the "Panhandle," a blockwide extension of Golden Gate Park, to protest and ultimately block its bisection by an expressway. The focus of our protests was not the highway's impact on places we could use to learn or teach about that part of San Francisco; it was about ambience, and maybe to a minor extent it was about kitsch, but it was mostly about community—what driving the freeway through that park, and hence through the neighborhoods that surrounded and valued it, would to do our sense of community. I think our motivations were pretty typical of those that fired the 1960s preservation movement, and that got translated—albeit in rhetoric derived from landmarks preservation and architectural history—into legal reality in the National Historic Preservation Act.

NHPA was the outcome of a study sponsored by the U.S. Conference of Mayors, with Ford Foundation support and a presidential blessing, whose findings and recommendations were published in a book called *With Heritage So Rich* (*WHSR*).[1] *WHSR* is made up of papers presenting a range of perspectives on historic preservation (though all are enthusiastically favorable). Faintly or with resonance, many of *WHSR*'s chapters reflect the preservation of community as a central purpose for the legislative initiatives the report recommends.

> Truly, the character of an area has its effects on people, and those who tamper with it against the wishes of the public are not blameless in the whole matter of the city's decline.[2]

> We already have on exhibition more historic houses and museums than we need, or are good for us as a nation. . . . Meanwhile, we urgently need to improve the quality of our lives and of our surroundings. Therefore, let us save what we have around us that is good, not for exhibition, not for "education," but for practical use as places to live in and to work in.[3]

> There are no fixed criteria of judgment. No matter how we approach the preservation of the architecture and the places and the objects of the past, our judgment must be subjective based on the interests and affects of the people.[4]

> Those who treasure a building for its pleasing appearance or local sentiment do not find *it* less important because it lacks "proper" historic credentials.[5]

But NHPA built on the Historic Sites Act of 1935, which was grounded in commemoration and illustration and uniqueness-representativeness, and to a minor extent on the 1906 Antiquities Act and the 1960 Reservoir Salvage Act,[6] which were more (in the case of the latter) or less (in the case of the former) grounded in the scholarly value school of significance interpretation. Perhaps more importantly, NHPA came to be largely interpreted and administered by people who were comfortable with schools of thought other than that of community value. The programs established by NHPA were lodged in the National Park Service, which for decades had managed the NHL program and others— HABS, the management and interpretation of historic National Park units, and the River Basin Archaeological Salvage program[7]—that employed commemoration and illustration, uniqueness-representativeness, and/or scholarly value models in deciding what to list, record, present to the public, or salvage. Ernest Connelly, the first head of the National Park Service's Office of Archaeology and Historic Preservation, was an academic architectural historian, whose bias could be expected to be toward the commemoration and illustration and ambience schools. The first keeper of the National Register, Bill Murtagh, had a similar background, and similar tendencies, which are reflected today in the National Register criteria.[8]

The scholarly value school became ascendant when President Richard Nixon issued Executive Order 11593[9] in 1972. The order for the first time caused such traditional archaeology despoilers as the Corps of Engineers, the Bureau of Land Management (BLM), and the Forest Service to pay attention to the historic places affected by their actions. The Park Service assigned three archaeologists to serve as "Executive Order Consultants," proselytizing federal agencies to the executive order's message. They were highly successful, and agencies like BLM, the Corps of Engineers, and the Forest Service began to hire archaeologists to run their historic preservation programs. To these new employees, of course, scholarly value was what could make a piece of ground significant, and they brought this worldview with them into the agencies.

Among the founders of the program that emerged from the enactment of NHPA, the late Robert R. Garvey Jr. was unique: he was *not* a professional in any of preservation's constituent academic disciplines. Garvey, one of the principal authors of NHPA and at the time of its enactment executive secretary of the National Trust for Historic Preservation,[10] was an entrepreneur, ex–Marine Corps fighter pilot, and former manager of Old Salem, an interpreted historic site in North Carolina. As executive director of the newly created Advisory Council on Historic Preservation, he brought a populist perspective to the national program that was, I think, more sympathetic to the community value school of thought than was common in NPS at the time. Most of the Advisory Council's early cases under Section 106 of NHPA dealt with properties that had been placed on the register for commemoration/illustration reasons—it could hardly have been otherwise, since at the time Section 106 applied only to effects on registered properties, and the early register reflected the existing list of National Historic Landmarks. The system of Section 106 review that Garvey created, however, emphasized open, public consultation, inevitably requiring that the significance of both properties and effects be understood from the community's point of view.

On the Road to Bulletin 38:
Robert Garvey and Tahquitz Canyon

My first encounter with Bob Garvey was a defining experience. It was my first Section 106 case, in the very early 1970s. I'd been retained by the Agua Caliente Band of Cahuilla Indians to help save the tribe's origin place, Tahquitz Canyon in Palm Springs, California, from a Corps of Engineers dam. In those days, under Section 106 an agency had to consider only its impacts on places that were actually included in the National Register, so my colleagues and I had prepared a nomination, and the canyon had been listed—both because of its archaeological sites and because of its association with the traditions of the Cahuilla. As part of Section 106 review, there was a public meeting in Palm Springs, attended by Garvey and one of the council's three or four other employees, Glennie Murray. As the tribe's archaeologists, my colleague George Jefferson and I made a presentation, with detailed maps of the canyon, discussions of our test excavations, and so on. Then there was a sort of pregnant silence, and then Garvey rumbled, "I'd like to hear what the *Indians* have to say."

Neither the Indians nor I had expected this; we thought Section 106 was all a pretty white-eyed archaeological sort of game. But Tony Andreas, the tribal historian, got up and made an eloquent statement about the canyon's place in the tribe's traditions. When all was said and done, the Corps of Engineers abandoned its project. Another flood control facility was built there many years later by the county, with the tribe's acquiescence after much consultation and redesign, but that's another story. The priority that Garvey gave that first time around to the tribe's view of the canyon's importance—its community value—made a lasting impression on me.[11]

Beyond Tahquitz Canyon: Warm Springs Dam and Mount Tonaachaw

Tahquitz Canyon was one of the first cases in which an Indian tribe used the Section 106 to protect a traditional cultural place. Working with the Cahuilla began to make me think about significance in ways for which my archaeological training hadn't conditioned me. My first encounter with Section 106 made me think that it was designed to make agencies pay attention to the cultural concerns of communities.

These impressions were solidified by my next Section 106 case, which allied me with the Dry Creek Band of Pomo Indians and other plaintiffs in a lawsuit seeking to halt construction of Warm Springs Dam on Dry Creek in Sonoma

County, California. *Warm Springs Dam Task Force v. Gribble*[12] was important for a number of reasons. First, it helped give the weight of law to the Advisory Council's then-new Section 106 "Procedures," which while they had been published in the Code of Federal Regulations were not yet unequivocally binding (the Advisory Council did not get clear-cut rule-making authority until some years later). Second, it was one of several events that occurred in the early to mid1970s that forced the Corps of Engineers to begin taking its NHPA responsibilities seriously and to hire archaeologists and—in the San Francisco District that had responsibility for Warm Springs—cultural anthropologists to carry out these responsibilities. Third, although it did not stop the dam, it did help cause the corps to undertake a quite comprehensive program of mitigation, including not only archaeological salvage and in-place preservation but things like replanting sedge and willow needed by the Pomo for basket making, all done in consultation with Pomo elders.[13]

Finally, it once again forced me to confront a disconnect with my archaeological roots. The reservoir area had been surveyed in the 1960s by the late Adan E. Treganza, my mentor at San Francisco State University, and he had literally written the place off, saying there was nothing there worth excavating. Trig had only recently died, and I revered (and still revere) his memory. I also understood that the historical, theoretical, and legal contexts in which he had made his judgments were different from mine. There had been no NHPA when he did his work, which involved advising the National Park Service about which of many destructive reservoir projects it should spend its limited archaeological salvage dollars on, not evaluating sites as such. But, still, I had to refute his premises, and develop arguments in support of my position that would stand up in court. Other archaeologists joined in this effort, but others viewed the enterprise with skepticism, and even as traitorous to Trig's memory. My allies were the Pomo, and while I was still thinking of archaeological sites as information mines, the consistency between the Pomo and Cahuilla ways of attributing significance to such places was beginning to make an impression on me.

While we were duking it out with the corps, a several amendments were enacted to the NHPA, including an obscure one that made the Trust Territory of the Pacific Islands[14] (TTPI) a "state" for purposes of the act. Accordingly, the Trust Territory began getting historic preservation grants from NPS, and its fledgling "State" historic preservation office began nominating places to the National Register.

Most of these were World War II sites, significant in terms of commemoration/illustration, but one of them was Mount Tonnachaw. Mount Tonnachaw is the traditional origin place of Chuukese civilization, where the culture hero Sowukachaw built his meeting house in the distant past and spread culture throughout the islands of Chuuk.

Ethnoarchaeological work on Tonnachaw, which the people of Iras and Mechchitiw Villages did in 1978–1981 with Pat Parker and me[15] gave some archaeological substantiation to the Sowukachaw tradition However, it was and is a tradition, not "history" in the Euro-American sense. In various renditions Sowukachaw is borne to Chuuk by a Frigate Bird, magically transports the top of the peak from another island, and floats to the island on a breadfruit leaf. The mountain was listed in the National Register because of its association with these traditions, which are of great significance in Chuukese culture.[16]

In 1977, through a rather improbable set of coincidences, I wound up in the TTPI as "Consultant in Archaeology and Historic Preservation to the High Commissioner," while Parker, who in a fit of confusion had married me, settled in at the base of Mount Tonnachaw to do ethnographic fieldwork for her Ph.D. dissertation at the University of Pennsylvania. Over the next two years, we mediated a dispute between the people of the two villages on the mountain—Iras and Mechchitiw—and the TTPI government and U.S. Navy over improvement and enlargement of Chuuk International Airport.[17] We used Section 106 review as our primary legal tool, and the memorandum of agreement (MOA) we negotiated among the Advisory Council, TTPI, navy, and villages under Section 106 provided the vehicle for addressing a wide range of village cultural concerns, including matters of land rights and access to traditional fishing and shellfishing areas.

Figure 2.1.   The Achaw, at the summit of Mount Tonaachaw, Wene Island, Chuuk. Photo by Patricia L. Parker.

Today, of course, we would recognize Tonaachaw as a TCP. At the time, it didn't seem like it needed any special categorization; it was obviously a culturally important place, and we negotiated ways to address its importance.

The Early 1980s: "Professionalism" and TCPs

Tahquitz, Warm Springs, and Tonnachaw had made me known to the Advisory Council.[18] When Pat and I returned to California, she great with child, me small with hepatitis, the Advisory Council's deputy executive director, Bob Utley, sat with us under my mother's walnut tree (within site of The Hill) and offered me either of two jobs. One was as the Advisory Council's senior archaeologist, the other a newly created position overseeing Section 106 review by all federal agencies nationwide. Utley flattered me with encouragement to consider the bigger, broader job, saying that my work and writings suggested that my perspective was broader than archaeology. I did not resist his blandishments.

So Pat, our son Tommy, and I continued east to Washington. As I became immersed in the Advisory Council's work, I gradually became aware of an evolutionary process that had begun in my absence, and that was gaining momentum, in the way the significance of historic properties was measured.

In the early days of NHPA, the National Register had flexible nomination standards. In the late 1970s these standards were tightening up for various reasons—criticism of the register by local governments and property owners and amendments to NHPA notable among them. The watchword had come to be *professionalism*—nominations and determinations of eligibility had to be professionally grounded, professionally defensible. This all seemed fine and rational, and a sign of the national historic preservation program's maturation. But professionalization carried with it an implication whose importance we did not recognize at the time—a profound implication for the way significance was understood.

Although there is, arguably, a "profession" of historic preservation, there is no academic discipline that embraces it. Preservationists are trained in one or more of several constituent disciplines—architectural history, historical architecture, archaeology, history. The academic programs in which such training is received are biased in one of two directions. "Historic preservation" programs emphasize architectural history and historical architecture, while "cultural resource management" programs are overwhelmingly archaeological.

The result was (and usually still is) that when a preservation practitioner sought to make a significance judgment professionally justifiable, he or she thought (and usually thinks today) about the professional standards of her or his natal discipline. Since the natal discipline of virtually all preservation practitioners in and around the federal government was either architectural history or archaeology, judgments about significance in the early 1980s were grounded in the mindsets of these two disciplines. Architectural historians tended to think in terms of the commemoration and illustration, uniqueness-representativeness, ambience retention, and kitsch models, while archaeologists were and are firmly attached to scholarly value. There weren't, and aren't, many professionals at the National Register, in the SHPO offices, or in the agencies who were or are closely attuned to community value.

The result was predictable. People were coming to think that in order for something to be eligible for the National Register, it had to be significant in commemoration and illustration, uniqueness-representativeness, ambience retention, kitsch, or scholarly value terms. Community value was falling through the cracks. This problem became apparent in the early 1980s, in two cases involving tribal spiritual places: the Helkau Historic District in northern California and the San Francisco Peaks in Arizona.

Devaluing Community Value: The GO Road, the San Francisco Peaks, and Other Lost or Threatened TCPs

What the National Register now calls the Helkau Historic District is a spiritual place to the Yurok, Hoopa, Karuk, and other tribes of northwestern California. It is a high point on the North Coast Range, on the Six Rivers National Forest. Traditionalists believe there is a hole in the sky over the Helkau, through which those properly prepared can receive wisdom and power; it is also a place where beneficial medicines can be gathered. It is a natural area, dominated by two peaks called Chimney Rock and Doctor Rock. Some religious practitioners have built small cairns of rock called "prayer seats," but it's the natural place that's important in the cultural lives of the local Indian people.

During the political struggles leading to creation of Redwood National Park, folklore that I have no reason to doubt has it that the timber industry offered to withdraw its opposition to the park if the government would agree to build a road across the mountains. The road would allow coastal sawmills to access timber in the interior. To be built by the Forest Service, the road would run between the towns of Gasquet and Orleans, and hence it was called the "G-O" or simply "GO" Road.

When plans for the GO Road were announced, the tribes objected that it would run through the high country where their spiritual place lay. The Forest Service initially blew them off; agency opinion held that it was unlikely the tribes still carried out ceremonies in the high country. Even if they did, the party line went on, this had no relevance to the Forest Service's environmental and historic preservation responsibilities. I remember writing letters objecting to these arguments, but my memory may well be faulty; I may have accepted them. I was pretty green. As things turned out, both the Forest Service and I, among others, learned a lot from the experience we were about to go through.

The GO Road went forward, and the outcry among the tribes grew in volume. Eventually, the Forest Service hired Dr. Dorothea Theodoratus to do an ethnographic study—the first, I think, designed specifically to reach conclusions about the eligibility of a "TCP" for the National Register. To make a long story short, Theodoratus's study documented that there *was* a place in the high country, in the GO Road right of way, that was of cultural religious importance to the Native people of the area. It is this area that now is known as the Helkau Historic District.

But by the time the study was done, the road was built up to what the register decided (with little plausible justification other than where the construction ended) were the boundaries of the district. By this time it was about 1983, and I was at the Advisory Council. The Forest Service unhappily entered Section 106 consultation, but there wasn't much they could realistically propose in the way of impact mitigation. They offered to shade the road's pavement in natural hues and to keep its shoulders narrow so people couldn't easily pull off and go watch the Indians doing their rituals.

Right, the tribes said; you're going to punch your road and its resident eighteen wheelers through our cathedral, and you say you'll make it all nice by painting it a pleasing color. We don't think so. The SHPO and the council backed the tribes, and we terminated consultation with the Forest Service.

As the regulations required, the council then rendered a comment to the Forest Service. It suggested backing off about seven miles and rerouting the road down another ridge, across a stream, up another ridge, and onward, thus avoiding both direct physical and most visual impacts on the Helkau. The Forest Service, as is its right under Section 106, said, Thanks, but we'll do it our way, and proceeded as planned. The tribes sued, charging violation of everything from 106 to the First Amendment. The case eventually went to the Supreme Court,[19] but not on Section 106 grounds. The district court recognized that the Forest Service had complied with Section 106 by taking the road's effects into account and by giving the council an opportunity to comment, in accordance with the regulations. So it dismissed the alleged Section 106 violation.[20]

While the GO Road case was going through its climax, another Forest Service Section 106 case was aborning. This involved the San Francisco Peaks in Arizona.

The Peaks comprise one of the revered four corners of the traditional Navajo world.[21] To the Hopi they are the home of the Katchina. In the late 1970s, the Forest Service proposed to permit expansion of a ski resort there.[22] It conducted an archaeological survey and found nothing. What a surprise, said the Hopi; Katchina don't leave tracks visible to an archaeologist. Nor did the

Figure 2.2. Chimney Rock, part of the Helkau Historic District along the GO Road right-of-way. Photo by Loretta Neumann.

First People, said the Navajo, and in a rare show of unity, the two tribes—traditional enemies—joined in litigation against the Forest Service.

Both the Advisory Council and the keeper of the National Register wrote to the Forest Service expressing concern. Sorry, said the Forest Service and SHPO, there's nothing there that the archaeologists think is significant—nothing of scholarly value—so therefore, there's nothing eligible for the National Register. Under the regulations then in effect (and, due to the amazing lassitude of the National Register, still technically so),[23] the Forest Service was able to determine that "no question existed" about the Peaks' ineligibility and was able to make this absurd contention stand up in court.[24] The project was permitted, though to some tribal amusement, it fell victim to a number of financing problems and was never built.

The GO Road case showed that agencies—the Forest Service, at least—were not doing much to address the community value aspect of historic property significance in their planning. The San Francisco Peaks case showed that agencies—again, the Forest Service, at least—would and could manipulate their understanding of NHPA to slime their ways out of considering impacts on places perceived to have such significance. These were not the only cases, and the Forest Service was not the only agency, to highlight these points. The city of Detroit, with funding from by the Department of Housing and Urban Development (HUD), decimated Poletown, an ethnic Polish neighborhood, to make way for a new Cadillac plant, ignoring Poletown's possible eligibility for the

National Register. The navy bombarded Kaho'olawe, an island claimed by native Hawaiians as sacred ground. The Pennsylvania Department of Transportation began planning an expressway through the middle of Pennsylvania's Old Order Amish country and couldn't see this as a historic preservation issue.

In short, it became increasingly clear—although I had not then organized my thoughts in quite this way—that agencies and SHPOs alike were coming to conceive of significance strictly in commemoration and illustration, uniqueness-representativeness, ambience retention, kitsch, and scholarly value terms, ignoring community value. I felt and feel that this is contrary to the intent of NHPA, plain wrong, and rather boring.

"Cultural Conservation"

In 1979, NPS archaeologists approached the Library of Congress's American Folklife Center about adding a living culture element to data recovery work along the Corps of Engineers' Tennessee-Tombigbee Waterway. The center eventually withdrew from the project on the (now rather quaint-seeming) grounds that taking money from the corps might be seen as supporting the destructive "Tenn-Tom." However, its director, Alan Jabbour, soon found himself working with the House of Representatives' redoubtable Loretta Neumann on an amendment to NHPA directing a more organic sort of collaboration. The amendment, enacted in 1980 as Section 502,[25] directed NPS and the center to prepare a report "on preserving and conserving the intangible elements of our cultural heritage such as arts, skills, folklife, and folkways."

The center and NPS, mostly represented by the office of the "Departmental Consulting Archaeologist,"[26] cobbled together funding to support Ormond Loomis of the Florida State Folklife Center to coordinate a study and report. When the report came out in 1983, it was entitled *Cultural Conservation.*[27] Jabbour comments:

> Exactly how the title of the final report came to be is a little mysterious. But it was clear to many of us that "intangible elements of our cultural heritage" would not suffice. The term "intangible" (which came from the world of archaeology and historic preservation, where tangible culture is the focal subject) is problematic in that it defines something by what it is not. Further, there was a strong sentiment within the Center staff—corroborated by our independent consultants—for making the report deal with the entire system of working with culture, not just a portion of it. . . . The question arose about giving the report a stronger, more positive title. A few words and phrases were kicked around. Then someone said "cultural conservation"; none of us can now remember how it came up, or from whom. We all murmured the phrase, then looked at each other. Our new phrase was positive and focused; it

provided an umbrella under which the various disciplines concerned with cultural action could unite; it chose a noun that resonated with the dynamic ecological models of natural conservation, as opposed to the static images of freeze-frame preservation; and finally, it alliterated.[28]

I participated in developing *Cultural Conservation* as the council's representative. Partly at my urging, though I was uneasy with the way the words wound up on the page, the report recommended, among other things, "Executive and legislative action to

[c]larify national policy in statutes including the National Historic Preservation Act of 1966, the National Environmental Policy Act of 1969, and the American Folklife Preservation Act of 1976 . . . to indicate the full range of cultural resources included under the protection of the law by defining cultural and historic resources to include historic properties, folklife, and related lifeways.[29]

During the Reagan administration, such clarification was the most ethereal of dreams, and by the time the administrations changed, the recommendation had dropped out of CRM's collective memory.[30] What *did* happen was that NPS and the Folklife Center embarked on a series of cooperative projects (some discussed in chapter 4) to document the cultural resources of particular places in a holistic manner.

Although I found it stimulating to work with the folklife people, they never seemed to me to relate to the rough-and-tumble world I was involved in—the world of Section 106—any better than the NPS archaeologists did. The archaeologists accepted the construction of destructive projects provided they could recover data from the sites such projects destroyed. The folklife people shied away from projects like the Tenn-Tom with righteous morality but did little to help the people whose traditional lives were upset by such projects—except to record their songs and stories for posterity, and to put on festivals to showcase their skills in the hope that they would thus be transmitted down the generations in some form or other. These are worthy enterprises, but they didn't engage the agents of change; they didn't confront the conflicts between tradition and modernity directly; they didn't help us with Section 106 review. They wouldn't help the Navajo and Hopi with the Forest Service or the people of Poletown with the Detroit city government.

For a while, it looked like things might work out otherwise. The center's Mary Hufford produced a fascinating report on the traditional culture of the New Jersey Pine Barrens (see chapter 4), including strong recommendations for management in respectful consultation with the "Pineys" who lived there.[31] She followed up with an edited volume called *Conserving Culture*, in which scholars from a variety of disciplines described and analyzed issues falling within the "cultural conservation" rubric. Several chapters dealt with conflicts and their resolution, and some of the solutions were creative. But what came out of the Pinelands exercise and others like it was not a process of conflict resolution but the notion of "heritage areas." A heritage area is a chunk of geography—often a river or some other kind of transportation corridor or an attractive agricultural or interesting industrial area—whose local governments decide that their distinctive culture is something they can capitalize on. They can petition Congress to designate their landscapes as National Heritage Areas or get them designated under state laws like Pennsylvania's pioneering Heritage Parks Program. They are then eligible for financial aid, tax relief, and technical assistance that permit them to retain what makes them culturally distinct; most then are marketed as cultural tourism destinations.[32]

Where self-defined cultural conservationists do confront crisis situations, they are often crises over community perceptions of cultural appropriateness versus those of governmental interpretive and planning bodies like the National Park Service and state parks departments.[33] Some cultural conservationists also work positively as advocates for traditional communities in local planning and land use activities,[34] but there is no systematic way for this to happen on a routine basis, particularly with respect to federal agency planning.

Meanwhile, the term *cultural conservation* has been appropriated in other countries to embrace virtually every form of cultural preservation and promotion activity known to humankind.[35] It seems to have come to mean anything of a generally cultural nature that anyone wants it to mean.

By the mid-1980s, it was clear that—at least in the then-prevailing political climate—"cultural conservation" was not anytime soon going to mean systematically helping traditional communities make sure their special places are given proper attention in agency decision making. And that was the problem that cases like the San Francisco Peaks and Poletown pressed on us at the Advisory Council.

Bulletin 38

In about 1985, in informal consultation with Pat—who by then had shepherded Tommy into elementary school and gone to work for the National Park Service—I began drafting a set of guidelines for agencies to use in Section 106 review when dealing with things like Native American spiritual sites, Micronesian origin places, Poletown, and Amish country. The idea was to use the persuasive powers of Section 106 to motivate agencies to pay attention to such places and the communities that valued them. This was pretty much a shot in the dark. It was at the height of the Reagan administration, and the Advisory Council was under attack from all quarters. One thing I'd learned by then about the government, however, was that one is unwise to be too doctrinaire; the opportunity to advance one's interests may emerge quite unexpectedly, among and even *from* those you might be inclined to view as enemies.

That's how it happened. With Garvey's support, I presented a draft of the guidelines to the council, whose members generally yawned and said fine. But the Interior Department objected, and since Interior had taken the point in the administration's effort to pull what few teeth the council had, this looked like a death knell for the guidelines.

Without much hope, Pat and I met with Dale Lanzone, then the Interior Department's main man on historic preservation political matters. And we found that the Department's problems were nothing of substance; they were all about turf. Significance is the National Register's schtick, Lanzone said, not the council's. Interior would support publication—indeed, would publish the document—as long as it was rewritten as a National Register bulletin.

So we sat down to rework the draft—Pat for NPS, me for the council—and the result was National Register Bulletin 38.

What Bulletin 38 Said

I'll discuss Bulletin 38 in detail in the chapters that follow. For purposes of this chapter, it's enough to say that it made the following points:

- A place can be eligible for the National Register based on its value in the eyes of a traditional community like an Indian tribe.

- Such a place need not be anything that's appreciated, or even perceivable as such, by an outsider.

- Entirely natural places can be eligible as TCPs, as can buildings, structures, archaeological sites, landscapes, and urban neighborhoods.

- TCPs are identified through consultation with communities.

- The significance of TCPs must be understood with reference to community perceptions—it's how the *community* perceives the place and its significance that matters.

We coined the term *traditional cultural property* as a broad umbrella to cover everything from Indian tribal spiritual places to traditional urban neighborhoods. A lifeless bureaucratic term, but we couldn't think of a better one.

It's worth emphasizing—because people don't always seem to realize it—that Bulletin 38 didn't really say anything new. It didn't provide a new criterion for National Register eligibility or "make TCPs eligible." TCPs—though without being so named, of course—had been found eligible for, and included in, the National Register since the register's inception. Even if one doesn't accept my premise that concern for TCP-like values was at the core of the movement that led to enactment of NHPA in the first place, one can hardly avoid the fact that places like Tahquitz Canyon and Mount Tonaachaw were included in the Register long before Bulletin 38 was even a gleam in Pat's and my eyes.

But however old hat it was, Bulletin 38 created a stir.

Agency Reaction and Congressional Response

Bulletin 38 was issued in 1990. Three important federal agencies—the Bureau of Land Management, the Forest Service, and the Bureau of Indian Affairs—all responded to it promptly by issuing guidance to their field offices. Mysteriously, all three memoranda said pretty much the same thing: Bulletin 38 is all very nice, but it's a National Park Service publication so it really doesn't apply to us.

This was ridiculous, of course. Whatever one thinks the National Register is,[36] it is not just for the National Park Service. NPS maintains the register, true, and resolves questions about what's eligible and what's not. It maintains the register for the whole government, however, and the questions it resolves are often raised by government agencies like those that found it inconvenient to be guided by Bulletin 38. Bulletin 38 was (and is) the register's guidance for the entire federal government (and everyone else). The fact is that the three agencies—or, to be more precise, the archaeologists who ran the three agencies' CRM programs—were uncomfortable dealing with places that were not archaeological sites. Places, indeed, that an archaeologist might not be able to distinguish from any other patch of dirt, rock, or trees. So they advised their field staff that while Bulletin 38 was all very fine for NPS, it really wasn't relevant to them.

Conveniently, work was under way at the time of amendments to the National Historic Preservation Act. Then-senator Wyche Fowler of Georgia was carrying the bill, and several Indian groups—notably the National Congress of American Indians and the Native American Rights Fund—were consulting with the senator's staff about language. The Indian groups were upset by what the three agencies were saying, because what they were saying amounted to "Listen to your archaeologists; ignore tribes." As a result, the amendments enacted in 1992 contained some clarifying language at Section 101(d)(6):

> Properties of traditional religious and cultural importance to an Indian tribe or Native Hawaiian organization may be determined to be eligible for inclusion on the National Register[37]

and

> In carrying out its responsibilities under section 106, a Federal agency shall consult with any Indian tribe or Native Hawaiian organization that attaches religious and cultural significance to [such] properties.[38]

Just as Bulletin 38 didn't "create" TCPs or make them eligible for the National Register, the amendments of 1992 didn't, either. All Congress did in adding Section 101(d)(6) was make it clear that agencies were wrong if they thought that only places important to archaeologists and other specialists were eligible for the register. Places in which a tribe or native Hawaiian group vested cultural or religious value could be eligible—and agencies needed to talk with tribes about such properties, and about things that might affect them.

Why didn't Congress speak to all kinds of TCPs—the Poletowns as well as the San Francisco Peaks? Simple: The tribes helped draft the amendment; others with concerns about TCPs didn't. This doesn't mean that places like Poletown or Amish country aren't eligible. Native American cultural places gained the attention of Congress because what BLM, the Forest Service, and BIA tried to do made the tribes mad, and the tribes told Congress about it. It might be said that Section 101(d)(6) gives tribal TCPs rather more stature in law than everybody else's TCPs, but they have such stature anyway, based on tribal sovereignty and the U.S. government's trust responsibility toward tribes. Places that are culturally important to non-Indian traditional communities are not made any *less* eligible for the National Register by the fact that Congress, in response to agency lassitude, singled out tribal TCPs for special mention in law.

The Development of TCP Practice

The purpose of Bulletin 38 was to guarantee for traditional communities the right to use the National Register and the Section 106 process—to make sure that such communities had access to the same planning tools that everybody else has. We have not yet achieved quite this even-handed condition; there is still much uncertainty about how TCPs should be identified and addressed in cultural resource management practice.

The notion of the National Register as a thing of primarily professional, pedagogical interest continues to haunt us. There's a tendency to try to make "TCP studies" into something that only particular kinds of professionals (usually ethnographers) do, according to detailed technical guidelines. We agonize over minutiae of documentation and standards and in doing so fail to engage the real communities and interests that make it important to address TCPs in the first place. But slowly, I think, some sort of responsible practice is developing.

Some who have read chapters of this book in draft have taken umbrage at what they take to be my "antiprofessional bias." I don't think I'm biased, but I do think that it's easy for us professionals to become pompous, self-congratulatory, and narrow-minded and to grab for ourselves and only for ourselves the protections and advantages that the cultural resource laws provide. Professionalism is a good thing when it's taken to mean responsible, informed practice by people who know what they're doing. Unfortunately, that's not always what it's understood to mean in American CRM; instead, it's taken to mean "archaeology for the archaeologists, buildings for the architectural historians, and never mind anybody else." Since Bulletin 38, some have amended this mantra to include "TCPs for the ethnographers." That was not what we were trying to accomplish with the bulletin.

Good ethnographic practice, like good practice in archaeology and architectural history, is admirable and necessary; I don't mean in any way to denigrate professional practice. But TCPs are places important to *communities,* and communities are the first authorities on them. Where the expertise of ethnographers, archaeologists, architectural historians, landscape historians, or astronauts is necessary to translate a community's values and beliefs into terms the planning process can absorb, it ought to be used and used well, but a professional's values or judgment ought not be elevated above those of a community. Such elevation is unfortunately a continuing tendency among CRM practitioners; we need to be alert to it and try to keep it under control.

"What You Do and How We Think"

Guidance from the National Register has been thin, and that's probably a good thing. The evolution of practice may be what we need right now, not direction. In 1993, the National Park Service published a special edition of its *CRM* newsletter (since expanded to near-magazine proportions), edited by Pat Parker and dedicated to TCP matters.[39] Rereading this issue today, I find myself wishing that someone—like me—had taken the time to abstract the key points made by its various authors into a concise little guidebook to "best TCP practices." *What You Do and How We Think,* as Pat titled the issue, covered just about every key issue that has continued to bedevil TCP practice, and many of its authors were both eloquent and specific in articulating the issues and proposing approaches to their solution. In the special edition:

Sally Thompson Greiser and T. Weber Greiser used their experience on the still-controversial Badger–Two Medicine oil and gas exploration program in Montana as the basis for exploring how the contrasting world views of tribes and Euro-American scientists and bureaucrats bedevil an agency's consideration of impacts on TCPs.[40] They offered recommendations for field research that remain relevant today. Frances Levine and Thomas W. Merlan provided similarly concrete recommendations from the useful perspective of *non*-Indian communities—providing the issue's only (but very articulate) reminder that TCPs are for everyone.[41]

Alan Downer and Alexa Roberts in one article, and Charles Carroll in another, articulated the difficulties inherent in addressing impacts on TCPs in the context of multiple, overlapping, sometimes seemingly contradictory, federal laws, notably NEPA and NHPA.[42] In a comment, I wistfully suggested that the Advisory Council might address this problem in its then-beginning rewrite of the Section 106 regulations—a possibility that unfortunately did not become reality.[43]

Lynne Sebastian tried to identify and correct several misconceptions about how Section 106 can and should be complied with in the context of TCPs and highlighted the fact that "[t]he fit between traditional cultural properties and Section 106 is inexact at best"[44]—a cautionary note that has proved prophetic. In the same paper, she articulated a piece of wisdom that I think of as *Sebastian's Dictum*—that she, in her role at the time as New Mexico SHPO, did not need to be provided with more information than she needed for purposes of Section 106.[45] We'll have occasion to return to this dictum.

Sebastian, Richard Hart,[46] and representatives of the Hopi and Zuni tribes[47] offered perspectives on archaeological sites as TCPs, and the tribal authors provided recommendations to archaeologists and others about how TCP studies should be conducted. Sebastian's concern about the poor fit between Section 106 and TCPs was underscored by Judy Brunson Hadley's account of her TCP troubles in connection with the proposed Fence Lake Mine in New Mexico.[48] David Cushman rethought a number of the key issues discussed in Bulletin 38; related them to the needs and worldviews of SHPOs, tribes, agencies and archaeologists; and offered recommendations to each group.

In about 1993, the Natural Resource Conservation Service contracted with me to produce a videotape on TCPs for use in training its field people, and when the National Register learned of the project, it quickly volunteered to participate in a management capacity. The result, *Through the Generations,* was released by the register in about 1995.[49] The video gave us something to use in introducing the subject of TCPs, but about its only contribution to practice was its reminder that impacts on TCPs that are *not* eligible for the National Register may need to be addressed in project planning under NEPA.

A Parallel Track: The Stoffle Tradition

While archaeologists and other CRM specialists were beginning to absorb Bulletin 38, cultural anthropologists led by Richard Stoffle, of the University of Michigan's Institute for Social Research and subsequently of the Bureau of Applied Research in Anthropology (BARA) at the University of Arizona, were refining a body of related practice under NEPA and AIRFA. Much of the early work of Stoffle's group was done in connection with studies of alternatives for the disposal of nuclear waste, which pumped a good deal of money into studies of tribal land use and cultural values during the 1980s.[50] What might be thought of as the BARA approach is a kind of social impact assessment that emphasizes the cultural uses of land and land resources, particularly plants, and the cultural value of landscapes. As the 1990s progressed, the Stoffle group developed its methods into a highly organized system for in-depth, iterative consultation with tribal representatives and the conduct of "cultural triage"—assigning different resources and resource classes to different levels of importance, as determined through consultation and systematic polling. Although they have often been involved in work with traditional tribal cultural values under NHPA, and hence have had to think about National Register eligibility, they tend to shy away from very specifically evaluating TCPs as such. This is apparently based on the inaccurate assumption that TCPs must be of some specific, relatively small, size; they have preferred to think of places important to tribes as rural historic landscapes.[51]

Hot Cases

There have been a number of difficult TCP cases in the decade since Bulletin 38 was published (some still ongoing), and each has contributed in one way or another to the evolution of our practice. At Mount Shasta in California, at the Bighorn Medicine Wheel in Wyoming, and at Okmulgee Old Fields in Georgia (among other places), the National Register's preoccupation with boundaries has been a problematic issue. At Las Huertas Canyon on New Mexico's Cibola National Forest, litigation has given us some direction about what a "reasonable and good faith effort" to identify TCPs should look like; ongoing litigation in the case of Fence Lake Mine and Zuni Salt Lake promises to give us more guidance about this matter, one way or another. On Mount Graham in Arizona, the proper nature of consultation has been at issue; on Enola Hill in Oregon, the question was how specifically TCPs need to be identified, and by whom, in order to qualify them for consideration. On Lake Superior and at the Grand Canyon, issues of scale have been debated, with mixed results. In Virginia, three nonfederally recognized tribes ascribe traditional cultural value to the entire

Pamunkey and Mattaponi River systems. At Kaho'olawe Island in Hawaii, long used in naval shore bombardment exercises, the U.S. Navy has had to confront how to manage an entire island that is regarded as culturally important by native Hawaiian groups, who need access to it for religious and cultural purposes. At Badger–Two Medicine in Montana, an expansive natural-cultural landscape, the Forest Service has been frustrated in trying to address the specific impacts of particular oil and gas exploration activities on particular TCPs, while the Blackfeet who value the area see the whole place as the significant property. Similar issues of particular place versus expansive landscape are at issue in the Glamis Imperial Mine case in southern California and in connection with geothermal energy development on northern California's Medicine Lake Highlands. At Mole Lake, Wisconsin, and Black Mesa in Arizona, we're dealing with the cultural qualities of underground water, and over Taos Blue Lake and the Hualapai Reservation the issue is intrusions on culturally sensitive airspace. These are knotty, complicated issues that don't really have simple answers. Unfortunately, there's some tendency in CRM practice to want simple answers and to throw up one's hands in despair if they aren't readily apparent. We continue to experience conflict between a practice of TCP identification and management that must be very soft, flexible, and organic, and standard practices in CRM based on archaeology, history, and architectural history that—for all their grounding in the social sciences and humanities—tend to seek hard-edged, black-and-white solutions.

Our problems in U.S. cultural resource management are not unique, however—though we certainly give the problems some peculiar spins. People all over the world are grappling with similar issues, dealing with similar places. Theoreticians are theorizing, practitioners are practicing, and traditional communities are just trying to hold their own, using whatever legal and procedural tools they can. In the next few chapters, we'll look at how TCP-like places are being addressed outside the United States and at some of the extrageographic interpretive frameworks that can be applied to understanding such places.

Notes

1. U.S. Conference of Mayors 1966.

2. Christopher Tunnard, Landmarks of Beauty and History, in *With Heritage So Rich*, report of a Special Committee on Historic Preservation under the auspices of the United States Conference of Mayors (Random House, New York, 1966), 33, emphasis in original.

3. Walter Muir Whitehill, The Right of Cities to Be Beautiful, in *With Heritage So Rich*, 55.

4. Carl Feiss, Our Lost Inheritance, in *With Heritage So Rich*, 130.

5. U.S. Conference of Mayors, *With Heritage So Rich,* 207.

6. An act authorizing the Park Service to fund archaeological salvage in areas flooded by U.S. Army Corps of Engineers Reservoirs. Many of us archaeological graybeards got our starts in this kind of salvage—that is, quickly excavating endangered sites before they're destroyed.

7. Established shortly after World War II by the Park Service and Smithsonian Institution, this program funded salvage in many reservoirs and led to the Reservoir Salvage Act.

8. 36 CFR 60.4.

9. Directing agencies to identify and nominate properties to the National Register and to treat eligible properties as though they were actually on the register. At the time, Section 106 of NHPA itself required consideration of impacts only on places already included in the register. The law was later amended to require consideration of eligible properties as well as those already listed.

10. A congressionally chartered private nongovernmental organization that promotes historic preservation; its full title is the National Trust for Historic Preservation in the United States, to distinguish it from its predecessor and model in Great Britain.

11. For the later history of project review in Tahquitz Canyon and the results of major research carried out there in the 1990s, see Lowell J. Bean, Silvia Brakke Vane, and Jerry Schaefer, *Archaeological, Ethnographic, and Ethnohistoric Investigations at Tahquitz Canyon,* 3 volumes (Cultural Systems Research, Inc., in press, Ballena Press, Ramona, CA, publication anticipated ca. 2004).

12. 378 F. Supp. 240 (N.D.Cal. 1974).

13. See Vera-Mae Fredrickson and David W. Peri, *Mihilakawna and Makahmo Pomo: People of Lake Sonoma* (U.S. Army Corps of Engineers, Sacramento, 1984); U.S. Army Corps of Engineers, *The Environment and the Engineers at Lake Sonoma,* videotape (San Francisco District, Corps of Engineers; Interface Video Services, Washington, D.C., 1989).

14. Now the Commonwealth of the Northern Mariana Islands, Republic of Palau, Federated States of Micronesia, and Republic of the Marshall Islands, then administered by the United States under a United Nations Trusteeship Agreement as a result of their seizure from Japan during World War II.

15. Thomas F. King and Patricia Parker, *Pisekin Nóómw Nóón Tonaachaw: Archaeology in the Tonaachaw Historic District, Moen Island,* Micronesian Archaeological Survey Report No. 18 (Southern Illinois University at Carbondale Center for Archaeological Investigations Occasional Paper No. 3, Carbondale, 1985).

16. For details, see King and Parker, *Pisekin Nóómw Nóón Tonaachaw.*

17. King and Parker, *Pisekin Nóómw Nóón Tonaachaw.*

18. Together with involvement in a number of archaeological matters in California, New York state, and nationally, and a year of work with NPS in Washington, D.C.

19. *Lyng v. Northwest Indian Cemetery Protective Ass'n.,* 485 U.S. 439.

20. *Northwest Indian Cemetery Protective Assn. v. Peterson,* 565 F. Supp. 586 (N.D. Cal 1983); 764 F. 2d 581 (9th Cir. 1985).

21. See Kelli Carmean, *Spider Woman Walks This Land: Traditional Cultural Properties and the Navajo Nation* (AltaMira, Walnut Creek, CA, 2002), 59–65.

22. See Carmean, *Spider Woman Walks This Land,* 134–42.

23. 36 CFR 63, which conflict directly with the Section 106 regulations at 36 CFR 800.4(c).

24. *Wilson v. Block,* 708 F. 2d 735 (D.C. Cir.).

25. 16 U.S.C. 470a note.

26. Department of the Interior archaeologists outside NPS have always had some trouble with this title.

27. Ormond H. Loomis, *Cultural Conservation: The Protection of Cultural Heritage in the United States* (American Folklife Center, Library of Congress, Washington, D.C., 1983).

28. Alan Jabbour, The American Folklife Center: The First Twenty Years, *Folklife Center News* XVIII:1/2 (Library of Congress, Washington, D.C., 1996).

29. Loomis, *Cultural Conservation,* 74.

30. I believe that NEPA *does* extend to all cultural resources, though NHPA, of course, does not.

31. Mary Hufford, *One Space, Many Places: Folklife and Land Use in New Jersey's Pinelands National Reserve* (American Folklife Center, Library of Congress, Washington, D.C., 1986).

32. See Shalom Staub, Cultural Conservation and Economic Recovery Planning: The Pennsylvania Heritage Parks Program, in Mary Hufford (ed.), *Conserving Culture: A New Discourse on Heritage,* published for the American Folklife Center at the Library of Congress (University of Illinois Press, Urbana, 1994), for a description of Pennsylvania's program.

33. See Douglas DeNatale, Federal and Neighborhood Notions of Place: Conflicts of Interest in Lowell, Massachusetts, in Hufford (ed.), *Conserving Culture,* for a classic example.

34. See Dale Rosengarten, "Sweetgrass Is Gold": Natural Resources, Conservation Policy, and African-American Basketry, in Hufford (ed.), *Conserving Culture.*

35. For example, Sharon Sullivan's weighty and informative Australian volume *Cultural Conservation: Towards a National Approach* (Special Australian Heritage Publication Series Number 9, Australian Heritage Commission, Australian Government Publishing Service, Canberra, 1995), seems to cover approximately what in the United States is called "historic preservation," while the African Cultural Conservation Fund (www.theculturebank.org/projects.htm) supports activities like skills exchanges among weavers in Africa and the United States. I have even found a website for the Canadian Cultural Conservation Program (www.geocities.com/Capitol/Hill/Lobby/3862/cccp/cccp.htm), whose stated purpose is to "ensure conformity (among cultural web-based

resources) to Official Canadian Culture." I am not at all sure that this one is not a joke, however.

36. I'm personally rather biased against it; see Thomas F. King, Stupid TCP Tricks, in *Thinking about Cultural Resource Management: Essays from the Edge* (AltaMira, Walnut Creek, CA, 2002), 19–25.

37. NHPA Section 101(d)(6)(A).

38. NHPA Section 101(d)(6)(B).

39. Patricia L. Parker (ed.), *Traditional Cultural Properties: What You Do and How We Think, CRM* Special Issue (National Park Service, Washington D.C., 1993); with most of the papers presented at a symposium at the 1993 annual meeting of the Society for American Archaeology, organized by Lynne Sebastian and Charles Carroll.

40. Sally T. Greiser and T. Weber Greiser, Two Views of the World, in Parker (ed.), *Traditional Cultural Properties*, 9–11.

41. Frances Levine and Thomas W. Merlan, Documenting Traditional Cultural Properties in Non-Indian Communities, in Parker (ed.), *Traditional Cultural Properties*, 55–64.

42. Alan S. Downer and Alexandra Roberts, Traditional Cultural Properties, Cultural Resources Management, and Environmental Planning, in Parker (ed.), *Traditional Cultural Properties*; Charles Carroll, Administering Federal Laws and Regulations Relating to Native Americans: Practical Processes and Paradoxes, in Parker (ed.), *Traditional Cultural Properties*.

43. Thomas F. King, Beyond Bulletin 38: Comments on the Traditional Cultural Properties Symposium, in Parker (ed.), *Traditional Cultural Properties*.

44. Lynne Sebastian, Protecting Traditional Cultural Properties through the Section 106 Process, in Parker (ed.), *Traditional Cultural Properties*, 26.

45. As she presented it at the time, it was a bit more narrowly phrased and focused entirely on eligibility determination: "I need to know about a property's association with a historic personage, with historic events, etc. I don't need to know, and don't wish to know, about the layers of confidential, sensitive, sacred knowledge associated with this historic property" (Sebastian, Protecting Traditional Cultural Properties, 25). I think it's fair to generalize it, though, as a reminder that each Section 106 review requires a particular body of data, and no more needs to be revealed about properties or their uses than is absolutely necessary for the purposes of the particular review.

46. E. Richard Hart, The Fence Lake Mine Project: Archaeology as Traditional Cultural Property, in Parker (ed.), *Traditional Cultural Properties*.

47. T. J. Ferguson, Kurt Dongoske, Leigh Jenkins, Mike Yeatts, and Eric Polingyouma, Working Together: The Roles of Archaeology and Ethnohistory in Hopi Cultural Preservation, in Parker (ed.), *Traditional Cultural Properties*; Andrew L. Othole and Roger Anyon, A Tribal Perspective on Traditional Cultural Property Consultation, in Parker (ed.), *Traditional Cultural Properties*.

48. Judy Brunson Hadley, Traditional Cultural Properties: Pros, Cons, and Reality, in Parker (ed.), *Traditional Cultural Properties*.

49. National Register, *Through the Generations: Identifying and Protecting Traditional Cultural Places,* videotape (National Park Service, in collaboration with the Natural Resources Conservation Service and Advisory Council on Historic Preservation, Washington, D.C., 1995).

50. As well as into sociocultural impact assessment not directed specifically toward tribes; see Richard W. Stoffle (ed.), *Cultural and Paleontological Effects of Siting a Low-Level Radioactive Waste Facility in Michigan: Candidate Area Analysis* (Institute for Social Research, University of Michigan, Ann Arbor, 1990); Lauri K. Sommers, Yvonne R. Lockwood, Marsha MacDowell, and Richard W. Stoffle, Folklife Assessment in the Michigan Low-Level Radioactive Waste Siting Process, in Hufford (ed.), *Conserving Culture.*

51. See David B. Halmo, Richard W. Stoffle, and Michael J. Evans, Paitu Nanasuagaindu Pahonupi (Three Sacred Valleys): Cultural Significance of Gosiute, Paiute, and Ute Plants, *Human Organization* 52(2): 142–50, 1993; Richard W. Stoffle and Michael J. Evans, Holistic Conservation and Cultural Triage: American Indian Perspectives on Cultural Resources, *Human Organization* 49(2): 91–99, 1990; Richard W. Stoffle, David B. Halmo, John E. Olmsted, and Michael J. Evans, *Native American Cultural Resource Studies at Yucca Mountain, Nevada* (Institute for Social Research, University of Michigan, Ann Arbor, 1990); Richard W. Stoffle, David B. Halmo, Michael J. Evans, and Diane E. Austin, *Piapaxa 'Uipi (Big River Canyon): Ethnographic Resource Inventory and Assessment for Colorado River Corridor, Glen Canyon National Recreation Area, Utah and Arizona, and Grand Canyon National Park, Arizona* (Bureau of Applied Research in Anthropology, University of Arizona, Tucson, 1993). Not calling them TCPs doesn't make much difference as long as the places are found to be eligible for the National Register. Where the whole eligibility determination process is sidestepped, however, places—whatever they're called—are denied the consideration they merit under Section 106.

Chapter Three

Tcps in Broader Perspective

Examples from Far and Wide

Every culture dreams its present and re-imagines its past.
—R. H. MacDonald (1994:42)

Introduction: TCPs in Context

THE process by which TCPs—and particularly indigenous spiritual places—got singled out for attention in U.S. historic preservation law and policy was part of something bigger. Several somethings, actually.

One was the American Indian movement—by which I mean not only the organization that took that name but the general movement toward tribal self-determination and self-respect that grew during the 1960s in parallel with the civil rights movement. This movement resulted in the passage of new legislation in the 1970s,[1] encouraged young tribal members to take up the practice of law, stimulated the establishment of important if sometimes short-lived activist organizations, and created a cadre of legally and politically savvy tribal advocates in Washington and across the nation. Members of this cadre, reflecting the frustrations of their tribes and elders, were instrumental in making Washington officialdom—myself included—pay attention to the concerns of tribal communities.

The civil rights movement itself had influence. Respecting places valued by local people is all about "power to the people." The fact of an increasingly educated, widely traveled, and prosperous U.S. population played a role, as did the post–Vietnam War suspicion of the wisdom of central government. The American public's love–hate relationship with science has been an influence, and I suspect that it may be a bigger one in the years to come. While we are great fans of science (and technology, of course), we have become skeptical of the notion that everything is amenable to scientific analysis. A healthy skepticism about

45

science as the one and only way to understand the universe is necessary to taking things like TCPs seriously.

But in this chapter and the next two I'd like to look at another "something" of which the recognition of TCPs has been a part—the growing worldwide interest in the "power of place." The word *place* and the notion of "place power" mean different things to different groups of people—landscape architects, urban and regional planners, philosophers, conservationists, anthropologists, New Age spiritualists—but whatever it's taken to mean, a lot of people have been thinking about it in the last twenty years. This interest is reflected in a growing literature on places and the roles they play in cultures around the world—the subject of this chapter. It's also been expressed in writings about North American cultures outside the context of CRM—the subject of chapter 5. Finally, it's expressed in works of theory and synthesis; some of these are the subjects of chapter 6.

It's useful for those of us who work and live with the U.S. CRM laws and regulations to appreciate these larger contexts, for at least two reasons. First, I think it's helpful to know that we aren't alone. Every government in the world has issues to deal with involving places that communities hold culturally dear. Few if any governments have yet dealt with such issues systematically. Those that have tried—Australia, for example, with regard to aboriginal land rights and heritage sites—have had mixed success.

The other useful thing about the "big picture" is that it highlights commonalities among places of community cultural value—some common attributes of such places, some common place types, and some common kinds of ascribed value. These commonalities can help us better understand the kinds of TCPs that we in the United States have to work with, and the factors that make them important. This, in turn, may help us craft effective management tools.

TCPs around the World—A Whirlwind Tour

Some sense of the breadth of interest in places of traditional cultural importance—and a sense of how important such places are coming to be seen in maintaining cultural integrity—can be grasped from a brief skim through *Cultural Survival Quarterly,* a journal that highlights issues of concern to traditional communities around the world. In the spring and fall 1996 issues of *CSQ* alone, for example, there were articles on the importance of traditional places in the cultural lives of the U'wa of Colombia,[2] indigenous communities in Palawan (Philippines),[3] the Wanniya Laeto of Sri Lanka,[4] and the Kaya of Kenya.[5] The relationships of more or less exotic communities to more or less faraway places are the meat and potatoes of magazines like *National Geographic.*

Beyond such popular descriptive works, TCP-like places of some parts of the world have been the subjects of quite intensive research. Let's look at a few of them.

Australia

The beliefs of aboriginal Australians about how the ancestral spirits of the Dreaming[6] created the landscape, and how their doings are reflected there, are well-known analogs to the beliefs of many American Indian groups. Many places in the Australian landscape are much like American Indian spiritual TCPs.

Anthropologists have studied Aboriginal society and its connections to the landmarks of the Dreaming since the discipline's earliest days. As in the United States, however, legislative and judicial actions over the last fifteen years, impelled by an increasingly educated and activist Aboriginal population, have resulted in intensified interest in indigenous land–society relationships. In 1992, in *Mabo and Ors v. the State of Queensland,* the Australian High Court upheld Aboriginal land claims based on indigenous customary law, thus introducing into the legal system the principle that such law could confer land title to Aboriginal people. Prior to *Mabo* and the 1993 enactment of the Native Title Act, it was assumed that precolonial Australia was *terra nullius,* without laws assigning land titles.[7]

Since Aboriginal customary law was of course unwritten (except in the land), the anthropological analysis of traditional land rights became a hot topic. Anthropological interpretations were dissected in courts of law and in the National Native Title Tribunal set up by the Title Act, and new research was undertaken to address needs not met by existing data. Anthropologists and Aboriginal groups found themselves working closely together, with specific reference to the ways in which contemporary society is tied to the land.[8] Such ties are typically represented by association with ancestral beings that operated in the Dreaming. While not all of the recent research has been motivated by the requirements of land title adjudication, these needs have generated a high level of interest in and support for such research, resulting in a burst of new analyses and publications.

Certainly the most widely known Aboriginal traditional place is Uluru, previously known as Ayres Rock. Uluru is a huge monolith that protrudes from the sandy red plains of central Australia. Believed to have been built of mud by spirits in the Dreaming, Uluru is the focus of many traditions; its folds, indentations, protuberances, overhangs, and the billabongs at its base are held to reflect the activities of the Dreaming spirits—cooking, eating, digging, hunting, fighting. Although originally part of an Aboriginal reserve established partly in recognition of its spiritual importance, Uluru and its vicinity were carved out to become a national park in 1958. After much negotiation, the land was returned to Aboriginal people in 1985, with the agreement that they would lease it back to government for park use, under the management authority of a board with a majority Aboriginal membership.

Uluru and the nearby rock outcrops of Kata Tjuta are only two of innumerable places associated with traditional beings and events of the Dreaming. *Associated* is actually too lifeless a word. Robert Layton writes that the landscape of the western Australian desert, to its Aboriginal people, is "fundamentally determined by the actions of beings during the *tjukurpa*, the 'time of the law.'" Ancestral beings "went into the ground" at specific named places in the landscape. "It is at these places," Layton says, "that their [the beings'] fecundity is concentrated." A living individual's identity is expected to mirror that of the ancestral being with which the individual has a relationship, and this relationship has geographic referents, particularly based on where the stub of a person's umbilical cord falls off. Places are sometimes spoken of as though they were themselves the ancestral beings with whom they are associated, and people are expected to know the stories associated with the places where their "fathers" went into the ground or performed other feats. Senior Aboriginal men pointed out to Layton "individual stones identified with their fathers. *Mama ngayuku palatja*, 'father mine just there,'" said one.[9]

Aboriginal Australians feel responsibility toward the land in which their ancestral places exist, and their responsibility toward such places is important to their cohesion as a society. To "hold" (have rights to) a "country" (land around a base camp), one must live there and look after its traditional places. Such places, Layton writes, "are fixed reference points to which individuals and coalitions are anchored . . . and permit . . . the precarious achievement of society in an environment where dispersal is the norm and the problem is how to draw sufficient people together to facilitate social interaction."[10]

Nancy Williams and Daymbalipu Munonggurr report that

> [d]uring their travels through Yolngu country [in the Northern Territory], wangarr spirit-beings left signs of their activities, both everyday events and those of religious import. They also left their appurtenances (such as digging sticks, dilly bags, and spears), and marks or impressions at the places where they sat or ate or slept. Most sacred of all, they left parts of their very beings in the sites that are most important to the Yolngu. . . . It is because the Yolngu landscape is saturated with signs that bear meanings and are still immensely

important to Yolngu that they regard it as potentially dangerous to disturb the features of the landscape.[11]

Howard Morphy argues that "interaction with the landscape is part of the process whereby the Dreaming as a component of the cultural structure of Aboriginal society is reproduced." "The ancestral beings," he says, "fixed in the land, become a timeless reference point outside the politics of daily life to which the emotions of the living can be attached."[12] Both individual and group identity are defined with reference to the landscape. Individual identity, Morphy says, "is so closely associated with the landscape that the one can act on the other. Ill treatment of the land—the breaking of taboos or disrespect of sacred sites—can result in illness or death for those who were born into that land. Conversely, the death of someone associated with an area of land can cause it to become a dangerous or barren place." At the same time, the association of ancestral beings with kin-based social groups means that kinship is "mapped onto landscape." As a result, "an individual, as he acquires knowledge of his kinship to others, can express it in terms of landscape. This, in turn, influences his perception of landscape. Kinship affects where he can go and what he can do at particular places; it can make a landscape . . . safe or dangerous."[13]

Neither the landscape nor the relationships of people to the landscape is unchanging, of course. Relationships are particularly fluid; one group may die out and another take over its territory, with the consequent need to reinterpret the area's traditions. However, the traditional past, encoded in the landscape, "though changed and reproduced through present human action, is absorbed as a precedent for future action, for marrying a particular person, for avoiding a particular place, for disposing of food remains in a particular way."[14]

In short, in Australia landscape features represent the identities of both living people—as individuals and as groups—and ancestral beings, and they integrate the living with the ancestors in the Dreaming. "Human identity thus is shared with something that has an existence independent of the person and which has the same origin: the ancestral past."[15]

An important feature of the way the Australian landscape is conceived of by its Aboriginal inhabitants is that everything is connected—it's not just empty space with landmarks in it. Peter Bridgewater and Theo Hooey[16] say that although Aboriginal sites are often separated by long distances, they are interconnected by trade trails and the paths of ancestral beings. They recommend thinking of such places as parts of networks rather than individually and in isolation. Robert Layton and Sarah Titchen make much the same point about the Uluru vicinity, though they describe the landscape more as an entity in itself than as the space occupied by a network.[17]

Africa

Some African societies—or perhaps those who have studied them—seem prone to ascribe spiritual power to humanly created structures more than to natural features of the landscape. For example, among the Bukusu of western Kenya, Simiyu Wandibba records three types of sacred sites: two types of constructed sacrificial shrines plus graves.[18] However, to the Bamenda of Cameroon's Western Grassfields, Mary Maimo Mumah says that "a sacred site is not necessarily a building, but is a powerful place or spot, an area or feature believed to be a residence of God."[19] The Mijikenda of coastal Kenya built walled enclosures that they call *kenda* as places of spiritual ritual, but places with special natural characteristics were selected for their construction. According to H. W. Mutoro, kenda are always "in the heart of dense forests."[20]

Spiritual places among the Muslim Swahili and Digo, also on the Kenyan coast, are "with a few exceptions, . . . not 'made' for such purposes, but are 'found.'" Found places may be constructed things—tombs and abandoned mosques—but they may also be "forests, caves, open-air sites, rock shelters, . . . and large trees (baobab and fig)."[21] Similarly in the south part of the continent, "found" spiritual places are often natural, though sometimes with evidence of cultural use by prior people. "Certain rock shelters with San paintings and rocky hills with San engravings . . . continued to have spiritual significance to the Bantu-speaking agriculturalists who displaced the San."[22]

According to Awo Fa'lokun Fatunmbi, the Yoruba believe that "altered states of consciousness that facilitate direct communication with specific Forces of Nature . . . [are] enhanced by certain natural settings called *Igbodu*. When a town is established in the Yoruba areas of the rain forest, the Ifa elders of the community search for those power spots that can be used as *Igbodu*."[23] These power places are then typically marked by constructing shrines; for example, "Igbodu Oshun in the city of Oshogbo is located in a cluster of trees along a bend in the Oshun River. The exposed roots of ancient trees appear to be long fingers leading into the water. Mud statues of mythic events in the life of Oshun are woven into the natural setting of the forest."[24]

Many writers have discussed a less mystical kind of African place that is nevertheless of considerable cultural value—the residential compound. Deborah Pellow, for example, writes of the attachment residents feel for their compounds in Adabraka, a low-rent neighborhood in Accra: "The compound yard—what in other circumstances is the courtyard—is the space that carries particular meaning for the compound dwellers. People feel attached or are attached to the compound yard because of what it offers, because of the actions that are part of its system."[25]

The "system" of which she writes is a system of traditional order that creates, in the compound, "an arena of informal socialization regarding gender roles, household and occupational responsibilities, and social and physical boundaries between occupants of [the compound's] rooms."[26]

The compound yard, then, represents and teaches its denizens about correct social relationships and cultural values, and is valued accordingly by the society and its members.

Several of the papers in Ezekial Kalipeni's and Paul Zeleza's edited volume, *Sacred Spaces and Public Quarrels: African Cultural and Economic Landscapes*, look at culture–place relationships from the interesting perspective of public health. Wilbert Gesler[27] discusses "therapeutic spaces"—landscapes and locations that aid in curing disease or in keeping a community healthy. Even a group as mobile as the !Kung—the very epitome of transient hunter-gatherers—carry out rituals to release curing spiritual energy, called *num,* in specific, socially sanctioned places, in their case the fires of their camps. These places are thought to contribute to cures: "Each !Kung group seems to favor its own fire: one healer says it is easier to kia[28] when he is dancing at his own camp. The camp thus becomes a community healer."[29]

In the same volume, Charles Anyinam discusses the relationships among African "sacred spaces," ecosystems, and the health of communities. African traditionalists ascribe spiritual qualities to many aspects of the natural environment:

All trees are thought to have souls of their own and some are regarded as the dwelling places of other powerful spirits who take temporary abode there. Many villages have a sacred tree.[30]

Wells, springs, rivers, lakes and the sea are believed to have spirits dwelling in them and in some cases great cults are made of the naiads. The greatest nature god of the Ashanti in Ghana is the Taro River.[31]

Landscapes and landscape features become objects of veneration:

In various parts of Africa, features of the landscape are selected as natural shrines. Shrine cults in Zambia, Ghana, Uganda, Kenya, and many other African countries tend to have a strong ecological emphasis and hills, imposing trees, caves, streams, falls and rapids become associated with invisible entities and become objects of veneration.[32]

Places are valued not only for their spiritual associations per se but because they embody a people's history. Tamara Giles-Vernick reports that the Banda "express history, or *guiriri,* as a spatial-temporal phenomenon rather than a temporal sequence of past events."[33]

Ascribing spiritual life to places, Anyinam says, and building traditions of veneration around them, encourages or even forces people to respect and protect them. This in turn maintains the health of the ecosystems represented by the "sacred spaces, which in turn maintains their ethnomedicinal (and subsistence) value." "As Schoffeleers reports of the Malawians, the indigenous people maintain 'a ritually directed ecosystem.'"[34]

In Africa as elsewhere, however, modern economic and political changes, population growth, and the breakdown of traditional systems of belief and social control are leading to the devaluation of spiritual space, and generating needs and conditions that lead to the destruction of such space. Anyinam warns that this contributes both to ecosystem degeneration and to the loss of community cultural integrity.[35]

Efforts to control such loss are not widely reported in Africa, but in Cape Coast, Ghana, one of the continent's first local historic preservation ordinances is reportedly designed not only to protect historic architecture but a shrine area at the edge of the city where chiefs go to carry out ceremonial activities and have ritual baths, and where returning "Africans of the diaspora" are given traditional names.[36]

China

China is well known for *feng shui,* a set of rules that can be applied to places to achieve, it is thought, a fruitful and safe relationship with one's surroundings.[37] Feng shui posits the flow of the spiritual power called *ch'ï* through the landscape. The fortunes of a house, office, or factory, and of those who live or work in it, are thought to be powerfully affected by the way ch'i flows through them, which depends on how they are situated in the landscape. The flow of ch'i makes places powerful (for good or ill) in ways that would be familiar to an Aboriginal Australian or an American Indian. Eugene Anderson comments:

> One of my consultants said that good and evil influences propagate through the world like radio waves, and a well-sited house or grave will pick up the good luck as a radio picks up radio waves. Others talked of the flow of ch'i. At some points it concentrates, and these are apt to be fortunate. It flows past other sites, and carries away their fortune, or even brings bad fortune to them. Still others speak of particular conformations or configurations of hills, or of good spirits attached to particular landmarks.[38]

Mountains, particularly high, rugged, wooded mountains, are regarded as places of concentrated ch'i. Trees can also be reservoirs of power, especially big, old trees and, among these, especially small-leafed banyans. This power can express itself in wry wisdom:

> The great philosopher Chuang Chou [ca. fourth century] . . . once asked a sacred tree how it had reached such veneration. He dreamed that the tree replied that it had worthless fruit, worthless lumber, and so acrid and stinging a sap that no one dared to bother it. "Thus," said the tree, "I have achieved great age, and people respect me." Chuang awoke with the reflection: "All know the use of use, but none know the use of uselessness!"[39]

Ch'i may concentrate in dramatic rock outcrops, recognized, perhaps, through many generations' observation of the land and its transformative powers. "In north and west China," Anderson reports, "where earthquakes are frequent, . . . one can often feel the earth quite literally move at such places."[40]

As elsewhere, in China community attachment to places can thwart development; this is one way, Anderson says, in which feng shui can be "a major builder of unity within communities." A village "will stand together in opposing a new and dangerous road, constructing a new and desirable pagoda, and protecting their sacred grove."[41] Reminiscent of the Chuukese village whose attitudes toward the "sacred" mountain I so misunderstood (see chapter 1), "They will also stand together in demanding compensation or mitigation from the government when the latter tries to force a major project on them. One bitter government agent told me: '*feng-shui* means money.'"[42] This reminds us of the danger in too readily assigning a loaded term like *sacred* to traditional places. "The Chinese language," Anderson points out, "has no word for 'religion'—in the Western sense—and literally cannot express the distinction between managing and venerating the landscape."[43] Respectful management of a landscape might embrace compensation while veneration might not.

Mongolia

According to Caroline Humphrey:[44]

> A Mongolian landscape seethes with entities which are attributed with anything from a hazy idea of energy to clearly visualized and named spirits. Each planet, mountain, river, lake, lone tree, cliff, marsh, spring, and so forth, has some such "supernatural" quality, as do animals, birds, fish, insects, humans, and even artifacts, such as tools, or guns, or man-made hay meadows.[45]

Even "the most featureless plain has its gentle curves, or bushes, or marshy patches, and even such entities are credited with powers of some kind."[46] Much as in North America and Australia, "people have their own relationships with particular mountains, cliffs, or trees, which they feel to be especially influential in their lives."[47]

In Mongolia, however, there are two contrastive traditional perceptions of the landscape—one associated with chiefly lineages, the other with shamans. Ordinary people apparently draw perceptions from both traditions, emphasizing one or the other more or less opportunistically. Chiefs see the landscape in ways that support patrilineal, hierarchical power relationships—for example, giving emphasis to altars on mountains. Shamans see landscape as more varied, imbued with many powers that must be appeased by individual actions. Under both traditions is a common belief in principles called *yos*, which articulate natural law and direct people in maintaining harmony with nature. An American land developer frustrated by TCPs might be grateful not to have to deal with yos.

> The yos essentially state that any unnecessary disturbance of nature must be avoided, and this includes inanimate entities. So it is wrong to move stones pointlessly from one place to another, or scuff the ground and make marks on it. Such marks must be wiped out with the foot before leaving a place. The circle left on the ground by a kettle should be erased. Burying things in the ground is done only with special rituals. It is wrong to interfere with the reproduction of nature: one must not take eggs, catch nestlings, or hunt young or pregnant animals. Grass should not be torn out by the roots—only withered grass should be collected.[48]

Chiefly lineages ascribe special significance to "mountains" under the authority of "land masters," or *gazarin ezed*—"landlords" in the post-Soviet vernacular, but traditionally spirit beings from whom permission had to be gotten to use land. In flat country, such "mountains" may be "no more than mounds, hardly visible except in the slanting rays of the setting sun. But nevertheless any particular mountain is the site at which to call upon the spirits of the whole landscape relevant to the agent (the social group or individual)."[49]

In the shamanistic landscape, the earth is female and the sky is male. Caves are equated with wombs and are venerated by cave cults, but many other landscape features have spiritual associations. There is, Humphrey says, an "infinite multiplicity of beings which people feel to have power."[50]

Eastern Arctic

In the hinterland of the Barents Sea, the Nenets ascribe cultural and spiritual importance to natural places and leave offerings there. O. V. Ovsyannikof and N. M. Terebikhin describe such places; they suggest that most have gone out of use since Christianization of the area, but at one major site, the Kozmin Copse, trees were hung not only with copper and bronze bells and other items of arguable antiquity but also with "dolls, teapots, a thermos flask, an alarm-clock, and the steering-wheel of a tractor."[51]

In southern Norway, Sweden, Finland, and northwestern Russia, the Saami people ascribe spiritual power to large stones, ground and shaped by wind, water, and ice. Although their veneration is no longer "officially" sanctioned, Saami "are taught how to conceal the existence of these places, so that they will remain unknown to the uninitiated."[52]

Eastern Andes and Amazonia

On the eastern slope of the Andes in central Peru, Fernando Santos-Granero suggests that the Yanesha "write history into the landscape" via a "protowriting system" based on what he calls "topograms."[53] A topogram is a landscape feature "imbued with historical significance through myth and ritual." Topograms are combined to form "topographs," units of narrative about both Yanesha occupation and consecration of the land and its despoliation by others. Yanesha tradition recounts how the solar and lunar divinities *Yompor Ror* and *Yachor Arror* traveled across the land siring children, dismembering rivals, struggling with enemies, creating living creatures and transforming some into stones. These stories, Santos-Granero suggests, reflect Yanesha movement into their present-day territory out of the Amazon lowlands at the expense of the area's prior occupants. The travel routes of Yompor Ror and Yachor Arror mirror the archaeologically and historically documented pathways along which the Yanesha ancestors apparently spread into the territory. Santos-Granero also shows how modern "desecration" of the area as part of the government's Pichis-Palcazu Special Project (a road-building scheme) has been "written into the landscape" through stories of upset spirit beings and bloodthirsty throat cutters associated with particular areas and landforms along the expanding road system. The meaning of the various topograms, and the topographs they make up, is maintained and reinforced in community memory through reciting traditions and through ritual activities. Santos-Granero suggests that similar topographic writing systems are used by the Paez of highland southwestern Colombia and the Wakuenai of lowland Venezuela.[54] Joanne Rappaport, in one of the sources cited by Santos-Granero, says, "Paez historical referents are encoded and interpreted through a localized sacred geography. Each community has its own topographical referents which structure its local historical accounts."[55]

Oceania

Polynesians, Micronesians, and Melanesians have elaborate bodies of tradition in which both land places and sea places are of central importance. The spiritual powers of Hawaiian deities like the volcano goddess Pele are widely known and give special importance to whole mountains and to places on and around them.[56] In New Zealand, places known to Maori as *waahi tapu*, "provide cultural and *iwi* [tribe] markers which, together with *whakapapa* [genealogy] mark the people and the traditional landscape, providing physical, historical and emotional links to the *tupuna* [ancestors]."[57]

Among Micronesian navigators, "places" in the open ocean are recognized as having special natural and supernatural characteristics, though the two categories are not usually distinguished from one another. Traditional chants describe these places and the relationships between them, providing "maps" to guide canoe voyagers over vast ocean distances.[58] Land areas are similarly mapped in traditional characterization. Mount Tonaachaw in Chuuk is characterized in *itaang* tradition as a huge octopus whose tentacles stretch out to landmarks on the fringing reef and whose ear—to the uninitiated a nondescript grassy place on the mountainside—harbors barracuda watchmen who keep a lookout on events in the world below.[59]

In Fiji, where the Melanesian and Polynesian linguistic areas flow together, Christina Toren reports that people constantly talk about "the passing of time, often in terms of places and landmarks that function as reference points for the succession of events." This commentary has a purpose. "The awareness of 'time emplaced,'" she suggests, "informs the process through which Fijian villagers constitute their identities, their sense of themselves, as rooted in their natal land."[60]

Rootedness in the land is important to Native Fijians, who Toren says see themselves as belonging to the land more than it belongs to them.[61] As a result, Fijian songs "regularly celebrate their villages and countries by name, the song of the birds that live there and the smell of the flowering trees and plants that grow there."[62]

Toren's mention of smell is worth noting. We often think of traditional places in terms of vision—not only vision questing, in some cases, but simply the visual qualities of the landscape. In making decisions about management of a TCP, it is visual impacts that often first come to mind as management issues. Auditory qualities are sometimes considered, where the sound of a stream or the wind in the trees is important—or the rumble of a subway train, the rattle of a taxi. But smells can be key, valued characteristics of a treasured place, too. Years ago, an urban planning study of place values in San Francisco, California mapped the smells of the districts south of Market Street.[63]

In Fiji smells can evoke deep associations between people and places: "The smell of a place can be a mark of certain ancestors: this is true of the vanilla-like scent of the sand at a beach near Sawaieke, while an inexplicable bad smell in the house alerts one to the potentially malign presence of 'the two ladies.'"[64]

Fijians experience continuity with the past "through the sights, sounds, and smells of the land," but the significance they ascribe to places is not frozen in time. Continuity is mediated by relations with others, which are constantly changing. This "makes the ancestral past continue into the present even while, for any given person, it effects transformations in the meanings of the past and thus in the meanings that 'the land' can have for present and future generations."[65]

New Guinea

Steven Field has studied the place associations of the Kaluli of Bosavi in Papua New Guinea, a rainforest people who, he finds, often define places acoustically. The Kaluli's is an environment where "the locational information available from sound . . . often greatly exceeds that available from vision, in both variety and salience." So the Kaluli use sound to define the key attributes of special places. However, "audition is always in interplay with other senses, particularly in a tense dialectic with vision. This is because much of the forest is visually hidden, whereas sound cannot be hidden."[66] Field finds this dialectic reflected powerfully in Kaluli poetics, which evoke places in terms of sight versus sound, hidden versus revealed.[67]

Places and place names are important in Kaluli life and in the identities of individuals and communities. Linguistic forms that attach possessive markers to place names ("his stream"; "her tree") tie "place to person, identity to locality, and heightens the affective resonance of placenames."[68] Places are mapped in memory through songs and laments built around "paths" or *tok*, which reveal "the connectedness of . . . places, and with that connectedness, a connectedness of people, experiences, and memories."[69] As in other cultures, Kaluli places don't exist in isolation from one another, but as webs of relationship, which reflect and give coherence to relationships among people, and between people and environment.

> Ulahi [a Kaluli singer] once told me that every one of her songs was like a mogan on a creek. I take her to mean that every song is a pool, a swirl, something that centers and circles in place for some moments, then turns and flows downstream to mingle and merge in other pools. In this sense, Ulahi's songs, like the Wo:lu creek where she sang them, meander and flow through Bosavi communities, reverberating through Kaluli lives and our own by linking places together and suggesting that these paths always connect stories about people's memories and feelings.[70]

Madagascar

We've seen many similarities among the ways people value traditional places in cultures across the world, but Maurice Bloch, writing about Madagascar, provides a cautionary note. The Zafimiry of that island nation, he finds, while they ascribe cultural value to places, do it very much in their own way.[71] The Zafimiry way may be a little difficult for a European or American environmentalist or historic preservationist to relate to.

The Zafimiry practice shifting horticulture in the rainforest, so Bloch naturally expected that they would value places expressing rainforest characteristics—fine groves of trees, dappled shadows on the forest floor. But he found that the Zafimiry are happiest when *clearing* the forest; they like to see it gone.

Bloch's initial impression—reminiscent of my response to the Chuukese willingness to "sell the sacred mountaintop"—was that the Zafimiry outlook on the environment was, as he delicately puts it, "purely utilitarian." Living with them, however, he came to realize that the Zafimiry assigned great cultural value to aspects of the natural environment—they just didn't like the closed-in rainforest.

What Zafimiry appreciate, it turned out, is what Bloch calls "clarity"—a clear view across open space. "The Zafmiry," he writes, "are as enthusiastic as are the Guide Michelin and municipal authorities about good views."[72] Whenever he was with a group of Zafimiry and they came upon a "view afar," they would stop and look at it, discuss its qualities, talk of its beauty—especially the clarity and spaciousness of the view.

But the forest grows back, and the Zafimiry themselves return to the soil of the forest floor. They commemorate the dead with rather elaborate mortuary structures, but in the end the identities of the dead are forgotten; they become parts of the uncaring forest landscape. So it is the places that rise out of that landscape, that can be seen from afar, that are affirming to the Zafimiry.

> They are looking at summits, many of which have villages on them and the others, it is presumed once had such villages. These summits represent their history, the achievements of their ancestors who have inscribed themselves on to the unchanging land, especially on those points which rise out of the chaos of the forest and the mist and stand clear and certain in the sunshine.[73]

Yet when they see such hilltops standing in all clarity above the forests, the Zafimiry often sing melancholy songs. Bloch attributes this to a recognition of their place in the environment, that in the end, the achievement of the ancestors, and of themselves, "is slight, many of the 'villages' have returned to forest, the viewed landscape and especially its contours seem in the end, unaffected by human activity, and the ultimate fruit of human efforts at immortality are nothing but rocks."[74]

TCPs are not always happy places, the Zafimiry remind us, but they are places that make us think about our place in time and space. And what triggers such thoughts in one group is not necessarily what does so in another.

Urban Japan

"Miyamoto-cho," a neighborhood in Tokyo studied by Theodore Bestor,[75] illustrates a somewhat different way that people ascribe cultural value to the places they frequent. Bestor shows how the traditional urban life of the *Shitamachi* neighborhoods—working-class neighborhoods along the shores of Tokyo Bay and at the mouth of the Sumida River—has been valued in Japanese culture as a "distinctive, cohesive, integrated way of life."[76] Though the extinction of this way of life was confidently predicted in the 1950s and 1960s with the growth of the new Japanese middle class, these predictions proved, in Bestor's words, to be "paradoxically premature." In fact, he says, "[t]hroughout the Shitamachi wards of Tokyo today there is a renaissance of Shitamachi consciousness."[77] It seems that when threatened with loss of the old, valued lifestyle, people sought to retain and revitalize them, with specific reference to the places with which they were associated. Moreover, "*Shitamachi* consciousness" has been appropriated by others—like the residents of the historically unrelated Miyamoto-cho, who think their district to "resemble Shitamachi in its social character. By this I think they mean to attribute to themselves the qualities of friendly, open, informal interactions within the context of a rich community social life."[78]

What makes Miyamoto-cho particularly relevant to the understanding of TCPs in the United States is that its valued cultural qualities are not exactly native to it; they're appropriated. A purist might argue that Miyamoto-cho isn't a legitimate representative of the Shitamachi tradition because it is not, as it were, traditionally Shitamachi. But Bestor argues that "[t]he ability to appropriate and manipulate the cultural symbols of the *Shitamachi* ethos constitutes an important social resource."[79]

Israel

No tour of special places would be complete without what Europeans and Americans call the Holy Land—a place liberally endowed with places important to contemporary religious communities both resident and distributed worldwide. Everyone knows about many such places—the Temple Mount/Dome of the Rock, Calvary, the Tomb of Abraham, Bethlehem—and is painfully aware of the passions that surge around them, but the way such places actually interact with cultural identity seems to have been little explored. In an interesting exception, Tom Selwyn[80] looks at the way landmarks and the land *qua* land have been more or less explicitly employed in the twentieth century for sociopolitical purposes. Selwyn documents how landscape and its "holistic" experience were used early in the twentieth century to reinforce secular Zionist values, replacing God with nature and emphasizing relationships between society and landscape. More recently, he proposes, "the landscape seems to have become one of the means of re-establishing the link with God which was severed at the beginning of the century."[81] Today, he says, the landscape of Israel "continues to be used . . . to construct myths in which 'we' appear as its defenders against several different kind of people and forces who would seem to threaten it and, by so doing, threaten us too."[82]

A more traditional portrayal of spiritual places in the Holy Land—and one that conveys a sense not unlike those associated with places of cultural importance to Aboriginal Australian, Africans, Native Americans, and Mongolians—is Roger Wharton's discussion of Bethlehem and its environs as a sacred site. Wharton's description will resonate with anyone who has shared or heard about, the experiences of indigenous people with the spiritual elements of the natural world.

Although it has always been the Christian way to enclose sacred places within churches and buildings, Bethlehem remains unique in that it also preserves one of the few outdoor Christian holy sites. Located about two miles down the hill from the Church of the Holy Nativity are a field and cave, the traditional site where the angels announced the birth of Christ to the shepherds abiding in their fields by night. Sheep still graze in this field.[83]

As I walked down the path (into the field), I looked skyward and was greeted by a large flock of migrating storks who had stopped their migration to circle overhead. For a moment as I gazed upward, time was transcended. I was standing in the field on the night of the birth of Christ and angels were flying overhead proclaiming the Good News.[84]

Notes

1. Notably the Indian Self-Determination and Education Act of 1974, but also of importance for our purposes, the American Indian Religious Freedom Act of 1979.

2. *Cultural Survival Quarterly* (spring 1996):5.

3. *Cultural Survival Quarterly* (spring 1996):45–49.

4. *Cultural Survival Quarterly* (spring 1996):16–20.

5. *Cultural Survival Quarterly* (fall 1996):19–21.

6. A sort of time-outside-time, also referred to as the Dreamtime and the time of the law.

7. By acts of the various states from 1966 onward, Aboriginal groups had been given varying degrees of control over the reserves on which many of them were collected, and the Aboriginal Land Rights (Northern Territory) Act of 1976 established a process for adjudicating Aboriginal land claims in the Northern Territory, but these legislative acts did not reflect the recognition that Aboriginal groups had in fact *possessed* title prior to colonization.

8. For overview and analytical articles on applied anthropology and Aboriginal land claims, see Sandy Toussaint (ed.), Practicing Anthropology in Australia, *Practicing Anthropology* 23 (2001):1, Society for Applied Anthropology.

9. Robert Layton (ed.), *Who Needs the Past? Indigenous Values and Archaeology* (World Archaeological Congress, Routledge, London, 1989), 213–20.

10. Layton, *Who Needs the Past?* 229.

11. Nancy M. Williams and Daymbalipu Mununggurr, Understanding Yolngu Signs of the Past, in Layton (ed.), *Who Needs the Past?* 79.

12. Howard Morphy, Landscape and the Reproduction of the Ancestral Past, in E. Hirsch and M. O'Hanlon (eds.), *The Anthropology of Landscape: Perspectives on Place and Space* (Clarendon, Oxford, 1995), 187–88.

13. Morphy, Landscape and the Reproduction of the Ancestral Past, 197–98.

14. Morphy, Landscape and the Reproduction of the Ancestral Past, 205.

15. Morphy, Landscape and the Reproduction of the Ancestral Past, 205.

16. Peter Bridgewater and Theo Hooey, Outstanding Cultural Landscapes in Australia, New Zealand, and the Pacific: The Footprint of Man in the Wilderness, in B. von Droste, H. Plachter, and M. Rössler (eds.), *Cultural Landscapes of Universal Value—Components of a Global Strategy* (Fischer, Jena, Germany, 1995), 168.

17. Robert Layton and Sarah Titchen, Uluru: An Outstanding Australian Aboriginal Cultural Landscape, in von Droste et al. (eds.), *Cultural Landscapes of Universal Value*, 178.

18. Simiyu Wandibba, Bukusu Sacred Places, in D. L. Carmichael et al. (eds.), *Sacred Sites, Sacred Places* (Routledge, London, 1994), 117–18.

19. Mary Maimo Mumah, Sacred Sites in the Bamenda Grassfields of Cameroon: A Study of Sacred Sites in the *Nso Fondom*, in Carmichael et al. (eds.), *Sacred Sites, Sacred Places*, 100.

20. Mumah, Sacred Sites in the Bamenda Grassfields of Cameroon, 134.

21. George H. Okello Abungu, Islam on the Kenyan Coast: An Overview of Kenyan Coastal Sacred Sites, in Carmichael et al. (eds.), *Sacred Sites and Sacred Places*.

22. Johannes Loubser, Management Planning for Conservation, in David S. Whitley (ed.), *Handbook of Rock Art Research* (AltaMira, Walnut Creek, CA, 2001), 92.

23. Awo Fa'lokun Fatunmbi, Kekere Kan Ati Ase Ayie: The Ifa Concept of Work and the Power of the Earth, in J. Swan and R. Swan (eds.), *Dialogues with the Living Earth* (Quest, Madras, 1995), 69.

24. Fatunmbi, Kekere Kan Ati Ase Ayie.

25. Deborah Pellow, Spaces That Teach: Attachment to the African Compound, in R. Altman and S. Low (eds.), *Place Attachment* (Plenum, New York, 1992), 197.

26. Pellow, Spaces That Teach, 202.

27. Often citing Robin Kearns, Place of Health in the Health of Place: The Case of the Hokianga Special Medical Area, *Social Science and Medicine* 33 (1991):519–30.

28. That is, achieve enhanced consciousness, which contributes to cures. Wilbert Gesler, The Construction of Therapeutic Spaces, in Ezekiel Kalipeni and Paul T. Zeleza (eds.), *Sacred Spaces and Public Quarrels: African Cultural and Economic Landscapes* (Africa World, Asmara, 1999), 120.

29. Gesler, The Construction of Therapeutic Spaces, 121.

30. Charles Anyinam, Ethnomedicine, Sacred Spaces, and Ecosystem Preservation and Conservation in Africa, in Kalipeni and Zeleza (eds.), *Sacred Spaces and Public Quarrels*, 134.

31. Anyinam, Ethnomedicine, 134.

32. Anyinam, Ethnomedicine, 135, citing van Binsbergen (1978).

33. Tamara Giles-Vernick, Na lege ti guiriri (On the Road of History): Mapping Out the Past and Present in M'Bres Region, Central African Republic, *Ethnohistory* 43 (1996):2, 244–75.

34. Anyinam, Ethnomedicine, 139.

35. Anyinam, Ethnomedicine, 141–42.

36. James Reap, Info for Ghana Project. Request for advice, with proposed project description, forwarded to ACRA-L by Sue Henry Renaud, National Park Service, November 15, 2000.

37. Eugene N. Anderson, *Ecologies of the Heart: Emotion, Belief, and the Environment* (Oxford University Press, New York, 1995).

38. Anderson, *Ecologies of the Heart*, 18.

39. Anderson, *Ecologies of the Heart*, 20.

40. Anderson, *Ecologies of the Heart*, 21.

41. Evidently such solidarity has been unavailing in the case of China's Three Gorges dam and reservoir—possibly the biggest planned destruction of traditional cultural properties (and the living communities that value them) in recent history.

42. Anderson, *Ecologies of the Heart*, 24.

43. Anderson, *Ecologies of the Heart*, 18.

44. Caroline Humphrey, Chiefly and Shamanist Landscapes in Mongolia, in Hirsch and O'Hanlon (eds.), *The Anthropology of Landscape*.

45. Humphrey, Chiefly and Shamanist Landscapes in Mongolia, 141.

46. Humphrey, Chiefly and Shamanist Landscapes in Mongolia, 135.

47. Humphrey, Chiefly and Shamanist Landscapes in Mongolia, 137.

48. Humphrey, Chiefly and Shamanist Landscapes in Mongolia, 141, citing Lattimore (1942) and Tatar (1984:321–22).

49. Humphrey, Chiefly and Shamanist Landscapes in Mongolia, 145.

50. Humphrey, Chiefly and Shamanist Landscapes in Mongolia, 151.

51. O. V. Ovsyannikof and N. M. Terebikhin, Sacred Space in the Culture of the Arctic Regions, in Carmichael et al. (eds.), *Sacred Sites, Sacred Places*, 67.

52. Inga-Marie Mulk, Sacrificial Places and Their Meaning in Saami Society, in Carmichael et al. (eds.), *Sacred Sites, Sacred Places*, 130.

53. Fernando Santos-Granero, Writing History into the Landscape: Space, Myth, and Ritual in Contemporary Amazonia, *American Ethnologist* 25(2) (1998):128–48, American Anthropological Association, Washington, D.C.

54. See Joanne Rappaport, Geography and Historical Understanding in Indigenous Colombia, in Layton (ed.), *Who Needs the Past?*; and Jonathan Hill, *Keepers of the Sacred Chants: The Poetics of Ritual Power in an Amazonian Society* (University of Arizona Press, Tucson, 1993).

55. Rappaport, Geography and Historical Understanding, 91.

56. See W. Bruce Masse, Laura A. Carter, and Gary F. Somers, Waha'ula Heiau: The Regional and Symbolic Context of Hawai'i Island's "Red Mouth" Temple, *Asian Perspectives* 30(1) (1991):19–56.

57. Hirini Matunga, Waahi Tapu: Maori Sacred Sites, in Carmichael et al. (eds.), *Sacred Sites, Sacred Places*, 221.

58. See Stephen D. Thomas, *The Last Navigator* (Ballantine, New York, 1987).

59. Thomas F. King and Patricia L. Parker, *Pisekin Nóómw Nóón Tonaachaw: Archaeology in the Tonaachaw Historic District, Moen Island,* Micronesian Archaeological Survey Report No. 18, Southern Illinois University at Carbondale Center for Archaeological Investigations Occasional Paper No. 3 (Carbondale, 1985), 55.

60. Christina Toren, Seeing the Ancestral Sites: Transformations in Fijian Notions of the Land, in Hirsch and O'Hanlon (eds.), *The Anthropology of Landscape*, 163.

61. Toren, Seeing the Ancestral Sites, 164.

62. Toren, Seeing the Ancestral Sites, 176.

63. Constance Ramirez (who did the study), personal communication to the author, 1996.

64. Toren, Seeing the Ancestral Sites.

65. Toren, Seeing the Ancestral Sites, 179.

66. Steven Field, Waterfalls of Song: An Acoustemology of Place Resounding in Basavi, Papua New Guinea, in Steven Field and Keith H. Basso (eds.), *Senses of Place* (School of American Research Press, Santa Fe, NM, 1996), 99.

67. Field, Waterfalls of Song, 107.

68. Field, Waterfalls of Song, 102.

69. Field, Waterfalls of Song, 103.

70. Field, Waterfalls of Song, 134.

71. Maurice Bloch, People into Places: Zafimiry Concepts of Clarity, in Hirsch and O'Hanlon (eds.), *The Anthropology of Landscape*.

72. Bloch, People into Places, 65.

73. Bloch, People into Places, 74.

74. Bloch, People into Places.

75. Theodore C. Bestor, *Neighborhood Tokyo* (Stanford University Press, Palo Alto, CA, 1989).

76. Theodore C. Bestor, Rediscovering Shitamachi: Subculture, Class, and Tokyo's "Traditional" Urbanism, in Rotenberg and McDonogh (eds.), *The Cultural Meaning of Urban Space* (Bergin & Garvey, Westport, CT, 1993), 52.

77. Bestor, Rediscovering Shitamachi, 53.

78. Bestor, Rediscovering Shitamachi, 55.

79. Bestor, Rediscovering Shitamachi, 57.

80. Tom Selwyn, Landscapes of Liberation and Imprisonment: Towards an Anthropology of the Israeli Landscape, in Hirsch and O'Hanlon (eds.), *The Anthropology of Landscape.*

81. Selwyn, Landscapes of Liberation and Imprisonment, 132.

82. Selwyn, Landscapes of Liberation and Imprisonment, 133.

83. Roger Wharton, But You, O Bethlehem of Ephrathah: Bethlehem as a Sacred Place, in Swan and Swan (eds.), *Dialogues with the Living Earth*, 129.

84. Wharton, But You, O Bethlehem of Ephrathah, 131.

Chapter Four

And Closer to Home . . .

The birthplace of the caribou is sacred to us, so that we do not enter it even in times of famine, although hunting would be easy for us there.

> —Joe Linklater and Faith Gemmill, representatives of Gwich'in Nation, writing about *Vadzih googii v dehk'it gwanlii*, the "Sacred Place Where Life Begins," on the Arctic National Wildlife Refuge (*Washington Post*, January 17, 2001)

The United States and Canada: Indigenous Places Not Called TCPs

SCHOLARS in the United States and Canada have written a good deal about what amount to traditional cultural places, under various names and reflecting the viewpoints and methods of several disciplines. Some of the recent literature—particularly that dealing with places important to Indian tribes in the United States—refers more or less explicitly to National Register Bulletin 38 and the requirements of NHPA and NEPA. We'll look at some of these studies in subsequent chapters.[1]

Other studies have been done on traditional places without reference to U.S. environmental and historic preservation laws, some of it by people who may think that *TCP* is the acronym for some kind of tissue paper. That's the literature I'd like to look at in this chapter, to help put Bulletin 38 and TCPs in perspective.

Indigenous Places in Canada[2]

In Canada, as in the United States and Australia, interest in and controversy around indigenous cultural places have surged in the last two decades. Canada's

"First Nations," like tribes south of the border, have vigorously and effectively made their identities known to government and the public alike. Land claims cases have resulted in investigations by government bodies, which have required studies of traditional beliefs about land and places on the land. Many of the important places and cases are summarized by Susan Buggey in a 1999 analysis prepared for the Historic Sites and Monuments Board Canada (HSMBC).[3]

Not surprisingly, the kinds of indigenous TCPs we deal with in the United States are also represented in Canada. For example, *Ninaistàkis* (Chief Mountain) in Alberta near the Montana border is regarded by the Niitsatapi (speakers of Blackfoot) as the home of the sacred Thunderbird, and it is a "traditional and continuing focus of their spiritual activity."[4] Some places are believed to "contain the powers of transformers or spirit beings"—examples being *Th'exelis* on the Fraser River[5] and *Xa:ytem* National Historic Site.[6] Other examples include the following:

- A rock, flooded by the creation of Lake Diefenbaker in Saskatchewan, believed by the Cree to be the gateway to the underworld. "Its explosion in conjunction with the lake construction ended forever their hope that the buffalo, disappeared from the Prairies for nearly a century, would return from their underground sojourn;"[7]

- The Annapolis Valley in Nova Scotia, traditionally created by the transformer *Glooscap;*[8]

- Bear Rock on the Mackenzie River, and a number of related sites widely spread over the Northwest Territories, believed by the Dene to be associated with the travels and accomplishments of the law giver *Yamoria;*[9]

- The routes taken by giant mythological serpents, reflected today in the main street pattern of Wendake in Quebec.[10]

Many indigenous cultural places in Canada are quite large, including multiple interrelated locations. For example, according to the November 1996 minutes of the HSMBC:

> The Sahtu Dene narratives create a mosaic of stories that envelop the cultural landscape of Grizzly Bear Mountain and Scented Grass Hills. The web of "myth and memory" spread beyond the mountains to cover the whole western end of Great Bear Lake, illustrating the complexity of the Sahtu Dene's landscape tradition.[11]

Places associated with spirits are thought to have special power, "where the combination of spirits and place create environments favorable for spiritual communication."[12] Such places may strengthen vision quest experiences but may also be dangerous. Some power places are reserved for use by shamans.

Traditional places are named and collectively constitute maps of indigenous groups' territories, each set of landmarks guiding its people through space and at the same time encapsulating their history, values, and beliefs.

> Recent field work focused on traditional place names and narratives in the North Slave Dogrib claim area, which has documented nearly 350 Dogrib place names, has shown that "[a]s part of a knowledge system, traditional place names serve as memory 'hooks' on which to hang the cultural fabric of a narrative tradition. In this way, physical geography ordered by place names is transformed into a social landscape where culture and topography are symbolically fused."[13]

Buggey offers an interesting indigenous classification of cultural places, which gives an idea of the range of properties considered "traditional" and "cultural" in Canada both by indigenous people and by government. Dogrib elders, she says, classify "sacred sites" in their landscape as:[14]

- reflections of the activities of culture heroes;

- locations of "spirit animals," usually malevolent;

- locations where the dreaming of culture heroes is associated with landscape features;

- places where important resources (e.g. ochre, stone) are found; and

- graves.

Places that are not exactly "sacred" may also be important. Landscapes and features reflecting traditional use of the land for social and economic purposes—places where people customarily camp, hunt, fish, trap, cross rivers, come together in summer congregations—are parts of a group's relations with its country, its past, and its culture. "Many groups identify summer gathering places to which they returned over centuries as among the most important places representing their heritage."[15]

Indigenous "Sacred Sites" in the United States

One of the intellectual traditions that produced Bulletin 38, and one of the sociopolitical imperatives that required its production, was the growth of interest in, and concern about, American Indian "sacred sites" that began (as in Canada) during the 1980s. While some have identified the publication of Bulletin 38 itself as a contribution to this "movement," it would be fairer to say that the "sacred sites movement" gave us direction in producing the bulletin.

Andrew Guilliford's *Sacred Objects and Sacred Places: Preserving Tribal Traditions*[16] describes many of the better-known (and some not-so-well-known) indigenous spiritual places in the United States and also discusses repatriation, museum issues, and living cultural traditions. A handsome "coffee table" book edited by Jake Page—*Sacred Lands of Indian America*[17]—offers evocative photos and text (the latter, alas, not always very accurate)[18] on such famous spiritual places as Mount Graham in Arizona, Bear Lodge (Devil's Tower) in Wyoming, and Mount Shasta and Medicine Lake in California. Both books are worth reading for overviews of often-referred-to sites and, in the case of Guilliford's book, some of the major issues surrounding tribal spiritual places in the United States.

Some analytical work with tribal "sacred sites" has been done in the Southwest, particularly among the Navajo. Typically such work has been stimulated by cultural and land use conflicts resulting from mineral development and the "settlement" of conflicting Navajo and Hopi land claims.[19] Studies from the 1970s and 1980s were summarized, together with the results of their own original work, by Klara Kelley and Harris Francis in their 1994 *Navajo Sacred Places*.[20]

Kelley and Francis interviewed members of thirteen Navajo chapters (the administrative divisions of the Navajo Nation) in different parts of the reservation. They identified 164 culturally significant places, three-fourths of which they classified as "sacred" because of their associations with stories, customary activities, or both.[21]

As in Australia and the Andes, spiritual places in the Navajo landscape are associated with stories about ancestral beings. Sometimes they are the ruins of the towns build by the ancestral puebloan people who lived in the area before the Navajo came; in other cases they are natural features, sometimes with incidental evidence of human use, sometimes without. For example: "mountains, hills, rock outcrops, canyons, springs and other bodies of water, natural discolorations on rocks, areas where certain plants grow, mineral deposits, isolated trees, places where rocks produce echoes, air vents in rocks, sand dunes, flat open areas, lightning-struck trees and rocks."[22]

The stories associated with some such places—for example, some places where plants and minerals are gathered and places like "flat open areas"—may be the kinds of tales that, as we'll see, Keith Basso would record among the Cibicue Apache as more or less secular pedagogical parables. Other place types whose "sacred" quality might be questioned are those "where Navajos have left evidence of customary Navajo activities—certain types of cairns, traps for ceremonial hunting of antelope, deer, and eagles."[23]

Whether an anthropologist calls a place "sacred" or not may depend more on the anthropologist's orientation than on the way Navajo or other indigenous people view it. The division between sacred and secular so dear to the hearts of Euro-American political scientists doesn't make much sense in the Navajo worldview.

> Often, people choose a place for customary activities because "a story goes with it." These locations are connected to Navajo origin stories, family stories, or stories about some other event that conferred some special power on the place.[24]

> "[S]acred" in the Navajo context embraces much more than it does in the national principle that separates "church and state." One could almost say that Navajo life and the stories and beliefs and customs that go with it are Navajo religion.[25]

Among the important points made repeatedly by Kelley and Francis is that "sacred places" aren't isolated little pieces of land, spots of sanctity in a spiritually neutral landscape. Instead, they comprise coherent networks, which impart significance to—or derive significance from, or share it with—the landscape over which they are cast.

> The places where successive episodes of a particular story or set of interrelated stories occur make up a culturally significant landscape just as the episodes make up the story. The places where actions relating to a particular ceremony occur make up a landscape just as the acts make up the ceremony.[26]

Kelley and Francis attempt to assign the places they recorded to types, and summarize the similar efforts of others. The lists are long and particularized, and Kelley and Francis are careful to note that a given place may fall into several different types. Generally the taxonomies they discuss are based both on physical characteristic (mesa, rock outcrop, waterfall) and function (prayer, ceremony, medicine gathering). Overlying physical characteristic and underlying function are the stories of Changing Woman, the Great Gambler, and other ancestral figures.[27]

Place as Metaphor: Keith Basso

Keith Basso of the University of New Mexico has devoted much of his life to understanding the Western Apache, giving particular attention to the village of Cibecue and the ways in which Cibecue Apache people use places to communicate. Basso's pivotal book, *Wisdom Sits in Places,* documents in rich detail how a

Cibecue woman or man can tell a whole story, illustrating an important life lesson and conveying a wide range of emotions, simply by referring to a named, known place.

"It happened at Line of White Rocks Extends Up and Out, at this very place," a woman tells her friend, who is worried about the foolish actions of her younger brother. The friend knows, without another word being spoken, that she is being reminded that young people always do stupid things but usually survive and learn from them.[28] She knows this because her friend's reference to the place, Line of White Rocks Extends Up and Out, evokes an image in her mind that connects with a traditional story that teaches that lesson. "It happened at Whiteness Spreads Out Descending to Water," another friend throws in, evoking a complementary story. The sister is comforted, perhaps is given something to say to her brother, and is able to put her worry into a larger, culturally coherent context.

Basso discusses the roles played by dozens of named places in the landscape around Cibecue, most of them descriptively named natural places like "Scattered Rocks Stand Erect," and "Water Lies with Mud in an Open Container."[29] Each name evokes a picture, and each picture tells a story.

> Place-names are used in all forms of Apache storytelling as situating devices, as conventionalized verbal instructions for locating narrated events at and in the physical settings where the events occurred. Thus, instead of describing these settings discursively, an Apache storyteller can simply employ their names, and Apache listeners, whether they have visited the sites or not, are able to imagine in some detail how they might appear. In this way, to borrow Hoijer's felicitous phrase, narrated events are "spatially anchored" at points on the land, and the evocative pictures presented by Western Apache place-names become indispensable resources for the storyteller's craft.[30]

What the storyteller is about, in many cases, is literally helping his or her listeners achieve wisdom.

> Incorporating places and their meanings into a compact model of mental and social development, the [Apache] theory of [wisdom] proposes that the most estimable qualities of human minds—keen and unhurried reasoning, resistance to fear and anxiety, and suppression of emotion born of hostility and pride—come into being through extended reflection on symbolic dimensions of the physical environment.[31]

Because place-associated stories reflect Apache oral history and belief, the use of place names as metaphors in Apache storytelling does more than simply permit the efficient delivery of food for thought. It also helps ground speaker and listeners alike in the values and history of the community.

> And so it happens, on those occasions when Apache people see fit to speak with place-names, that a vital part of their tribal heritage seems to speak to them as well. For on such occasions . . . participants may be moved and instructed by voices other than their own, [and] . . . are addressed and may be affected by the voices of their ancestors.[32]

All this gives places in the landscape tremendous cultural and psychological importance in Apache life.

> As Apache men and women set about drinking from places—as they acquire knowledge of their natural surroundings, commit it to permanent memory, and apply it productively to the workings of their minds—they show by their actions that their surroundings live in them. Like their ancestors before them, they display by word and deed that beyond the visible reality of place lies a moral reality which they themselves have come to embody.[33]

To the Western Apache as described by Basso, then, places in the landscape both embody tribal history (as among the Yanesha; see chapter 3) and serve as the containers and transmitters of tribal wisdom. In essence, they constitute the historical and ethical literature of Apache culture.

TCPs in the City: U.S. Urban Anthropology

Urban anthropological research almost by definition involves the study of people and communities in specific places, but most often it's aimed at adducing patterns of behavior and the principles that underlie them, rather than on place relationships themselves.[34] Some urban anthropological studies have been attentive to such relationships, however, seeking the roles places play in culture and the ways in which people feel attached to them.

In the relatively early work *Soulside,* Ulf Hannerz studied Winston Street in Washington, D.C., a "narrow, one-way ghetto street" whose resident community he divided into two contrasting but overlapping and interacting groups that he called "the mainstreamers" and "the swingers." Hannerz showed how the neighborhood and its institutions—bootlegging, numbers gaming, storefront churches, "running mouths" on front steps and street corners, music, and the pervasive notion of "soul"—formed a culturally cohesive whole. The neighborhood is important to its residents, he said, because of "the significance of a ghetto-specific culture to community integration."[35]

A more recent study, and one that is germane to the ways traditional community values are (or aren't) addressed in planning by governments and other change agents, is Steven Gregory's *Black Corona*.[36] Corona is a largely African American neighborhood hard by La Guardia airport near New York City, whose residents found their ways of life threatened by the development plans of the Port Authority of New York and New Jersey. Gregory's book recounts (among other things) how the people of Corona organized to fight the proposed development. Along the way Gregory illustrates what it is about Corona that made it, in the eyes of its people, worth fighting for. Gregory's detailed account of Corona's history and contemporary ethnography would, I think, provide a good basis for arguing that Corona is eligible for the National Register as a TCP, though it's unlikely that Gregory, for one, would be interested in doing so. In fact, he argues that

> [t]he notion of a community "bounded" by a common history, social identity, or sense of attachment to place not only elides (institutional and social) heterogeneity but also obscures the central role that efforts to define the meaning and limits of community play in the lives of urban residents and in the construction of their collective identities and commitments.[37]

Black Corona is about political activism, not about "place" per se, but it's redolent with Corona's sense of place, as viewed through the eyes of its activists and their families. Corona's people are clearly attached to the place, define themselves with reference to the place, and are deeply involved in the history that ties them to the place.

Usefully, Gregory illustrates that the history of a place like Corona, as remembered by those who value it, is not just a matter of objective fact; it's something that has social utility and that is constructed and reinvented to serve social purposes:

> While doing my fieldwork it quickly became apparent that activists continually recollected and reworked Corona's history to provide meaning and context, as well as narrative authority, to interpretations of contemporary social conditions. . . . Indeed, when Corona activists recalled the past, it was more often than not to interpret and communicate why they acted in the past, and why they should continue to act in the future.[38]

Like the Cibicue Apache, the people of Corona recall traditions in order to interpret, communicate, and set courses of future action. And Corona's people, like those of Cibicue, remember and talk about their history in place-focused terms. Gregory begins the book with a vignette from an interview with two elderly community activists, who recall their lives and times with reference to community landmarks like the El Dorado Moving Picture Theater (later Antioch Baptist Church) and the Corona Congregational Church.[39]

Even earlier, Gregory writes of his own motivations in writing the book. He refers back to a boyhood trip with his father to Richmond, Virginia, to visit and view the mostly vanished scenes of the elder Gregory's youth:

> It was as though he wanted me to see the places where he had endured and overcome the day-to-day brutalities of racism in America. It was not enough to talk about them—to give words to experiences that were far too life-shaping to convey through language. Rather, he wanted me to relive them with him—to rehearse the constraints and struggles of the past against the noisy promises of the future. And in the process he taught me a great deal about human dignity, courage, and resolve.[40]

Chinatowns are commonly cited as examples of urban TCPs—in National Register Bulletin 38, for example. On the other hand, they are often disparaged as mere fictions created to make money from tourists. Rambles through San Francisco's Chinatown at many hours of the day and night have convinced me of its legitimacy as a culturally distinct community, but detailed ethnographies demonstrating this fact are not common.

A recent and useful exception is Jan Lin's *Reconstructing Chinatown*.[41] Lin studied New York's Chinatown in ethnographic detail and historical depth, and he uses it to illustrate the history and cultural character of Chinatowns throughout the United States. He portrays Chinatown as an evolving community of multiple interest groups that interact with each other, with China, and with the world economy around a core of tradition. Chinatown, he says, is simultaneously a "sanitized ethnic tourist village" and a "gritty, littered urban district that still functions as a vital residential and employment center for a low-income immigrant proletariat."[42] It is a place in flux, reflecting interactions among its component social and economic groups and the outside world—both locally and globally—but it is a place whose cultural values, as defined by its inhabitants, are important to them. Yet—and this is an important point with respect to the way we approach TCPs —those values themselves are fluid, subject to evolution, redefinition, and manipulation. And there is nothing necessarily wrong with that. "I recognize community, ethnicity, and 'place' as social constructions or contingent solidarities that have the power to mobilize and reinforce networks of association and influence, confer human roles and identities, and grant an affective meaning to physical space."[43]

Not all traditional cultural neighborhoods are as "ethnic" as a Chinatown or a Black Corona. The East End neighborhood of Cincinnati, Ohio, studied by

Rhoda Halperin,[44] is an example of a multiethnic working-class semiurban community that—like Corona—has fought to maintain its identity in the face of development.

Like many TCPs, the East End is hard to define as a bounded physical entity. It is "not a traditional urban ethnic community, for it is neither urban nor ethnic in the classic sense."[45] It is made up of families with—generally—five or six generations' time depth in place. Many, both black and white, have roots in Appalachia, but not all do; some trace their roots to Europe or the rural American South. Although officially classified as one of the city's urban neighborhoods, its residents resist "impersonal urbanism" and "urban institutions (most notably, large schools, large hospitals, and large bureaucracies)." Halperin concludes that in some contexts, at least, "community identity—as expressed in the phrases 'we are East Enders' or he is a 'real East Ender'—is a code for class or, as one community leader put it, 'the common people.'"[46] At the same time:

> Community is not just a place, although place is very important, but a series of day-to-day, ongoing, often invisible practices. These practices are connected but not confined to place. To maintain the East End community for East Enders requires residents and leaders alike to take community personally. The stakes are high—community, identity, heritage, and survival.[47]

Halperin's study spanned a time when the community was confronted with unwanted condominium development. The people of the East End "practiced community," in Halperin's evocative term, by struggling with the city and developers against what they saw as a threat to their identity. Halperin quotes a letter written to the developers by a fourteen-year-old East Ender girl:

> We love our street just the way it is. We don't need condos. . . . We ain't got much but what we do have is special and East End is all we got, take that you have nothing no future, just a big place with rich snobby people. . . . Take away the East End we have nothing! After all if someone took away your family . . . what would you have? So now do you get my point! East End is our family and you're slowly ripping us apart![48]

Other studies in urban anthropology also touch on the felt relationships between people and place, though few that I know of are as richly detailed as Halperin's. Halperin, like Hannerz, Gregory, Lin, and others, but with more intensity, evokes the role that place plays in the identities of a city's social groups. At the same time, she illustrates that the place per se is not exactly the issue. The East End won't go away even if it is built up in wall-to-wall condos; it will still be a physical place. But if its people aren't able to live there, or if the physical and social characteristics that make it theirs are transformed—if they are no longer able to "practice community" as East Enders—then it will truly have been "taken away" from them.

Documenters of Folklife

In the beginning there was folklore—stories, myths, "tall tales." The study of folklore has been pursued by academics and avocationals for many years. Folklore always has a "place" referent—you don't find tales of Paul Bunyan in Arizona—but these referents tend to be pretty general. Other aspects of folk expressive culture—music, poetry, painting, handwork—and folk material culture as expressed in tools, handcrafts, and the like—similarly have regional connections but are seldom very explicitly tied to particular places.[49]

Folklore and folk expressive culture came together to beget "folklife"—the study of how "folk culture" operates and operated on the ground. Folklife studies tend to be at least region-specific and often address specific places. The differences are small between folklife studies and the descriptive ethnographies done by anthropologists, usually focusing on such groups as the Amish.[50] Indeed, folklife specialists refer to their fieldwork as ethnography.

In chapter 2 I described how the American Folklife Center in the Library of Congress set out in the 1980s to explore the relationships between research in folklife and historic preservation, under the rubric "cultural conservation." This effort, in which I was marginally involved, helped form my perception of what TCPs are.

Mary Hufford's work in the Pinelands was particularly influential.[51] The Pinelands, a million acres or so of piney woods and cranberry bogs along New Jersey's Atlantic shore east of Philadelphia, had recently been designated a National Reserve by Congress, and a comprehensive plan for the area was being developed. Hufford and her team set out to document the traditional life of the "Pineys."

Whatever their connections with the rest of the world, the Pineys are a self-identified, localized community, or network of communities, whose members relate to the Pinelands through residence and an intimate involvement in their environment. They hunt and fish in the marshes, run oyster boats out from the bays or "garveys" and "sneakboats" in the channels, harvest cranberries in the bogs, and fight the fires that sweep through the forest in the dry seasons. They have songs and stories and folktales, even their own special monster, the Jersey Devil. They understand themselves as linked to the Pinelands and its special places—special to them, if not to outsiders—and that linkage is fundamental to their identity.

Hufford wrote a short but rich account of the Pineys and their world; as I reread it now, it seems like one of the best "TCP studies" I've seen, except that of course it doesn't include an analysis of National Register eligibility.[52] It does lead to explicit management recommendations, though—seemingly very reasonable ones. I'm afraid to look into the extent to which anyone in authority has attended to them, for fear of being disappointed.

Meanwhile, the Folklife Center teamed up with the National Park Service (NPS) and the Utah SHPO to produce the first major published study of a place explicitly blending folklife and historic preservation perspectives. The subject was Grouse Creek, a Mormon Cowboy community in Utah.[53] Grouse Creek is a cluster of long-established working cattle ranches, which was evaluated as a historic property with reference to the relationships between the overall place and the way people lived and worked there.

At the time the study was done, it seemed quite exciting—an effort to bring living culture, as it relates to place, into the ambit of the National Register. Rereading the report today is an odd experience; it seems stilted and academic, almost lifeless despite its detailed description of Grouse Creek's richly textured sociocultural life through time.

This is not solely the fault of the authors' attempt to relate their work to the National Register, though that is a large part of the problem. Folklife as a discipline is oriented toward documentation, "preserving" things by getting them down on paper, in other media, in museums. Like the National Register, it has a certain disengaged quality that can suck the life out of its products.

But the Grouse Creek report has value, not only as a piece of history in itself but for what it says about what makes the community eligible for the National Register. Not *all* of what it says; there's a dreadful, turgid bit about how the place reflects various "contexts"—the National Register's preoccupation in the late 1980s[54]—but

> [t]he connections between people and the past were revealed by the examination of the cultural landscape—the arrangement on the land of buildings, fences, irrigation systems, and the like. The connection was also evident . . . "in the things people do." While things have changed and will continue to change, the way of life that was established in Grouse Creek during the late nineteenth and early twentieth centuries continues to exert a powerful influence on contemporary activities and practices.[55]

What the Pinelands and Grouse Creek and other folklife studies of specific places do is to show the relationships among place, people, and perceptions—perceptions of value, of appropriate ways to live and interact with others, of what's important in the environment, of what makes a good tool or house or fence or duck-hunting spot or irrigation ditch. In other words, the ways in which place creates tradition and tradition gives value to place.

Community-Oriented Landscape Architects and Planners

Landscape architects and planners interested in community identity have studied, documented, and sought to preserve TCP-like places. The work of Randolph Hester, a landscape architect at the University of California, Berkeley, and his colleagues is notable. Hester's approach is neatly summarized in his 1987 article in the landscape architecture journal *Place,* entitled "Subconscious Landscapes of the Heart."[56] His example is the small coastal community of Manteo, North Carolina.

Manteo, a once-busy port that had been languishing in oblivion since it was bypassed by highways in the 1950s, was trying to revitalize itself but wanted to avoid suffering "the eventual demise of existing community traditions, destruction of valued places, and replacement by a phony folk culture."[57] The community engaged Hester to help. He and his colleagues consulted with the residents, administered a questionnaire, observed people at work and play, mapped where they unconsciously interacted, and developed a map and list— ranked and weighted—of places the community seemed to value. This they took back to the community for discussion and correction.

The places identified through this study

> were almost universally unappealing to the trained professional eyes of an architect, historian, real estate developer, or upper middle-class tourist. As a result, in Manteo only two places among the Sacred Structure were protected by historic preservation legislation. Only a few were protected by zoning law. Even to locals the sacred places were outwardly taken for granted. Their value resided in the community's subconscious.[58]

Being lodged in the subconscious, such places—referred to by one of the town's leaders as its "perfect jewels"—were not easily discussed with outsiders. Community members assumed that outsiders would look down on them. "Since they were somewhat ashamed of these places when outsiders were around, it was important for us outside design experts to say these places were fine. Otherwise townspeople would tell us only about places that tourists would value, and we would never have been able to uncover truly important places."[59]

The listed and mapped places were given a collective name in consultation with the community, which has been adopted in much of Hester's subsequent work. The name generates a feeling of déjà vu in a TCP type like me, discovering Hester's work only lately;[60] they called the places Manteo's "Sacred Structure."[61]

Notes

1. Though in point of fact few explicit TCP studies have made it into the readily consultable literature, either as published pieces or as widely circulated manuscripts.

2. Canada has wisely thus far avoided creating a National Register, so "TCPs" aren't dealt with in the same sort of legal context we have to contend with in the United States, and the term itself is not widely used. Canadian indigenous cultural places are indistinguishable from similar places in the U.S., however.

3. Susan Buggey, *Approach to Aboriginal Cultural Landscapes* (Historic Sites and Monuments Board of Canada, Parks Canada, Ottawa, 1999).

4. Buggey, *Approach to Aboriginal Cultural Landscapes*, 5; Brian Reeves, Ninaistakis—The Nitsatapii's Sacred Mountain: Traditional Native Religious Activities and Land Use/Tourism, in D. Carmichael et al. (eds.), *Sacred Sites, Sacred Places* (Routledge, London, 1994), 265–95.

5. Buggey, *Approach to Aboriginal Cultural Landscapes*, citing Mohs (1994:189–95).

6. Buggey, *Approach to Aboriginal Cultural Landscapes*, 6, citing Lee and Henderson (1992) and Smyth (1997), together with minutes of a 1997 meeting of the Historic Sites and Monuments Board.

7. Buggey, *Approach to Aboriginal Cultural Landscapes*, 6, citing personal communication from Dr. George MacDonald.

8. Buggey, *Approach to Aboriginal Cultural Landscapes*, 6, citing Carpenter (1985).

9. Buggey, *Approach to Aboriginal Cultural Landscapes*, 6, citing Blondin (1997) and others.

10. Buggey, *Approach to Aboriginal Cultural Landscapes*.

11. Quoted in Buggey, *Approach to Aboriginal Cultural Landscapes*, 7.

12. Buggey, *Approach to Aboriginal Cultural Landscapes*, 6.

13. Buggey, *Approach to Aboriginal Cultural Landscapes*, 8, citing Andrews and Zoe (1997) and Andrews (1990:4).

14. Buggey, *Approach to Aboriginal Cultural Landscapes*, 6.

15. Buggey, *Approach to Aboriginal Cultural Landscapes*, 10.

16. Andrew Guilliford, *Sacred Objects and Sacred Places: Preserving Tribal Traditions* (University Press of Colorado, Boulder, 2000).

17. Jake Page (ed.)., *Sacred Lands of Indian America* (Abrams, New York, 2001).

18. For example, contrary to page 24, the lawsuit against the National Park Service at Bear Lodge did not go "up to the U.S. Supreme Court before being thrown out," and the discussion of Executive Order 13007 on page 51 is oversimplified to the point of being misleading.

19. See, for example, John J. Wood and Walter M. Vannette, A Preliminary Assessment of the Significance of Navajo Sacred Places in the vicinity of Big Mountain, Arizona, ms., Bureau of Indian Affairs (Navajo Area Office, Window Rock, AZ, 1979).

20. Klara B. Kelley and Harris Francis, *Navajo Sacred Places* (Indiana University Press, Bloomington, 1994). Alan Downer's 1989 Ph.D. dissertation, Anthropology, Historic Preservation and the Navajo, reports related research. Also see Kelli Carmean, *Spider Woman Walks This Land: Traditional Cultural Properties and the Navajo Nation* (AltaMira, Walnut Creek, CA, 2002), for a recent somewhat similar study.

21. Kelley and Francis, *Navajo Sacred Places,* 40.

22. Kelley and Francis, *Navajo Sacred Places,* 39.

23. Keith H. Basso, *Wisdom Sits in Places: Landscape and Language among the Western Apache* (University of New Mexico Press, Albuquerque, 1996).

24. Basso, *Wisdom Sits in Places.*

25. Basso, *Wisdom Sits in Places,* 40.

26. Basso, *Wisdom Sits in Places,* 43.

27. Basso, *Wisdom Sits in Places,* 81–82.

28. Basso, *Wisdom Sits in Places,* 79.

29. Basso, *Wisdom Sits in Places,* 13. Not all place names are beautiful. One site is called "Shades of Shit" (23–28). Nor are all descriptive; some are commemorative, like "Two Old Women are Buried" and "She Became Old Sitting" (29).

30. Basso, *Wisdom Sits in Places,* 47.

31. Basso, *Wisdom Sits in Places,* 146.

32. Basso, *Wisdom Sits in Places,* 101.

33. Basso, *Wisdom Sits in Places,* 146.

34. See Elliot Liebow, *Tally's Corner: A Study of Negro Street Corner Men* (Little, Brown, New York, 1967), for an early and classic example.

35. Ulf Hannerz, *Soulside: Inquiries into Ghetto Culture and Community* (Almqvist & Wiksell, Stockholm, 1969), 158.

36. Steven Gregory, *Black Corona: Race and the Politics of Place in an Urban Community* (Princeton University Press, Princeton, NJ, 1998).

37. Gregory, *Black Corona,* 11.

38. Gregory, *Black Corona,* 14–15.

39. Gregory, *Black Corona,* 3.

40. Gregory, *Black Corona,* xii.

41. Jan Lin, *Reconstructing Chinatown: Ethnic Enclave, Global Change* (University of Minnesota Press, Minneapolis, 1998).

42. Lin, *Reconstructing Chinatown,* 203.

43. Lin, *Reconstructing Chinatown,* 204.

44. Rhoda H. Halperin, *Practicing Community: Class Culture and Power in an Urban Neighborhood* (University of Texas Press, Austin, 1998).

45. Halperin, *Practicing Community,* 3.

46. Halperin, *Practicing Community,* 4.

47. Halperin, *Practicing Community,* 5.

48. Halperin, *Practicing Community,* 15.

49. There are exceptions. For example, Gerald Milnes in a study focusing on West Virginia fiddle music features "Shelvin' Rock," a fiddle tune associated with a rock outcrop under which lived generations of the Carpenters, a famous fiddling family. See Milnes, *Play of a Fiddle: Traditional Music, Dance, and Folklore in West Virginia* (University Press of Kentucky, Lexington, 1999), 39.

50. Tom Greaves, The Amish of Lancaster County, Pennsylvania, in Tom Greaves (ed.), *Endangered Peoples of North America: Struggles to Survive and Thrive* (Greenwood, Westport, CT, 2002), chap. 10; John A. Hostetler, *Amish Society,* 4th ed. (Johns Hopkins University Press, Baltimore, 1993).

51. Mary Hufford, *One Space, Many Places: Folklife and Land Use in New Jersey's Pinelands National Reserve* (American Folklife Center, Library of Congress, Washington, D.C., 1986).

52. Another is Gordon Mohs, Sto:lo Sacred Ground, in D. L. Carmichael et al. (eds.), *Sacred Sites, Sacred Places* (Routledge, London, 1994).

53. Thomas Carter and Carl Fleischhauer, *The Grouse Creek Cultural Study: Integrating Folklife and Historic Preservation Field Research* (American Folklife Center, Library of Congress, Washington, D.C., 1988).

54. Carter and Fleischhauer, *The Grouse Creek Cultural Study,* 54–59.

55. Carter and Fleischhauer, *The Grouse Creek Cultural Study,* 61.

56. Randolph T. Hester, Subconscious Landscapes of the Heart, *Place* 2(3) (1987):10–22; see also Randolph T. Hester, *Planning Neighbourhood Space with People,* 2d ed. (Van Nostrand Reinhold, New York, 1997).

57. Hester, Subconscious Landscapes of the Heart, 10.

58. Hester, Subconscious Landscapes of the Heart, 15.

59. Hester, Subconscious Landscapes of the Heart.

60. For which I am very grateful to National Park Service Landscape Architect Lisa Duwall.

61. Hester, Subconscious Landscapes of the Heart, 13.

Chapter Five

Tcps in Broader Perspective

Theoretical and Synthesizing Perspectives

When places are actively sensed, the physical landscape becomes wedded to the landscape of the mind, to the roving imagination, and where the latter can lead is anybody's guess.

—Keith Basso (1996:197)

Why Is a TCP?

"WHAT is truly thought-provoking," Eugene Anderson writes, noting that *feng shui* experts, landscape painters, and tourists all gravitate to the same places, "is why such places capture our imagination."[1] Anderson says that "no one has even begun to explain" this phenomenon, and that's probably true, but several writers have recently tried.

Many of the sources cited in the last two chapters attempt to account for place attachment in particular cultural and geographic contexts. But what I propose to dip into in this chapter is some of the explicitly theoretical "sense of place" literature and the burgeoning body of relevant synthetic work. Only a shallow dip; a deep dive would take us into some strange places, where it would be easy to get lost.

While much of the literature summarized in chapters 3 and 4 is about indigenous cultural places, most of the theoretical and synthetic literature is not, or deals with such places only as parts of a bigger universe. This is good, for the purposes of this book. It's easy, in the United States, to fall into thinking of TCPs only in terms of "Indian sacred sites." Charismatic as such places are, the theorists and synthesizers remind us that we all have, and treasure, special places, and that we have shared reasons for doing so.

Yi-Fu Tuan

One of the best-known place theoreticians is the geographer Yi-Fu Tuan, whose *Space and Place: The Perspective of Experience* is a classic. Like other writers on the subject, Tuan sees the perception of significance in places—not based on specific, objectively definable characteristics but because they *feel* significant—as a legitimate and important quality of humanness, that has been largely overwhelmed in modern society by analytical objectivity. "Analytical thought," he says:

> has transformed our physical and social environment. . . . We are so impressed that to us "knowing" is practically identical with "knowing about," and Lord Kelvin has gone so far as to say that we do not really know anything unless we can also measure it. Much of human experience is difficult to articulate, however and we are far from finding devices that measure satisfactorily the quality of a feeling or aesthetic response. What we cannot say in an acceptable scientific language we tend to deny or forget.[2]

Feelings about places are not measurable or objectifiable but can be compelling. Tuan notes that in some societies there is "the belief, quite unsupported by geography, that . . . their sacred place is at the earth's summit." Similar beliefs are often associated with Native American spiritual places, including some of the TCPs that present federal land managers with the greatest challenges. But these beliefs are not exclusively the property of tribes and other extraliterate[3] groups. Tuan provides examples from China and Mongolia and then notes that:

> [a] common belief in Rabbinical literature is that the land of Israel stands higher above sea level than any other land, and that the Temple Hill is the highest point in Israel. Islamic tradition teaches that the most sacred sanctuary, the Kaaba, is not only the center and the navel of the world, but also its highest point. . . . This is why prayers said in its sanctuary are most clearly heard.[4]

But a place need not be as officially sanctified as the Temple Hill or the Kaaba, or as geographically circumscribed, to be an emotional touchstone. Tuan devotes considerable attention to the attachment that people can feel for what they define as their homelands, which may be expansive landscapes.

> Landscape is personal and tribal history made visible. The native's identity—his place in the total scheme of things—is not in doubt, because the myths that support it are as real as the rocks and waterholes he can see and touch. . . . The whole countryside is his family tree.[5]

[A] strong attachment to the homeland can emerge quite apart from any explicit concept of sacredness; it can form without the memory of heroic battles won and lost, and without the bond of fear or of superiority vis-à-vis other people. Attachment of a deep though subconscious sort may come simply with familiarity and ease, with the assurance of nurture and security, with the memory of sounds and smells, of communal activities and homely pleasures accumulated over time.[6]

A treasured place need not be visually striking, though it may be made so because it is treasured. "[D]eeply-loved places are not necessarily visible, either to ourselves or to others. Places may be made visible by a number of means: rivalry or conflict with other places, visual prominence, and the evocative power of art, architecture, ceremonials and rites."[7]

Interestingly for our purposes, Tuan does not see organized historic preservation—the "cult of the past"—as very relevant to the connection of people to place. "The cult of the past has little in common with the fact of being rooted in place. The state of rootedness is essentially subconscious; it means that a people have come to identify themselves with a particular locality, to feel that it is their home and the home of their ancestors."[8] And "[a] truly rooted community may have shrines and monuments, but it is unlikely to have museums and societies for the preservation of the past."[9]

E. V. Walter

In *Placeways,* E. V. Walter coins the word *topistics* for the study of placeways—that is, the ways in which people connect with valued places. Like Tuan's, Walter's approach is holistic and experiential, and like Tuan he has little use for analytical objectivity. The disastrous consequences of urban renewal, he suggests, were products of an outside, "surgical" model, calling for the excision of "cancerous," "blighted" neighborhoods. "This kind of 'therapy' requires objectivity," he observes, "because few surgeons would want to operate on their own parts. The people who clear the slums never dwell in the regions they clear."[10]

A place is valued, Walter says, because people experience something there[11]—not necessarily a specific event but a feeling of something beyond yet connected with the self. But he makes it clear that to him it is person, not place, that is the active player in the generation of experience. "A place has no feelings apart from human experience there. But a place is a location of experience. It evokes and organizes memories, images, feelings, sentiments, meanings, and the work of imagination."[12]

Having identified place as a passive location where the human mind experiences feelings, Walter repeatedly treats it as active. For example, he describes a place as "a matrix of energies, generating representations and causing changes in awareness."[13] It is not clear (to me, at least) whether he thinks these energies exist outside the human mind, within it, or in some kind of mind/place inter-action.

Wherever it operates, the experience of places is not necessarily or pri-marily visual; it is a much more holistic kind of thing. Borrowing from Kent Bloomer and Charles Moore, Walter refers to the way we experience mean-ingful places as "haptic."[14] Haptic sensing, he says, is "a sense of touch that means not just contact with the fingers or the skin but an entire perceptual system conveying sensations of pressure, temperature, pain and the sense of movement within the body as well as the feelings of the body moving through space."[15] "Haptic perception," he says, "reminds us that the whole self may grasp reality without seeing, hearing, or thinking. It also calls attention to a primitive way of knowing that resembles mythical thought, in contrast to the analytical stages of seeing, thinking, and acting—a unified structure of feeling and doing."

Haptic perception doesn't yield easily to objective analysis but can be extremely influential. Some places where people experience feelings that aren't quite assignable to sight or sound or touch, or that go beyond them, come to be regarded as spiritual or sacred.

> People build or discover sacred places to experience hidden presences. In the feelings and meanings of a sacred space, and in the sacred places of all times, worshipers express a religious longing to recover a lost unity. Dynamists seek connections to invisible forces. Animists strive for relationships to spirits. And theists reach for God.[16]

Walter credits Plato with an understanding of haptic perception. Again seeming to contradict his assertion that "a place has no feelings," he writes approvingly of Plato's (perhaps metaphorical) notion of place as an "active receptacle" of human experience, as opposed to its characterization by Aris-totle as a neutral container of such experience. He deplores the fact (as he sees it) that the Aristotelian interpretation undid the Platonic, discrediting those aspects of place (among many other things) that could not be objectively measured.[17] He criticizes (and pities) Freud for exacerbating this state of affairs by fathering a psychology that disconnects self from place.[18]

Two millennia of Aristotle and a century of Freud, Walter suggests, have brought mainstream Western thinking—including the thinking of architects and planners—to a point at which the notion of place as something with which we actively interact, which influences us at a deep emotional level in ways that cannot be objectively construed, has been thoroughly devalued. As

a result—coming back to the failed logic of urban renewal—we came to identify slums and suburbs as respectively bad and good. In fact, however,

> [w]hile some slums are good places to dwell—warm and lively environments
> with a rich and complex social life—others are cacotopes, generating misery in
> the households and death in the streets. And while some suburbs remain inter-
> esting, nourishing communities, others are dead places, where nothing moves
> but station wagons and lawn sprinklers.[19]

To create a "fully human environment," Walter proposes, we need to overcome
the obstacle of "ungrounded reason and the absence of topistic awareness. . . .
We need to recollect the unity of a place as a location of experience and a matrix
of energies."[20]

Edward S. Casey

The philosopher Edward S. Casey has written extensively about "place" in Western intellectual history. His magnum opus, *The Fate of Place*,[21] traces the con-
ceptual relationships between "place" and "space" over the two millennia–plus
since Plato. He is more kindly disposed toward Aristotle than Walter is but
arrives at broadly the same conclusions, along the way relating his thinking to
that of virtually every major figure in Western intellectual history. In an introduction to Steven Field's and Keith Basso's edited collection, *Senses of Place*,[22] he
has handily summarized his thinking about space/place relationships and specifically about whether the latter is simply a chunk of the former.[23]

This may seem like a nonquestion: How can places be anything *but* chunks
of space? But it's a philosopher's business to cause us to question assumptions,
and Casey does a good job of it, in the process deepening the mystery of why
we attach such value to places.

Casey begins by highlighting the "article of faith" in anthropology and other
sciences that "*place* is something *posterior to space,* even made from space. By
'space' is meant a neutral, pre-given medium, a *tabula rasa* onto which the par-
ticularities of culture and history come to be inscribed, with place as the pre-
sumed result."[24]

As examples of this assumption, Casey cites works by James Weiner in
Papua New Guinea and Fred Myers with the Pintupi of central Australia. Myers
is quoted as discussing "[t]he process by which space becomes 'country,' by
which a story gets attached to an object,"[25] but Casey notes that:

> the Pintupi themselves think otherwise, as Myers himself avers: "To the Pintupi
> . . . , a place itself with its multiple features is logically prior or central." . . .

Whom are we to believe? The theorizing anthropologist, the arsenal of his natural attitude bristling with explanatory projectiles that go off into space? Or the
aborigine on the ground who finds this ground itself to be a coherent collocation
of pre-given places—pre-given at once in his experience and in the Dreaming
that sanctions this experience? For the anthropologist, Space comes first; for the
native, Place; and the difference is by no means trivial.[26]

Without attempting to follow Casey through his intricate and engaging analysis, let's cut to the chase: he agrees with the Pintupi. "True concreteness," he says,
"belongs to place—plain old place, the place under our feet, before our eyes and
in our ears."[27] However, "I do not take place to be something simply physical.
A place is not a mere patch of ground, a bare stretch of earth, a sedentary set of
stones. What kind of thing is it then?" He answers:

> A place is more an *event* than a *thing* to be assimilated to known categories. As
> an event, it is unique, idiolocal. Its peculiarity calls not for assumption into the
> already known—that way lies site, which lends itself to predefined predica-
> tions, uses, and interpretations—but for the imaginative constitution of terms
> respecting idiolocality (these range from place names to whole discourses).[28]

This may all seem pretty obscure—philosophers often are, at least to me.
But Casey's notion of the primacy of place speaks to a disquiet I feel with TCPs
(by whatever name) as simply cultural constructs, impositions of human
assumptions onto an impersonal spacescape. Indigenous spiritual places, at least,
are not that to the people who value them—they are, indeed, more like events.
Although I've described them as things whose significance lies in people's heads
(i.e., is attributed, not intrinsic), I find that description unsatisfying, and it's nice
to find that Casey does, too.

Tony Hiss

In his short, snappy *The Experience of Place*,[29] Tony Hiss writes about place values from an urban planning (and New Yorker's) perspective.[30] Like Walter, he
proposes that we appreciate places holistically, via what he calls "simultaneous
perception"—that is, perceiving with all the senses.[31] Hiss is less the abstract
thinker than Walter and more interested in speaking to ordinary people (particularly planners). His central concern is about "how our health and well-being
are affected by changing what we can experience in a place."[32]

Although many of Hiss's examples are historic places like parks designed by
the Olmsted brothers, many are not,[33] and like Tuan and Walter, he seems to be
no fan of organized historic preservation. He would like to see planning recognize the value "not just of architectural beauty but of the character of a place, or

its essential spirit, or the quality of life there, or of its livability, genius, flavor, feeling, ambience, essence, resonance, presence, aura, harmony, grace, charm, or seemliness."[34]

Amos Rapoport

Amos Rapoport is primarily concerned about designing space in ways that relate meaningfully to users, but many of his observations are relevant to why a quite ordinary seeming place can be meaningful to those who know it. People, he says (rather self-evidently), "react to environments in terms of the meanings the environments have for them."[35] Unfortunately, he adds, too much design reflects meaning ascribed by designers, rather than by the space's users.

Rapoport sees perceptions of meaning in the environment as culturally patterned and acquired through enculturation. As a result, the environment "can . . . be seen as a teaching medium. Once learned, it becomes a mnemonic device reminding one of appropriate behavior."[36]

Hence place attachment is a way in which people come to understand and adhere to socially appropriate ways of living, and find comfort and fulfillment in doing so. "This mnemonic function of the environment is equivalent to group memory and consensus. In effect, the setting 'freezes' categories and domains, or cultural conventions." "How well this process (of encoding and decoding information in the environment) works can be very important indeed. It has been argued that anxiety ('the disease of our age') is generated in an individual when he or she has to choose a course of action without having sufficient information on the basis of which to make up his or her mind."[37]

Altman, Low, and Their Colleagues

Irving Altman and Setha Low's 1992 edited book *Place Attachment*[38] brought together practitioners in several disciplines to discuss how and why people are attached to places. The contributors viewed their work as being very much in progress; each chapter includes recommendations for further research. All focus on the interface between culture and individual psychology; two of the most explicitly theoretical, or at least generalizing, contributions have to do with the formation of place attachment in childhood.

Claire Cooper Marcus, a landscape architect, writes of having her students do "environmental autobiographies" based on their recollections of significant places in their lives—a large-scale version of the kind of exercise we went through in chapter 1. Not surprisingly, she finds that "earliest childhood places are powerful images, resonating into adulthood via memories, dreams, even the creative work of some adult designers."[39]

Louise Chawla writes that people experience four forms of attachment to childhood places. One such form is affection—feelings of fondness, warmth, association of the place with one's roots. Another, perhaps contrasting attachment is what Chawla calls transcendence—the feeling, through place, of a dynamic relationship with the outside world. Identification with a place of origin may be "complicated by the tension that it embodies family weaknesses or social injustice and stigma," creating ambivalence. Finally, Chawla says, in adolescence many people experience an idealized attachment to an abstract environment, an example of such attachment being patriotism.[40]

Winifred Gallagher

Journalist Winifred Gallagher provides a fascinating and pleasant-to-read synthesis in her 1999 *The Power of Place*. Gallagher ranges over a wide array of place-related topics—climatic influences on behavior, city versus country, the womb as a place. Two of her chapters are particularly relevant to TCPs— particularly, as usual, to that most charismatic of TCPs, the spiritual place.

Chapter 5, "Subtle Geophysical Energies," summarizes the work of geophysicists and others interested in how the human mind and body interact with the Earth's electromagnetism and similar forces. "The surfaces of cells are waving forests of electrochemical receptors," one of her interviewees observes,[41] which provides a basis for thinking that geomagnetism and similar earth forces could influence us in ways that we don't readily apprehend with the senses we're accustomed to using. Apparently, they can also be impressive to those senses we *do* routinely use, like sight, by releasing ball lightning and other light phenomena.[42]

Chapter 6, "Sacred Places," is built largely around the work of psychologist Michael Persinger, who is interested in how geophysical forces might concentrate in particular locations and cause reactions in the human body. Persinger's research suggests that such forces, often tectonically induced, may act directly on the human limbic system.[43] People exposed to such forces "might think they're getting ideas from outside their own minds, experience odd tastes, entertain thoughts from childhood, or have the sensation of being detached from the body."[44] Since tectonic forces concentrate stress in particular locations, such locations may come to be seen as spiritually energetic.

The Ordinary Landscape Movement

In 1951, John Brinckerhoff Jackson began publication of a magazine called *Landscape* that had as its purpose the study, appreciation, and celebration of the everyday landscapes in which we live and work.[45] Jackson effectively invented the idea of the "cultural landscape" and kicked off something of a movement among historians, landscape architects, and students of land use. Paul Groth and

Todd Bressi have recently pulled together a series of readings on the subject.[46] "Landscape," to Groth and Bressi, "denotes the interaction of people and place: a social group and its spaces, particularly the spaces to which the group belongs and from which its members derive some part of their shared identity and meaning."[47]

The cultural landscape movement is guided by some basic principles; as articulated by Groth and Bressi, these are as follows:

- Ordinary, everyday landscapes are important and worthy of study.

- Subjects . . . are likely to be urban as well as rural, focused on production as well as consumption.

- Contrasts of diversity and uniformity frame essential and continuing debates within cultural landscape interpretation.

- Landscape studies call for popular as well as academic writing.

- The many choices of theory and method in landscape studies stem from the subject's interdisciplinary nature.

- Within cultural landscape methods, the primary of visual and spatial information is a central theme.[48]

Given the pedagogical and humanistic assumptions embedded in these principles—that what cultural landscape studies are all about is documenting and teaching about landscapes so they can be better appreciated—it is not surprising that most of the essays in Groth and Bressi's book, while interesting and often thought-provoking, don't really delve seriously into why cultural landscapes are important to people and groups. One exception is a chapter on urban landscape history by Dolores Hayden, who draws on the work of Tuan and of Low and Altman to suggest that places are important to us because they encapsulate important memories—implicitly, memories that are culturally meaningful to us. Places, Hayden says, "make memories cohere in complex ways."[49]

Public History Perspectives

During the 1970s and 1980s, academic historians became increasingly interested in better relating their work to the interests of the public. In part this interest was driven by the same economic factors that shortly before had caused archaeologists to invent CRM—decline in academic jobs and increase in opportunities for extra-academic employment. No doubt another factor was the desire for relevance that characterized much of academia in the post-Vietnam era. In any event, historians began seeking ways to apply themselves to work that arguably served the public interest, and built programs to address such interests under the rubric of "public history."

One way that historians can relate to the public is via historic preservation; indeed, early in public history's history it was not uncommon for historians to complain that *historic* preservation, after all, really should be about *history*, so there ought to be lots more jobs for historians in the field, rather than for the bloody archaeologists and architects.

The problem was that historical research isn't necessarily very directly linked to buildings and sites and other places on the ground. Even when it involves analysis of something that happened on the ground—a battle, the development of an industry—it doesn't necessarily have much to say about what that something left behind. A lot of public historians have wound up simply providing background information for CRM reports written or edited by archaeologists.

But public history has matured, and one of the major ways it has found to relate to living people is through where they live—through the history of communities. This has made the study of places valued by communities very relevant to public history, and vice versa. As a result, there is a growing public history literature that deals with communities and their emotional attachments to place.

Some public history works seem to be mostly concerned with justifying public history to communities on the one hand and to the historical establishment on the other. Dolores Hayden's *The Power of Place: Urban Landscapes as Public History*,[50] for instance, provides examples of how place-based urban history can be used as a means of maintaining community identity and integrity. The examples are admirable and interesting, but they speak more to the power of history than to that of place.

On the other hand, Robert Archibald's *A Place to Remember: Using History to Build Community*[51] is much more evocative of the emotional power of place than its title implies. Archibald writes eloquently of the power of places—often quite ordinary sorts of places—to connect people and communities to their roots. Places enable us to remember stories about who we are, where we come from, what our values are.

> We know that objects, whether built environments or small personal effects, are symbolic memory devices; that is, they facilitate remembering. As public historians we understand that memory is an ongoing process through which we create usable narratives that explain the world in which we live, stories that inevitably connect us to each other, history that builds community. . . . Places, memories, and stories are inextricably connected, and we cannot create a real community without these elements.[52]

As a onetime SHPO and a continuing active participant in urban planning, Archibald is refreshing in his efforts to relate his thinking about place to the works of government. He insists on a relativistic approach to the significance of places; places are important to people, individually and in communities, so broad consultation among multiple groups is necessary to achieve a "common story" as the basis for public policy.[53] Nobody's story is necessarily more important than anybody else's, and everybody's treasured places deserve respect. Such respect is vital because places help give people and groups stability as the world—and they—necessarily change: "The persistence of [culturally valued] places is central to an environmental debate with future implications, but it is also reflective of a deep-seated need to find refuge from the complexities and insecurities of contemporary life in places that set humans in context, that provide constancy in the midst of profound and rapid change."[54]

Much of Archibald's writing about place is highly personal, relating to places that are connected with his own history, that evoke emotional responses in him. He never directly grapples with the practical problem of our obvious inability to preserve everybody's treasured places, but his strong implication is that change, including loss of treasured places, can be more palatable if perceptions of significance and feelings of loss are not ignored but rather are respected and confronted through consultative planning.

New Age Beliefs

New Age mysticism ascribes spiritual power to many landscape features, both natural (mountains, springs) and built (e.g., Stonehenge, the Chaco Canyon ruins). The New Age literature is replete with claims of power experienced and spiritual enlightenment attained at such places. However extravagant and unlikely many of these claims may be, they reflect a widespread perception of places as energetic—as "active receptacles of experience," though both Walter and Plato might be less than comfortable with New Age mystics as advocates for their way of thinking.

I have delved into New Age writings only deeply enough to be frustrated by them. Like the literature surrounding such mysteries as the disappearance of Amelia Earhart,[55] the New Age books tend toward unsubstantiated allegations and assumptions masquerading as facts. But, of course, so does the Bible and probably every other religious text. So does a tribal elder when he tells me about little people in the spring or the power of a juniper tree. I suppose that we look at New Agers with greater skepticism than we do traditional tribal elders (who are not always very old) because they are *us,* people of our own, shared cultural tradition, rather than "others" whose beliefs are grounded in life experiences we assume to be very different from our own.

But if nothing else, the New Age literature reflects the beliefs of fairly large numbers of people and illustrates the breadth of popular attachment to the kinds of places that we often call traditional cultural properties. Here are a few examples, rather randomly chosen from a substantial selection at my local bookstore:

The Road Within: True Stories of Transformation[56]—an edited volume in which writers recount their travels to and through places where they believe they experienced spiritual transformations;

Sacred Sites of the West: A Guide to Mystical Centers[57]—a guidebook to places in the American West thought by New Age practitioners to have spiritual power. Many of these, of course, are indigenous spiritual places, where the interests of tribes and New Agers sometimes come into conflict;

Secrets of Sacred Space[58]—provides not only instructions on how to find "places of power" but directions about how to create them;

Places of Power[59]—a children's book that explains New Age place beliefs in simple terms with attractive illustrations;

Dialogues with the Living Earth—a compilation of papers from a series of five annual seminars organized by James and Roberta Swan between 1988 and 1993 on "The Spirit of Place: The Modern Relevance of an Ancient Concept"—aimed at helping "restore the wisdom of the past about the significance of place and explore its meaning in modern times."[60]

"Fringe Science"

Standing rather by himself as a self-described "fringe scientist," Paul Devereux has undertaken apparently objective research on megalithic sites in Great Britain and elsewhere, trying to determine whether the "spiritual power" of such places can demonstrably be detected and measured. Although far from conclusive (as Devereux is the first to acknowledge), his work has, he says, in some cases revealed anomalously high levels or peculiar patterns of geomagnetism and radiation, associated with sightings of mysterious lights and reports of strange sounds.[61] Sometimes, he suggests, these anomalies are associated with fault lines and similar areas of geological activity. Devereux's research recalls that of Michael Persinger,[62] mentioned earlier, which suggested that geomagnetic and geoelectrical forces might influence human perception.

Relating All This to Traditional Cultural Properties

This chapter represents a brief immersion in the deep, wide, choppy pool of theory and speculation about "sense of place," "power of place," and related concepts. If it shows nothing else, it shows that there is more to places than just the physical space they occupy. Places connect with human experience and human belief in many complicated ways.

Places teach things; places embody moral lessons.

Places are where we are grounded, they form and become parts of our identities, as individuals and as groups.

Places are *felt* in ways we don't entirely understand, and some of them may actually have unusual power to affect our nervous systems.

People who feel the power of places, who feel bound to them, repelled by them, or otherwise somehow touched by them, are not necessarily deranged; in fact, they are not out of step with respected bodies of contemporary thought. With Walter, we might acknowledge that they're out of step with post-Platonic thinking about the nature of reality, but Walter, Casey, Tuan, and the others would also say that this is all to the good.

> As I was walking around the site, flags in hand [to mark the locations of artifacts], I began to walk toward a small grove of trees . . . when suddenly I began to feel a flow of energy. At first it was weak, yet the tingling sensation was familiar. I looked up to assess my location and set down a flag to mark my spot. I slowly walked forward toward the grove and as I did so the energy became stronger until I could walk no further. I set down another flag. The sensation was so strong I felt as if I had walked up to a glass wall. I could see through this invisible barrier yet could not pass through it. The distinct impression I was receiving from the flow of energy was that I should not enter because I am female. The message was not malevolent, rather I was simply being informed that I should show respect. This was a place meant for men not women.[63]

That's how Yolanda Chavez, a Native American CRM practitioner with graduate education in anthropology, described her encounter with a place charged with spiritual energy related to what an Aboriginal Australian might call "men's business."

What did Chavez feel? Was it "just" in her mind, or was it external, or—like everything we experience, of course—a product of interaction between the external and internal, between nature and neurons?

When we're dealing with this sort of "power of place," the mind trained in the traditions of Euro-American science is likely to be skeptical. One may be wise enough, and sensitive enough, not to reveal one's skepticism, but it's probably there. There's nothing wrong with this; there's no law, rule, regulation, or ethical code that says you have to believe in the little people in the spring; you only ought to respect the beliefs of those who think they're in there.

But what about it? Is there anything about spiritually energetic places that makes sense in the context of science as we currently define it? If there is, then maybe managers would feel more comfortable about paying attention to such places, and maybe we could find better ways than we now have of managing impacts on them. Or maybe not, but the question tends to trouble the mind, whether its answer has any practical consequences or not.

Whatever it was that Chavez encountered was not entirely unexpected. She was engaged in a survey, with an archaeologist and other tribal experts, to identify culturally important sites in advance of a construction project. She had some reason to suspect that such a place might exist in the area.

Well, a skeptic may scoff, so she just made it up or was influenced to sense it because she expected to.

Maybe, but one could say the same thing of an archaeologist who, having predicted that an ancient village site will be found on this or that ridge, goes out and finds it. Of course, the archaeologist can demonstrate the validity of her discovery by producing physical evidence, but often this evidence is something that only another archaeologist can appreciate, and archaeologists have on occasion been known to disagree about how to interpret an observation or artifact. Similarly, the power of a place experienced by one spiritual practitioner may—or may not—be experienced by another. If one cares to do so, one can set up ways of achieving intersubjective verification or disverification. I hasten to add that I don't recommend this, though it may be necessary in some extraordinary cases.

It is easy for someone whose education is grounded in Western empiricism and whose personality tends toward cynicism—like me, for instance, and like many colleagues in archaeology, historic preservation, and public service—to question giving credence to claims about spiritual energy and the places it energizes. Often, as Dorothy Parker said in a quite different context about Oakland, California, there is no there there—the place is "just" a rock, a grove of trees, a spring, an island, a stretch of river. We can't see anything that expresses the power that we're told the place has. Or if there *is* something there—a burial site, a monument—we may view it as something interesting for purposes of archaeology, or history, architecture, engineering, but its special power eludes us. *We don't feel it.*

But quite a lot of people seem to, and the belief that such places have power is by no means limited to nonindustrial, non-"Western" cultures. If it were, it would hardly make it illegitimate—who better to appreciate the special powers of nature than those who live in it? But there are plenty of nonindigenes who believe in such power and who in some cases have developed bodies of theory to account for them. There's Michael Persinger, for example, with his experimental data indicating that low-level geomagnetic forces can influence human perception. Very closely related to Persinger's work are Paul Devereaux's claims to have documented unusual radioactivity and magnetic anomalies at reputedly "sacred" sites in Great Britain. Farther yet removed from the mainstream scientific pale are people like Frank Joseph and the O'Reillys, who accept and pass on all kinds of evocative if anecdotal accounts of power experienced at "sacred sites."

Sure, sure, New Age nut cases, the skeptic scoffs. Maybe so, and maybe all those Native Americans, Africans, Chinese, Mongolians, and Australians are more or less nut cases too, centuries out of synch with the Enlightenment. Or maybe not. Maybe, as E. V. Walter might say even if he didn't buy the idea of a place as energetic in itself, it's we products of the Enlightenment who are out of synch, led down the garden path of dogmatic objectivity by Aristotle and Freud.

My own opinion, for what it's worth, is that the only thing we can be sure of about reality is that we don't understand it very well. When scientists tell us with straight faces that we live in a relativistic universe of warped spacetime, perhaps only one of an infinite number of universes that may bud off into one another and interact in strange ways, perhaps made up of minute strings of something-or-other vibrating in all kinds of dimensions, it strikes me as the height of folly to suppose that *anything* is impossible. Skepticism is a fine thing, until it becomes unskeptical of its own canons. I suggest keeping an open mind—neither accepting nor dismissing anything uncritically. But whether you *accept* them or not, it's of fundamental importance to *respect* the beliefs of those who think that the spiritual power of places is real.

In the spirit of such respect, I realize that to some who believe in "place power" as a matter of faith and received or perceived truth, even to speculate about how such power might work in the "real" world may seem disrespectful. I mean no disrespect by bringing the matter up, and—again strictly as my opinion—it seems to me that thinking of human beings as packages of electrical energy organizing and mobilizing the matter we call our bodies and interacting with larger patterns of energy in the environment's special places isn't much different from thinking of souls interacting in such places with worlds of the spirit.

Whether the power of place is actually in places, in our brains and nervous systems, or in interaction between the two, it exists somehow, it's influential, it's important to individuals and cultures, and it ought not be ignored simply because an archaeologist or other professional can't fit it into a category that he or she understands. Chavez, in reflecting on her experience with the grove, comments, "The spectacle that was presented that day was, the archaeologists were looking for physical evidence of human activity while we were looking for spiritual evidence. . . . Both are important. Both must be considered."[64]

Even when it's not a matter of spiritual energy, when the place is not a "sacred site" but simply a place that people value because it's tied up with their community's identity somehow—a nexus for stories, a place of familiar practice—places have power. Even when nobody suggests that power is in the place itself, a place exerts influence on those who value it. This emotive power of place is worth considering in planning, and worth trying somehow to maintain in order to enrich our lives as individuals and communities.

Which—to descend from the cosmic to the acronymous—is why we consider impacts on TCPs under the U.S. CRM laws.

Notes

1. Eugene N. Anderson, *Ecologies of the Heart: Emotion, Belief, and the Environment* (Oxford University Press, New York, 1996), 21.

2. Yi-Fu Tuan, *Space and Place: The Perspective of Experience* (University of Minnesota Press, Minneapolis, 1977), 200.

3. That is, groups whose knowledge base is grounded in oral tradition rather than in literature. The widely used term *nonliterate* really doesn't apply to such societies today; most are entirely literate, but if their cultural wisdom is set down on paper it has been set down only relatively recently, and often by people from other cultural traditions.

4. Tuan, *Space and Place*, 40.

5. Tuan, *Space and Place*, 157–58.

6. Tuan, *Space and Place*, 158.

7. Tuan, *Space and Place*, 178.

8. Tuan, *Space and Place*, 194.

9. Tuan, *Space and Place*, 198.

10. E. V. Walter, *Placeways: A Theory of the Human Environment* (University of North Carolina Press, Chapel Hill, 1988), 20.

11. Walter, *Placeways*, 117.

12. Walter, *Placeways*, 21.

13. Walter, *Placeways*, 131.

14. According to the Haptic Community website's Research page (haptic.mech.nwu.edu/HapticResearch.html): "of or relating to the sense of touch; tactile"; Greek *haptikos*, from *haptesthai*, "to grasp, touch."

15. Walter, *Placeways*, 134.

16. Walter, *Placeways*, 95.

17. Walter, *Placeways*, 121.

18. Walter, *Placeways*, 105–12.

19. Walter, *Placeways*, 204.

20. Walter, *Placeways*, 212–13.

21. Edward S. Casey, *The Fate of Place: A Philosophical History* (University of California Press, Berkeley, 1996).

22. Steven Field and Keith H. Basso (eds.), *Senses of Place* (School of American Research Press, Santa Fe, NM, 1997).

23. Edward S. Casey, How to Get from Space to Place in a Fairly Short Stretch of

Time: "Phenomenological Prolegomena," in Steven Field and Keith H. Basso (Eds.), *Senses of Place* (School of American Research, Santa Fe, NM, 1997).

24. Casey, How to Get from Space to Place, 14, emphasis in original.

25. Casey, How to Get from Space to Place, citing Myers (1991:67).

26. Casey, How to Get from Space to Place, 15, citing Myers (1991:59).

27. Casey, How to Get from Space to Place, 46.

28. Casey, How to Get from Space to Place, 26, emphasis in original.

29. Tony Hiss, *The Experience of Place* (Random House, New York, 1991).

30. Hiss is in the tradition of urban excellence advocates like Kevin Lynch (1960, 1981) but is a bit more focused on specific places and what makes them resonate with people. For a similar but more academic perspective, see Christopher Alexander, *The Timeless Way of Building* (Oxford University Press, New York, 1979).

31. Hiss, *The Experience of Place*, 6–7.

32. Hiss, *The Experience of Place*, 14.

33. Anonymous country roads, for example, and landmarks like Times Square, whose social significance is based on more than history and architecture. An inadvertently chilling example is the World Trade Center, where Hiss identifies a perspective that, when the buildings still stood, he said conveyed to the viewer a sense of weightlessness. I was intrigued when I read his description and wanted to check it out. "Next time I'm in Manhattan . . . ," I thought.

34. Hiss, *The Experience of Place*, 15.

35. Amos Rapoport, *The Meaning of the Built Environment: A Nonverbal Communication Approach* (Sage, Beverly Hills, 1982), 13.

36. Rapoport, *The Meaning of the Built Environment*, 65–68.

37. Rapoport, *The Meaning of the Built Environment*, 81.

38. Irwin Altman and Setha M. Low (eds.), *Place Attachment* (Plenum, New York, 1992).

39. Clare Cooper Marcus, Environmental Memories, in Altman and Low (eds.), *Place Attachment*, 89.

40. Louise Chawla, Childhood Place Attachments, in Altman and Low (eds.), *Place Attachment*, 75.

41. Ross Adey, quoted in Winifred Gallagher, *The Power of Place: How Our Surroundings Shape Our Thoughts, Emotions, and Actions* (HarperCollins, New York, 1994), 81.

42. Gallagher, *The Power of Place*, 80, 96.

43. Specifically the amygdala and the hippocampus; Gallagher, *The Power of Place*, 93.

44. Michael Pensinger, quoted in Gallagher, *The Power of Place*, 93.

45. For a reflective summary of the issues brought out in *Landscape*, see John Brinckerhoff Jackson, *A Sense of Place, a Sense of Time* (Yale University Press, New Haven, CT, 1994).

46. Paul Groth and Todd W. Bressi (eds.), *Understanding Ordinary Landscapes* (Yale University Press, New Haven, CT, 1997).

47. Groth and Bressi, *Understanding Ordinary Landscapes,* 1.

48. Groth and Bressi, *Understanding Ordinary Landscapes,* 3–18.

49. Dolores Hayden, Urban Landscape History: The Sense of Place and the Politics of Space, in Groth and Bressi (eds.), *Understanding Ordinary Landscapes,* 133. For similar perspectives with specific reference to houses, see Janet Carsten and Stephen Hugh-Jones (eds.), *About the House: Levi-Strauss and Beyond* (Cambridge University Press, Cambridge, 1995).

50. Dolores Hayden, *The Power of Place: Urban Landscapes as Public History* (MIT Press, Cambridge, 1995).

51. Robert A. Archibald, *A Place to Remember: Using History to Build Community* (AltaMira, Walnut Creek, CA, 1999).

52. Archibald, *A Place to Remember,* 24.

53. Archibald, *A Place to Remember,* 62, 104–5.

54. Archibald, *A Place to Remember,* 204.

55. With the notable exception of T. F. King, R. Jacobson, K. R. Burns, and K. Spading, *Amelia Earhart's Shoes: Is the Mystery Solved?* (AltaMira, Walnut Creek, CA, 2001).

56. Sean O'Reilly, James O'Reilly, and Tim O'Reilly, *The Road Within: True Stories of Transformation and the Soul* (Travellers' Tales, San Francisco, 2002).

57. Frank Joseph (ed.), *Sacred Sites of the West: A Guide to Mystical Centers* (Hancock House, Surrey, B.C., 1997).

58. Chuck Pettis, *Secrets of Sacred Space* (Llewellyn, St. Paul, MN, 1999).

59. Michael DeMunn and Noah Buchanan (illustrator), *Places of Power* (Dawn, Nevada City, CA, 1997).

60. James Swan, Working with the Spirit of Place, in James Swan and Roberta Swan (eds.), *Dialogues with the Living Earth* (Quest Books; Theosophical Publishing House, Wheaton, IL, 1996), 3.

61. Paul Devereux, *Places of Power: Measuring the Secret Energy of Ancient Sites* (Blandford, London, 1990).

62. See n. 43.

63. Yolanda Chavez, personal communication to the author, June 25, 2002, quoted with permission.

64. Chavez, personal communication.

Chapter Six

What Makes a TCP?

"Does this island have a name?" Dora asked him. "No, no," he
answered, "but it's my island and I'm pretty well attached to it."
—Mary Hufford (1986:37)

From Spirit Places to Urban Ghettos—
The Diversity of TCPs

CHAPTERS 3 and 4 suggest the kinds of places to which communities ascribe
cultural value. Chapter 5 summarizes some ideas about what we value
about such places, and why. This gives us a basis, I hope, for appreciating the
diversity of places, and of values, which the notion of traditional cultural properties embraces.

As it's reflected in National Register Bulletin 38, this diversity is partly a
matter of historical accident. The two cases that particularly motivated Pat
Parker and me to start writing—the ski facility on the San Francisco Peaks and
the destruction of Poletown—were superficially about as different from one
another as two cases could be. One was rural, the other urban; one dealt with a
large chunk of natural space, the other with a modest piece of Detroit's built
environment. One was a place important to Indian tribes, the other to Polish
Americans. One was ascribed spiritual significance; the other was not—at least
not explicitly.

All they really shared was that the importance of the places lay in the minds
of the plain, ordinary, local people who valued them and was largely invisible to
professionals in the standard historic preservation disciplines. Had the hot cases
of the time all involved, say, Native American spiritual places, the bulletin's scope
might not have been so broad. As it was, once we concluded that our objective
was to get agencies to pay attention to what regular old folks in communities

thought was important, we were committed to dealing with a very broad range of places.

But there *are* some attributes that TCPs share, though none necessarily exhibits them all. In this chapter we'll look at the attributes that tend to characterize TCPs. Understanding these attributes, and how they interact, can be important to making management decisions. Then we'll turn to some questions that can't be avoided when dealing with places whose value lies in the minds of communities—what if the people lie, and what is a "community," anyhow? Finally, we'll look at some examples of identified TCPs —without, I should stress, much detail. Others have provided such detail to some extent,[1] and it's far beyond the scope of this book.

What TCPs Share

The value that communities ascribe to TCPs tends to be expressed in terms of five attributes. Not all TCPs reflect all five; probably few do. But every TCP reflects at least one. These attributes are important because they influence—may even define—how a community is likely to want its TCPs managed. You can do things with places exhibiting certain attributes that you can't so readily do with places whose attributes are different.

The five attributes that I think can make a place a TCP are spiritual power, practice, stories, therapeutic quality, and remembrances.

Figure 6.1.   The Medicine Lake Highlands, California, an extensive spiritual landscape. Mount Shasta is in the distance. Photo by the author.

Spiritual Power

A TCP may be thought by some group—an Indian tribe or its elders, an Aboriginal Australian community, African animists, specialists in feng shui—to have some kind of "supernatural" character.[2] In the eyes of the group, there is something a bit weird about such places. The group may know what it is—know the spirit or spirits associated with the place and know what they do—or it may simply understand that the area has spiritual associations. The place is usually thought to have some kind of ability to *act* on people and things. The place and its power may be helpful or dangerous, or both, or neither, but whatever it is, it can affect people. As David Carmichael puts it, such places are "where power is received or where power is needed for protection from spiritual danger."[3] People who visit such a place may have visions, or gain enlightenment, or be terrified, or go mad, or die. Such a place usually needs to be treated with care; to do otherwise is to tempt fate. The preservation of such a place may be seen as vital to the preservation of the world, or the tribe, or humanity, or the universe, or its power may be seen as more limited geographically and socially.

Famous examples abound: in the United States, Mount Shasta, the San Francisco Peaks, and the Bighorn Medicine Wheel; in Australia, Uluru and other famous places where ancestral beings have gone into the ground; in England, Stonehenge; in France, Lourdes. These represent only the tiny tip of a huge iceberg. Every community that relates intimately with its environment probably knows of places that people think have spiritual power.

Practice

A TCP may be important because of what people do there. The practice may be spiritual in character, or it may not.

The Karuk Tribe in northern California holds its World Renewal ritual along the banks of the Klamath River. To the Karuk, the Klamath is where the ritual *must* be carried out, if the world is to continue. It's safe to guess that the Karuk regard the Klamath as having spiritual power, but its association with the ritual would give the river cultural significance even if the river itself were not regarded as spiritually energetic. The ritual involves traveling along specific trails and performing functions—prayers, lighting fires, shooting arrows—at specific places. Some of these places are doubtless thought to have power, but the whole river valley is where the spiritual practice of world renewal must be carried out.

A practice may not be formally ritualistic but still have spiritual qualities that it shares with the places where it is carried out. Many if not most indigenous groups ascribe spiritual qualities to plants and animals. As a result, areas where the plants or animals live may have to be treated carefully, out of respect for their residents.

Or the practice may be more ritualistic than spiritual. Boatmen running the Colorado River—both Indian and non-Indian—often stop for a moment of silence at Vulcan's Anvil above Lava Falls, a particularly dangerous rapid. Some might say that Vulcan's Anvil has power to keep them safe in the rapids, but I daresay most would simply say that it's a convenient, somewhat awe-inspiring place to take stock, scout the rapids ahead, and gather one's forces for the ordeal to come.

Finally, the practice may not be spiritual at all. Gathering to watch fireworks on the Fourth of July may give value to the city park. Customary use of a bridge or path or hilltop as a place to propose marriage, looking out over the countryside from the top of a pile of mine spoil, the sale of *punchkes*[4] by Polish bakeries in Detroit on Fat Tuesday—all these thoroughly secular activities can give cultural value to the places where they happen.

Stories

A story, or a cluster of stories, is often an important TCP attribute. The stories may have spiritual qualities. The stories of the Dreaming among aboriginal Australians account for the desert's rocks and ridges and billabongs through association with spirit ancestors. The story associated by practitioners of the Latter-Day Saints religions with the place in Missouri they call "Adam ondi-Ahman" has Adam setting up an altar there and blessing his children.[5]

Figure 6.2.   A TCP building: The Jewish Community Center, Petaluma, California, center of secular and religious life for the town's Jewish community since the 1920s. Photo by the author.

Often the stories have to do with the group's ancestors. Often but not always, the sites associated with ancestor stories are what archaeologists call archaeological sites. They may also be cemeteries, shrines, or simply places in the landscape where ancestors are believed to have done something.

The place referents may be quite specific or very general. The summit of Mount Tonnaachaw in Chuuk, for example, discussed in chapter 2, is a very specific location associated in Chuukese tradition with the specific deeds of the culture bringer *Sowukachaw* and the mystic land *Kachaw.*[6] In contrast, Hopi and Zuni people ascribe spiritual value to all places reflecting their ancestors' presence, whether or not they figure in particular stories, simply because they are associated with the ancestors' trek through the Southwest to the pueblos where their descendants live today. The African Burial Ground in New York City is important to African Americans for its association with enslaved ancestors, even though its location was lost for generations, and any specific stories associated with it have dissipated.[7]

Stories may connect a place with a group's origins, often under supernatural conditions. Tahquitz Canyon in California is where Cahuilla people believe their ancestors emerged from a lower world at the beginning of time. Chequemagon Bay on Lake Superior is where Ojibwe legend says the ancestors were led from the great salt sea by the sacred *Megis* shell. The Hopi, Zuni, and other tribes trace their origins to the Grand Canyon. Or the stories may recount heroic or desperate or otherwise memorable acts of the ancestors. The Kiks.adi Survival March Route in Alaska is associated with the heroic withdrawal of the Tlingit from the guns of the Russians in 1804—a sort of Tlingit Dunkirk.

The stories may be ways of "writing history in the land," as the Cibicue Apache and the Yanesha of eastern Peru do. As Keith Basso has shown, they may teach moral lessons and perform socializing functions. The stories of loss and heroism associated with the World Trade Center site in New York and the crash site of United Flight 93 near Shanksville, Pennsylvania, are already powerfully associated with American identity.

Finally, stories may simply lend special character to a valued place, making it more exciting and emotionally charged than it would otherwise be. "The Rocks," near San Juan Bautista, California, are associated with stories of outlaws and stagecoach robbers that lend character to the local cultural environment.

Therapeutic Quality

The power to cure is ascribed to some TCPs (consider Lourdes), and therapeutic practices—medicine gathering, the administration of medicines, physical therapy, spiritual healing—may be among the practices that make a place important. In a broader sense, Wilbert Gessler has described places that are regarded as inherently therapeutic; these can be natural landscapes and landscape features, or socially created places like the vicinity of a !Kung campfire.[8]

Remembrances

Robert Archibald writes movingly about the importance of remembrance in the valuation of place:

> I crave Lake Superior. It was present in my childhood map of [Marquette, Wisconsin]. Now I cannot imagine the place without its frigid, clear, beautiful blue-green waters. . . . This lake is inside me, the exact center of my emotional map of the world. I do not know who I would be without it. This water is my definition of splendor, beauty, tranquility, violence, chill, ice, winter, spring, life and death. This water cascades through my mind incessantly as though over craggy rocks, with me everywhere, in faraway places, dreams and waking. It is what makes this place and me different from all others.[9]

Archibald's Lake Superior is clearly a place that he, at least, experiences (and has experienced) "haptically" in Walters' terms,[10] via "simultaneous perception" in Hiss's.[11] Losing such places can leave us psychologically adrift. We are sometimes at a loss to explain what it is that makes such places important to us. They are simply those places where, in Yi-Fu Tuan's words, a "deep though subconscious" sort of attachment comes "simply with familiarity and ease, with the assurance of nurture and security, with the memory of sounds and smells, of communal activities and homely pleasures accumulated over time."[12]

It must be these kinds of deep, complex patterns of remembrance that gives people their attachments to the East End of Cincinnati or to Corona, New York. It's what makes Chinatowns comfortable to Chinese, the hills and arroyos of Grouse Creek dear to its Mormon cowboy families, Poletown worth chaining one's self to the church door to save from demolition.

The places that become dear in one's memory can be surprising. Consider Stiltsville, an undistinguished group of houses built on stilts in Biscayne Bay, Florida. The National Park Service has gained control of the bay and wants Stiltsville removed in order to return the place to its natural condition. Fighting the demolition order, the residents were tricked by the Park Service into nominating the place to the National Register—an ill-advised and predictably doomed undertaking. In trying to demonstrate the cultural value of the place, however, the residents amassed a remarkable collection of letters, statements, resolutions from city councils, and other expressions of belief that Stiltsville was a vital and beloved part of the Biscayne Bayscape. It was a place that people remembered and associated with the bay; it gave the bay a special identity. The fact that the buildings were undistinguished, and of relatively recent origin (being prone to blowing away in hurricanes), while impressive to the keeper of the National Register, was of no importance whatever to the people and organizations that rallied to Stiltsville's defense. Its significance lay simply in its being remembered, as a defining characteristic of Biscayne Bay.[13]

Attachment to places that define our identities through memory can be powerful—powerful enough even to overcome strong cultural biases against expressions of such attachment. Tony Hiss describes the reaction of Amish farmers in Pennsylvania—a notoriously reticent lot—to plans for construction of an expressway through their area:

> The Amish, traditionally, do not participate in the public process, but in 1988, on the night of the Lancaster County scoping meeting, more than a thousand Old Order Amish drove their buggies to the meeting hall and expressed their concern by simply sitting quietly in the audience in their black homespun suits while testimony was taken. The silent eloquence of their unprecedented turnout produced a dramatic impact of its own—a short time later, Pennsylvania's governor, Robert Casey, announced that he had ordered the Pennsylvania Department of transportation to abandon work on the proposed alignment for the new road and to find a more suitable alternative.[14]

Attribute Clusters

The attribute "spiritual power" overlaps the attribute "practice"; spiritually energetic places are often places where spiritual practices are carried out. But not always. Some places are so powerful that one doesn't approach them, so one can't possibly carry out practices of any kind there. This was a source of confusion when the Forest Service was evaluating the San Francisco Peaks back in the early 1980s. Seeing no sign that people had been performing ceremonies there, the Forest Service concluded that the peaks were not spiritually significant. But to the Navajo and Hopi the fact that no one goes there reflects the very spiritual significance of the place. Had there been evidence there of human activity, it would have been at best irrelevant to the peaks' significance, and it might even have evidenced desecration. And of course, the cultural practices with which a place is associated may not be spiritual at all but still be viewed as culturally important.

Similarly, spiritual power may or may not cluster with the attributes "stories" and "therapeutic value." The stories associated with places may or may not be spiritual in character, and many but not all spiritual places are thought to have therapeutic qualities, but the ascription of therapeutic value doesn't require that a place be viewed as spiritual.

The attributes "practice," "stories," and "remembrance" tend to cluster. Generally one remembers places where one does something, performs some practice. One tends to remember stories about such places. But "practice" and "stories" tend to have the implication of group activities, while "remembrance" can be solitary. And each of these attributes can stand solidly on its own. The stories associated with a place where people gather reeds for basketry may be only anecdotes ("That's where Sylvia fell in the creek trying to reach that tall willow shoot"), but that doesn't make the practice of gathering, or the place, less important. Conversely, a place about which stories are told may be important for that reason even though nobody practices anything there. The place referred to by Cibicue Apache as "Shelters of Shit" teaches an important set of moral lessons through a story about selfish people who got uncomfortably bound up in their shelters, but if people do anything there today, it probably has little to do with the hoarding of food or defecation. The haptic experience of place by a Robert Archibald or a resident of Poletown, Stiltsville, the Amish countryside, or the East End of Cincinnati is no less powerful for being grounded in remembrances that may have little to do with practice or specific stories.

The attribute "therapeutic" is also pretty self-contained, though it may attach itself to spiritually energetic places or places ascribed spiritual importance, and there may well be stories and practices associated with it. The medicinal plants gathered by Chamorro medicine makers on Guam's Anderson Air Force Base give the installation's rainforest therapeutic value, which would exist even if there were no stories attached to it, and that value would exist even if the medicine makers were prohibited by the air force from carrying out their practices (thankfully, they are not).

The important thing about the attributes that consistently are associated with TCPs is not that they're mutually exclusive—they're not—or that they cluster together to form obvious "types"—they can be made to do so, but I don't think much is gained by it.[15] What's important is simply that they exist, that one can look for them, think of a place with reference to them, and sometimes get a hint of what will and will not be seen by the community as an appropriate way to treat the place. Conversely, if one *doesn't* think about the attributes the place is likely to have and what those attributes may mean to management, one may propose something that makes one look an utterly irredeemable barbarian in the eyes of the community. We'll look at how attributes influence management and mitigation in chapter 9.

But first, and before we even get to the core subjects of Bulletin 38—identification and evaluation of TCPs—there are two big questions that we might as well address, because the ways one answers them influence the way one does everything else.

Does the Place's Story Have to Be "True"?

Often, association with a story or stories is among the attributes that a community values about a place. There's a natural tendency among the historians and archaeologists who do most CRM work to try to validate or disvalidate stories about the past—is this "really" what happened, or is it "only folklore"?

Few would try to validate or disvalidate a story about spiritual power; there's no point. Where a tradition has spiritual qualities, we have little difficulty—in most cases—accepting it simply as something that people honestly believe. Out of respect for the people, we can acknowledge the belief as vesting the place with significance even though we can't demonstrate that what's believed actually happened. We are unlikely to find archaeological evidence of a burned bush on Mount Sinai or to be able to link it to *the* burning bush if we do, but that hardly deflates the significance of the mountain to Jews, Christians, and Muslims.

But what about a story that's not spiritual in character at all but more like secular history, a belief that something happened there—but there's evidence to suggest that the story's not true? Do we accept the significance of the place even though we think the story is bogus? Consider the case of "The Rocks."[16]

The Rocks, as their name implies, comprise a group of rock outcrops; they lie along U.S. Route 101 in Central California. In local tradition this is a place where highwaymen—*bandidos*—hid to waylay stagecoaches and unwary passers-by. In some versions, the famous bandits Joaquin Murrieta and Tiberio Vasquez used The Rocks as an ambush site. When improvements were planned to the highway in the vicinity, the state highway agency—Caltrans—had a "cultural resources" study done that did not identify The Rocks as a significant place.

Local people commented critically on the draft environmental report, recounting the bandido legends and their importance in defining the character of the area. The Rocks, the commenters indicated, played an important role in their valued traditions.

The authors of the environmental report replied that their historians and archaeologists had considered the matter and concluded that there was no factual basis for the legend. The legend, they said, was reflected only in anecdotal accounts. One might counter that anecdote is rather the stuff of legend, and vice versa, but the authors hedged their bets by going on to suggest that even if robberies were committed at The Rocks, this didn't "convey" much significance, because "the association (created by a robbery) is fleeting, and is duplicated in numerous other locations." As a result, they said, The Rocks were not eligible for the National Register.[17]

Never mind why a "fleeting" association is insufficient to make a place significant (it's easy to think of "fleeting" events that people think are pretty important—President Kennedy's assassination, the destruction of Hiroshima, the events that took place in a couple of hours on the morning of September 11, 2001). Never mind that if only properties in no danger of duplication were eligible for the register the vast majority of archaeological sites and examples of vernacular architecture would be excluded. What's interesting about the environmental analysts' position is the priority they give to professional historical analysis and documentation over local values.

The analysts went on to "agree that it might not always be essential for associated events to be proven, or even true, in order for a . . . resource to qualify as a TCP," but they promptly contradicted themselves by saying that since there should be written documentation if robberies had taken place, and they hadn't found any, the legend might "be just a later myth."[18]

There are lots of technical holes that can be punched in the environmental analysts' arguments, but suppose there weren't? What if research convinced us that the bandido stories absolutely, certainly are not true—that stagecoaches never rolled through The Rocks, and Murrieta and Vasquez suffered from lithophobia?

Bulletin 38 says that to resolve such issues, one ought to consult a wide range of both background literature and contemporary authorities.[19] Looking back over a dozen years of practice with the bulletin, I now think that's simplistic. Or in a way, unduly complicated. If a TCP is important because of the role it plays in a community's cultural life, then does it really matter whether the qualities ascribed to it are "real"? If such attributes exist in the minds of the community's members and make the place play a role in the community's life, doesn't that in itself make the place a TCP worthy of being considered in planning? I think it does.[20] Of course, I'm not speaking for the keeper of the National Register; the keeper might be sufficiently impressed by dismissive research results to determine the place ineligible. But still it would seem to me to need consideration under laws like NEPA, whose scope of concern for the cultural environment isn't limited by the bounds of National Register eligibility.[21]

But doesn't this mean that there are no standards at all? That anything anybody says has any kind of importance at all can be allowed to impede important public projects and the enjoyment of private rights to improve one's land? I don't think so, but I'd like to delay explaining why I don't think so until a bit later. First, let's look at a related but even more difficult question about the "reality" of a TCP's significant qualities.

What If They're Lying?

Since figuring out whether a place is traditional and cultural involves talking with people, there's always the danger that the people you're talking with aren't just mistaken, as their critics would doubtless call those who value The Rocks, but that they're telling lies. There may be several reasons for this besides sheer cussedness.

They may be telling you what they think you want to hear. This often happens when the people you're interviewing are members of a relatively downtrodden social or ethnic group, and they perceive you as a member of the dominant society. There are also groups within which it's simply polite to tell people what will make them happy. You need to find out, going in, whether you're faced with this kind of situation, by reviewing what's been written about the group, by talking to knowledgeable people (anthropologists or sociologists who've worked with the group, other people who interact with the group regularly, members of the group who have enough "outside" perspective to advise you), and simply by thinking about it and watching people's behavior. Think about the political and economic circumstances of the group, past and present. Are there reasons for them to want to please you? Would they, for example, simply like for you to go away?

But the trickier problem is with people who may deliberately try to mislead. Maybe you're evaluating the impacts of a project that people really don't like for reasons that have nothing to do with their cultural values. Maybe it's strictly economic; maybe they'll benefit financially from one alternative approach to the project, so they make up TCPs to tip the balance away from others. Or maybe it's the influence of another group—organized environmentalists, say. Maybe they're even being bought off, directly or indirectly, by such a group. Or maybe it's just that they don't like the idea of change.

Or maybe they really do have cultural values that will be violated by the project, but they aren't attached to *places*. So they stretch things a bit to create a place attachment that doesn't really exist.

The reader (like the writer) may be feeling a bit conflicted about all this. It's easy enough to criticize, and want to dismiss the contentions of, a group that's "just in it for the money" (though what if it's a group that's economically disadvantaged; isn't a little fabrication understandable?). We may feel contemptuous of a group that's had the wool pulled over its eyes by somebody else and whose members have been beguiled into perjuring themselves, but how can we be sure that's what's happened? How do we reliably sort out relations between the groups and figure out just who's persuading who of what? And if the people really have a cultural problem with the project, or if their society is such that change isn't welcome, shouldn't that be considered in planning in its own right? Why should there have to be a *place* involved?

These are all difficult questions, but for a CRM practitioner the last is likely to be particularly vexing. If one believes that cultural resources should be given a fair shake in planning—and if one doesn't, one really should be in some other field—then how can one not squirm at the notion that a group's culture-based problems with a project shouldn't be considered unless they somehow involve a piece of land or a building? I found myself squirming thus—though luckily only briefly—when I was engaged by the Bad River and Red Cliff Bands of Great Lakes Ojibwe to help in evaluating the effects of underwater logging on TCPs.

The story of Chequamegon Bay[22] is a complicated one. Suffice it to say that one reason for the bands' disquiet with the grappling of sunken logs off the bottom of Lake Superior was that the logs represented trees that in their view had been stolen from them back in the nineteenth century—cut off their lands with thin legal justification, to line the pockets of non-Indians. The logs that had sunk before getting to the sawmills had been rescued from the thieves—some said by the powerful spirit *Mishebeshu*. For them to now be stolen back again was a serious affront. But was it related to *place?* To *a* place that might be eligible for the National Register?

Like other students of the matter, I eventually decided that it was—though another researcher argued strongly that it wasn't—and there were enough cultural values attached to the bay in which the logs lay to make the status of the logs themselves more or less moot. It was troubling, however, that we couldn't simply consider the culturally based objections of the Ojibwe in their own right.

Theoretically we could. Under NEPA, which isn't place fixated, we should in theory consider people's environmental concerns whether place-based or not. However, in NEPA practice we're troubled by a Supreme Court decision known rather fittingly as PANE[23] and a piece of the NEPA regulations[24] that collectively tend to discredit environmental impacts that are strictly social, economic, or psychological.[25] Since 1994, Executive Order 12898, on environmental justice (EJ), has encouraged consideration of such impacts, because they are often disproportionately visited on low-income populations and minority groups, but many NEPA practitioners don't pay much attention to EJ unless there are obvious, measurable physical impacts (typically via air or water pollution) on populations identified through census data as resident in an impact area. And neither NEPA nor the executive order set up the kind of consultation-based problem-solving system offered by Section 106, which of course requires some sort of place referent. If the bands wanted a reasonably guaranteed opportunity to negotiate to resolve their cultural concerns, they had to trigger Section 106 review, and that required a physical place. This is a common problem, and it can be frustrating for a traditional community.

Bulletin 38 discusses at some length the problem of efforts to mislead, along with that of inadvertent bias, concluding, "In general, the only reasonably reliable way to resolve conflict among sources is to review a wide enough range of documentary data, and to interview a wide enough range of authorities, to minimize the likelihood of inadvertent bias or of being deliberately misled."[26]

I recall thinking at the time that we were rather blithely dismissing a very complicated subject, about which I had conflicting views myself. I don't know that we could have done otherwise, but time has validated my unease. Two cases that have been discussed in print exemplify the problems surrounding truthfulness.

Point Conception, California

In 1978, a liquefied natural gas (LNG) terminal was proposed at Point Conception, on the south-central California coast. This is the historical territory of the Chumash, a once-large and sophisticated indigenous society represented today by a number of small groups, some recognized by the federal government, most not. Members of several such groups banded together and gained the support of archaeologists and others, in opposition to the project, asserting that Point Conception was the "Western Gate" through which the souls of the dead passed on their way to the spirit world. The Chumash fought the project vigorously, eventually even occupying the site in an act of rather effective civil disobedience. Eventually the project was canceled.

In 1997, anthropologists Brian Haley and Larry Wilcoxon published an article in the journal *Current Anthropology* in which they criticized the Chumash project opponents as liars and their archaeological supporters as dupes.[27] Haley and Wilcoxon argued that Point Conception was not traditionally the Western Gate, at least to most Chumash. The project opponents, they said, had reconstructed their culture based on ethnographic data, and to some extent made it up. They also asserted that some of the "traditionalists" were not even really Chumash and that some, at least, were trying to position themselves to make money in the contract archaeology game.

Current Anthropology publishes comments on its articles, and those that accompanied Haley and Wilcoxon's piece were generally laudatory. A few issues later, however, half a dozen anthropologists, archaeologists, historians, and Chumash took them to task for ethnocentric bias.[28] Not only were Haley and Wilcoxon wrong about many of their facts, these critics argued, but they were guilty of imposing their own cultural biases on the Chumash and interpreting their actions in this inappropriate light.

The seventh commenter on Haley and Wilcoxon's article, anthropologist Robert Winthrop, was a nonspecialist in the area and accordingly didn't get involved in particulars. He took a broader view, on which he elaborated in a subsequent article.[29] In essence, Winthrop questioned the very notion of trying to measure the historical authenticity of a TCP. His argument went like this:

1. The government considers things like TCPs in planning in order to allow groups to maintain valued cultural traditions.

2. The experience of Indian tribes over the last five hundred years has been one of vast sociocultural dislocation; many traditions have been nearly or entirely lost.

3. Even in a stable society that has not undergone such drastic disruptions, culture is not static; it evolves, and it is not uncommon for a group to reach back into its past, particularly across a historical diaspora, to collect and reinterpret its traditions. A student of Benedictine monasticism, Winthrop used the history of that order's evolution and self-reinterpretation to illustrate his point.

4. Hence the government's purpose can be achieved only by allowing for the evolution and reinterpretation of tradition, particularly among historically damaged groups like Indian tribes. He summarized:

[T]he objective of cultural resource management policy should not be to ensure the strict perpetuation of earlier practices, or to demand an unbroken continuity of ritual observance. Rather, to the extent feasible federal policy should be directed toward protecting and extending access to those resources and landscapes through which traditions can be adapted and renewed.[30]

Hindmarsh Island, South Australia

The second case is Australian, and hence it occurred in a somewhat different legal context than Point Conception—and one seemingly less relevant to most readers of this book. But the facts of the case, and the conclusions reached by one thoughtful commentator at least, are similar to those at Point Conception.

Since the *Mabo* decision and enactment of the Native Title Act—and in some cases under prior state laws and the Aboriginal Land Rights Act in the Northern Territory—Aboriginal groups assert rights in or title to places based on (among other things) traditional cultural associations. Even if this doesn't result in a transfer of ownership, it gives them some clout when projects are planned affecting such places. In the Hindmarsh Island case, a group of Aboriginal women opposed a bridge that was to be built connecting the island with the shore of the Murray River, in whose mouth the island lies. They asserted that the island was a place where "women's business" (women's religious ritual activity) was carried out and that its separateness from the shore had to be maintained in order to preserve the integrity of the "business." On the strength of this assertion, the minister of Aboriginal affairs in 1994 placed a ban on the construction—a ban subsequently overturned by a 1995 federal court decision. Shortly thereafter a television station in Adelaide asserted that the information on which the women had based their claim had been "fabricated" by Aboriginal men and the women's lawyer.

As in the case of Point Conception, the specifics of who was right and who was wrong at Hindmarsh Island are things that I certainly can't address, and they aren't entirely relevant. What's relevant is that in this case a historian, Austin Gough, entered the fray in June 1995 with a broadside against anthropological interpretations of traditional cultural values, insisting that they did not reflect objectively derived historical fact.[31] To this Haley/Wilcoxonesque attack, anthropologist James Weiner responded in an article that presaged much of Winthrop's argument, though neither scholar seems to have had knowledge of the other.

Like Winthrop, Weiner argues that "historical authenticity" is a very slippery concept. While it is the business of a historian to seek such authenticity, an anthropologist understands that it is really an artificial construct. "The enduring and stable in what we call culture and religion is always negotiated and made visible through the contingent and mutable conventions of the present; to the extent that there is never any perfect instauration of law or convention, then every conventional act or belief is . . . innovative, or 'new,' or 'fabricated.'"[32]

Weiner also makes a useful point about the "rediscovery" of tradition through study of the anthropological literature. "Now we have had the Magna Carta for centuries. The fact that I may have found out about it at school only two days ago may make my knowledge of it recent in terms of acquisition, but the knowledge itself is of long duration."[33]

The burden of Weiner's and Winthrop's arguments is that what is "true" about the cultural traditions that make TCPs (or indigenous TCPs, at least) important is not necessarily what's "true" in a strictly historiographic sense. Similarly, "historical significance" is not necessarily a function of historical accuracy as understood by historians. As Jon Erlandson said in his comment on Haley and Wilcoxon: "For [Indian people], the significance of Point Conception lies not just in its ancient sacredness but also in the transformative role it played in the revitalization of Chumash culture."[34]

Accordingly, I think Weiner, Winthrop and Erlandson would say that it's simplistic (at best) to judge truthfulness against the standards employed by historians.

So, then, is there no truth? Is there no yardstick we can hold up to measure which places are and which places are not TCPs? I think there is, but it is not a yardstick of historical accuracy or objectively definable truthfulness.

The question to ask, I think, is not "Is the place really what people say it is?" but "Do people really ascribe the significance to it that people say they do?" Or, to put it another way, does it play the sort of role in a community's cultural integrity that people say it does?

Suppose an indigenous individual claims that there's a hole in the middle of a proposed project area, which nobody can see but that is really there and is full of the spirits of the ancestors. Rather than sending archaeologists out to look for holes, or mediums out to interview the ancestral shades, or historians to find out whether the spiritual place was regarded as such a generation or two or ten ago, it seems to me that we should be interviewing broadly in the community to find out whether its members generally agree that there's a hole out there full of spirits— or agree that the tradition of such a hole is important to them. If they do agree, and it doesn't appear that they've been coerced or cajoled into saying something that they don't really believe, then the question of whether there is historical evidence of time depth to the tradition is no more important than that of whether there are "really" spirits in the hole.

This, of course, leads to another question.

How Many Must Believe?

If to validate a place we ought to find out how much the community values it, rather than whether it "really" has the powers or associations ascribed to it, we have to confront the sticky question of what the *community is.*

Often this isn't difficult. The community may be an Indian tribe or some other clearly defined social group—an organized neighborhood, a self-defined group of citizens, an ethnic or social or economic minority group. But what if it's not?

Or what if the group is of two minds, or three, or four? What if some neighborhood residents think the place is important, while others don't? Or some think it's got one kind of importance, while others ascribe some other kind of cultural value to it?

What if it comes down, really, to one person? Elder Joe says that Medicine Hole is a really important spiritual place, but nobody else much cares about it. Or maybe Joe isn't even an elder; maybe he's just a member of a tribe. Maybe not a federally recognized tribe. Maybe not a tribal member at all; maybe a white farmer, an Asian American auto worker. But he really, really believes that Medicine Hole is a special place.

We're getting perilously close here to something like my own "TCP," The Hill, and I don't mean to suggest that every place some pimply adolescent moons over ought to be given consideration in making public decisions— though I suppose we might have a more emotionally balanced population if we were all accorded such respect. But if The Hill has slippery slopes, the numbers game is tricky, too. What if Elder Joe is the last member of his tribe? Does that matter? What if there are *three* people who call Medicine Hole special? Where do we draw the line?

I don't know the answer to that question and suspect that it has to be left to the political process. Elder Joe is going to have to mobilize some support if he really wants to protect Medicine Hole. But that's an uncomfortable conclusion to reach, particularly since Elder Joe's ability to garner political support is likely to vary in direct proportion to his wealth and his public relations acumen. Meaning that Ted Turner's TCPs are going to get more attention than mine, and while I have the utmost respect for Mr. Turner, I don't think that's fair.

Nor can we forget the previous question: What if Joe Elder is lying? Presumably it would be harder for a dozen people to sustain a lie than it would for one person to do so, but the fact that only one person thinks something is true while everybody else thinks it's hooey doesn't automatically make it hooey. Consider Galileo.

I don't have an answer to the "How many?" problem, but there's a case that relates to it, that provides some food for thought.

Enola Hill,[35] in the foothills of Zig Zag Mountain in Oregon, is on the Mount Hood National Forest. Back in 1987, the forest proposed a "salvage" timber sale on the hill, to take out diseased trees that it argued posed a threat of infection to the surrounding forest.

Several tribes and multitribal reservations have traditional ties to the area—Yakama, Umatilla, Warm Springs. But it was Rip Lone Wolf, a Nez Perce who spent part of his youth at Warm Springs, who voiced specific concern about what the project would do to the hill's spiritual qualities. His main evidence for these qualities was the fact that he went there to seek visions, and he got them. He attracted the attention of others, both Indian and non-Indian, who felt that the logging would damage the scenic qualities of the hill, and eventually the cause of Enola Hill's defense grew legs.

The forest had a TCP study done by an ethnographer—Robert Winthrop. Winthrop did a creditable job of interviewing people in the tribes of the area and found that some tribal authorities said the hill had little or no cultural significance while others thought it did, identifying it both generally as a cultural or spiritual area and specifically as a seasonal camp, a huckleberry-collecting area, and a source of physically and spiritually pure water, as well as sweat lodge stones. On balance, he concluded, the hill might well be eligible for the National Register.[36]

The Forest Service didn't want to hear it and put together a kangaroo court of archaeologists and lawyers (they called it an "evaluation committee"), who systematically if on very flimsy grounds rebutted Winthrop point by point, providing the Forest Service with the basis for deciding that Enola Hill was *not* eligible.[37] At the time, I described the Forest Service's report as "an egregious exercise in the manipulation of information,"[38] and I've seen no reason since to change my mind.

Meanwhile, the Yakama had written to the secretary of the interior saying that the hill was a sacred site, but the Confederated Tribes of the Warm Springs

Reservation issued a position paper "oppos[ing] the voices of those individuals about the importance of Enola Hill." Later the Warm Springs general manager argued, in effect, that because the logging would be done "to insure the forest health of Enola Hill," it should go forward, denying "any tribal government request to consider Enola Hill as a 'traditional cultural property' eligible for inclusion in the National Register."[39]

To make a long and convoluted story short,[40] the case went to the keeper of the National Register, to the Advisory Council, and to court[41] before the project was rescued by Congress in a rider on the 1995 Emergency Supplemental Appropriations and Rescissions Act, authorizing it to go forward without completion of normal environmental reviews. After almost ten years of wrangling, the logging finally took place in 1996.

Not long afterward, I was taken to Enola Hill by one of the non-Indian citizen activists who had fought the project. It was to be his first visit since the "desecration."

We drove up the winding but not much used logging road. Only then did I learn that the logging had been done by helicopter.

We eventually came to a rock outcrop that was identified as one of Rip Lone Wolf's vision quest sites. Looking out from it, I could see nothing but what looked like pristine forest. My host tried to point out clear spots in the woods, and maybe they were there, but throughout the whole trip the only serious damage I saw was a rather ugly helipad that probably could and should have been located someplace else.

I am, of course, an outsider who never saw the place in its prelogged condition, but it looked to me like the Forest Service had done a very creditable job of low-impact logging. I feel confirmed in my impression by the fact that anthropologist Frank Occhipinti, who *did* see the hill before logging, reports a similar reaction and quotes an activist as stating with some enthusiasm that the hill "would still qualify for NHPA eligibility."[42]

So, what we seem to have had here was a justifiable project, carefully designed to minimize impacts, supported by a tribe with interests in the area because of its positive impacts on forest health (surely a cultural resource in itself, in the Pacific Northwest), which got bogged down for almost ten years in a thoroughly unnecessary fight over eligibility—largely, I suspect, because the question of eligibility was raised by one person, Rip Lone Wolf, whose "credentials" the Forest Service felt were suspect. Mr. Lone Wolf, aptly named, was not regarded as a "community." He and his supporters then attempted to get community backing and got it from the Yakama, but the Forest Service got backing from Warm Springs, and the fat was in the fire.

I have to wonder what would have happened, had the Forest Service said, OK, Mr. Lone Wolf, you think Enola Hill is eligible for the National Register;

let's assume it is. We need to do this logging for the health of the forest; how can we do it in a way that doesn't mess up your vision questing?

Lone Wolf might have said there's no way, but if the tribes were at the table with him, and the Forest Service presented its plans for helicopter logging, I have a hunch that agreement would have been reached, pretty quickly, on doing essentially what the Forest Service in the end did, but perhaps doing it at times when it wouldn't disturb Mr. Lone Wolf's vision questing. I think it's likely that if discussion had been focused on the project's effects on the hill and its use, rather than on the hill's cultural character, it would have been far, far less contentious and the project could have gone forward much sooner, at less cost to the Forest Service, and without the anguish that it must have caused to both the Yakama and Warm Springs Tribes and certainly caused to Mr. Lone Wolf and his supporters.

So my suggestion about how to deal with very small or otherwise marginal-seeming "communities" that allege impacts on TCPs is to take them, initially, at their word. Assume they're legitimate and that their concerns are, too. Sit down at the table with them. The chances, I believe, are excellent that you'll never have to get embroiled in trying to validate them and their claims. If you respect both the group and its concerns and look for ways to resolve them, you may very well find them, at a lot less cost in money, time, and heartache than will be the case if you try to *invalidate* either one.

Of course, there will be instances in which such a happy alternative won't be found; when there's no middle-ground solution to conflict between a perceived public need and the interests of a questionable community about a questionable place. When that happens, the ante inevitably goes up, and higher levels of "proof" are going to be required. Had Rip Lone Wolf insisted that even the most benign helicopter logging was impermissible on Enola Hill (something that as far as I know he never had the opportunity to insist on), then it would be perfectly legitimate to insist that he explain himself, not only to the Forest Service but to the tribes with concerns about forest health. He would have either to persuade others to join his "community" and to demonstrate that Enola Hill shouldn't be touched by so much as a helicopter skid, or to give way.

I think the standards we employ should vary with the complexity and contentiousness of the consultation. Initially, when we're figuring out what concerns should be addressed, the standards should be very loose. You have an issue? Fine, sit down; let's talk. Everybody should have a seat at the table, and every concern should be considered. If we find ourselves in intractable conflict, the standards may have to be tightened. "We're willing to talk about the importance of your sacred tree, Mr. Smith, but we don't think it's important enough to make us spend the extra ten million bucks it would cost to avoid damaging it. If you have more evidence you can supply to change our minds, or more people you'd like to bring in to support your position, fine, but if not, then it's bye-bye, Tree."

What we should *not* do, I think, is what the Forest Service did in the Enola Hill case—get so involved in discrediting the apparently marginal community and place that we never get to find out whether the apparent conflict is real or if it's easily resoluble. We shouldn't make unnecessary trouble for ourselves and everyone else just because we aren't impressed by the legitimacy of the people who oppose us.

Some Examples

In the years since Bulletin 38 was issued, a number of places have been more or less officially recognized as National Register–eligible TCPs—occasionally through listing in the National Register, more often by being treated as eligible under Section 106. I've mentioned some such places already and will discuss others as we go along, but it may be helpful here to have a short list of examples, to illustrate the kinds of places that often are identified as TCPs—and to highlight some that aren't but probably ought to be.

Mountains are often recognized as TCPs, typically because of spiritual values attached to them by Indian tribes and other indigenous people. Mount Shasta[43] in California is actually venerated not only by tribes but by some Buddhists, quite a few New Age groups, and (to judge from their advertising before the mountain's significance became controversial) the local Chamber of Commerce. Mount Graham[44] in Arizona is a spiritual place to the Apache, and has been the scene of intense controversy over the construction of astronomical observatories on its summit. Kilauea, the active volcano on the Big Island of Hawai'i, is equated by native Hawaiians with the volcano goddess Pele.[45] Kuchamaa,[46] on the Mexican border in Southern California, is a spiritual place of the Kumeyaay tribe and is one of the few TCPs that has actually been placed on the National Register.

Whole mountain ranges can also be TCPs. The Lakota view the Black Hills in South Dakota as their origin place, and the Chuska Mountains are regarded as spiritually powerful by the Navajo. The Navajo also revere the four mountains that make up the corners of their traditional world—Mount Blanca in the Sangre de Cristo Mountains, Mount Taylor in the San Juans, Humphreys Peak in the San Francisco Peaks, and Mount Hesperus in the La Planta Mountains.

Other high places are often identified both as spiritual power places and because people go there to carry out spiritual practices, such as vision quests. Examples include Bear Butte, an outlier of the Black Hills, a spiritual place to the Lakota and other Plains tribes that has been the focus of contentious Section 106 consultations.[47] Another well-known high place on the margins of the

Black Hills, Devil's Tower or Bear's Lodge,[48] will be discussed in some detail in chapter 12. The Sweetgrass Hills in Montana, spiritually powerful for a number of tribes, has also been the site of a complicated Section 106 case[49] regarding proposed gold mining. The Helkau Historic District in northern California, the site involved in the GO Road case, is at the crest of the North Coast Range, with expansive views in all directions. Woodruff Butte in Arizona, a Hopi shrine site, is (or was, until it was substantially torn up for gravel) an isolated desert peak.[50]

Landscapes, often quite expansive landscapes, can be TCPs and can be eligible as such for the National Register. The Indian Pass/Trail of Dreams area in Imperial County, California, is an example—a desert landscape comprising hundreds of square miles, laced with trails along which Quechan tribal traditionalists travel both physically and in their dreams to places of spiritual enlightenment— now threatened by the proposed Glamis Imperial gold mine.[51] The Medicine Lake Highlands[52] in northern California is a rugged volcanic caldera with lakes, lava beds, and hot springs, where Pit River, Shasta, and other tribal practitioners come to seek spiritual power. The even larger Badger–Two Medicine[53] landscape—a complex of watercourses, mountains, and wooded ridges in Montana—is an area of spiritual power for the Blackfoot. The Hualapai treat virtually the entire landscape of their reservation as having spiritual power, though there are specific mountains and canyons that are most often used for power seeking and medicine making. The extensive landscape surrounding and including the Bighorn Medicine Wheel in Wyoming went unnoticed by visitors and land managers for decades after the site of the wheel itself was designated as a National Historic Landmark, and is now causing heartburn to people who concern themselves with historic property boundaries.

The Grand Canyon is another extensive TCP landscape, within which are smaller canyons, streams, springs, salt seeps, and other places important to the tribes of the region.[54] Many other canyons, like Tahquitz in Palm Springs, are associated with important tribal traditions, as Tahquitz is with the origin tradition of the Cahuilla.

Springs and pools, like Panther Spring on Mount Shasta and the hot springs at China Lake Naval Weapons Station in California, are often regarded as the homes of spirits or spirits themselves. The springs that feed into *Mushgigagamongsebe*, or Swamp Creek,[55] and ultimately into Rice Lake on the Sokaogon Ojibwe's Mole Lake Reservation in Wisconsin, are the sources of pure water used by the tribe in ceremonies. Waterfalls and rapids along rivers are also often seen as spiritually energetic. At Kootenai Falls on the Kootenai River, Section 106 review in the 1980s focused on the reduction of water flow over the falls, which in the eyes of Kootenai traditionalists could deprive the place of its spiritual power and anger its spirits.[56]

Whole rivers can be TCPs for a variety of reasons. The Mattaponi and Pamunkey Rivers in Virginia are regarded as spiritually energetic by the Mattaponi, Pamunkey, and Upper Mattaponi Tribes. The tribes also hunt and gather food and medicine in the wetlands along the rivers, and the rivers support their economically and culturally important shad fisheries. More subtly, the rivers are simply basic elements of each tribe's identity; they have always been associated with one another. As a result, impact on the rivers has been an important issue during Section 106 consultation on a proposed reservoir that would draw water from the Mattaponi. The marshes along Mushgigagamongsebe in Wisconsin are similarly important to the Sokaogon Community, as is Rice Lake, which is fed by its water and supports the wild rice that is central to the community's traditional way of life. The marshlands at Okmulgee Old Fields in Georgia, though no longer used by the Creek (forcibly removed long ago) contribute to the character of the site.[57]

Lakes themselves, like Rice Lake, are not infrequently found eligible for the National Register as TCPs. Probably the most famous is Zuni Salt Lake[58] in New Mexico, where the keeper has determined eligible not only the salty lake, thought by the Zuni to represent the spirit being Salt Woman, but also an expansive "neutral zone" surrounding it. I've argued elsewhere that Lake Superior can be regarded as eligible for the National Register for its association with the traditions of the Ojibwe, though the major focus of my study was a stretch of lake shore around Chequemegon Bay. The bay is associated not only with the tradition of the Great Migration, central to Ojibwe identity, but also with the subsequent history of the Ojibwe and their Midewiwin religion, and with the lake's fish, game, and wild rice.[59]

Islands in lakes, rivers, and the ocean have been identified as TCPs. The best-known instance is probably Kaho'olawe in Hawaii, whose cultural significance, argued extensively in court, was instrumental in forcing the U.S. Navy to stop using it as a training site and clean it up for eventual management by native Hawaiians as a place of spiritual refuge.[60]

Groves of trees can be associated with important cultural traditions. On the island of Pohnpei during my 1970s tenure in Micronesia, an issue arose with a village about the proposal to put a road through a grove of palm trees near the shore. The grove, in tradition, was the pubic hair of the supernatural being whose body made up that part of the island. The road was relocated. Rocks and other landscape elements can be similarly associated with important stories. The road on Pohnpei had to be rerouted at another point after construction inadvertently disturbed a large rock standing in a stream. The rock was regarded as the body of an adulteress turned to stone, associated with a story used by local people to teach moral lessons.

Places that archaeologists and other CRM specialists are more used to dealing with—burial and effigy mounds, petroglyph and pictograph sites, and ancestral habitation and special-use sites—may of course also be TCPs, though what makes them so may be quite different from what gives them importance to archaeologists. A Cheyenne elder once told me that he got a kick out of visiting a site with an archaeologist because the archaeologist would get so excited about flakes of stone. "I don't care a thing about the flakes," he said. "I get excited finding the plants."

And then there are places that look, to the outsider, like nothing in particular at all—not a mountain, not a pond, not a grove, just a place. On the upper east face of Mount Tonaachaw in Chuuk, for example, there's a steeply sloping grassy place that the average passer-by wouldn't give a second glance. But the mountain as a whole, in *itang* tradition, is the head of the great octopus *kùùs*, whose tentacles spread out to connect all the islands and seamarks of Chuuk Lagoon, and the grassy spot is his ear. From being the octopus's ear, in another permutation it becomes *Neepisaram*, "saffron island place," home of the protector-spirit *Saraw*.[61] Lots of significance in the eyes of itang practitioners, but just a grassy slope to anyone else.

Finally, there are all kinds of other places—notably including lots of nonindigenous places—that have not typically been identified explicitly as TCPs though they easily could be and though their cultural significance is often widely recognized. Smith Island, Maryland, for example, on the Chesapeake Bay, a traditional watermen's community with deep roots in Maryland's history. The Amish countryside of Lancaster County, Pennsylvania. The East End of Cincinnati. Corona. The "Sacred Structure" of Manteo, North Carolina. Innumerable Chinatowns, Hispanic barrios, the African American fishing communities of coastal Georgia, and the stands of plants along the South Carolina coast that make traditional African American basket making possible.[62] Folklife specialists, urban anthropologists, rural sociologists, and landscape architects document these places and worry about their potential for survival. Sometimes historic preservationists nominate them, or their buildings, to the National Register for their association with local history or their architectural merit. But we seldom manage to see as a basis for National Register eligibility—and hence for Section 106 review when they're threatened—their traditional cultural significance, as perceived by those who live in them or use them. Is this a problem? I think it is, because it can allow us to ignore the issues of community identity that we should really be addressing in Section 106 review—the issues that, as I've suggested, the National Historic Preservation Act was designed to address.

The reader looking for nonindigenous TCPs in this book will be disappointed; most of the discussion is about places important to tribes and other Native Americans and the issues they raise, because these places and these issues have been the main subjects of discussion about TCPs in the years since Bulletin

Figure 6.3.   Spiritual high places are not necessarily very high in absolute terms. Spirit Hill, a place of spiritual power for the Sakaogon Ojibwe, just east of the Mole Lake Reservation, Wisconsin. Photo by Anna Willow.

38. Without in any way denigrating the importance of indigenous places, I wish it were otherwise, but the fact is that at this writing, no one has spent much time dealing with nonindigenous TCPs under NHPA, so there isn't much for me to say about them that hasn't been better said by people like Randolph Hester in his writings on "sacred structure."

Perhaps this will change. I hope so. TCPs are, after all, for everyone.

Notes

1. See Andrew Guilliford, *Sacred Objects and Sacred Places: Preserving Tribal Traditions* (University Press of Colorado, Boulder, 2000), 201, admittedly only with reference to tribal "sacred" sites.

2. I put *supernatural* in quotation marks because I have no confidence whatever in my ability, or anybody else's, to put limits on what's "natural."

3. David L. Carmichael, Places of Power: Mescalero Apache Sacred Sites and Sensitive Areas, in David L. Carmichael, Jane Hubert, Brian Reeves, and Audhild Schanch (eds.), *Sacred Sites, Sacred Places* (Routledge, London, 1994), 91.

4. A jelly doughnut said to be "so delicious you remember them all your life." I am indebted to Elaine Blender of the U.S. General Services Administration for this example.

5. Fawn Brodie, *No Man Knows My History: The Life of Joseph Smith* (Random House, New York, 1971), 211.

6. See Thomas F. King and Patricia L. Parker, *Pisekin Nóómw Nóón Tonaachaw: Archaeology in the Tonaachaw Historic District, Moen Island,* Micronesian Archaeological Survey Report No. 18 (Southern Illinois University at Carbondale Center for Archaeological Investigations Occasional Paper No. 3, Carbondale, 1985), 54.

7. See Terrence W. Epperson, The Politics of "Race" and Cultural Identity at the African Burial Ground Excavations, New York City, *World Archaeological Bulletin* 7 (1997):108–17.

8. Wilbert Gessler, The Construction of Therapeutic Spaces, in Ezekiel Kalipeni and Paul T. Zeleza (eds.), *Sacred Spaces and Public Quarrels: African Cultural and Economic Landscapes* (Africa World, Asmara, 1999).

9. Robert A. Archibald, *A Place to Remember: Using History to Build Community* (AltaMira, Walnut Creek, CA, 1999), 126–27.

10. E. V. Walter, *Placeways: A Theory of the Human Environment* (University of North Carolina Press, Chapel Hill, 1988).

11. Tony Hiss, *The Experience of Place* (Random House, New York, 1991).

12. Yi-Fu Tuan, *Space and Place: The Perspective of Experience* (University of Minnesota Press, Minneapolis, 1977), 158.

13. See chapter 8 for further discussion of Stiltsville.

14. Hiss, *The Experience of Place,* 173–74.

15. For typologies of TCP-like places, see Carmichael et al. (eds.), *Sacred Sites, Sacred Places,* 10; Hirini Matunga, Waahi Tapu: Maori Sacred Sites, in Carmichael et al. (1994), 222; T. Sole and K. Woods, Protection of Indigenous Sacred Sites: The New Zealand Thesis, in J. Birckhead, T. de Lacy, and L. Smith (eds.), *Aboriginal Involvement in Parks and Protected Areas* (Aboriginal Studies Press, Canberra, 1993), quoted in Carmichael et al. (1994), *Sacred Sites, Sacred Places,* 11; Gabriel Cooney, Sacred and Secular Neolithic Landscapes in Ireland, in Carmichael et al. (1994), *Sacred Sites, Sacred Places,* citing Barrett (1989); David L. Carmichael, Places of Power: Mescalero Apache Sacred Sites and Sensitive Areas, in Carmichael et al., *Sacred Sites, Sacred Places,* 91–95; Gordon Mohs, Sto:lo Sacred Ground, in Carmichael et al. (1994), *Sacred Sites, Sacred Places,* 192–99; Alan S. Downer, Anthropology, Historic Preservation and the Navajo: A Case Study in Cultural Resource Management on Indian Lands, Ph.D. diss. University of Missouri–Columbia, 1989, 162–63; Susan Buggey, *Approach to Aboriginal Cultural Landscapes* (Historic Sites and Monuments Board of Canada, Parks Canada, Ottawa, 1999), 12, citing UNESCO (1996).

16. A.k.a. Pinecate Rocks—see California Department of Transportation (Caltrans), Negative Declaration and Finding of No Significant Impact: Realignment of Route 101 Southbound Lanes Near Pinecate Rocks (Sacramento, 1999).

17. Caltrans, Negative Declaration, 31.

18. One wonders what a "myth"—that is, a legend, or tradition—would be if not "later." Whenever Homer wrote the *Iliad,* it probably wasn't *before* the Trojan War.

19. National Register, *Guidelines for Evaluating and Documenting Traditional Cultural Properties* (National Park Service, Washington, D.C., n.d. [sometimes (accurately) dated 1990]), 9.

20. In fairness to the authors of the dismissive environmental analysis, I should note that they acknowledged, in a backhanded kind of way, that perceived value to a community might make The Rocks eligible. However, they went on to argue, based on no discernible data, that there really wasn't a community involved with the traditions of The Rocks anyway.

21. In another remarkable case, the Minnesota Department of Transportation got away with regarding a grove of trees as ineligible for the National Register despite its traditional association with ancestral tribal burial practices. Dendrochronology showed that the trees were not old enough to have held scaffold burials. Whether particular living trees had ever held bodies was irrelevant, of course; the point of the grove's significance was that in tradition the grove, as a living community of trees, had been and still was associated with the passage of the dead to the spirit world. In both this case and that of The Rocks, I imagine that the highway agencies were motivated in large measure by a desire to avoid the stringent requirements of Section 4(f) of the Department of Transportation Act, which would have been triggered had the properties been determined eligible. The trouble is that the method they chose to avoid these rather draconian requirements effectively deprived the properties of any consideration whatever.

22. See Thomas F. King, In the Light of the Megis: The Chequamegon Bay Area as a Traditional Cultural Property, report to the Bad River and Red Cliff Bands of Lake Superior Tribe of Chippewa, Bad River and Bayfield, Wisconsin, 1999a.

23. *Metropolitan Edison Co. v. People against Nuclear Energy.* 460 U.S. 766, 103 S. Ct. 1556 (1983).

24. 40 CFR 1508.14.

25. In fact, neither PANE nor 40 CFR 1508.14 says such factors shouldn't be considered; they simply say that by themselves their existence isn't enough to force preparation of an Environmental Impact Statement. The effect of the decision and regulatory language, however, has been to devalue consideration of social, economic, and psychological variables.

26. National Register, *Guidelines for Evaluating and Documenting Traditional Cultural Properties*, 9.

27. Brian Haley and Larry Wilcoxon, The Making of Chumash Tradition, *Current Anthropology* 38(5) (1997):761–94; my description is a very simplified gloss on a many-faceted paper.

28. Jon M. Erlandson et al., The Making of Chumash Tradition: Replies to Haley and Wilcoxon, *Current Anthropology* 39(4) (1998):477–501; see also Brian Haley and Larry Wilcoxon, Reply, *Current Anthropology* 39(4) (1998):501–8.

29. Robert H. Winthrop, Contribution to Erlandson et al., *Current Anthropology* 39(4)(1998a):496–99; Robert H. Winthrop, Tradition, Authenticity, and Dislocation: Some Dilemmas of Traditional Cultural Property Studies, *Practicing Anthropology* 20(3)(1998b):25–27.

30. Winthrop, Tradition, Authenticity, and Dislocation, 27.

31. Austin Gough, Hindmarsh Island and the Politics of the Future, *Adelaide Review* (June 1995):8–9.

32. James Weiner, Anthropologists, Historians, and the Secret of Social Knowledge, *Anthropology Today* 11(5) (1994):6.

33. Weiner, Anthropologists.

34. Erlandson et al., The Making of Chumash Tradition, 480.

35. The Enola Hill case has been ably summarized and analyzed by Frank D. Occhipinti (2002) in one of the very few detailed analyses of a TCP controversy I've seen. We could use more analyses like his.

36. Robert H. Winthrop, Enola Hill Ethnographic Reconnaissance, ms., Mount Hood National Forest, Gresham, OR, 1991.

37. Beth E. Walton, Enola Hill Project Area Cultural Resources, ms., Mount Hood National Forest, Gresham, OR, 1992.

38. Thomas F. King, Comments on Studies of Enola Hill, ms. supplied to Michael V. Nixon, attorney for plaintiffs in *Native Americans for Enola et al. v. U.S. Forest Service* (CV 92-1534-JF), District of Oregon, Portland, 1994.

39. Frank D. Occhipinti, American Indian Sacred Sites and the National Historic Preservation Act: The Enola Hill Case, *Journal of Northwest Anthropology* 36(1) (2002):26–31.

40. For details, see Occhipinti, American Indian Sacred Sites, 30–37.

41. *Native Americans for Enola v. United States Forest Service*, 832 F.Supp. 297 (D. Or. 1993)

42. Occhipinti, American Indian Sacred Sites, 37.

43. See Guilliford, *Sacred Objects*, 154–57.

44. Guilliford, *Sacred Objects*, 131–35. See also *Apache Survival Coalition v. United States*, 21 F.3d 895 (9th Cir. 1994) and *Apache Survival Coalition v. United States (Apache Survival. II)*, 118 F.3d 663 (9th Cir. 1997).

45. See Masse et al. 1991.

46. Source: Bureau of Land Management nomination documentation on file with the National Register.

47. Guilliford, *Sacred Objects*, 144–48; Jake Page (ed.), *Sacred Lands of Indian America* (Abrams, New York, 2001), 39–41.

48. Guilliford, *Sacred Objects*, 162–67.

49. Probably more complicated than it needed to be. See Guilliford, *Sacred Objects*, 149–54.

50. See Christopher McLeod (producer/director), *In the Light of Reverence,* videotape, Sacred Lands Film Project (Earth Image Films, La Honda, CA, 2000).

51. Andrew R. Pigniolo, Jackson Underwood, and James H. Cleland, *Where Trails Cross: Cultural Resources Inventory and Evaluation for the Imperial Project, Imperial County, California* (Environmental Management Associates, Inc., Appendix L to Draft Environmental Impact Statement/Environmental Impact Report, Imperial Project, Imperial County, CA; U.S. Department of the Interior Bureau of Land Management and County of Imperial Planning/Building Department, El Centro, CA, 1996), provide a general, somewhat archaeo-biased portrayal of the area. Advisory Council on Historic Preservation (ACHP), Comment to Secretary of the Interior Bruce Babbitt, pursuant to Section 106 of the National Historic Preservation Act, regarding the impacts of the proposed Glamis Imperial Mine, Imperial County, California, letter dated October 19, 1999 (ACHP, Washington, D.C.), and Thomas F. King, Letter to Bruce Babbitt, Secretary of the Interior, regarding Glamis Imperial Mine and impacts on Quechan Trail of Dreams landscape (March 29, 1999b) (rather obscure sources) provide broader views with specific reference to Bulletin 38 and Section 106.

52. Page, *Sacred Lands,* 49–53.

53. Page, *Sacred Lands,* 77–81.

54. See Richard W. Stoffle, David B. Halmo, Michael J. Evans, and Diane E. Austin, *Piapaxa 'Uipi (Big River Canyon): Ethnographic Resource Inventory and Assessment for Colorado River Corridor, Glen Canyon National Recreation Area, Utah and Arizona, and Grand Canyon National Park, Arizona* (Bureau of Applied Research in Anthropology, University of Arizona, Tucson, 1993).

55. Another traditional cultural landscape; see Larry Nesper, Anna Willow, and Thomas F. King, *The Mushgigagamongsebe District: A Traditional Cultural Landscape of the Sokaogon Ojibwe Community,* report submitted to the Corps of Engineers, St. Paul District, by the Mole Lake Sokaogon Community of Great Lakes Chippewa Indians, Crandon, WI, 2002.

56. Although the spiritual significance of Kootenai Falls is well known, during Section 106 review of a project that would have reduced flow over the falls, in the early 1980s, the sensitivity of some of the cultural data developed for purposes of eligibility determination was such that the National Register alone was permitted, by court order, to review the pertinent documents. As a representative of the Advisory Council, I was given limited access to the data. This was another step in my education leading to Bulletin 38.

57. Brockington and Associates and Ethnoscience, Inc., National Register of Historic Places Determination of Eligibility (Draft), Ocmulgee Old Fields Traditional Cultural Property, ms., Georgia Department of Transportation, Atlanta, 1999.

58. See E. Richard Hart, The Fence Lake Mine Project: Archaeology as Traditional Cultural Property, in P. L. Parker (ed.), *Traditional Cultural Properties: What You Do and How We Think, CRM* Special Issue (National Park Service, Washington, D.C., 1993);

ACHP, New Mexico and Arizona: Construction of Fence Lake Mine, spring 2002, Case Digest on ACHP website, www.achp.gov/casesspg02NM-AZ.html.

59. King, In the Light of the Megis.

60. See Vincent R. Shigekuni, The Kahoʻolawe Use Plan: Non-traditional Planning for Traditional Use, *CRM* 23(7)(2000):36–40; *Aluli v. Brown*, 437 F.Supp. 602 (D. Haw. 1977).

61. King and Parker, *Pisekin Nóómw Nóón Tonaachaw*, 399.

62. Or the Jewish Community Center in Petaluma, California (see Kenneth Kahn, *Comrades and Chicken Farmers: The Story of a California Jewish Community* [Cornell University Press, Ithaca, NY, 1993]), which I managed to miss entirely, together with the context it represents, in 1988–1989 when I prepared a videotape for NPS on "historic contexts" (now, thankfully, no longer available from NPS as far as I can tell).

Chapter Seven

Bulletin 38 Revisited

Identifying TCPs

For reasons that are both frustrating and hard not to respect, native tribes are loath to engage in the distribution of cultural information when the purpose does not clearly reflect tribal interests.
—John Hockenberry (2002: unpaginated)

NATIONAL Register Bulletin 38 is about identifying TCPs and judging their eligibility for the National Register of Historic Places. After a dozen years of practice with the bulletin, what have we learned about these subjects? In this chapter, we'll look at identification; in the next, we'll consider eligibility determinations.

Beginning at the beginning, I think we've learned some things, and need to learn more, about the circumstances under which we need to identify TCPs and about constructive alternatives to identification. This is as good a place as any to start.

To Identify or Not to Identify

CRM practitioners tend to think about TCPs only when they're dealing with places associated with indigenous people and conversely *not* to think about them with reference to other ethnic and cultural groups. But even plain old white-eye redneck honkies find places dear to them. I think we'd have a much broader, sounder sort of CRM if we tried to make the cultural concerns of all communities the centerpiece of our practice. We'd certainly have a CRM that's better understood and more widely supported by the public, because we'd be dealing with what concerns real people, not just what's of interest to academicians and bureaucrats.

So give it a thought as you set out to identify historic places. Are you dealing with urban neighborhoods? Rural landscapes? Family farms? Don't think about your subject just in terms of architectural history, or history, or landscape history, or the historical development of agriculture. Ask yourself—and, more important, ask the folks who live in the area—whether there are things about the area that are important to the community, that its members don't want to lose. Look at Bulletin 38 and see whether it applies to your situation. You might have TCPs to deal with, even if they have nothing whatever to do with indigenous groups. If you do, you ought to think about it and address the possibility in your analysis. If you don't, you may disregard places that are eligible for the National Register or propose forms of treatments that, while perhaps professionally sound, are anathema to the people to whom such places are important.

A classic example of missing the traditional cultural significance of a place is the Mark Gob Pile in north-central Illinois.[1] North-central Illinois is about as flat a place as you'll find. Things that stick up out of the landscape are at a premium and tend to be valued. The Mark Gob Pile was a pile of refuse from a defunct surface mine, near the small town—Mark—that had grown up as a result of the mine and had managed to develop a diversified enough economy to survive its demise. In the mid-1980s, the Office of Surface Mining and Reclamation (OSM) in the Department of the Interior proposed to assist the state in reclaiming the mine, basically by pushing the Gob Pile into it.

OSM recognized that it had Section 106 responsibilities, and that the Gob Pile might conceivably be eligible for the National Register. An evaluation was done in cooperation with the SHPO; the resulting documentation emphasized the continuing role of the pile in the cultural life of Mark:

> The mine gob is climbed almost daily by young people and those young at heart. From its peak one can observe a most beautiful view to a distance of a 34 mile radius. The mine gob and especially its peak forms a beautiful background to the local baseball field, play grounds, shelter and community hall. It has served as a focal point for the town's annual homecoming celebration as hundreds of former residents return to their or their ancestors' coal mining roots.[2]

The SHPO supported the Gob Pile's eligibility as "a significant product of the coal mining industry of the state." OSM was unsure and sent the documentation to the keeper. The keeper rather snootily responded that "[a]t best, an industrial waste dump might constitute a contributing feature to [a historic mining] district if it provided information important in completing the total picture by which the mining process could be understood and interpreted," but as an isolated property, the Gob Pile didn't even fall into one of the register's standard divisions of reality—district, site, building, structure, or object.³ The keeper found the Gob Pile ineligible without any consideration of its importance to the community, and that was that; the Gob Pile went back into the pit.

I don't think there's any doubt that if the Gob Pile had been evaluated with reference to Bulletin 38, as a TCP, it would have been found eligible—which of course might or might not have resulted in its preservation but at least would have ensured that preservation was considered. As a TCP, it really didn't matter whether the Gob Pile was a good example of mining technology; it could have been a wholly natural feature, if such things existed in that part of the world, and be eligible. But because its evaluation was filtered through the lens of commemorating or illustrating mining history and technology, rather than through that of community value, the community's interests in the pile were ignored.

I'm told that in recent years at least one or two similar piles in Illinois have been determined eligible for the register. And in fairness to the keeper, the evaluation happened four years before Bulletin 38 was issued. But the fact remains that Mark, like innumerable other communities, had a TCP that got destroyed because it didn't fit into an architectural, historical, or archaeological pigeonhole. This shouldn't happen.

Considering the possibility that TCPs are present doesn't necessarily mean that you have to do a detailed study to identify them. One of the most important lessons I've learned since publication of Bulletin 38, I think, is to look for ways to *avoid* having to identify specific TCPs. By this I don't mean to make another Mark and ignore TCPs; what I mean is to look for ways to consider impacts on them, in a responsible way, without identifying specific places, or at least without documenting them in much detail.

There are a couple of practical reasons to avoid identifying specific TCPs if you can. Where you're dealing with spiritual places, the community may want to keep them as secret as possible. Sometimes it's believed that revealing information about them, at least to outsiders or others who don't have a culturally appropriate relationship to the information holder, will cause the spiritual power of a place to be diminished or pose dangers to those who reveal the information, those who receive it, the community, or the world. Sometimes people don't want outsiders to know what they do in a place—whether it's vision questing, medicine gathering, rites of passage, or quiet meditation—for fear that the outsiders will pry, make the practitioners into tourist attractions. Sometimes there's concern about physical or spiritual desecration—chipping petroglyphs off rocks, digging up ancestral burials, using a place for inappropriate rituals. Whatever the reasons, the perceived need to "tell all"—or even some—about a place may cause traditional knowledge bearers to want to do the opposite. In extreme cases, they may even prefer to leave the place to its own devices, hope that its own spiritual power will protect it, or let it be destroyed, rather than reveal what they know or believe about its character. Obviously if you can avoid having to identify the place, you can avoid putting people in this kind of uncomfortable, even agonizing, situation.

The other major reason for minimizing identification is to avoid overkill. You may just not need much information about a place in order to consider it in planning. An example of such overkill is what happened to the Federal Aviation Administration (FAA) in considering TCPs on the Hualapai Reservation in Arizona.

Under the National Parks Overflights Act,[4] FAA was required to develop plans for controlling air tours over the Grand Canyon and adjacent areas, notably the Hualapai Reservation. It was evident that impacts on TCPs—generally characterized in this case as "Hualapai sacred sites"—would be an issue, so FAA set out to identify TCPs that might be affected by air tours.

Pursuing standard Section 106 practice, FAA figured that it had to identify each particular TCP and apply the National Register Criteria to it, based on enough information to satisfy itself, the Hualapai THPO, and possibly the keeper of the National Register that each property was or was not eligible. To do this, it very responsibly contracted with the Hualapai Tribe to conduct a TCP survey.

The survey cost tens of thousands of dollars and took many months—particularly since the air tour routes FAA was considering kept changing, requiring changes to the area subjected to survey. It also generated a good deal of argument between FAA and the tribe over things like property boundaries—not because FAA necessarily objected to boundaries proposed by the tribe, but because even *assigning* boundaries to spiritual places, medicine-gathering areas, and the like was a hard thing for the tribe to embrace. More generally, the whole process put the tribe's cultural resource specialists in the difficult position of having to ferret a lot of specific information out of the elders—about things like boundaries, that often cause elders' eyes to glaze over because they make no sense in the elders' worldview.

What made this overkill was that FAA didn't *need* a lot of specific information in order to assess the impacts of air tours on TCPs. All it really needed to know was that X mountain or Y canyon was culturally sensitive in such a way that the auditory or visual impacts of overflights could be a problem. With this knowledge in hand, FAA could begin talking with the tribe about what kinds of impacts were and were not problematic and about what might be done to control them. FAA could have saved itself a lot of time and money, and saved the tribe a good deal of angst, by focusing on the information it really needed, as opposed to that which it did not need for any reason but compliance with what it (and the tribe) thought were standard procedures.

But can an agency avoid detailed identification and be in compliance with Section 106? Easily. The statutory requirement of Section 106 is that agencies "take into account" the effects of their actions on historic properties. Were the FAA to assume that anyplace the Hualapai said was culturally significant was eligible for the National Register and to take the effects of overflights on each such place—or all such places collectively—into account, it would have met this requirement. Section 110(a)(2)(E) of NHPA requires that agencies identify and evaluate historic properties subject to possible effect by agency actions, but it doesn't say how to do either thing. 36 CFR 800.4 requires a "reasonable and good faith effort" to identify historic properties subject to effect, and refers agencies to the *Secretary of the Interior's Standards and Guidelines for Identification* for further guidance. Standard #1 of the *Secretary's Standards* says that "Identification of historic properties is undertaken to the degree required to make decisions."[5]

In regulating air tour overflights, FAA could have made most if not all of its decisions based on the general information I've suggested above. It's possible that to make particular decisions they'd need more—for example, perhaps to assess the impacts of a particular route they'd need to know when a particular place was used, or what viewsheds were and were not important. It's even possible that there would be such a conflict between a given place and a particular decision that in order to protect itself legally FAA would have to insist on getting all the information the keeper would like to have for an eligibility determination, but there's no point in assuming at the outset that such information is needed on every property, with respect to every possible conflict.

FAA could have started off with minimal data and moved to the collection of more detailed information only if and when needed to deal with a specific problem. I think it very likely that it would never have been necessary to collect such detailed information—in part because, by not requiring the tribe to report stuff that its members had trouble revealing, FAA would have facilitated consultation about effects, shown itself to be sensitive to the tribe's cultural values, and almost certainly have had a more congenial, cooperative program of consultation.

Of course, what works in one case won't work in another, but I think the path of wisdom lies in starting out with a question based on Sebastian's Dictum: "what's the minimum information I need in order to make my decision?"[6] In some cases the answer will be "a whole lot," even "a completed National Register nomination form," but I suspect that such cases are very much a minority. In some cases, the answer will be "virtually no information at all," while in most cases it will fall somewhere in between.

But how do you ask such a question, and how can the answer define how you identify TCPs? Through scoping.

Scoping: The Critical First Step

Early in its discussion of identification, Bulletin 38 talks about "establishing the level of effort"—that is, figuring out what you need to do to identify TCPs. This guidance intersects neatly with the direction in both the NEPA and Section 106 regulations to plan one's analysis through scoping.

Scoping under the NEPA regulations means determining "the range of actions, alternatives, and impacts to be considered."[7] The Section 106 regulations talk about determining the scope of identification by determining the project's area of potential effects, reviewing background information, and seeking information about historic properties and identification issues, all leading to a decision about how to take "the steps necessary to identify historic properties."[8]

In specifying "establishing the level of effort" as the first step in TCP identification, Bulletin 38 notes that "what constitutes a 'reasonable' effort depends in part on the likelihood that (TCPs) may be present. The likelihood that such properties may be present can be reliably assessed only on the basis of background knowledge of the area's history, ethnography, and contemporary society developed through preservation planning."[9]

So it's during scoping that you can ask and negotiate about identification methods. The word *negotiate* is an important one; everyone involved should be prepared to discuss, compare notes, and where necessary argue about what sort of identification is appropriate.[10]

There's no single way of identifying TCPs. What you ought to do depends on the character of the project you're considering, its likely effects, the local environment, what kinds of communities are involved—a host of factors. Scoping is the way we can deal with this variability and uncertainty, establishing effective standards tailored to the needs of each project.

There aren't many good guidelines for scoping, and this has had unfortunate results. In the NEPA world, too often scoping is reduced to a public meeting or two—often highly structured and formulaic, perceived merely as regulatory hoops through which to jump rather than as opportunities to reason together—and exchanges of correspondence with regulatory agencies. In Section 106 practice, it often involves little besides consulting the SHPO or THPO, and even that may involve a mere exchange of form letters. This kind of "scoping" is seldom worth much as a way of figuring out how to identify TCPs and impacts on them.

Probably the first thing to ask during scoping is, What communities may be concerned about the proposed action? What Indian tribes or other indigenous groups live nearby or previously occupied the vicinity? Remember that such groups may have been forced off the land decades or centuries ago and may live somewhere else today. What nonindigenous communities are nearby—what towns, villages, urban neighborhoods? Have these been around for awhile? Do their residents see themselves as having a particular identity? Muslim cowboys? Jewish autoworkers? Survivalists? Amish? What about dispersed communities—ranchers, farmers, loggers, fishermen? In short, who are the people with whom you'll need to talk?

Next question: How should you consult with these folks? Are they all native speakers of English, or will you need interpreters? When and where will you need to hold meetings in order to make it easy for people to participate? Who are the community leaders you'll have to communicate with in order to gain access to knowledgeable people? Note that these may not be the official leaders or only the official leaders. Although protocol, and law in some cases, require consultation with government representatives, the community's traditional leadership may lie elsewhere. Are there likely to be special barriers to, or opportunities for, effective consultation? Are there particular social forms that should be followed in contacting people, in meeting with them, in seeking information, opinions, or agreement?[11]

Then there's the question of what you need to consult *about,* which has a lot to do with the kind of action that's being planned. Obviously the FAA needed to be concerned a lot about auditory and visual impact issues in the Hualapai case, but not about the impacts of earth moving. In the case of a pipeline, these priorities would be reversed.

Figure 7.1.   Pool of the sacred eels, Pohnpei. You can't consult with the eels about this place, but you must consult with the people who hold the eels sacred, in a way that makes sense to them. Photo by the author.

Thinking about these questions, discussing them with knowledgeable people, and reviewing pertinent government guidelines, planning documents, and the relevant professional literature should make it possible to create a scope of work for identification—which is really what scoping is all about.

I realize that getting answers to all these questions costs money and takes time, and I realize that almost nobody actually does it. Most agencies put out a stock scope of work attached to a stock request for proposals, after—or maybe before—doing a "background records check" with the SHPO or THPO. The fact that such "scoping" is standard practice doesn't make it the smart thing to do. Up-front investment in planning identification will pay for itself many times over in research efficiency and improved relations with affected communities.

Considering TCPs When Establishing the APE

The area of potential effects (APE) of a project is the area (or areas) within which the action has the potential to affect historic properties—directly or indirectly, physically or visually or audibly or in any other way.[12] Because many TCPs are vulnerable to things like visual and auditory effects, they may demand the recognition of expansive APEs.

In the late 1980s, San Ildefonso Pueblo in New Mexico needed increased electrical power, and the Bureau of Indian Affairs (BIA) and Rural Electrification Administration (REA)[13] set out to construct a new power substation. The site they chose was on the border between pueblo land and the surrounding unincorporated mostly Hispanic community known as El Rancho.

Thinking only about potential impacts on archaeological sites, BIA and REA confused the project's APE with its footprint, where physical ground disturbance would occur. They had an archaeological survey done and found nothing. They began construction. Work was under way when the people of El Rancho complained. The project was adjacent to the graded parking lot surrounding their cantina, they pointed out, and the parking lot was where they carried out their *Matachines* dance—an important cultural tradition dating back to the days of the conquistadores.

Give us a break, said BIA and REA—it's a &^*&^%$ parking lot.

Es verdad, replied the people of El Rancho, but it's a parking lot that's eligible for the National Register as a TCP, and you're going to have visual and auditory effects on it. You've got to consider those under Section 106.

El Rancho prevailed in court,[14] but not until BIA and REA had virtually completed the project. The pueblo couldn't throw the switch and get its power, however; the court halted the project pending Section 106 review. The SHPO thought the parking lot was eligible for the register; BIA and REA did not, so it went to the keeper.

Figure 7.2. The Matachines Dance Site at El Rancho, New Mexico. Photo by the author.

The keeper sided with El Rancho and the SHPO; the property was eligible as a TCP for its association with performance of the Matachines dance. It took almost ten years to finally resolve the case through Section 106 review,[15] during all which time the pueblo was deprived of the power that the station would have provided.

The problem resulted, of course, from the failure to consider potential visual and auditory effects on TCPs (or other kinds of historic property) beyond the construction site. Had the APE been drawn to include areas where visual and auditory effects would occur, and had the identification effort been designed to find TCPs as well as archaeological sites, the importance of the parking lot would have been discovered, and the project could have been relocated to any of innumerable alternative pieces of desert. So, the APE needs to be drawn broadly enough to include places where visual or auditory effects might occur, as well as physical effects, social effects, economic effects, effects on land use, and all other kinds of effects.

Talking with People

The one invariable—or near-invariable—thing about TCP identification is that it involves consulting the communities that may value the places you're interested in identifying—talking with real live people.

There are commonsense semiexceptions to this rule. When I was engaged to analyze the eligibility of Chequemagon Bay on the Lake Superior shore of Wisconsin—a very important place to the Ojibwe[16]—I expected to do a great deal of face-to-face consultation, but as it turned out, virtually everyone I needed to talk with had already been talked with by one or more of four researchers who had worked in the area immediately before me. It would have irritated them to have still another researcher come beating on their doors. It also turned out that the significance of Chequamegon Bay was extensively documented in published and unpublished literature; my main challenge was relating all these data to the National Register criteria. I spent only about three days in face-to-face consultation and tried not to irritate people by asking the same questions that others had asked them. Usually, though, identification involves a lot of talking.

Who do you talk with? The people most likely to know about TCPs and how they may be affected by a project are usually the traditional culture bearers, the elders. But that's not always the case, and even if it *is* the case you may not be able to speak directly with the elders. There may be intermediaries—official spokespeople, designated cultural resource staff, relatives, or just people who walk the boundary between the traditional and contemporary worlds. You may be talking with them, and they may be talking with the elders. This may introduce a layer of complexity, but it also may simplify things, because the intermediary is able to make it clear to the elders what the hell you're talking about, in ways that would be difficult for you to do yourself. In the end, you talk with those the group wants you or will allow you to talk with.

What do you talk about? Obviously, I imagine someone thinking, you talk about where and what the TCPs are. That seems like it ought to be the case, but actually it isn't. For one thing, if you start asking people where their TCPs are, they may be confused. What are *teecees,* and why does this guy want to know where they urinate? You can't always, or even often, use shorthand jargon. Try to think about how they may conceptualize the kind of place we call a TCP, and try to speak their language. Do it respectfully; you're asking them about places that are important to them, not about some abstract type of real estate.

But asking someone what's important to her may be problematic, too. What do you mean by "important"? Particularly where you're talking with tribal people or other ethnic or social minorities, it may be difficult for them to quite figure out what this outsider is after. It may be best to come at the matter from the direction of the action's possible effects, like this:

We're considering helping Farmer Brown improve his sheep pasture on Muffin Meadow. Do you think this will cause any problems for you?

Well, it's not going to mess up this bog over here, is it? That's where I gather my medicine.

Ah-ha; the bog may be a TCP, so let's find out a little more about it.

Actually, it might mess it up quite a bit, but maybe we can keep that from happening. Can you tell me anything more about the bog? What makes it a good place to get medicine?

And so on. Even if you conclude at the end of this interview that the bog isn't a TCP, or maybe is a TCP but isn't eligible for the register, you've probably gotten useful information about the environmental impacts of the Muffin Meadow Pasture Improvement Project, which will need to be considered under NEPA. And the medicine person you're talking with may feel—rightly—that you've listened to her and tried to address her problems, which is a lot better than having her feel that you've been trying to pry private information out of her for some surreptitious purpose.

There's quite a bit of published guidance about how to elicit information from people.[17] Much of it is designed to guide data gathering for academic research purposes, however, and some of it for use in criminal investigation. Neither may be entirely relevant to your needs. Remember that what you need is the minimum necessary to define and try to resolve impacts.

The Role of Ethnography

When we wrote Bulletin 38, we came under a good deal of pressure to say that identification of TCPs required studies by ethnographers—that is, professionals[18] who specialize in describing living cultures. We resisted, though in retrospect I don't think we resisted as much as we should have. As a result, the bulletin says:

Culturally sensitive consultation may require . . . the conduct of studies by trained ethnographers, ethnohistorians, sociologists, or folklorists. . . . Particularly where large projects or large land areas are involved, or where it is likely that particularly sensitive resources may be at issue, formal ethnographic studies should be carried out, by or under the supervision of a professionally qualified cultural anthropologist.[19]

Full-scale, professionally directed ethnographic studies are certainly sometimes appropriate and necessary—particularly where there are questions about whether people are telling the truth or where there's a very skeptical change agent or regulatory agency that needs to be convinced. But don't assume automatically that an ethnographic study is necessary or that only an ethnographer can do it.[20]

So what *is* necessary, and who *can* do it? Talking with people is the major necessary thing, and the person who does the talking should above all else be a good listener, who knows how to behave in the culture. In one case I worked on in the Black Hills of South Dakota, the tribes flatly rejected the proposal that they work with anthropologists, and it turned out that the best person to talk with them was a Forest Service engineer. He had grown up in the area and knew how to sit down at people's kitchen tables and listen. A good ethnographer can do that, too—should be trained to do it and be able to do it better than your average engineer—but that's not always the case, and as in the Black Hills case, ethnographers sometimes carry baggage that can get in the way of their work.

Of course, an advantage of performing some sort of more or less standard ethnographic study—probably employing what have come in some quarters to be called rapid ethnographic assessment procedures (REAP)[21]—is that the results may at least appear to be more reliable, more "scientific," than just talking with people. That appearance can be misleading, however. At base, ethnography *means* talking with people, together with watching them and sometimes participating in what they do. Putting a professional-sounding label on the activity (with an acronym, yet) may create only the illusion of reliability. And it may result in doing things that aren't really necessary, in order to meet professional standards that don't really need to be applied. For example, in REAP, as explained in one recent article, "more than one researcher is always involved," and multiple methods are employed in "triangulation." These are important standards to apply in some cases, such as in an overall social impact assessment, but they can be overkill when you're simply trying to find out whether there are TCPs in an area and what people think about them.

Or, they may *not* be overkill; as usual, it all depends on the particulars of the case—how complex or controversial it is, how complicated the roles are that TCPs play in a community, how factionalized the community is, and how its members feel about being "assessed." I'm not for a moment saying that one need *never* do formal ethnographic assessments, whether rapid or leisurely, but neither should one assume that formal ethnography, carried out by professional ethnographers, is always the best or only way to identify TCPs.

Inside and Outside

This may seem self-evident, but to identify TCPs or issues surrounding TCPs, you need to work substantially from within the community. This is not to say that CRM practitioners shouldn't apply their professional training or provide an outside perspective, but the idea is to relate what the professional can do to what the community knows and thinks, in a complementary manner.

The work of Randolph Hester and his colleagues, discussed in chapter 4, is an admirable example of such complementarity—made more so by the fact that it's the work of people who might well not know a TCP from a PCB. Hester and his team undertook a "community goals survey," including a questionnaire administered through the local newspaper, to identify concerns. Among these concerns, "affection for place was mentioned frequently."[22] So they interviewed in more depth and also—applying their own, outside expertise—undertook "behavior mapping"—a technique much like an ethnographer's participant observation:

> For several weeks we sat in various locations and recorded what people did and where. The resulting maps showed us activity settings for the daily patterns of townspeople. While people had described some of these in the goals survey, most had not been mentioned. Activities like newsing (exchanging gossip) at the post office, hanging out at the docks, and checking the water (tides, shoreline, fishing catches, weather, and gossip) recurred in the same places each day.[23]

Combining the survey results and the behavior mapping, they constructed a tentative list of important places and took it to the community. This consultation resulted in corrections and—in a rather eerie convergence with Stoffle's "cultural triage," a "ranked and weighted list of significant places"—the "Sacred Structure"[24] of Manteo. They wound up with a list and map of the places that were most important to the community in retaining its identity.

Of course, Hester had the advantage of working *for* the community and hence being able to get more cooperation than he might if he had been hired by a change agent or an agency of nonlocal government. But whoever we work for, we're not going to identify TCPs if we don't try to visualize their importance through the eyes of the people—even when they can't explicitly articulate that importance. Hester and his colleagues provide some useful tools for this enterprise.

Objections to Objectification

When looking for TCPs, you're trying to record objective data, but they're objective data about subjective phenomena—not necessarily about what *is* but about what *people think is*. I've never gone up Tahquitz Canyon looking for the obsidian cave from which the Cahuilla say the spirit Tahquitz ventures out in the form of a blue comet to steal people's souls. It might be interesting (if risky) to do so, but I probably wouldn't see anything but rocks and sagebrush. This doesn't mean that in some kind of reality the cave isn't there, and it really doesn't matter whether it's there. What matters is that people *think* it's there. As Roger Wharton has commented, it doesn't matter whether Jesus was born at Bethlehem; what matters is that people think he was and are inspired by the belief.[25]

How do you objectively pursue what people think? Anthropologists and sociologists do this all the time, often using survey instruments like questionnaires. Questionnaires give you objective boxes in which to put information, and enable you to put numerical values on things. X percentage of the population thinks Tahquitz is up there; Y percentage thinks he's not.

Objectifying devices like questionnaires have their place, but I think one ought to be very wary of relying on them. Klara Kelley and Harris Francis have pointed out that using a questionnaire can be seen as disrespectful, putting the interviewer in a seemingly superior position and not properly honoring the knowledge given by an interviewee.[26] Survey instruments can also become crutches and can isolate the researcher from the human qualities of the data.

I've been impressed with the community-based "cultural triage"[27] used by Richard Stoffle and his colleagues as a means of eliciting resource rankings from people who are not very inclined to rank things. But as their methods have matured they have become more and more questionnaire based, and I've become more and more uncomfortable with them. I have the sneaking feeling that quantification can so insulate the anthropologist from those consulted that it becomes unclear whether they're eliciting rankings or imposing them on their data.

Questionnaires and other objectifying devices can be useful, and necessary at times, but one shouldn't begin with the assumption that they must be employed. A softer-edged, less "scientific" approach—simply hearing people out and trying to capture their thoughts on paper or other media—is usually, I think, the way to start. One of the best quick TCP studies I've ever seen was done by John Anfinson, an archaeologist who at the time worked for the Corps of Engineers in St. Paul, Minnesota. Anfinson spent a couple of days on Chequemagon Bay talking informally with tribal members and captured the essentials of the bay's traditional significance in a half-dozen-page memorandum.[28] The corps didn't regard his conclusions as sufficient,[29] and two years later the Red Cliff and Bad River Bands of Chippewa had to spend several thousand dollars on a TCP study—by me—that really didn't wind up saying much more than Anfinson had. I just used more words.[30]

Social Impact Assessment

In illustrating how the scope of identification varies with the nature of the project's likely effects, Bulletin 38 uses the example of building rehabilitation:

[A]s a rule the rehabilitation of historic buildings may have relatively little potential for effect on [TCPs]. However, if a rehabilitation project may result in displacement of residents, "gentrification" of a neighborhood, or other sociocultural impacts, the possibility that the buildings to be rehabilitated, or the neighborhood in which they exist, may be ascribed traditional cultural value . . . should be considered.[31]

This rather elliptical recommendation applies to more than rehabilitation. Wherever a project may have social impacts on a community, the possibility that some of those effects may involve TCPs should be considered. If they may be involved, then Section 106 review may be in order.

In theory, social impacts are routinely considered in NEPA analyses, under the rubric of social impact assessment (SIA). Social impacts have been defined as

the consequences to human populations of any public or private action—that alter the ways in which people live, work, play, relate to one another, organize to meet their needs and generally cope as members of society. The term also includes cultural impacts involving changes to the norms, values, and beliefs that guide and rationalize their cognition of themselves and their society.[32]

The analysis of impacts on TCPs, and on the community values that give TCPs their importance, should be a part of SIA, but this doesn't often happen. Usually, TCP analyses are done as parts of cultural resource impact assessments (by whatever name) carried out by archaeologists and other historic preservation specialists, while SIA is done (if it's done) by a different group of people, usually economists and sociologists, under a separate scope of work.[33]

The scope of an SIA may also not be conducive to examining impacts on TCPs. The practice of SIA seems to be rather schizophrenic—practitioners talk about looking broadly at the social environment and how projects may affect it,[34] but often what actually gets analyzed are only those social variables that can be reduced to numbers—things like how many kids are enrolled in school and how many families have flush toilets. This is particularly the case where—as often happens—*socioeconomic* impact assessment is substituted for real SIA. Socioeconomic impact analysts try hard to be real scientists who work with hard, quantifiable data. Anything as soft and squishy as how a community feels about a valued place is likely to make such an analyst roll his eyes. This is too bad, and contrary to the fundamental principle of SIA that one should "deal with issues and public concerns that really count, not those that are just easy to count,"[35] but it's often the way things are, and it makes for little overlap between SIA and CRM.

So, it's a good idea—indeed, it's vital to the kind of interdisciplinary analysis called for by NEPA—to try to make your analysis of TCP impacts relate to whatever SIA is being done. But this may not be possible, and if it's not, this doesn't mean that sociocultural (and socioeconomic and other social) impacts involving TCPs don't have to be analyzed. You'll just have to do the analysis without the help of SIA.

Following the Rules

Particularly where a TCP is thought to be spiritually energetic or where it figures in ritual, there are likely to be rules about how it's discussed or about how one should behave in its vicinity. There may also be rules about how traditional cultural information in general is transmitted, to whom it can be transmitted, and in what forms. And there may simply be rules of courtesy, ways that one is supposed to interact with others. Some of these strictures may seem strange to an outsider, and even offensive. Bulletin 38 gives some examples: "Some groups forbid visits to such [spiritual] locations by menstruating women or by people of inappropriate ages. The taking of photographs or the use of electronic recording equipment may not be appropriate."[36]

We had some trouble prevailing upon the National Register to include the bit about menstruating women; it was felt to be offensively personal. That, Pat and I insisted, was precisely the point. Anyone working with TCPs had better be prepared for rules that clash with one's own values, and if one objects to abiding by such rules one should get into a different line of work. The traditional rules of some groups certainly seem sexist, or ageist, or discriminatory in some other way, or they may be just plain embarrassing. They may make it impossible for male researchers to pursue some studies, and for female researchers to pursue others. It may be necessary to hire graybeards to interview people about things they can't share with young folks. There's nothing for it; you have to play by the group's rules.

Of course, there are limits. Shortly after Bulletin 38's issuance, Maryland SHPO Rodney Little pointed out to me that if carried to its logical conclusion, the bulletin would suggest respecting the segregation of restroom facilities in parts of the South. There may well be community rules that a responsible and lawful researcher cannot follow. Luckily I have yet to find myself confronted with such a rule, but if I were, I think my own rule of thumb would be this: If the rule requires something that is clearly unlawful or that would be generally held to be morally reprehensible, I shouldn't go along with it, but if it simply makes me uncomfortable or seems repugnant to me, personally, I should swallow my objections and get on with the job.

How do you find out what the rules are? That may be a problem. I don't know of anything to do but to try to be prepared in advance; review the pertinent literature; consult knowledgeable people. Someone—a tribal government official, a group's cultural resource coordinator, an experienced ethnographer—should be able to advise.

But don't get carried away. This is the twenty-first century, and you shouldn't assume that traditional people are locked in the nineteenth, or twelfth, or that they aren't flexible enough to accommodate the odd ways of outsiders. Don't try to pretend you're "one of them." Don't wear beads or feathers when you go to visit a tribe, unless they're part of your routine attire. Don't insist on a prayer at the beginning of the meeting if nobody you're consulting with seems to want one. On the other hand, try to avoid behavior or appearances that might give offense. Elders in many communities are put off by dress that shows too much of the body or the wrong parts, and the federal employee who went into a meeting with tribal members wearing his sidearm got a distinctly cool reception. It's not "going native" to cover your upper arms if you're a woman in Chuuk; it's just polite.

Avoiding Overburdening the Community

One of the unintended consequences of Bulletin 38, and of the 1992 NHPA amendments that clarified requirements for tribal consultation, has been a deluge of notification letters coming through every Indian tribe's mail slot.

> Dear Tribe:
>
> The Bureau of Redundant Development is planning a project in Deepdark Canyon. Please advise us of any traditional cultural property concerns you may have. . . .

Tribes complain of being overwhelmed by letters asking for their comments on proposals—often written in obtuse bureaucratic language and demanding responses within fixed deadlines. Agencies and applicants for federal approvals complain of notification letters going into tribal black holes from which no light of response escapes. These linked problems result from two linked, or mirror-imaging, facts of life. Agencies don't have the money, time, or staff to undertake detailed consultation on each and every thing they do, so they resort to form letters—often using forms and formats that aren't exactly reader- or responder-friendly. Tribes don't have the money, time, or staff to handle the flood of requests and to figure out the form letters, so they don't respond.

Groups that are not tribes—urban neighborhoods, rural villages, dispersed rural communities—are burdened not only by lack of time and money to respond to queries from agencies, but by the fact that queries aren't even made, or are made only in media to which they have little or no access (e.g., the *Federal Register* or legal notices in a newspaper). They often have trouble even finding out that an action is being considered and have no regular way to make their concerns known. And in tribes and nontribes alike, local perceptions of time, protocol, and priorities may make it impossible for the group to respond on the sort of schedule an agency might like.

Agencies that honestly want to engage in real, fruitful consultation with tribes and other groups—BLM and the Forest Service in California come to mind as examples, along with a number of military bases, and some Department of Energy facilities like the Hanford Site in Washington state—have backed up and viewed the problem programmatically, sitting down with communities when they're *not* considering some potentially threatening project and working out mutually agreeable ways of interacting when such projects come along. Sometimes these agreements are formalized in consultation protocols, memoranda of understanding, or other formal instruments.[37] Such an instrument will typically distinguish between those kinds of projects the tribe or group wants to be consulted about and those it doesn't. It goes on, usually, to designate formal points of contact in the tribe/group and in the agency and to specify when and how contacts will be made and consultation will be carried out.

Such agreements can greatly simplify consultation for all concerned. They make things more predictable and reduce the overall workload, allowing everyone to focus on the important stuff rather than the trivia.

Where a federally recognized Indian tribe is involved, such an agreement can help solve the often-sticky problem of government-to-government consultation. The U.S. government is supposed to maintain a government-to-government relationship with each tribal government.[38] This is generally taken to mean that a line officer of the relevant agency—a forest supervisor, a National Park superintendent, a military base commander—should meet and consult with the head of the tribal government. But the base commander and the tribal chairman can't be expected to sit down and reason together over every little training exercise or placement of underground fiber optics; there has to be a more efficient way. A consultation agreement can solve this problem. The federal line officer and the tribal chairman meet (after appropriate staff work) to negotiate and sign the overall agreement that then guides their staffs in ongoing, day by day interaction.

One remarkable example of such a programmatic approach to consultation—all the more so because no land management agencies were involved, and most of the tribes live on reservations out of state—is the "tribal summit" sponsored in 2000 by the Iowa Department of Transportation (IDOT) and the Federal Highway Administration. All fifteen[39] tribes with cultural connections to Iowa were invited to a meeting, their expenses covered by the agencies. The meeting featured workshops on Section 106 and NEPA review, so that everyone had a common understanding of the legal context in which they were consulting. The centerpiece of the summit was consultation about how to maintain ongoing interaction, and this led to the formulation of a clever coordination letter. The letter is a two-part form, designed to cover a package of project documents. IDOT fills out one part, providing basic data on the project and what's known about its potential impacts. It's then sent to each tribe that's expressed interest in the county in which the project is planned, and the tribe fills in a series of check boxes: we don't want further information; we do want further information; we want a site visit; we're really concerned about this. The tribal representative then folds the form over, staples it, and drops it in the mailbox; IDOT's address is preprinted on the outfolded side, and postage is prepaid.[40]

I hasten to say that there are things I think are unfortunate about IDOT's form. It's biased toward archaeology, and it's based on some peculiar assumptions about the Section 106 process.[41] But it's a good example of a simple means of maintaining communication that respects the workload of the tribal representatives—a good example of people reasoning together to find ways of meeting legal and ethical responsibilities with minimum bureaucratic folderol.

One caveat, though: Be careful about the agreements you prepare and about signing those that are put before you, by tribes or anyone else. There are tribes and intertribal groups who seem to believe that an agreement about how to deal with Section 106 review is something that every agency must execute, as an expression of its respect for tribal sovereignty, whether the agreement makes any sense or not. Some such agreements—particularly those promoted by eastern tribes and intertribal groups, for some reason—are very strange manglings and regurgitations of the standard Section 106 process that if followed would greatly complicate the lives of both agencies and tribes while placing agencies neatly in noncompliance with the Section 106 regulations and other authorities. A particularly bizarre but not atypical example was executed in 2003 by the Louisiana Army National Guard with a number of tribes, the SHPO, and others[42] and rather astonishingly blessed by the ACHP. Don't sign such a tribal agreement if it doesn't make sense to you—and to others who will have to interpret or implement it—no matter what kinds of authorities (like the ACHP) have lined up behind it.

How Not to Do It

In the early 1990s, the Cibola National Forest in New Mexico was planning transportation and recreation facility improvements in Las Huertas Canyon, near Albuquerque and Sandia Pueblo. The forest staff knew that they had to do Section 106 review on the project. Knowing, too, that tribal TCPs might be among the historic property types affected, the forest sent out a form letter to local tribes. The letter asked each tribe to notify the forest staff, within thirty days, of any TCPs in the canyon. They were to explain where each one was, describe its significance and boundaries, and attach a 7.5-minute U.S. Geological Survey quadrangle map with the site's boundaries marked.

Whenever I tell this story in class, everybody laughs. Who could possibly expect a tribe to provide the specific mapped locations of their TCPs to a federal agency? With boundaries marked, yet! On 7.5-minute quadrangles!

In fact, though, federal agencies expect that kind of thing all the time, both from tribes and from others; they're just not usually as blatant about it as the Cibola was. It's not uncommon for an agency, or the applicant for a permit, to send out a form letter saying, "Tell us everything that you think is important about this area, and do it within thirty days, or we're going to assume you have no interest and the 'dozers are gonna roll." They may even say, "Nominate your special places to the National Register, and if they're accepted, we'll consider impacts on them."

What the change agent is doing in such a case is shifting the legwork of Section 106 review to the recipient of its letter. It's not the responsibility of a tribe, or any other group, to identify historic properties for an agency; it's the agency's responsibility to do so. And sending out a letter saying "tell us or else" is not a very effective means of identification.

Remember your own TCP, that you brought to mind back in chapter 1? Suppose the Olympus Mons Development Corporation from Mars is planning a new spaceport in your area and sends you a letter asking you to notify the corporation of all your TCPs (only they probably call them Fleeblewhackies), with maps showing their metes and bounds and a clear explanation of why you think each one is significant. How would you respond?

Of course, in many cases letters are necessary as a first step in consultation, but when you prepare such a letter, put yourself in the shoes of the recipient and think about what you might find relatively easy to respond to. Tailor your letter accordingly. Where you're dealing with a federally recognized tribal government, of course, you'll have to be sure that the letter is signed by the appropriate official in the agency and sent to the tribal government, but whatever you're doing and whoever you're writing, try to make the form of communication fit the circumstances, and expect to have to follow up by telephone, in person, or both.

Richard Stoffle and his colleagues report using a "video-letter" as an initial way to contact the several tribal groups concerned about Fajada Butte in New Mexico, concluding that the letter—apparently a video sent to tribes explaining the work and asking their cooperation—was an "effective tool for communicating about a complex study to a number of tribal governments in a short time." There are doubtless lots of other creative approaches.[43]

Looking at the Land

Most CRM practitioners are used to doing archaeological surveys, and project planners are fairly used to contracting for them. As a result, archaeological survey is taken as the basic model for all kinds of surveys, to locate all kinds of historic properties (or even all kinds of cultural resources).

In many parts of the country, pretty clear-cut survey standards have been promulgated or adopted by SHPOs, agencies, and archaeological organizations. Not that they're necessarily thoughtful, effective, or in keeping with the requirements of law,[44] but they *are* clear-cut and are typically quite well understood by archaeologists. There is a natural tendency to try to apply the same standards to TCP identification.

An assumption about TCP identification based on an archaeological survey model might go like this:

> To identify archaeological sites and determine their eligibility, the standard requirement is to do Phase I.B. survey. This involves having qualified archaeologists walk over the ground no more than ten meters apart examining the surface and recording everything they see. A TCP survey must involve the same level of work—qualified TCP identifiers spaced no more than ten meters apart looking at every square meter of the surface. . . .

Even if traipsing archaeologists over the landscape at specified intervals were always an appropriate way to identify archaeological sites (and it's not), this wouldn't make it an appropriate way to identify TCPs. TCPs aren't necessarily visible on the surface of the ground, and walking transects at standard intervals is unlikely to reveal them even if they are. It may be very helpful for knowledgeable people— elders, or people instructed by elders—to go out onto the ground and look for TCPs, but that doesn't mean they have to walk transects or inspect the ground, or even look at every part of the area under investigation.

At the other end of the spectrum from those who try to identify TCPs like archaeological sites are those who think they never need to do in-field TCP surveys at all. After all, the argument goes, if TCPs are important in the ongoing cultural integrity of the community, their locations and character must be known to the community, or at least to the elders, so why should anybody need to go look for them?

Plenty of reasons. First, the place may be known in the abstract, but not in particular. Tradition may have it that the ancestors went from place to place over the country and left marks of their passing. Belief in the existence of those marks may be important in maintaining the community's sense of itself, but few or none of the marks may actually have ever been seen by anybody. If the marks (e.g., rock art, or archaeological sites, or particular natural features) are out there and may be affected by a project, they need to be found, and the only way to find them is for somebody who knows what they look like to go look for them.

Or consider the case of a tribe that was forcibly removed from its land, or ceded it, and hasn't been able to get back on it for the last century or so. Tribal tradition may tell of culturally important places in the land to which the tribe no longer has access, but knowledge of their specific locations may have faded.

And, of course, elders—those who tend to know about such things as TCPs—have a discouraging tendency to be old. It's quite possible that a group's elders haven't visited an area in many years simply because they're too feeble, and they've forgotten a lot of specifics about where things are and what they're like. Field visits can often refresh memories.

Finally, the places may be so fully embedded in people's sense of self, sense of community, that they're difficult for people to tease out and hold up for the visiting investigator's inspection. Remember Manteo, where "even to locals, the sacred places were outwardly taken for granted."[45]

Some Relevant Case Law

In the Las Huertas Canyon case, the Forest Service got little response to its request for mapped TCP locations. Nobody sent in marked-up quadrangle maps. The Pueblo of Sandia did, however, advise the Forest Service that its people regarded the whole canyon as having cultural and spiritual value and that it wanted to be consulted as planning went along.[46] The Forest Service , seeing no attached quadrangle, decided there were no historic properties subject to effect and proceeded with planning, whereupon the Pueblo went to court. After several years, the case of *Pueblo of Sandia v. United States*[47] ended with a finding by the Tenth Circuit Court of Appeals that the Forest Service had not made the "reasonable and good faith effort" to identify historic properties required by the Section 106 regulations.[48] In articulating this finding, the court essentially established standards for what a "reasonable and good-faith effort" to identify TCPs ought to entail. The standards for "reasonableness" can be summarized as follows:

- The level and kind of effort needed to identify TCPs must be established on the basis of all the information available to the agency (i.e., on good scoping). Just writing letters and compiling responses isn't enough.

- Bulletin 38, on which the court relied extensively, is guidance that should be considered carefully in planning and conducting identification.

- Reluctance to reveal information about sensitive cultural matters should be thoughtfully considered; the implication is that identification must be planned with such possible reluctance in mind, and an agency can't just say, "Well, they won't tell us, so there's nothing we can do."

As for "good faith," the court focused on the quality of consultation, saying essentially that good-faith consultation must be informed consultation—the agency can't hide information from other parties and say it's acting in good faith.[49] One might paraphrase the court as saying that agencies have to be honest.

I hasten to add that it's important not to overplay the Tenth Circuit's findings. Two other cases, both in the Ninth Circuit, indicate that a tribe (or, presumably, other affected party) cannot sit on its hands and expect an agency to perform TCP identification appropriately. Nor can a tribe prescribe precisely what kind of study an agency will do.

In *Muckleshoot Indian Tribe v. U.S. Forest Service,*[50] the Ninth Circuit found that the Forest Service's failure to perform a general TCP survey when a tribe demanded it but didn't provide evidence that TCPs might be present was "in tension" with Bulletin 38 and indicated that the Forest Service "could have been more sensitive to the needs of the tribe." However, the court found, it "probably [did] not provide sufficient grounds to conclude that the Forest Service failed to comply with NHPA."

In *Morongo Band v. FAA,*[51] the same court found the Federal Aviation Administration to be in compliance with Section 106 even though it ignored the tribe's suggestion that TCPs might be affected by its action, in this case changing airline flight patterns in and out of Los Angeles International Airport. FAA was in compliance, the court said, because it ignored the tribe not in the context of identification but in that of determining that the action under consideration had no potential to affect historic properties. Since the action couldn't affect historic properties, the court reasoned, the FAA's "failure to identify specific potential sites or properties is irrelevant." The court also found that FAA had not failed to comply with Section 106 by failing to do an EIS on its action, or by failing to get tribal consent, since Section 106 requires neither.

In a nutshell, *Sandia, Muckleshoot,* and *Morongo* collectively indicate that an agency cannot simply rely on a group to tell it where and what all its TCPs are, but tribes and others do *not* have carte blanche to require agencies to do particular forms of TCP identification, or to expect agencies to identify TCPs without any help at all.

So . . .

The court findings give us a good ending point for this chapter. There is no standard way to identify TCPs. Identification strategy must be developed on a

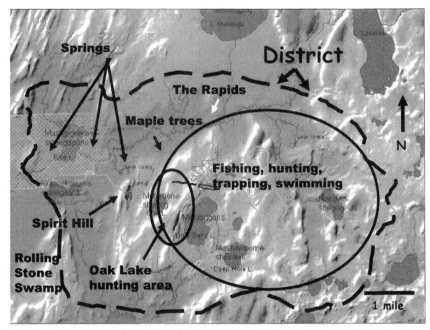

Figure 7.3.   Approximate boundaries of Mushgigagamonsebe, a Sokaogon Ojibwe TCP landscape defined by the author and colleagues based on interviews with tribal consultants, background historical research, and review by the tribe. Contributing elements include spiritual locations, traditional hunting and fishing areas, springs, medicine gathering areas, and the quality of the district's water. Source: Nesper et al. 2002; base map from Great Lakes Indian Fish and Wildlife Commission.

case-by-case basis, taking into account all the information that may be pulled together during scoping (or before, or after).

Identification planning needs to take guidance like Bulletin 38 into account. It needs to appreciate people's reluctance to provide detailed information about places they regard as culturally significant and spiritually powerful. It needs to include good-faith, honest consultation.

And everybody has a part to play. The agency is the primary responsible party, but others have to participate if they expect their interests to be considered.

I think that if one is guided by these precepts in putting together an identification strategy at the scoping stage and doesn't get sidetracked by what somebody thinks is the standard way of doing identification or into filling out unnecessary forms or recording unnecessary data, a reasonable and good-faith identification effort should result.

Notes

1. I'm grateful to the Illinois SHPO and Dr. Robert Jeske for improving the accuracy of my description of the Mark Gob Pile case.

2. From the "Statement of Significance" section of a National Register nomination form prepared 1986 for the Mark Mine Gob Pile, on file with the Illinois SHPO.

3. Keeper's determination of ineligibility dated January 19, 1986, on file with the Illinois SHPO.

4. Public Law 100-91.

5. *Secretary of the Interior's Standards for Identification,* 48 FR 44720.

6. See chapter 2, n. 42. Collect, or at least share with consulting parties, only such information about TCPs or their uses as is necessary for purposes of consultation.

7. 40 CFR 1408.25.

8. 36 CFR 800.4(a) and (b).

9. National Register, *Guidelines for Evaluating and Documenting Traditional Cultural Properties* (National Park Service, Washington, D.C., n.d. [sometimes (accurately) dated 1990]), 38:5.

10. Bulletin 38, on page 4, discusses "preservation planning," the basis for understanding the area's history, ethnography, and contemporary society, partly in terms of "historic contexts," an unfortunate concept with which NPS and to some extent this author were enamored at the time. Fortunately, it goes on to note that such planning must include contacting and consulting with concerned groups and that historic contexts should "reflect the history and culture of such groups as the groups themselves understand them, as well as their history and culture as defined by Euroamerican scholarship."

11. Identifying and dealing with such variables is an important part of addressing environmental justice concerns. In the context of ecosystem management, Daniels et al. (1996) provide an excellent example of how to identify interest groups and opinion leaders, in connection with development of a National Forest reforestation program. See S. E. Daniels, G. B. Walker, M. S. Carroll, and K. Blatner, Collaborative Learning and Fire Recovery Planning. *Journal of Forestry* 94(4)(1996):4–9.

12. See 36 CFR 800.16(d) for APE definition, 36 CFR 800.5(a) for range of effects to be considered, for pertinent case law see *Colorado River v. Marsh*, 605 F. supp. 1425 (C.D. Cal. 1985).

13. REA's functions today are administered by the Rural Utilities Service.

14. *El Rancho La Comunidad v. United States,* No. 90-113 (D.N.M. May 21, 1991).

15. The resolution finally agreed to involved plantings to screen the station visually and audibly from the dance site.

16. Thomas F. King, In the Light of the Megis: The Chequamegon Bay Area as a Traditional Cultural Property, report to the Bad River and Red Cliff Bands of Lake Superior Tribe of Chippewa, Bad River and Bayfield, Wisconsin, 1999a.

17. See Steven L. Schensul, Jean J. Schensul, and Margaret D. LeCompte, *Essential Ethnographic Methods,* vol. 2 of the Ethnographer's Toolkit (AltaMira, Walnut Creek, CA, 1999), on standard ethnographic methods; James Beebe, Basic Concepts and Techniques of Rapid Appraisal, *Human Organization* 54 (1995):42–51, on rapid appraisal.

18. Usually cultural anthropologists, folklorists, or sociologists.

19. Bulletin 38:7.

20. See Thomas F. King, Stupid TCP Tricks, in *Thinking about Cultural Resource Management: Essays from the Edge* (AltaMira, Walnut Creek, CA, 2002), 15–18.

21. See D. H. Taplin, S. Scheld, and S. M. Low, Rapid Ethnographic Assessment in Urban Parks: A Case Study of Independence National Historical Park, *Human Organization* 61(2000):81, for a concise summary of REAP; related aconymous methodologies are rapid rural appraisal or RRA (see Beebe, Basic Concepts) and participatory rural appraisal or PRA (see R. Chambers, The Origins and Practice of Participatory Rural Appraisal, *World Development* 22[7] [1994]:953–69).

22. Randolph T. Hester, Subconscious Landscapes of the Heart, *Place* 2(3) (1987):11.

23. Hester, Subconscious Landscapes, 12.

24. Hester, Subconscious Landscapes, 13–14.

25. Roger Wharton, But You, O Bethlehem of Ephrathah: Bethlehem as a Sacred Place, in James Swan and Roberta Swan (eds.), *Dialogues with the Living Earth* (Quest Books; Theosophical Publishing House, Wheaton, IL, 1996), 127.

26. Klara B. Kelley and Harris Francis, *Navajo Sacred Places* (Indiana University Press, Bloomington, 1994), 63.

27. Richard W. Stoffle and Michael J. Evans, Holistic Conservation and Cultural Triage: American Indian Perspectives on Cultural Resources, *Human Organization* 49(2) (1990): 91–99; and see chap. 12.

28. John Anfinson, Lake Superior Sunken Log Permits: Interviews with Red Cliff and Bad River Chippewa Bands, memorandum for CEMVP-CO-R, U.S. Army Corps of Engineers, St. Paul District, July 16, 1997.

29. And in fairness to the Corps, neither did Anfinson.

30. King, In the Light of the Megis.

31. National Register n.d. 38:6.

32. Interorganizational Committee on Guidelines and Principles for Social Impact Assessment, Guidelines and Principles for Social Impact Assessment, *Environmental Impact Assessment Review* 15(1) (1993):11; and see Frank Vanclay, Conceptualizing Social Impacts, *Environmental Impact Assessment Review* 22 (2002):183–211, for a thoughtful critique and correction.

33. This is essentially an accident of history. While archaeologists were inventing "cultural resource management" and defining it implicitly as addressing impacts on archaeological sites, sociologists and other students of living communities were inventing SIA; the two have never really gotten together.

34. For example, in Interorganizational Committee, Guidelines and Principles.

35. Interorganizational Committee, Guidelines and Principles, 31.

36. National Register n.d. 38:8.

37. Darby C. Stapp and Michael S. Burney, *Tribal Cultural Resource Management: The Full Circle to Stewardship* (AltaMira, Walnut Creek, CA, 2002), 119–51, provide excellent examples of tribal protocol development, and consultation in general.

38. See Charles F. Wilkinson, *American Indians, Time, and the Law: Native Societies in a Modern Constitutional Democracy* (Yale University Press, New Haven, CT, 1988), for a discussion of tribal sovereignty and related issues; and Stapp and Burney, *Tribal Cultural Resource Management,* for applications to tribal CRM programs.

39. Or more, depending on how they're counted.

40. Tribal Notification Form, Iowa Department of Transportation.

41. Furthermore, the programmatic agreement that puts it and other mechanisms in place is almost a caricature of a Section 106 agreement document, embodying in a single document virtually everything that one can possibly do to make such a document pointless, confusing, and misleading.

42. Louisiana Army National Guard, Programmatic Agreement among the Louisiana Army National Guard, the Alabama Coushatta Tribe of Texas, the Caddo Tribe of Oklahoma, the Chitimacha Tribe of Louisiana, the Coushatta Tribe of Louisiana, the Jena Band of Choctaw Indians, the Mississippi Band of Choctaw Indians, the Quapaw Tribe of Oklahoma, the Tunica-Biloxi Indians of Louisiana, the Louisiana State Historic Preservation Officer, the Louisiana State Archaeologist, and the Advisory Council on Historic Preservation Regarding Undertakings That May Affect Historic Properties, Jackson Barracks, New Orleans, 2003.

43. Richard W. Stoffle, Michael J. Evans, M. Nieves Zedeño, Brent W. Stoffle, and Cindy J. Kesel, *American Indians and Fajada Butte: Ethnographic Overview and Assessment for Fajada Butte and Traditional (Ethnobotanical) Use Study for Chaco Culture National Historical Park, New Mexico,* report to New Mexico State Historic Preservation Officer and Regional Ethnographer, Southwestern Regional Office, National Park Service, by the Bureau of Applied Research in Anthropology (University of Arizona, Tucson, 1994), 11.

44. See Thomas F. King, How the Archaeologists Stole Culture: A Gap in American Environmental Impact Assessment and What to Do about It, *Environmental Impact Assessment Review* 18(2) (1998b):117–34, and King, Stupid TCP Tricks, 147–53, for critiques of common archaeological approaches to CRM in general and identification in particular.

45. Hester, Subconscious Landscapes, 15.

46. The Forest Service also had other sources of information indicating the cultural importance of the canyon.

47. 50 F.3d 856 (10th Cir. 1995).

48. 36 CFR 800.4(b)(1).

49. The court explicitly discussed consultation with the SHPO, from whom the Forest Service had withheld information about the Pueblo's concerns, but it seems likely that the same standard would apply to an agency's dealings with other consulting parties.

50. 177 F.3d 800 (9th Cir. 1999).

51. 161 F.3d 569 (9th Cir. 1998).

Chapter Eight

Bulletin 38 Revisited

Evaluating Eligibility

> Boundaries have to be assigned. It may not be fair, and it may not
> be right, but . . . they have to be assigned. This is bureaucracy.
> —State historic preservation officer statement
> in interagency/intertribal meeting on
> TCP management along a major western
> river system, from meeting minutes;
> specific attribution withheld

THERE'S no standard way of identifying TCPs or any other kind of historic
property, but if you have to evaluate a place's significance—which in Section 106 Land means determining whether something is eligible for the
National Register—it's a bit different. When one embarks on an eligibility determination, one is treading on the National Register's turf, and that means following some rules.

Not necessarily the register's rules, however. The register would like to see
its standard nomination forms completed for each evaluation. There are 16
pages of regulation and 147 pages of guidelines on how to complete these
forms.[1]

One certainly *can* follow the National Register's rules.[2] The trouble is, the
rules are pretty nit-picky, they weren't designed with TCPs in mind, and some
of the information they elicit—detailed boundary definitions, for instance—is
often irrelevant to TCPs and difficult if not impossible to record in a way that
(1) makes sense and (2) isn't offensive to the people who value the property.

The alternative is to collect and document only the information you actually
need to judge the eligibility of the place you're looking at—which may or may
not resemble what you'd collect and document in order to fill out a nomination

form. How to do this? It depends on the circumstances, but in this chapter I'll offer some suggestions, followed by an example of how one agency did both identification and evaluation very well by—in a sense—doing neither.

Avoiding the Nomination Trap

Section 106 extends the same consideration to places that are *eligible* for the National Register as it does to those that have actually been registered, but would-be protectors of TCPs sometimes get misled—intentionally or otherwise—into thinking that they must get their places registered in order to get them considered. This is what happened to the residents of Stiltsville.

We touched on Stiltsville in chapter 6. It is (or was, if by the time this book is published its residents have lost their fight) a collection of stilthouses in Biscayne Bay, Florida. Beginning in the early twentieth century with a few fishing shacks, it grew to include a notorious bar and a number of more or less elaborate recreational residences. Every time a hurricane blew through, much of Stiltsville would disappear, but it would always be rebuilt. In the eyes of many (though certainly not all) denizens of the bay's shores, it came to be regarded with some fondness as a kinky part of the area's ambience.

Then the bay came under the jurisdiction of the National Park Service, which decided that intrusions on the natural scene had to go. Stiltsville was built on leaseholds which NPS inherited, so NPS could and did advise the residents that their leases would not be renewed and they'd better demolish their homes forthwith.

In making its decision, NPS had to comply with Section 106, but through either ignorance or malice, its representatives interpreted Section 106 to the Stiltsvillians like this: If you nominate the place to the National Register and get it included, we won't be able to terminate your leases. So the residents drummed up the money to prepare a nomination. Since Stiltsville was made up of buildings they hired an architectural historian, who prepared an excellent nomination but couldn't get past the fact that most of the buildings had been blown away and rebuilt in the 1960s; they just weren't very old. It was easy for NPS (in which, of course, the register is lodged) to convince the keeper that Stiltsville didn't meet the register criteria. The people of Stiltsville then hired me, and we renominated the site as a TCP, with the buildings as incidental contributing elements. I think we made a respectable case, but not respectable enough to overcome the Park Service's by then frenzied desire to see the buildings gone. I'm fairly sure that if it had been the nasty old Corps of Engineers proposing that Stiltsville go, the keeper would have accepted the site with open arms, but since it was her own colleagues, indeed her own boss, who wanted to rid the bay of the eyesore, the keeper ignored our arguments for Stiltsville's traditional cultural value, focused once again on the age of the buildings, and tut-tutted the site into ineligibility. The Stiltsvillians continue to fight, but they've lost the Section 106 round and spent a good deal of their own money doing so.

Would they have won if they had *not* nominated? There's no guarantee, but the argument would have been differently framed if instead of nominating they had insisted that NPS do its job and determine eligibility—and then dogged the determination process to make sure it was done correctly. NPS would have been forced to defend *its* opinions, rather than being able to require the Stiltsvillians to defend theirs. The Stiltsvillians could have taken the offensive as critics of any flaws in the NPS analysis, rather than being humble petitioners for the keeper's blessing.

A few years ago, I advised an Indian tribe against nomination and was sternly taken to task by the tribe's Tribal Historic Preservation Officer (THPO). If white guys could get their rinky-dink old buildings on the register, the THPO railed, why shouldn't his Sovereign Tribal Nation (STN)[3] be able to get its important places listed?

I was puzzled, because it seemed to me that the Sovereign Tribal Nation's sovereignty was an excellent reason *not* to nominate. The STN wouldn't beseech the government of France or China or Botswana to list the STN's historic places on their national schedules; why should they petition the United States to do so? If they felt that things needed to be listed, why not create their own Sovereign Tribal National Register? Why not design their own nomination forms, collecting the information that *they* think is important rather than what some representative of the Great White Father in Washington likes to see? Why not maintain their own inventory data, and then tell the U.S. government that it can bloody well regard all tribally registered places as eligible for the U.S. National Register and treat them accordingly under Section 106? Where was the sovereignty, where the national pride and self-respect, in playing the game according to another government's rules? I did not convince the THPO, who I suppose is happily spending his days filling out the register's forms. I still don't understand his point of view.

There *are* reasons to nominate. Some tax advantages and grants are available only to listed properties, and some state and local laws give special protection to listed properties. And there's certainly some psychological cachet to being included in the register, so sometimes it's worth doing. But don't assume that it's always worth doing, or always a good thing to do. And remember that although occasionally it's *strategic* to nominate, it's never *necessary* in the context of Section 106 review. Nomination is irrelevant to Section 106.

"But what about Section 110?" I imagine someone asking. Section 110 of NHPA includes a subsection—110(a)(2)(A)—requiring each agency to have a historic preservation program. This program is supposed to include nomination of properties under the agency's jurisdiction or control. However, Section 110(a)(2) does not say that *everything* has to be nominated; in fact, when the act was amended in 1992, a requirement to nominate "all" properties under agency control was removed, specifically to give agencies the flexibility to avoid wasting time and money on nomination where it wasn't warranted. So the agency's program needs to *include* nomination, but there's no requirement to include it in any particular way. An agency can nominate only properties in which it wants to invest money, or only properties it intends to sell to nonfederal parties, or only properties it plans to paint pink. Nomination is one tool that agencies can use in carrying out their general management responsibilities under Section 110; it ought to be used where it's useful. Where it's not useful, don't use it.

I am *not* saying, "Don't use the National Register Criteria (36 CFR 60.4)." You have to use the criteria in the context of Section 106. But there's a huge difference between *using* the criteria—which are, if a bit convoluted, at base pretty flexible and commonsensical—and nomination. Using the criteria is a way of organizing one's thoughts and communicating using common terms. There's nothing wrong with that; indeed, it's necessary. Nomination is another matter— an administrative process that requires the collection of specific data regardless of their relevance to the issues at hand, and that creates a supplicant–benefactor relationship that's entirely at odds with the democratic notion that government should pay attention to what citizens think is important, not vice versa. It also almost inevitably breeds conflict, because people react to a property's formal "designation" as a historic place with far more angst than they do a simple decision to recognize that the place has some historical or cultural value. And conflict is almost always conflict over things that don't have much management utility, like boundaries.[4]

Respecting the Keeper

There are two ways to "determine eligibility," though some would say that one of them is not a "determination" at all. An agency and SHPO or THPO can agree to *regard a place* as eligible for purposes of Section 106; this is sometimes called a "consensus determination" and sometimes as simply an agreement to treat the place as eligible. Or an agency can ask the keeper of the National Register for a formal determination. My very strong advice is to avoid the latter course of action if you possibly can. I am not promoting disrespect for the keeper or suggesting that you not use her in the roles the regulations assign to her. My advice is simply a paraphrase on that given about the czar by the rabbi in *Fiddler on the Roof:* "Bless the keeper and keep her—far away from us."

Besides ruling on nominations and promoting the register as a research and educational tool, the keeper's job is to make final decisions in cases of contested or questionable eligibility. This is a useful and important role, but it's not one that any keeper has ever particularly liked doing, and it's not one that any keeper has always done well. The keeper inevitably applies nomination standards when determining eligibility, and that can result in a lot of nit-picking about things like boundaries, what kind of property the place is, and which particular criteria apply. Since the Section 106 regulations require neither keeper review (except in contested or questionable cases) nor any particular level or kind of documentation, in the vast majority of cases there's no reason to subject oneself to the keeper's attentions. The best rule, I think, is to try to resolve all questions about eligibility without involving the keeper. In most cases where anybody really cares about the property at issue (which by definition includes any case involving a TCP), this will mean agreeing that the property is eligible for the register.

An extreme example of the application of this rule is provided by the case of a putative Medicine Wheel in Boulder, Colorado.

The General Services Administration (GSA) proposed to construct new facilities for two agencies on a parcel of federally owned land in Boulder. The land, largely vacant, was bordered by housing developments, the residents of which used the federal land for running, walking dogs, and other kinds of low-impact recreation; it was valued open space for them but hardly definable on that basis alone as either historically or culturally important. The residents were not wild about losing it, however, and particularly about losing it to a new federal office campus.

Figure 8.1.   One limb of the putative medicine wheel at Boulder, Colorado. Photo by the author.

As NEPA review got under way on the project, people in the neighborhood began to talk about their belief that a "sacred Indian medicine wheel" existed on the property. Medicine wheels are circular, spoked arrangements of stone that occur in various places on the northern Plains; the most famous—a National Historic Landmark and the subject of one of the most famous recent TCP-based Section 106 cases—is the Bighorn Medicine Wheel on the Bighorn National Forest in Wyoming.[5] They are viewed as important spiritual places by the Northern Arapaho, Eastern Shoshone, Northern Cheyenne, Crow, and other tribes. A medicine wheel at Boulder would be a bit outside the seeming normal range of such sites, but at about the same time another such wheel was the subject of controversy at Fort Hood, clear down in Texas,[6] so it wasn't beyond belief that the Boulder site could be for real. There really were alignments of boulders in the field.

On the other hand, historical air photos showed that the alignments tended to coincide with old fence lines, raising the suspicion that they simply represented the rocks thrown aside by farmers clearing fields. There were accounts of rocks being scraped into windrows at some point in the past to create a baseball diamond on the site. And no tribes came to GSA to complain about the proposed project; it was all local citizens. Bundles and strings of feathers and colored ribbons began showing up attached to bushes near the alignments, and corn meal was found in hollows in the rocks; somebody was doing something somewhat akin to traditional tribal religious practices, but

Figure 8.2.   One of the offerings that suggested its spiritual use. Photo by the author.

was it "real" traditionalists, or were local residents making the whole thing up to impede the project?

GSA decided that the only thing to do was consult the tribes. However, a lot of tribes have more or less resided in the Boulder vicinity over the years. In the end, GSA sponsored three tribal workshops that brought together representatives of fourteen tribes to consider the putative spiritual character of the "wheel." There was much head scratching and chin rubbing, I'm told, and no one was terribly enthusiastic about the "wheel" itself, but the belief was expressed by several tribal representatives that the general area, and particularly the land upslope of the proposed construction site, had spiritual characteristics and should be protected and kept accessible to tribal religious practitioners.

At this point GSA and its very creative cultural resource consultants did something that raised eyebrows at the SHPO and Advisory Council offices and made me a bit uncomfortable, too—but on balance, I think it was pretty smart. They decided to gloss over the question of the "medicine wheel's" eligibility for the National Register, and indeed on the eligibility of anything, and jump immediately to a memorandum of agreement (MOA) with the tribes, leaving the Advisory Council and SHPO out in the cold. The rationale, which I think was an excellent one, was that a great deal of money and time could be dumped into determining whether anything was "really" eligible within the project's area of potential effect and that much of this work could be taken as disrespectful to the tribes—who were, after all, saying that the area was culturally important even if they weren't willing to commit themselves to the "wheel." Rather than go to this kind of trouble and expense, GSA figured, let's just cut to the chase. So they did, executing an MOA with the fourteen tribes that found, among other things, that "rather than permit additional archaeological studies," it would be better to consider the federal land from the wheel on up into the foothills "special and sacred under the provisions and criteria of the American Indian Religious Freedom Act." The MOA provided for designing the project's buildings to minimize impact, for developing a management plan, and for granting the tribes an easement on the property, thus staving off future development and guaranteeing tribal access.[7] So the apparent conflict was resolved, and the effects of the project were taken into account, without ever deciding whether or not anything eligible was there.

I quibble with aspects of what GSA did; I think, for example, that the MOA could have been done as a regular Section 106 document, making everybody less vulnerable to criticism for playing fast and loose with the law. All that would have been needed was to persuade the SHPO and Advisory Council to go along. This might or might not have been hard; I don't know whether GSA tried. But this *is* a quibble. The Boulder case is an example of the lengths to which an agency will go to avoid seeking a formal determination of eligibility, and I think that on balance it was a sensible approach. It accomplished the purposes of Section 106, not only taking effects on (possible) historic properties into account but resolving them, and it did so in a way that kept the keeper (to say nothing, in this case, of the Advisory Council and SHPO) where the keeper has always been happiest—far from the trenches of Section 106 review.

Where it *is* necessary to go to the keeper, it's essential to provide her with as full a body of information as possible, but it's not helpful just to throw all available paper at her and let her sort through it. Organize the data; organize your arguments. The more you can make the data resemble a National Register nomination, the better the keeper is likely to like it. If there's some piece of standard register documentation that you can't supply, explain concisely but thoroughly *why* you can't supply it. And frame your arguments with specific reference to the National Register Criteria and pertinent register guidance, notably National Register Bulletin 15—the general guidelines for applying the eligibility criteria—and Bulletin 38. Where the property involved is an expansive landscape, Bulletin 30 on rural historic landscapes may be helpful, too, and depending on the type of property you're looking at, other bulletins may be relevant. Bear in mind, though, that the different bulletins were prepared by different people, with different professional backgrounds and views of the world, and the register has made little effort to achieve consistency among them. So, the more bulletins you use, the more inconsistencies and contradictions you may have to contend with. This can be a sort of interesting challenge, if you have nothing more useful to do with your time, but as a rule, the whole business of developing detailed eligibility documentation is a good thing to avoid. The only way to do that is to work out eligibility questions among the parties who really care about the place and whatever may affect it, without recourse to the keeper unless there's no way to avoid it.

Semantic Pitfalls

The processes under which TCPs are identified and considered in planning are bureaucratic processes, operated by bureaucrats. They use language in exotic ways, using acronyms (like *TCP* and *CRM*, for example) and giving special meanings to ordinary words (like *integrity*). It's important to understand what special meanings particular words and phrases may have for them. Miscommunication can have disastrous consequences.

A classic example of such miscommunication, and its consequences, is the case of the Kiks.adi Survival March Route "Trail" in Alaska.

In 1802, the Tlingit people of what is now the vicinity of Sitka drove the Russians out of Alaska, but in 1804 the Russians returned with warships and began bombarding the Tlingits' fortified village. After a seven-day battle the Tlingits were forced to flee to safety across what is now part of Tongass National Forest. The story of this epic trek has come down the generations as the tradition of the Kiks.adi Survival March. In modern times the march has been recreated several times by Sitka tribal members, and the story is important in the tribe's traditional history.[8]

In 1993 the National Forest embarked on planning for several timber sales. One of these, the Northeast Baranof Sale, would involve lands crossed by the traditional route of the Kiks.adi Survival March. The Sitka Tribe became concerned about the effects of the timber sale on the March route.

For reasons that have never been clear to me, the tribe decided (or perhaps was told) that it should nominate the March route to the National Register, in order to trigger Section 106 review of the timber sale. So, tribal members drafted a nomination package for what they called the "Kiks.adi Survival March Route Trail." They sent it to the SHPO for an informal review. The SHPO was dubious, and sent it to the keeper's staff for *their* informal opinion.

The response was negative. The register staff did not think the route was eligible as a trail because there were no wagon ruts or other marks of passage, as there are on trails like the Santa Fe, and no documented landmarks along the way as there are along the route of the Lewis and Clark expedition. Moreover, the keeper's people advised, the route wouldn't qualify as a TCP because there was no evidence of "continuing use. The tribe, and the authors of Bulletin 38, objected, pointing out that:

- to leave wagon ruts one needs wagons, which the fleeing Tlingit had not possessed;

- to document landmarks along the route, one needs literate personnel with the time and historical interest to document them, which the fleeing Tlingit had not possessed;

- considering the nature of the terrain, the Tlingit would not have marched single-file like good little Indians but would have spread out over the landscape to hunt and gather the food they needed as they traveled;

- the general course of the retreat was known through oral history at a level of accuracy sufficient to satisfy the tribe—in other words, the route was known well enough in the eyes of the tribe; and

- it was unreasonable to expect continuing use in the absence of continuing Russian bombardment; oddly enough, the Russians have not lately bombarded Alaska.

The register and SHPO predictably dug in their heels and did not deign to respond to the tribe or its supporters. The Forest Service apparently did make efforts to document the trail route but did so applying the standards laid down by the keeper's staff, and so naturally it did not succeed. The Forest Service determined that no historic properties would be affected by the sale, and proceeded.[9]

What could the tribe have done to avoid this outcome?

First, of course, they could have avoided doing the Forest Service's work for it. It wasn't the tribe's responsibility to nominate the route; it was the Forest Service's responsibility to determine its eligibility. The minute the tribe took on the agency's responsibility, it shifted the burden of proof to itself, and the minute it agreed to nominate the route, it committed itself to meeting irrelevant and misleading nomination standards that wouldn't have had to be met if it had been consulting with the Forest Service about eligibility.

But the particular point I want to highlight here is that the tribe used the fatal word *trail*. This instantly brought ruts and historically documented trail markers to the minds of the SHPO and National Register reviewers. Once these reviewers had gone on record with what they portrayed as the authoritative word about the nature of trails and TCPs, they were committed to their position and could in good bureaucratic conscience do nothing but stonewall the tribe's complaints. Had the tribe simply referred to the property as the Kiks.adi Survival March *Route* and categorized it as a landscape, they would have had a fighting chance of being understood.

So the lesson here—besides not to nominate—is to be careful about the words you use in describing a TCP. Think about the way reviewers are likely to use and understand words, and try to make sure it speaks to them in words that—to the extent possible—they can't misinterpret.

Using National Register Guidance

Bulletin 38 lays out (I like to think) a logical way of relating a TCP's significance to the arcane criteria and procedures used by the National Register. To whatever extent you have to document your conclusions about eligibility, it's a good idea to relate your argument to the guidelines in the bulletin.

The bulletin lays out a series of evaluative steps[10]; let's follow them through.

The TCP as "Property"

Bulletin 38 says that the first step is to "ensure that the entity under consideration is a property."[11] Some people dislike the word *property* because it implies to them something that can be possessed ("That ring of power is *my* property!").

That wasn't what we intended; we were simply trying to relate to the statutory definition of "historic property" in NHPA.

The "property" requirement means that the entity has to be physical; it can't be an intangible cultural resource like a dance form or a tradition per se. This is not to say that intangible characteristics aren't important—both in general and to the significance of historic places. Arguably, the significance of every historic property is "intangible" (What is "association," or "information," if not an intangible characteristic?). But to be eligible for the National Register of Historic *Places*, there has to be a *place* involved.

Bulletin 38 makes it clear that "districts, sites, and objects *do not have to be the products of, or contain, the work of human beings* in order to be classified as properties,"[12] but people continue to misinterpret the "property" requirement as one that demands the presence of human handiwork.

Another misinterpretation is that the "property" requirement somehow means that the place can't be too big. How *much* too big is anybody's guess, but it's irrelevant; the bulletin doesn't say the place has to be small.[13] The universe is a "property" in the sense of being made up (in part) of physical matter.

Judging integrity, the bulletin's second step, is complicated enough to require detailed discussion, a bit later, so let's go on to the third step.

Evaluation Using the National Register Criteria[14]

Most TCPs are found eligible under Criterion A, for association with events or patterns of events. These events or patterns don't have to be assignable to specifically definable time periods; they can refer to "traditional time"—the Aboriginal Australian's Dreamtime. "As long as the tradition (with which the place is associated) is rooted in the history of the group, and associates the property with traditional events, the association can be accepted."[15]

On the other hand, the bulletin insists that "association . . . must be documented through accepted means of historical research," going on to list various of kinds of research that may be appropriate. In most cases, you don't need to document the property's association in great detail; as we've noted, under the Section 106 regulations an agency and SHPO or THPO can agree to treat something as eligible on the basis of whatever documentation suits them. But if you're going to take a case to the keeper for a determination, such documentation *will* be demanded.

What about Criterion B—association with important people? According to Bulletin 38, *people* "can be taken to refer both to persons whose tangible, human existence in the past can be inferred on the basis of historical, ethnographic, or other research, or to 'persons' such as gods and demigods who feature in the traditions of a group."[16]

In other words, "history" as understood by Euro-American historians is not given precedence over traditional history. The fact that in the former the spirit being Tahquitz doesn't exist doesn't vitiate his association with Tahquitz Canyon in Cahuilla tradition.

The other criteria, C and D, sometimes apply to TCPs but are nowhere nearly as important or commonly applicable as the two above.

Applying the "Criteria Considerations"

This is the fourth and final step. The considerations are treated in some detail in the bulletin[17] because, taken on their face, some of them seem to make certain kinds of TCPs categorically ineligible. Notable among these is Criteria Consideration A, the "religious property exclusion," which we'll treat in chapter 12. Other often-tricky considerations are those dealing with cemeteries, commemorative properties, and properties achieving significance within the last fifty years. It's a good idea to familiarize yourself with the bulletin's discussion of each pertinent consideration and to frame arguments about the application of each with reference to what the bulletin has to say.

Interbulletin Conflict

Interbulletin conflict is something to be prepared for, as noted earlier. Bulletin 42 on mining properties, for example, is written entirely from the point of view of mining history, so if one were evaluating the Mark Gob Pile looking only at that bulletin, one would never think to consider its traditional cultural aspects. Bulletin 30 on rural historic landscapes requires that such landscapes "possess tangible features, called landscape characteristics, that have resulted from historic human use." This leaves districts made up of natural features hanging out to dry. Bulletin 30 does go on to reference Bulletin 38 as the source to use when addressing "natural areas that embody important cultural values but have experienced little modification."[18] Of course, many areas are both rural historic landscapes *and* TCPs.

Perhaps the trickiest interbulletin conflict is between Bulletin 38 and Bulletin 15, the register's general guidance on how to apply the National Register Criteria. One can construct arguments for or against almost anything's eligibility using Bulletin 15, and TCPs are no exception. With regard to religious properties, for example, at one point Bulletin 15 says that Criteria Consideration A applies if the property being evaluated "is used for religious purposes." This implies that such properties are not ordinarily eligible, though the wording of the discussion is so agonizingly twisted that it's hard to be sure. A few bullets later, though, we're told that a "religious" property can be eligible if it is "significantly associated with traditional cultural values." About the only thing that

Bulletin 15 is definite about on this point is that Criteria Consideration A applies if you check the "Religion" box in the "Significance" section of the register form.[19]

All this suggests that you need to be very careful about the words you use (think culture, not religion), and about which blocks you check on the nomination form if you use it. But the bottom line is this: If you have to develop a detailed argument for or against the eligibility of a TCP, you need to know and use Bulletin 38, but you also need to know Bulletin 15, and whatever other bulletins may apply to the kind or place you're dealing with, and be alert to inconsistencies that may trip you up.

Boundaries

Remember your own personal TCP, from chapter 1? Try to get it back into your head and think about what its boundaries are. Maybe it's easy—maybe your TCP is Grandma's kitchen, and the walls represent its boundaries. But did the kitchen have windows? Was the view outside important? If so, how far did it go? In the case of my TCP, The Hill, I suppose I can establish some kind of boundaries—the limits of my view while lying under my favorite scraggly live oak, maybe. But what am I, or what are you, defining boundaries *for?* My view from the live oak establishes visual boundaries, but what about auditory boundaries? Olfactory boundaries? Do these matter? Does it matter if a testing facility for emergency vehicle sirens or a raw sewage lagoon is put in just outside the boundaries of your TCP or mine? Do boundaries really matter?

Government-sponsored historic preservation in the United States, and indeed everywhere, through the good offices of the various colonial powers, has its roots in the European practice that the British call "scheduling." In the tradition of this practice, the government schedules, lists, or registers a place as an historical monument, and by doing so it commits itself to protecting the monument more or less absolutely, through legal prohibitions on its destruction, controls on its alteration, and financial arrangements to support its maintenance. In such a system, it is obviously necessary to establish the property's boundaries rather carefully.

When the National Historic Preservation Act—largely inspired by European models—was enacted, it contained a scheduling device—the National Register. Although the register in its early days was not very sticky about boundaries (or much of anything else), it soon fell in with its European progenitors. Clearly marked, justified boundaries became an essential part of every register nomination package.

When the register began doing determinations of eligibility in the early 1970s, it understandably took the position that such a determination should be supported by about the same level of documentation as a nomination. After all, if you need a given body of data to recognize a goose, surely you need the same to identify a gander. As part of this tendency toward equivalence, the register came routinely to insist on clearly defined boundaries whenever a property was submitted for an eligibility determination.

But determining a place eligible for the National Register serves a different purpose than does actually listing it. Listing is a formal action that conveys permanent status, at least in the eye of the beholder, and often in law. Determining a place eligible simply represents a judgment that for purposes of the action under review, the place appears to meet the National Register Criteria. Sometimes making this determination, or determining what effects an action may have on a place, requires considering boundaries; other times boundary definition is irrelevant—as it would be to me, and I suspect it would be to you, if Olympus Mons Development planned a sewage lagoon just outside the boundaries of our respective TCPs.

We're stuck with the National Register, however, and as a result, it's generally understood among people who do historic property documentation that such documentation must define boundaries.[20]

This leads to some pretty silly debates and unnecessary complications. Consider Mount Shasta.

Mount Shasta is a volcano in northern California, a beautiful, symmetrical mountain that can be seen for miles around. Every tribe whose members can see it (and some who can't) have stories about it; to many it's a very spiritual place, even a powerful living being.

In the late 1980s, the Forest Service was considering another of the ski facilities that naturally bedevil an agency whose lands tend to be in mountains. This one was on the slopes of Mount Shasta not far from a particular spiritual site known as Panther Meadows. The Forest Service initiated Section 106 review and opined that there were several eligible properties within the project's area of potential effects. One of these was Panther Meadow, but another, naturally enough, was the mountain itself.

In documenting its determination, the Forest Service felt compelled to specify boundaries for each eligible property. For the eligible part of the mountain, it set the boundary at timberline. Everything above timberline was eligible, it said, and everything below (except Panther Meadow and a few other specific locations) was not. Ridiculous, said the tribes. We don't make the timberline distinction; to us the whole mountain, from its tip to its toes, is the significant entity, so the whole mountain ought to be eligible.

The Forest Service could not bring itself to agree, so the matter went to the keeper. The keeper agreed with the tribes; the boundary should be set at the base of the mountain. Unfortunately, this boundary enclosed a good deal of private

Figure 8.3. Mount Shasta. Where's the boundary? Photo by the author.

property, and under a rather ill-considered provision of California law, a federal determination of eligibility triggers the imposition of some administrative burden on the owners of the eligible property. So the Mount Shasta property owners objected vociferously to the determination. Their congressman threatened legislation prohibiting the recognition of natural areas as eligible for the register—almost certainly an idle threat, by a relatively powerless congressman, but it doesn't take much political pressure to make the keeper squirm.

The keeper visited the mountain in the company of local interests and the Forest Service (but without visiting the tribes) and noted with astonishment and shock that large areas of the lower slopes had been logged and converted to plantation forest years ago. On the strength of this allegedly compromised integrity, the keeper reversed himself and found that the Forest Service's timberline boundary had been right all along. The tribes cried foul, pointing out that the keeper was violating National Register Bulletin 38's principle of judging integrity in the eyes of those who value the property. The keeper ignored them.[21] The Forest Service went on to review the proposed ski facility under Section 106 and NEPA and, to its great credit, in the end decided not to permit it.

Did it really matter where the Forest Service set the boundary? Yes, but not for the reason you might think. If the ski facility had not been proposed to extend above timberline,[22] you might think that using timberline as the boundary would relieve the Forest Service of the responsibility to consider effects under Section 106. But this is not true. The project's area of potential effects—considering visual, auditory, and perhaps other effects—would still include lands above timberline, as well as Panther Meadow, so limiting the boundary wouldn't kick the project out of the Section 106 process. Nor did it affect the way the Forest Service reviews the impacts of other projects on the mountain,[23] except—and here's the point—to make such reviews more complicated than they need to be.

Suppose the Forest Service recognized the whole mountain as eligible and then wanted to build a road on its slopes. Under Section 106, the Forest Service would need to consult with tribes and others and try to find ways to avoid or reduce impacts on the mountain's culturally important qualities. Having done so, and adopted such measures as it could via a Memorandum of Agreement or received the Advisory Council's comments, the Forest Service would decide what to do and do it. Three to four steps: determine effects, consult about how to resolve adverse effects, and then either execute and implement an MOA or obtain council comment and decide what to do.

In contrast, assume that the Forest Service did what it actually did—recognized only the slopes above timberline as eligible, together with Panther Meadows and a few other spots—and then proposed a road. Under Section 106, the Forest Service would first need to consult with tribes and others and identify and evaluate properties subject to impact. Considering that to the tribes the whole mountain actually *is* significant, the Forest Service would almost inevitably find itself with eligible properties even if its road went nowhere near timberline or any of the specific locations it identified as eligible back in the mid-1990s. Having identified such properties, the Forest Service would *then* be at the beginning of our previous scenario—ready to consult about effects and their mitigation. Four to five steps, or more, since identification and evaluation can become complicated.

So arguably—always assuming that the Forest Service follows the Section 106 regulations—the Forest Service folks have actually *complicated* their management of the mountain by failing to recognize the whole place as eligible. Rather than knowing in advance that it has an eligible entity subject to effect, it has to go out and check, each time it undertakes a project. Each such check involves consultation and, probably, wrangling over eligibility.

In addition, by arguing about eligibility the Forest Service extended the Section 106 review on the ski facility by a year or more, and generated antagonism on the part of the tribes. Meanwhile, the argument over eligibility enflamed the passions of the non-Indian community, leading to the political pressure that so troubled the keeper.

How could the Forest Service have avoided such consequences? It could have recognized that the mountain, *qua* mountain, is culturally important to the tribes (and others) and hence eligible for the National Register, and gotten on with its real job of considering the ski facility's impacts on it. This could have been done without involving the keeper, and then integrated into ongoing management of the mountain so that in subsequent project planning the mountain's significance would be automatically considered without renewed arguments about which of its particular bounded elements made it so. It wouldn't have even necessarily had to define very specific boundaries, or get involved in whether the private lands were included. It could have simply said, We'll assume the mountain is eligible, and treat it as such in the management of the lands under our jurisdiction.

Or consider Ocmulgee Old Fields, in Georgia. This site, or complex of sites, or cultural landscape, is associated with one of the four founding towns of the Muscogee Creek. Creek people today regard the site as the cradle of their nation. It runs for something like nine miles (as the crow flies) along the Muscogee River south of Macon and is anywhere from two to six miles wide—depending on whose argument you accept about boundaries. Portions of the site have been documented for years, but the significance of the whole landscape as a TCP became an issue when the Georgia Department of Transportation (DOT) proposed to construct a new highway through it.

Georgia DOT and the Federal Highway Administration (FHWA) consulted with the several Creek tribes and undertook archaeological and ethnographic studies to determine just what was eligible for the register. These studies, and hence highway planning, became bogged down in boundary questions. Where should the boundaries of this very expansive "site" or landscape be drawn? Which clay pits, factories, and developed roads should be excluded? Archaeologists made suggestions, the Creek Nation passed resolutions, the keeper was queried and gave advice; further studies were done by archaeologists, historians, and ethnographers.[24] The case is still a hotly contested one and at this writing has not been resolved.

The federal undertaking here is a highway—a long, skinny thing running across the river valley that makes up the Old Fields landscape. Several long skinny things, actually, since several alternatives are under consideration and most of them cross the Old Fields. But still, long skinny things whose areas of potential effects cannot possibly extend to all the boundaries of the site—no matter which boundaries you pick. It certainly appears, to me at least, that the contentious question of boundaries is largely irrelevant to the questions of what effects the various alternatives may have, and what can be done about them. So why are boundaries holding up planning? Apparently, because it was taken for granted that before one could determine effect one had to determine eligibility, and to determine eligibility one had to define boundaries, and so, we're off to the races.

There are situations where boundaries can and should be defined, but this is rarely the case with most kinds of TCPs. Often, as in the case of Mount Shasta and Ocmulgee Old Fields, boundaries simply don't matter, and in many cases they can't be defined in any meaningful way. What are the boundaries of Mount Sinai's cultural significance to Jews, Christians, and Muslims?

The basic question to ask about boundaries is, Do we need to define them in order to consider impacts? If we don't, there's no earthly reason to get involved in the complex, usually arbitrary, exercise of defining them. I think this rule applies to all sorts of historic properties, but it applies in spades to TCPs, whose boundaries can so often be established only by fiat.

If you *do* need to define boundaries, try to make sure they make sense both in cultural terms and in terms of management. Susan Buggey, writing about the problem from a Canadian perspective, points to national park and biosphere reserve zoning as a possible model, together with the methods used in very large protected areas like the Yellowstone to Yukon corridor and the Mesoamerican Biological Corridor.[25] Alan Downer and Alexa Roberts[26] suggest the use of ecosystem boundaries. These are good suggestions where they apply, but they're not formulae. I don't think there is any "right" way to define boundaries; the best approach depends on the place, its significant qualities, the administrative circumstances surrounding its consideration, the potential effects that are under review—the usual host of factors. But the key thing to think about, I believe, is whether it's necessary to define boundaries at all.

Integrity: In the Eye of the Beholder

In analyzing integrity, Bulletin 38 says we should address both "integrity of relationship" and "integrity of condition."[27] The former means that the group that values the place must perceive a relationship between the place and whatever tradition or traditional activity gives it significance; the latter that the property must not be so messed up physically that it no longer can fulfill its cultural purpose. Both kinds of integrity are supposed to be analyzed from the viewpoint of the group that ascribes significance to the property.[28]

The principle of viewing integrity of *relationship* through the eyes of those who value the property means that it's inappropriate to interpose some external standard on the relationship. If the community believes that the only place it can hold the annual owl ceremony is in Green Grove Gulch, it's not appropriate to dismiss the relationship between the ceremony and the gulch just because it seems to an outsider that they could perform the ceremony just as well on Pine Tree Peak. It may be entirely appropriate to discuss relocating the ceremony to Pine Tree Peak as a *mitigation measure* if Green Grove Gulch really must be used to dispose of nuclear waste, and such a relocation may turn out to be all right, but the fact that relocation might be a feasible mitigation measure doesn't mean that Green Grove Gulch lacks integrity of association with the owl ceremony.

What's sometimes harder for CRM practitioners to get their arms around is the notion that integrity of *condition* also must be judged through the eyes of those who value the place. The erstwhile keeper of the National Register illustrated the ease with which professionals can fall away from Bulletin 38's guidance when he decided—without even troubling to talk with the tribes—that everything on Mount Shasta below timberline had lost integrity because it had been logged and converted to plantation forest. The tribes didn't see logging as having compromised integrity; they might not have liked it much, but it didn't much change the way the mountain looked from a distance, and from a distance is the only way it can be seen in its entirety. In just the same way—and this one the keeper *did* get right—the fact that the land where the people of El Rancho, New Mexico, carry out their Matachines Dance had been graded for a parking lot didn't compromise its integrity, because as far as the dancers and their audiences were concerned, it only created a better dancing place.

A few years ago, there was a dramatic eruption of Kilauea Volcano on the Island of Hawaii, and the Waha'ula or "Red Mouth" Heiau—a temple associated with the volcano goddess Pele and for this reason and others[29] regarded as an important spiritual place—was engulfed by a lava flow. The temple—like all *heiaus*, made up of basalt walls, platforms, and enclosures—is now thoroughly entombed in hardened lava. At the time of the eruption, archaeologists and others quoted in the newspapers bemoaned the "destruction" of the heiau. When I've asked native Hawaiians about it, it's been pretty clear that they don't necessarily regard the site to have been destroyed (i.e., to have lost integrity). Some have even suggested that in being "taken back" by Pele it's *gained* integrity.

The Other Kind of Integrity

Historic properties are not the only things that can have or lack integrity. So can people—notably CRM practitioners. The NEPA regulations call for maintaining "the professional integrity, including scientific integrity, of . . . discussions and analyses,"[30] and the codes of ethics of virtually every CRM-related profession call for honest and honorable practice, but we don't always meet these standards very well.

The easiest kind of poor integrity to recognize and bemoan is that sometimes displayed by consultants for change agents who dismiss the importance of TCPs in order to advance the interests of their clients in damaging projects. But the opposite can be true, too; an advocate of preservation can become so convinced of the rightness of The Cause that it may seem justifiable to lie or to ascribe to people beliefs that they don't really have.

I experienced both kinds of problem a few years ago. In one case, the contractor for a project proponent conducted a TCP study in which he interviewed members of a tribe and was told of their spiritual beliefs about a water body, its surroundings, and its contents. He then concluded that these beliefs did not warrant treating the place as an eligible TCP because only "a handful" of people held them and the traditional culture of the area was in fact "dead." In another case, an ostensibly neutral contractor for a federal oversight agency failed to reveal her personal opposition to the project under review, and then organized her TCP study in such a way as to "demonstrate" an intractable, irremediable conflict between the project and the values of a tribe. In the first case, I was hired by the tribes opposing the project to conduct an independent review, but certainly with the expectation that I would poke holes in the proponent's study. In the latter case I was engaged by the project proponents to review the contractor's study. I had no trouble ascribing a lack of integrity to the authors of both the studies I reviewed, but this left me in an uncomfortable position. I was as much a hired gun as the other researchers, so what about *my* integrity?

We obviously have to reach conclusions, and we have to apply our best professional judgment when doing so. How do we do this honestly, without letting our biases or economics color our interpretations? Objective analysis of cultural phenomena is of course something that ethnographers are supposedly trained to do, so this may be an argument for the routine employment of ethnographers to conduct TCP studies. However, in one of the two cases I just summarized, the contractor *was* an ethnographer (the other was a historian), and the report the ethnographer produced was embarrassing in the transparency of its bias. So professional training does not seem to be the whole answer, though it probably helps.

I expect to struggle with this problem every time I undertake a TCP study (or probably any other kind of applied work). Thus far I've come up with only two techniques for dealing with it.

One is simply to be scrupulously honest with myself and with my client about what I think, just as soon as I have some idea what I *do* think. "I don't play golf, so I can't get very excited about the course you want to put in on the mesa where the tribe performs spirit quests, but I'll try to help you talk with the tribe about whether there are ways for the project to go forward without driving them crazy. No guarantees."

But how can I really be sure what I think about a project, or a place? How can I avoid deluding myself in order to justify getting paid to help a change agent, or to help an opposition group stop a project? The only way I've found to clarify my point of view—my second technique—is to undertake a thought

Figure 8.4. Jaeger Island, in the Hanford Reach on the Columbia River, has been churned up by artifact diggers and erosion, and arguably has lost archaeological integrity, but it is still an important ancestral place to the tribes of the area. Photo by the author.

experiment. I imagine that I'm advising "the other side." If I'm working for a tribe that doesn't want a mine to go in, I imagine myself working for the miners, and vice versa. Then I ask myself whether I'd tell my imaginary client the same thing I'm telling my real one. I don't expect myself to use the same words or not to couch what I say in terms my imaginary client can relate to, but I try to think honestly about whether I'd offer the same bottom-line advice. If I would, then I think I'm all right. If I wouldn't, then something's wrong and I need to reconsider what I'm doing.

This is not to say that I can't be an advocate for a particular group or point of view. For example, I've provided advice to the Bureau of Land Management and the Advisory Council as an advocate for the Quechan Tribe's opposition to the Glamis Imperial Mine—a proposed gold mine in the middle of the tribe's "trail of dreams" spiritual landscape. No two ways about it; I don't think the mine should be permitted. But having thought carefully about what I'd be saying to the mining company if I were advising them instead of BLM and the tribe, I'm certain that my distaste for the mine arises from its actual conflict with a real traditional cultural landscape about which Quechan people feel real, deeply meaningful concern. I'm not making up the importance of the landscape because I just don't like surface mines. In another case, I'm working for a change agent whose project is opposed by a tribe. Imagining myself advising the tribe, given the circumstances of the case and the places and issues involved, as the tribe has described them, I think I'd advise the tribe to make a deal, letting the project go forward in return for some negotiated version of the mitigation that's being offered by my actual client.

Am I kidding myself to think I can use thought experiments to cushion my professional integrity against the temptations served up by my need to make a living or the attractions of being a white knight? Maybe, but the use of thought experiments is the best technique I've come up with, and I recommend it. Or whatever else seems to work; whatever you can do to confront the subtle challenges that the rough-and-tumble world of CRM presents to your integrity. As in recovery from an addiction, the first step is to acknowledge the problem.

Doing It Right: Planning for MX Missile Deployment

At the end of the day, what I've recommended in this chapter and the one preceding it boils down to this: We can best identify TCPs and define the issues surrounding them by talking with people—openly, honestly, with sensitivity for their cultural values and feelings, and with as little attention as possible to the esoteric fine points of National Register eligibility. And often, the best "identification" is no explicit identification at all.

The classic example of how such anti-identification can work is the well-known, and now rather hoary, case of the U.S. Air Force's deployment of MX Missiles in Minuteman silos.

The air force, back in the 1980s, needed to deploy "Peacekeeper" (MX) Missiles—MIRVed ICBMs, in what now seems like nostalgic Cold War terminology—in silos designed to house the single-warhead Minuteman missile. The silos were distributed over a landscape controlled by Francis E. Warren Air Force Base in Wyoming.[31] The deployment would require an upgrade of command and control facilities, involving installation of new fiber-optic lines among the silos, control buildings, and so forth. The cables would be put in trenches, which would of course disturb the landscape.

The air force undertook preparation of an environmental assessment (EA) on the project under NEPA and soon learned that the landscape had cultural value in the eyes of nearby Cheyenne and Lakota groups. It comprised, or contained, what we would now call TCPs; there were rumors of burial sites and other more or less specific spiritually significant locations.

Had the Air Force done the kind of thing the Forest Service was doing at about the same time not too far away in Badger–Two Medicine, and would do years later at Las Huertas Canyon, it would have sent letters to the tribes asking them to send in maps of their TCPs. The tribes would have told the air force to bug off and then either suffered their losses in stony silence or begun writing nasty letters and dusting off their lawyers. But the air force did something much smarter.

It contracted with an intertribal group to help in consultation with the tribes. *Help*, not *do*; consultation with an Indian tribe is a government-to-government matter, but there's nothing to keep an agency from getting expert assistance. The group had good relations with the tribes and helped the air force find out what kind of consultation the tribal governments and their elders would like. The air force accommodated. A meeting of tribal officials, elders, air force officers, and representatives of the SHPO and Advisory Council was held in the field. A sweat lodge was constructed, and everyone had a purifying sweat. Food was shared, a pipe circulated, speeches were made, gifts exchanged, and then they got down to business.

I wasn't the Advisory Council's representative, unfortunately, but I understand that the conversation went like this:

AIR FORCE OFFICER (pointing at map): We need to run a fiber-optic line from this silo to that silo, right along here.

ELDER (after conversing with his colleagues): That's not a very good place.

AIR FORCE OFFICER: Well, what about if we ran it over here?

ELDER: Hmmm. Sorry, that's worse.

AIR FORCE OFFICER: Over here?

ELDER: Ah, that's better.

In the end, the consultation produced a map of routes to be followed that were acceptable to the tribes and their elders and that met the air force's needs. An MOA was drawn up specifying the routes to be followed, and that was that. Section 106 had been complied with, in a manner consistent with AIRFA, tribal sovereignty, the government-to-government relationship, and the federal government's trust responsibility to tribes, broadly construed—and nobody had to identify anything. Efficient for the air force, comfortable for and respectful toward the elders, and adverse effects on TCPs either avoided or at least managed in a way that the tribes could live with.

We can't always do what the air force did; not all projects are as flexible as rewiring missile silos. But we may be able to go a long way in the same direction, or in comparable directions using other strategies, if we can shake off the presumption that there's a standard way in which we must do identification and evaluation—indeed that we must always identify and evaluate in order to manage. We

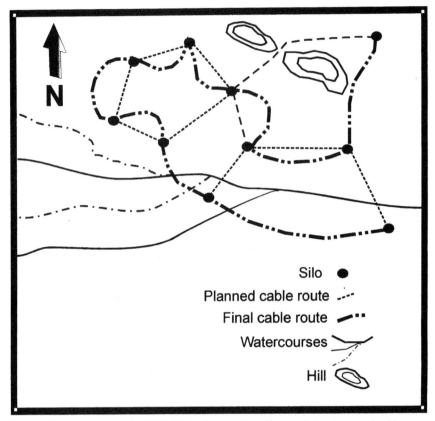

Figure 8.5. Schematic of the "MX Missile Solution." Landforms, silo locations, and cable routes are entirely fictitious but based on reality.

don't, and it may be the most efficient, respectful, culturally appropriate strategy to try not to.

The bottom line is management, of places and of impacts. Identification and evaluation are tools used to achieve the objective of careful, thoughtful management. If they're useful, they ought to be used; if they're not, they shouldn't.

Notes

1. 36 CFR 60; National Register n.d. 15, 16A, and 16B. Plus, of course, a host of specialized bulletins, including Bulletin 38.

2. See Scott Anfinson, National Register of Historic Places nomination for *Maka Yusota* ("Boiling Springs"), Savage, Minnesota (Minnesota Historical Society, St. Paul, 2002), for an example of a quite good TCP nomination.

3. Not its real name, of course; I keep the tribe anonymous to avoid offence and in hopes that it will change its mind and follow my advice.

4. See Ellen Prendergast, Perceptions of the National Register Nomination Process: A Case Study at *Chelhtenem*, Point Roberts, Washington, master's thesis, Western Washington University, 1998, for a classic example.

5. See Andrew Guilliford, *Sacred Objects and Sacred Places: Preserving Tribal Traditions* (University Press of Colorado, Boulder, 2000), 135–44; and Jack F. Trope, Existing Federal Law and the Protection of Sacred Sites: Possibilities and Limitations, *Cultural Survival* 19(4) (1995):30–35.

6. Michael J. Quigg, Charles D. Frederick, and Dorothy Lippert, *Archaeology and Native American Religion at the Leon River Medicine Wheel*, U.S. Army, Fort Hood, Archaeological Resource Management Series Research Report No. 33 (Fort Hood, Texas, 1996).

7. General Services Administration, Memorandum of Agreement between the U.S. Department of Commerce, the U.S. General Services Administration, and the Southern Ute, the Ute Mountain Ute, the Northern Ute, the Jicarilla Apache, the Apache of Oklahoma, the Kowa of Oklahoma, the Comanche of Oklahoma, the Cheyenne and Arapaho of Oklahoma, the Pawnee of Oklahoma, the Eastern Shoshone, the Northern Arapah, the Northern Cheyenne, the Oglala Sioux, and the Rosebud Sioux, regarding The Department of Commerce Campus, Boulder, Colorado (GSA, Denver, November 21, 1995).

8. See Nora M. Dauenhauer and Richard Dauenhauer, The Battle of Sitka, 1802 and 1804, from Tlingit, Russian, and Other Points of View, in R. A. Pierce (ed.), *Russia in North America: Proceedings of the 2nd International Conference on Russian America* (Limestone, Fairbanks, AK, 1990), for general historical context.

9. The tribe took the Forest to court in *Hoonah Indian Association v. Morrison* (170 F.3D 1223 [9th Cir. 1994]) and lost. In reading the decision of the Ninth Circuit Court of Appeals in the case, I was impressed with how poorly the tribe's attorneys appeared to have argued their client's NHPA case; they seemed much more knowledgeable about, and focused on, claims arising from the Alaska National Interest Lands Conservation Act. Notably, they like the Forest Service did not question the conclusions of the SHPO and keeper, which could have been readily, amusingly, and (I think) effectively assaulted.

10. J. C. Russell, C. M. Woods, and J. Underwood, *Imperial Sand Dunes as a Native American Cultural Landscape* (EDAW, Inc., for Bureau of Land Management California State Office, Sacramento, 2002), provide a very clean example of how to follow these steps, in their case concluding that the property evaluated is not eligible for the Register.

11. National Register, *Guidelines for Evaluating and Documenting Traditional Cultural Properties* (National Park Service, Washington, D.C., n.d. [sometimes (accurately) dated 1990]) 38:9.

12. National Register, n.d. 38:9.

13. See Thomas F. King, Stupid TCP Tricks, in *Thinking about Cultural Resource Management: Essays from the Edge* (AltaMira, Walnut Creek, CA, 2002), 129–33.

14. National Register, n.d. 38:11.

15. National Register, n.d. 38.

16. National Register, n.d. 38.

17. National Register, n.d. 38:12–15.

18. National Register, n.d. 30:2.

19. National Register, n.d. 15:25.

20. See National Register, n.d. 38:18–19, for discussion.

21. The keeper did resign his keeperhood, passing the mantle to his deputy, who had plausible deniability.

22. But in fact it did extend higher, leaving one to wonder what the Forest Service thought it accomplished by drawing the boundary where it did.

23. Assuming, of course, that the Forest Service carries out such reviews in accordance with law and regulation; I rather suspect that this may not be the case.

24. See Brockington and Associates, Inc. and Ethnoscience, Inc., National Register of Historic Places Determination of Eligibility (Draft), Ocmulgee Old Fields Traditional Cultural Property, ms., Georgia Department of Transportation, Atlanta, 1999.

25. Susan Buggey, *Approach to Aboriginal Cultural Landscapes* (Historic Sites and Monuments Board of Canada, Parks Canada, Ottawa, 1999), 31.

26. Alan S. Downer and Alexandra Roberts, Traditional Cultural Properties, Cultural Resources Management, and Environmental Planning, in P. L. Parker (ed.), *Traditional Cultural Properties: What You Do and How We Think, CRM* Special Issue (National Park Service, Washington, D.C., 1993), 14.

27. National Register n.d. 38:10.

28. National Register n.d. 38:10: "If the property is . . . regarded by a traditional cultural group as important in the retention or transmittal of a belief, or to the performance of a practice, the property can be taken to have an integral relationship with the belief or practice, and vice-versa"; and "(a) property may retain its traditional cultural significance even though it has been substantially modified."

29. Not least being its legendary association with the introduction of human sacrifice into ancient Hawaiian religious practice. See W. Bruce Masse, Laura A. Carter, and Gary F. Somers, Waha'ula Heiau: The Regional and Symbolic Context of Hawai'i Island's "Red Mouth" Temple, *Asian Perspectives* 30(1) (1991):19–56, for a detailed discussion of the site.

30. 40 CFR 1502.24.

31. F. E. Warren's missile fields are scattered over Wyoming, Nebraska, and Colorado.

Chapter Nine

Beyond Identification

Managing Effects

The idea that a person who may have a real interest in gaining access to an area of land is obliged to accept the bald assertion that it is a sacred site or face the prospect of prosecution is not one with which many people would live comfortably.

—Justice J. Maurice (1985:84–85, quoted in Ritchie 1994:232)

Determining Effects

SUPPOSE the Advisory Council on Historic Preservation wrote guidelines for managing impacts on TCPs. What might they look like?

They'd probably be built around the "Criteria of Adverse Effect" in the council's regulations; they'd talk about how to apply each "criterion" to TCPs. But that would only be part of the picture. Once you've established that there'll be adverse effects, you need to figure out what to do about them. So I imagine there would be two parts to the council's guidance. Let's consider what each might look like.

Applying the Core Criterion of Adverse Effect

Although Section 106 practitioners routinely talk about the "Criteria of Adverse Effect, there is really only one criterion. According to 36 CFR 800.5(a)(1), an action has an adverse effect if it "may alter, directly or indirectly, any of the characteristics of a historic property that qualify the property for inclusion in the National Register in a manner that would diminish the integrity of the property's location, design, setting, materials, workmanship, feeling, or association."

There are some commonly used shortcut ways of applying this criterion. One is to highlight the National Register criterion under which the property is eligible. If it's eligible under Criterion D, for example—that is, if it may contain data significant in history or prehistory—then it's an adverse effect if the action will muck up whatever it is that contains the data (e.g., the ground), and it's not an adverse effect if it won't. Of course, to use this method reliably, you need to be sure what makes the place eligible.

But TCPs are usually found eligible under Criterion A, for their association with "events that have made a significant contribution to the broad patterns of our history." How does a project alter characteristics of association? If we bulldozed Mount Vernon into the Potomac, would it no longer be associated with George Washington? It seems to me that the association would still be there, though the building wouldn't.

Evaluators usually get around this problem by focusing on integrity. If we bulldozed Mount Vernon, it would lose its integrity; hence bulldozing it would be an adverse effect.

So how might we alter the integrity of a TCP? Well, as usual, it depends on how the people who value the place perceive it. What do *they* see as the critical elements of its integrity; what do they think will alter that integrity?

Sometimes a community's perception of what is or is not an impact on integrity will differ markedly from an outsider's assumptions. Pat Parker once told me of going with a tribal elder to see the juniper tree through which the tribe believes its elders communicate with the spirit world above. The tree stands on a ridge overlooking the reservation center. Next to it, Parker was startled to see the satellite dish used by the tribe's television station. Was this proximity a problem, she asked, implicitly asking whether the presence of the dish compromised the integrity of the tree. The elder looked confused. Why would it be a problem? he asked; we communicate with the sky through the tree, and we communicate with the sky through the dish; they're really quite compatible.

Conversely, something that doesn't seem damaging to an outsider may be seen as a threat by a concerned community. When I was at the Advisory Council, a proposal was made to add an antenna to an existing array on top of Mount Diablo, a spiritual place in the eyes of several California Indian tribes. The antenna was to be used by a fundamentalist Christian television station. Some of the tribes saw this as a very significant impact because of the conflict they perceived between the station's message and that of the mountain's spirits.[1]

So one thing an Advisory Council version of Bulletin 38 might say is, you've got to consider whether a potential change constitutes an adverse effect in the eyes of those who value the property. It doesn't matter whether it looks like an adverse effect to *you;* the question is, does it look like an adverse effect to the people?

Another way to think about adverse effect in the eye of the beholder is to remember Bulletin 38's distinction between integrity of association and integrity of condition. An action may diminish one without diminishing the other, and this might influence the way one judged the adversity of the effect. Integrity of association exists entirely in the mind, while integrity of condition has a more "objective," external quality. In the case of the juniper and the satellite dish, one could argue that the dish diminished the integrity of condition of the site where the juniper grew but that this really didn't matter because its integrity of association wasn't compromised. Conversely, broadcasting Christian messages from the top of Mount Diablo arguably compromised the mountain's integrity of association with tribal cultural values, even though the effect of adding a tower to the already tower-littered mountaintop had little or no effect on its integrity of condition. One might argue, though I'm not sure I'd want to push the argument very far, that integrity of condition is really irrelevant where TCPs are involved—that integrity of association is everything, and the only thing to be considered when applying the core criterion of adverse effect.

Using the Examples

But most people, most of the time, don't work with the core "alteration of integrity" criterion. Instead they apply a series of examples set forth at 36 CFR 800.5(a)(2). These are colloquially referred to as the "criteria." How might each apply to impacts on a TCP?

"Physical Destruction of or Damage to All or Part of the Property"[2]

What destroys a TCP in the eyes of those who value it? It's hard to imagine a case in which bulldozing, flooding, or bombing it out of existence wouldn't do the job, though I suppose it's possible. But what else? Depending on the nature of the place, there are lots of possibilities.

Consider the China Lake Naval Weapons Center in southeastern California, where Paiute traditionalists believe that supernatural beings live in the U.S. Navy base's hot springs. When a geothermal project was planned in the area, the danger that it would cause the springs to dry up was taken to be an adverse effect under Section 106, because as far as the Paiute were concerned it would have destroyed the habitat of the springs' spirit inhabitants. Similarly, the Mattaponi and Pamunkey Tribes in Virginia believe that withdrawing water from the rivers in which they fish, and which they regard as having spiritual qualities, may destroy both the fishery and the rivers' spiritual qualities. The controversial Fence Lake Mine case in New Mexico involves similar issues. The Zuni and other tribes regard Zuni Salt Lake as the deity Salt Woman. They fear that developing a surface mine some twelve miles from the lake, and drawing water out of the underlying aquifer for dust control, will cause the lake to dry up, and as a result they have been fighting ferociously to halt the project, using Section 106 review as one of their weapons.

Note that the regulations don't say that the property has to be completely destroyed in order to be adversely affected; damage in whole or in part is sufficient. And there's nothing that says the damage has to be permanent. So a reservoir that floods a TCP adversely affects it because it damages it, even though someday the reservoir may be drawn down and the site may emerge from the muck. Similarly, drawing water out of an aquifer that feeds a culturally important lake, marsh, spring, or stream can be an adverse effect if it damages the character of the water body, even temporarily.

"Alteration . . . That Is Not Consistent with the Secretary's Standards for the Treatment of Historic Properties"[3]

"Alteration" can be a tricky example to apply to TCPs. The regulations provide that an alteration that's consistent with the pertinent standards of the secretary of the interior and their supporting guidelines is *not* an adverse effect, while an inconsistent alteration *is* adverse. But suppose the property in question is a neighborhood whose people have modified their homes and businesses to reflect their cultural values, in ways that *themselves* are inconsistent with the *Secretary's Standards.* Covered up all the ornate detailing on the facades, let's say, with a facing of formstone that reminds them of the stone-walled buildings where they grew up in the Outer Hebrides. Removing the formstone and restoring the facades, which if carefully done would meet the *Secretary's Standards* would probably have an adverse effect on the character of the neighborhood in the eyes of the Hebridean community. Conversely, leaving the formstone on and even adding more would *not* be an adverse effect in the community's eyes.

In fact, the *Secretary's Standards* are broad and flexible enough to accommodate this kind of thing; they articulate the principle that changes made to buildings in the course of their history may have achieved significance in their own right and should be respected. But this can be a hard notion for a mainstream historic preservationist to apply to something that he personally finds offensive, like formstone and vinyl siding. It's easy to conclude either that the modified buildings just aren't eligible in the first place—that they've lost integrity—or that keeping and expanding the formstone *has* to be an adverse effect. Conversely, removing the formstone may seem like a good thing to do, because it makes the buildings look more like they did in, say, 1879 when they were built. But the people of the community don't give a fig for the 1880s; they like their homes looking like Hebridean farmsteads.

Applying the *Secretary's Standards* in nonbuilding cases is still more challenging, but it has been done. After the Corps of Engineers gave up its plans to dam Tahquitz Canyon back in the late 1970s, the City of Palm Springs obtained a grant[4] from the National Park Service to purchase the canyon's mouth as an "archaeological park." The city then did nothing about the land for ten years or so, whereupon the Riverside County flood control agency proposed to—what a surprise!—build a flood control facility there. Scaled back considerably from the corps' proposal, but still hardly in keeping with what the Agua Caliente Cahuilla Band thought appropriate, so the tribe complained to NPS. NPS pointed to an obscure standard clause in its grant contract with the city, requiring the city to ensure that any changes to the canyon were consistent with the *Secretary's Standards.* This would have been virtually impossible for the city to do. The city probably could have refunded the grant to NPS and been in the clear, but it would have been costly and looked bad in the press, so NPS's position gave a good deal of added authority to the tribe and its allies (NPS, the SHPO, the Advisory Council) in negotiating a memorandum of agreement under Section 106. In the end, flood control facilities were constructed, but with the tribe effectively specifying how they would be constructed and what they would look like.

"Removal of the Property from Its Historic Setting"[5]

This example is as straightforward in its application to TCPs as to any other kind of historic property. If the property involved isn't inherently movable like a canoe or a fishing boat, then moving it away from its native place is an adverse effect. Again, though, we have to consider whether such removal is seen by the community as adverse. Suppose the community is one that generations ago was relocated from its traditional lands to some other part of the country, and there's something "back home"—a big rock, let's say, or a community meeting place—that's really important to the group. It might—and I stress *might*—be seen as a positive, not adverse, effect to pick up the rock or meeting place and move it to where the group now lives. The thing might continue to have integrity of association—even improved integrity— despite its compromised integrity of condition, and the latter might not be regarded as important. I have trouble envisioning such a situation, but it's conceivable.

"Change in the Character of the Property's Use"[6]

Change in use can be a huge issue with respect to TCPs. If a project blocks access to a place, makes it unusable for traditional purposes, or if it causes a traditional use to be abandoned, that's an adverse effect, and often a very serious one. Consider the following two examples, of many that could be cited.

A Navajo traditional chanter once told a Navajo Nation TCP survey team about a source of medicine that lay at some distance from his home. He reported with regret that he couldn't use the source any more. When asked why not, he asked them whether they knew about the transmission line that had been constructed in the vicinity some time before. He couldn't cross under the power line to gather the medicine or bring it back, he said, because the power of the transmission line was incompatible with the spiritual power of the medicine. The power line was nowhere near the medicine source (or the chanter's hogan), but its construction had altered the site's use and therefore was an adverse effect.[7]

When the General Services Administration planned an expansion of court facilities in the old federal courthouse and post office in San Juan, Puerto Rico, an elegant restoration of the building was proposed. The building had suffered from slipshod and ill-considered "improvements" over the years; these would be corrected, and the courthouse returned to its original glory. The Postal Service would remove its facilities—a positive thing because it would reduce traffic congestion around the building. The Puerto Rico SHPO and local interests objected mightily, however, because the postal boxes in the building had made it a community meeting place for generations. Removing the Postal Service, even though it would result in no physical change (the boxes would be left in place; they just wouldn't be serviced), would alter the traditional use of the building, and hence was an adverse effect in the eyes of its traditional users.[8]

"Change in the Character . . . of Physical Features within the Property's Setting That Contribute to Its Historic Significance"[9]

Figure 9.1 shows the view (in about 1980) from the Helkau Historic District on the Six Rivers National Forest in California. The clear-cut blocks are far, far outside the prescribed boundaries of the National Register–eligible district, but the trees that grow there are clearly physical features of the district's setting. Cutting them down has pretty obviously changed their character, as well as the character of the once-wooded ridges on which they stood—at least temporarily.

But does the natural landscape of the setting contribute to the district's "historic significance"? I don't know, but the Helkau is a place where people go to communicate with the spirit world, to get visions.

Surely what one sees from a vision quest site is relevant to the site's significance. I would certainly think so, but it would be dangerous for me to assume it; I'd need to ask the people who seek spiritual communication in the district. And of course I'd need to be careful about what I asked them, to avoid prejudicing the answer. If I asked, "Does that clear-cutting mess up your vision questing?" the answer would very likely be yes, whether or not anybody had ever before perceived it as doing so. Perhaps instead, I'd ask whether there was anything especially important about the view from the district and see whether any-

Figure 9.1. Clearcutting in the viewshed of the Helkau Historic District. The photographer is standing in the visual APE of these projects. Photo by Loretta Neumann.

one volunteered that looking at a pristine environment was important, *and* that this importance had been diminished by the logging.

"Introduction of Visual, Atmospheric, or Audible Elements That Diminish the Integrity of the Property's Significant Historic Features"[10]

The clear-cuts in the viewshed illustrate this "criterion" just as they do "alteration of setting," but other, nonvisual impacts can also exemplify it. If natural quiet is an important characteristic, then the introduction of noise into the property's auditory environment can be a problem. Noise is an issue in consultation about the effects of geothermal development on the Medicine Lake Highlands in northeastern California—the geothermal plants would make noise, and the quiet of the highlands is important to those who seek out its spiritual qualities. Air tour operations and military overflights are other examples. FAA and the Hualapai have spent a good deal of time wrangling over how many decibels of increase over ambient noise levels are acceptable results of air tour operations over the Hualapais' cultural landscape. I once heard a Paiute tribal leader describe in vivid terms what it was like to be praying on a spiritual site when an F-16 from a nearby air base popped up out of a canyon on a terrain-hugging strafing run. A heart-stopping experience, he commented dryly.

Altitude is an interesting problem with aerial overflights. How close to the ground must the aircraft travel in order to have an adverse effect? To the

Euro-American eye or ear, there is no adverse effect if the thing is too high to see or hear,[11] but an indigenous group may feel otherwise. The Hualapai view the airspace above their spiritual landscape as part of the spirit world, so the passage of aircraft through it is a problem, regardless of whether people can see or hear anything. The people of Taos Pueblo have taken a similar position with respect to flights over their Blue Lake. This illustrates an important general point: many indigenous groups feel that they—and all humans—are responsible for respecting and maintaining the health of the universe or of the spirit world. Impacts on these worlds can occur without humans being aware of them, but it is the responsibility of humans to try to keep them from happening or to take the necessary ritual steps to compensate or seek forgiveness when they do happen.

Atmospheric impacts have not often been an issue—to my knowledge, at least—in TCP cases, but it's easy to imagine how they could be. In the Micronesian islands of Chuuk, people are very sensitive about bad smells and very appreciative of good ones. An action that introduced the former, or diminished the latter, would undoubtedly be seen as an adverse effect. Diminution of air quality in a culturally important viewshed could also be seen as adverse. The health hazards resulting from air pollution in urban neighborhoods often fall disproportionately on low-income and minority populations, making them environmental justice concerns; they could also be adverse effects on TCP neighborhoods.

"Neglect of a Property Which Causes Its Deterioration"[12]

"Demolition by neglect" has seldom been cited as an issue in cases that explicitly involved TCPs, but implicitly it's another matter. For example, one of the most notorious demolition by neglect cases concerns the Forest Glen Seminary, a strange and wonderful collection of exotic buildings in a Maryland suburb of the District of Columbia. Forest Glen is controlled and has been disgracefully neglected by the U.S. Army. The seminary has never to my knowledge been discussed as a TCP, but the very fact that it is a local community group that treasures the place for the ambience it gives the neighborhood[13] suggests that it could be so regarded. Destruction by neglect is something that traditional communities might do well to think about. Many places described as "archaeological sites," for example, might be given a higher level of protection by land management agencies if their neglect were seen as destroying their traditional cultural value as well as their significance to archaeologists.

This example of adverse effect in the regulation includes—or excludes—an interesting exception, carved out specifically to accommodate indigenous cultural groups: "except where such neglect and deterioration are recognized qualities of a property of religious and cultural significance to an Indian tribe or native Hawaiian organization."[14]

So if the tribe thinks that the right thing to do with the ancestors is to let them return to Mother Earth, it's not an adverse effect to let them deteriorate. Arguably, it *would* be an adverse effect from the standpoint of archaeologists and physical anthropologists, but this apparently doesn't matter; it would appear that the regulations are set up so that traditional cultural values trump scientific values. No doubt this establishment of priorities will eventually be challenged in court, with unpredictable results. For the moment, however, if deterioration is OK with the group that values the place, it's not an adverse effect—provided the group is an Indian tribe or native Hawaiian group, and provided the place is important for religious and cultural reasons.

"Transfer, Lease, or Sale of Property Out of Federal Ownership or Control without Adequate and Legally Enforceable Restrictions or Conditions to Ensure Long-term Preservation of the Property's Historic Significance"[15]

This is another example of adverse effect that has not been much of an issue in connection with TCPs, but that certainly could be. Consider two examples—one hypothetical, the other real.

Imagine that a military base has been closed and is up for transfer to the private sector. Suppose there are places on the base where indigenous medicine people or basket makers gather plants. Such places could well be eligible TCPs, and it could be an adverse effect to transfer them out of federal ownership without deed restrictions to ensure—to the extent anything can be ensured—that the plants would be protected and the people would have continuing access.

The real-world case that comes to mind is that of the Valley of the Chiefs, or Weatherman Draw, in Montana. Here, as in thousands of other cases, the Bureau of Land Management years ago leased mineral rights without Section 106 review. BLM's rationale, which is enshrined in policy and an ancient Programmatic Agreement with the Advisory Council,[16] is that after all, the lease by itself didn't authorize the lessee to do anything that might disturb the area. BLM would have another bite at the apple when it came time to issue a permit to drill or otherwise dig into the ground.

Note the archaeological bias here; it's assumed that digging in the ground is the issue. Moreover, it's implicitly assumed that whatever impacts the digging will cause can be mitigated in some not-too-difficult way, as through archaeological salvage. BLM would never admit to this assumption, but it has to be there. Otherwise, it would be obvious to BLM that by encouraging a lessee to invest in a piece of land, with the expectation that its exploitation would be feasible, it is setting up a situation in which expensive, difficult conflicts are inevitable.

This is what happened at Weatherman Draw. The Anschutz Exploration Corporation proposed to undertake exploratory drilling in an area to whose minerals it had a lease right. BLM undertook NEPA and Section 106 review, and discovered to its embarrassment that the area was, in effect, a complex of TCPs of spiritual importance to the Blackfeet, Cheyenne, and Crow. The tribes sought to stop the drilling. The SHPO said there was clearly an adverse effect. The Environmental Protection Agency weighed in with environmental justice concerns.[17] Anschutz, of course, cried foul; it had its lease, it had invested in the project; why hadn't BLM told it about this cultural resource problem up-front?

Clearly, BLM had an adverse effect on the Valley of the Chiefs as a TCP when it leased the mineral estate without imposing restrictions to protect the cultural integrity of the surface estate.[18] What might those restrictions have been? I don't know, but they should have been the subjects of Section 106 consultation. One thing is certain: Merely providing for archaeological data recovery or the physical protection of particular sites, which the logic of BLM policy offers as the only practical management measures, would not have been adequate to protect the valley's traditional cultural values, as these values were and are understood by the Blackfeet, Cheyenne, and Crow.

Adverse Effect is in the Eye of the Affected

So, the main thing to remember in applying the "criteria of adverse effect"—both the core criterion and the examples commonly referred to as the "criteria"—is to apply them from the perspective of those who value the property. Unfortunately, the core criterion—whether the action may diminish the integrity of whatever makes the place eligible for the National Register—can tempt CRM practitioners into precious professional pedantry. One can ponder at great and self-satisfying length which National Register criterion applies, what it is about the place that contributes to its eligibility, and precisely what gives each contributing element its integrity or nonintegrity. Such nit-picking glazes over the eyes and tests the patience of change agents and place protectors alike.

The same technique that can save TCP evaluation from irrelevance can keep us from miring determinations of adverse effect in academic hairsplitting. Just as we can accept a place as eligible if somebody holds it dear, we can assume that it's adversely affected if those who hold it dear think it is. Even though to ostensibly objective outsider eyes there seems to be no potential for adverse effect, if people think there will be such an effect then there's a cultural problem to deal with. This shouldn't be swept under the rug; it ought to be managed.

"But wait," I hear some reader asking who knows NEPA case law; "what about PANE?" In *Metropolitan Edison Co. v. People against Nuclear Energy*,[19] back in 1983, my reader protests, the Supreme Court found that beliefs, unsubstantiated by science, have no place in environmental review. People against Nuclear Energy (PANE) argued that AEC needed to do an Environmental Impact Statement on restarting the Three Mile Island Nuclear Plant in Pennsylvania because people in the area feared a meltdown. The Court found that without some associated impact on the tangible environment, purported psychological and social effects were not enough to require preparation of an EIS.

Which is the answer to my critical reader. The PANE threshold, if you'll excuse the pun, doesn't affect *consideration under NEPA* but *preparation of an environmental impact statement (EIS)*. The court didn't say that people's beliefs and fears don't deserve consideration under NEPA; it said that by themselves they were not enough to force preparation of an EIS. The PANE decision, as I read it, does not discourage agencies from trying to address people's beliefs, even when scientific analysis gives them no support. People's beliefs about the environment and what may affect it should be considered in screening categorical exclusions and in preparing environmental assessments, and in EISs when they're done. But perceptions alone, in the absence of effects for which there's scientific support, aren't enough to cause an EIS to be prepared. And in making a decision about an action that people believe will have beliefs, it seems to me that if the decision-making agency isn't going to be guided by these beliefs, NEPA demands that it either show that the beliefs really are unfounded, or acknowledge that it is going against them and show that there are overriding public interest reasons for doing so. And it ought to adopt such mitigation measures as it can to assuage the concerns that it has decided not to heed.

What to Do about Adverse Effects

We determine effects, of course, in order to figure out whether and how to mitigate them. How do we approach mitigation in the case of a TCP?

Can Impacts on TCPs Be Mitigated?

Is it even possible to mitigate adverse effects on TCPs? At least where spiritual places are involved, many Indian tribes say no. For instance:

> Mitigation of impact, a common way of dealing with historic properties, is often not an option for traditional cultural properties. The only known culturally acceptable way to mitigate impact . . . is not to have any impact at all by avoiding the property.[20]

This statement would be funny if it weren't so sad. Tribes who take the "can't mitigate, must avoid" position have bought into an archaeological view of what mitigation is all about. To many archaeologists, "mitigation" means archaeological data recovery, and physical avoidance of an archaeological site doesn't have "any impact at all." But does "avoiding the property" avoid visual, auditory, atmospheric, or other not quite direct physical effects on it? Of course not. If you build the road fifty feet from a traditional prayer site, the fact that you've avoided the *site* won't necessarily mean that you've avoided the *effects* of traffic noise and pollution on those praying.

When a traditional community buys into the standard archaeological definition of impact avoidance, it's misleading agencies into thinking that physical avoidance will automatically satisfy the community. It's putting itself in a position where an agency may avoid physical effects only and then say, "Look, it's what you *told* us was acceptable."

"Mitigation" does not equal "dig up" in any but archaeological parlance. The NEPA regulations define the term as follows:

> "Mitigation" includes:
> (a) Avoiding the impact altogether . . . ;
> (b) Minimizing impacts by limiting the degree or magnitude of the action . . . ;
> (c) Rectifying the impact by repairing, rehabilitating, or restoring the affected environment;
> (d) Reducing or eliminating the impact over time by preservation and maintenance operations . . . ;
> (e) Compensating for the impact by replacing or providing substitute resources or environments.[21]

So "avoidance"—of *impact,* not just of *place*—is a *form of mitigation,* and so are lots of other things besides archaeological excavation. Tahquitz Canyon is an example of how a number of mitigation approaches can be applied to TCPs.

At Tahquitz, after lengthy consultation about the county flood control agency's scaled-down facility, an MOA was worked out among the tribe, NPS, the SHPO, and the Advisory Council. It didn't avoid impacts altogether but did provide for the following:

- *Minimizing* impacts by lowering the height of the dam, increasing its base thickness, and planting it in native vegetation so that it blended into the landscape, and by naturalizing the flood channel and routing it to avoid physical impact on identified living, burial, rock art, and other sites (though not all of them);

- *Rectifying* the impact by funding the tribe's extensive archaeological study of all the sites that did have to be damaged, coupled with a detailed ethnohistoric and ethnobotanical study;

Figure 9.2. Tahquitz Canyon: detail of dam and channel immediately after construction. Photo by the author.

- *Compensating* for the impact through the archaeological and ethnographic work, by committing a substantial sum to the tribe's development of a cultural and curation center and by transferring all land in the canyon not actually occupied by flood control facilities to the tribe, to be brought into trust and added to the reservation.[22]

The MOA didn't satisfy everyone; some tribal members would have been much happier stopping the project altogether. This might have been possible, but more likely the city would have refunded its grant money to NPS, significantly reducing the leverage that the tribe had in Section 106 review.[23] As in most cases, the MOA represented a compromise—the best that the tribe could get under the circumstances. On balance, in this imperfect world, I'd say it was pretty good.

Another example of mitigation through compromise, also from California and much more recent, is the case of the Medicine Lake Highlands. Here two geothermal energy leases threatened the spiritual landscape. After consultation with concerned tribes, the Bureau of Land Management and Forest Service denied their permit for the operation that would have had the worst effects and permitted the one that would do less damage, at the same time committing themselves to developing a long-term management plan for the highlands. Here again the traditional tribal interests were not entirely satisfied (and did not sign the MOA), but I believe (as one who helped broker the deal) that on balance, given the situation, it was the best politically feasible solution to the conflict.[24]

A negotiated solution to conflicts between construction of Chuuk International Airport in Micronesia and the protection of Mount Tonaachaw involved redesigning dredge areas on the reef at the mountain's feet to minimize impacts on traditional fishing and shellfishing areas and funding a fishing and farming cooperative to help compensate for the loss of such areas that couldn't be avoided.[25] In the case of air tour overflights of the Hualapai spiritual landscape, FAA negotiated an agreement with the tribe prescribing routes that keep air tours as far as possible away from those portions of the landscape most used by traditional practitioners for spiritual purposes. In a case involving logging by a tribal timber program on tribal lands (handled internally by the tribe), mitigation took the form of mediation by the THPO between the timber program and the traditionalists who ascribed value to particular trees and groves. The THPO worked with the traditionalists to identify areas of concern and the kinds of logging operations that would be problematic and with both parties to set up a way for the logging to be as compatible as possible with the area's spiritual qualities.

What about an effect that's perceived (or feared) by a community but that science "shows" won't occur? In discussing the PANE decision earlier, I suggested that if the project decision was going to go against the beliefs of the community in such a case, mitigation ought to be provided. How do you mitigate an effect that's in the mind?

Sometimes, of course, you can't, and the decision maker is just going to have to say so. But sometimes there are measures that can be put in place. In one case I've worked on, for example, Indian tribes believe that drawing water out of a river will permit seawater to intrude up the river and impact its fish population. Science—or at least, the project proponent's science—says it won't happen. One of the mitigation measures set forth in an MOA proposed by the proponent is monitoring by the tribes or people acceptable to the tribes; if it turns out that the salt water is creeping up the river, the proponents would commit themselves to stop drawing water out. An acceptable measure? I don't know; consultation is in abeyance so we don't know what, if anything, can be worked out, but it's an example of the kind of thing that can at least be considered as a way of assuaging fears about scientifically unverified effects. I hasten to acknowledge that I have no idea how to mitigate a purely spiritual effect.

Deciding on Mitigation

There are no formulas for managing impacts on TCPs; everything is negotiable. But just saying "negotiate" and leaving it at that is a chicken way out. Surely there's something we can say about how to reach a negotiated resolution—some rules of thumb to be offered. And of course, there are such rules, most of them familiar to CRM practitioners of every stripe.

Start Early

Every environmental review guideline urges managers to start early in considering the impacts of a proposed action, but agencies continue to ignore this advice. Not explicitly, of course, but tacitly, by simply not thinking about potential problems until too late or by talking themselves into thinking that such consideration can be put off.

Weatherman Draw is a classic example of the bitter fruits of failure to start early—a cautionary tale illustrating that that one should start thinking about how to manage TCPs as soon as anybody starts talking about changing the way a piece of land is used. For the most practical of reasons—that in the long run it will cost money to delay and defer—agencies and other change agents should start dealing with TCPs at the very beginning of any land use planning process. Weatherman Draw seems to have worked out for the best—in the end the Anschutz Exploration Company agreed to walk away from the project, donating its rights to the National Trust for Historic Preservation, which will hold them until they expire while BLM identifies the area as unsuitable for future exploitation. But if BLM had started talking with the tribe much, much earlier than it did, a solution could have almost certainly been achieved with a lot less waste of time, money, and anguish on all sides.

Joseph Winter, in a 1993 paper on the Transwestern Pipeline,[26] provides a good example of how spiritually significant places on the Navajo reservation were identified, and effects on them minimized through project relocation and design. The key to success was early and effective consultation with knowledgeable Navajo people, notably medicine men. Winter also describes a case in which impacts could not be avoided but were mitigated in a manner that doubtless surprised Transwestern's project planners.

The pipeline was to pass through Schultz Pass in the San Francisco Peaks; these peaks, as you'll recall, are a tremendously important place in Navajo cosmology. There was apparently no practical way to route the pipeline elsewhere. In consultation with anthropologist Orit Tamir, Navajo medicine men decided that conducting a Blessingway ceremony might restore harmony to the mountain "as long as the Northwestern Pipeline Company was sincere in its efforts to restore balance by carrying out all of the proper formulae in approaching the medicine man (who would conduct the ceremony) and following all the prescriptions required." As a result, "A prominent medicine man who lived near the peaks and used them was willing to perform the ceremony. A representative of the pipeline company approached him in the proper manner and agreed to the necessary prescriptions. The ceremony was conducted in September of 1991. The pipeline was built through Shultz Pass shortly thereafter."

Winter emphasizes that the mitigation was not complete, nor to everyone's satisfaction. He quotes an unpublished work by anthropologist Klara Kelley that describes the conduct of the ceremony as, in the eyes of the Navajo participants, making "the best of a bad business."[27]

Ask—Carefully

To find out whether people perceive an adverse effect, of course you have to ask them. Asking about effects may be easier than asking about the places themselves. A person may have difficulty articulating why a place is important to her community or be impeded or even prevented from doing so by cultural barriers but perfectly able to talk about her reactions to a proposed change. In the Las Huertas Canyon case, the people of Sandia Pueblo weren't about to tell the Forest Service where all the TCPs were and why they were significant, but they were able to express their concern about alterations that might happen in the canyon. The elders consulted by the Air Force on the MX Missile deployment would probably have had a very hard time explaining what was spiritual about the landscape around the silos, but they could react to proposals for fiber-optic lines in specific locations.

But asking or answering questions about effects is seldom easy. When proposed airport construction in Yap threatened a collection of tombs, I asked the local community what they thought about the matter and whether excavating and reburying the people interred in the tombs might mitigate the impact. There was virtually no response; the idea of disturbing the graves was so outrageous that the people couldn't relate to it.

Actually, the Yap case illustrates a couple of points concerning how and why to consult about impacts on TCPs. As for the "how," I somehow stumbled into the practice of not asking directly about impacts but asking instead about mitigation. Had I asked the community if it would be a bad thing to bulldoze the tombs, there's little question not only that they would have said, "Of course, stupid," but that they would have been outraged. When I asked whether excavation and reburial would be the right things to do *if* it became necessary to build the airport on the site—asking this in the context of negotiations with the government about how the project might be designed to minimize tomb destruction—I avoided looking like an idiot and everyone was able to discuss the matter calmly. The community never actually said that it was all right to destroy the tombs that couldn't be avoided, provided their remains were excavated and reburied, but they tacitly acquiesced. We effectively reached agreement on a program that allowed the project to go forward while respecting the concerns of the community.

And the "why"? The Yap case was one in which the local community threatened litigation to halt the project. The litigation didn't happen, and I think an important reason for this was that the government negotiated in good faith with the community about how to minimize impacts on what the community valued. Even though we did not reach an agreement that the community was willing or even psychologically able to sign, the community couldn't say that the government hadn't tried, or hadn't respected its concerns. Had the government done otherwise—had it, for example, treated the tombs simply as archaeological sites and done data recovery without consultation—the case would certainly have wound up in court and the project might never have been built. I have mixed feelings about the need for and impacts of a modern airport in Yap, but that's not the point. The government felt that the airport was needed, and it was able to move the project forward with relative efficiency because we sat down with the community and sought ways to resolve its concerns.

Of course, the community didn't articulate its concerns as having to do with adverse effects on a TCP; they were concerns about respect for the ancestors. When I say one needs to ask "carefully" about adverse effects, I mean that one should ask in ways that make sense to the people. As with questions about the presence and significance of TCPs, it's usually best to jump over the fine points of regulatory process and get to the real-world issues. If the airport has to be built here, what can we do to respect the ancestors? We know you'd rather the airport *weren't* built here, and we're looking at alternatives (assuming we are—an important reason to consult early in planning), but if it turns out this is the best place to build it . . . .

In other words, try to put yourself in the shoes of the community and address their likely concerns as simply, straightforwardly, and directly as possible; don't be hung up on following the steps of the Section 106 process in rigid succession, and try to avoid using abstractions and jargon like "National Register eligibility" and "adverse effect." The relevant questions are, Do you have a problem with this proposal, and, if so, what can we do about it?

Forecasting Mitigation Options: Property Attributes as Clues

While the way to manage impacts on a TCP ultimately depends on the subjective beliefs of the community, you may get some early notion of what will and will not work by considering the likely attributes of the place you're dealing with. There is no particular magic in the attribute list presented in chapter 7, but we can use it to illustrate how TCPs with different characteristics may require different kinds of management.

Places perceived to have *spiritual energy*—spiritually energetic or power places—are likely to be associated with power that is both esoteric and thought to be dangerous. A manager's options for mitigating adverse effects on such places may be seen as very limited, even laughable. It's not uncommon for traditionalists simply to shake their heads over proposals to build something on or through or over or near such a place. "They want to do *that?* Those people really *are* stupid." There's sometimes the belief that the place will take care of itself, probably at the expense of those who violate its power, but it's often also feared that the place will visit its wrath on those charged with protecting it, or on the community or the world as a whole.

In his 1994 article on the Blackfoot spiritual mountain Ninaistàkis, for example, Brian Reeves identified an old oil well road on the Blackfoot reservation as a major source of tourism conflicts with the mountain's spiritual character and the values of its Blackfoot religious practitioners. In a postscript he reports that a major earthquake had shaken the mountain, causing the largest mudslide in a thousand years. "Blackfoot Elders are of the opinion that this event was the result of inappropriate Native and non-Native activities taking place at Ninaistàkis. The Blackfeet closed the area to all hikers and non-traditional users."[28]

In the Ninaistàkis case, the Blackfeet controlled the routes to the mountain and were able to close them to avoid angering its spirits further. Where (as usual) the concerned community does *not* control the situation, its traditionalists may warn those in control about the bad things that will happen if they don't do right, but beyond this they may simply shrug their shoulders and say, "They'll find out." Or they may quietly do what they can to assuage the spirits, with prayers and offerings and meditation. Either way, they will likely bear the emotional burden of having, in their eyes, failed to keep faith with the place, failed in their responsibilities as the interface between this world and the spirit world. Places thought to have the attribute of spiritual power can present intractable mitigation problems. On the other hand, spiritually powerful places may be amenable to forms of management and mitigation that most of us would never think of. Winter's Transwestern Pipeline case is a good example.[29]

Where *practice* is an important attribute, there may be more flexibility in the form of mitigation chosen. Years ago at Warm Springs Dam in northern California, the Corps of Engineers helped Pomo basket makers and traditional doctors relocate important basketry and medicinal plants out of the reservoir area and get them started in new gardens—a sort of compensatory mitigation.

Sometimes impacts on a practice place can be made up for through some seemingly unrelated form of compensation—particularly where it looks like the practice is going to be lost no matter what happens. In one case, a tribe facing impacts on a practice place agreed to mitigation in the form of a financial contribution to cultural programming on its radio station.[30]

Where the practice has place-specific spiritual overtones, of course, such compensatory mitigation may be unacceptable or irrelevant. If a dam were built on the Klamath River and flooded the trails where the Karuk carry out the World Renewal Rite, it would almost certainly not be possible to relocate the performance of the ritual to some other place or to compensate for its loss by paying for cultural programming. Or, more accurately, it might be possible, and might even happen over time, but it's nothing that a manager could propose without being bitterly laughed out of the room. If the project won't make the place entirely inaccessible to practitioners, however, or destroy it completely, other mitigation options may be feasible. On the Klamath, the California Department of Transportation (Caltrans) has tried to mitigate the impact of a road down the valley (put in decades ago) on the World Renewal Rites by designing dips in the road where the ritual trails cross. Traffic is stopped when the ritual is carried out, natural sand or soil is placed in the low spots, and the traditionalists can walk across without touching anything unnatural.

In one recent case, a new road required fill that would most efficiently come from a marina whose construction was proposed by a tribe at its lakeshore casino. The hill on which the casino stood, and at whose feet the proposed marina lay, turned out to be a place where curing rituals are carried out. The tribal elders believed that the construction of the casino had compromised this use, and building the marina would make things worse. In the end, however, negotiation led to the recognition that the integrity of the hill could be restored by conducting appropriate ceremonies. This was done, and construction proceeded on both the marina and the road.

Recordation may be a relevant mitigation measure where places associated with *stories* are involved. As with practice places, this is more likely to happen where the story is in imminent danger of being lost than in one where it is alive and vibrant in the culture. I'd imagine (though I may be very presumptuous in doing so) that if nobody at Cibique ever gets out anymore to look at Trail Extends across a Red Ridge with Alder Trees, and hence be reminded of its associated mildly pornographic story and moral implications,[31] then committing the story and images of the place to videotape might be an acceptable way to mitigate loss if the place had to be destroyed. The people of Cincinnati's East End might find some kind of folklife documentation to be an acceptable way to mitigate the impacts of condominium development, but only if they were pretty sure that the East Ender way of life was inevitably coming to an end. It's rather sad when documentation is adopted as a means of mitigation; it reeks of defeat, of acceptance of the inevitable. But of course, change of one kind or another *is* inevitable, and recordation can have profound long-term implications. Many California Indian tribes that virtually lost contact with their cultural roots during the nineteenth and early to mid–twentieth centuries are recovering and reconstructing them today based in large measure on what anthropologists like J. P. Harrington were able to record, sometimes through seemingly brutal deathbed interviews.

As with other TCP attributes, however, the more a story reflects spiritual beliefs, the less likely recordation is to be acceptable. Although recordation through archaeological and ethnohistorical research became part of the way impacts were mitigated in Tahquitz Canyon, this would never have been acceptable all by itself. Coupled with design to minimize physical and visual impacts, a land transfer to put the bulk of the canyon under tribal control, and contributions to a cultural center, recordation was agreed on, but had it been the only measure proposed, no agreement would have been possible.

Where a property is understood to have *therapeutic* value, the appropriateness of mitigation and management options depends on what gives it such value. If the place is therapeutic because of the medicinal plants that grow there, it may be feasible to transplant or replace them, but if it's therapeutic because of its comforting views or healthy air, these characteristics are unlikely to be replaceable. At the same time, sometimes it may not be the place itself that needs to be managed. If a clear view across a pristine landscape is what people find therapeutic in a given site, what happens to the site itself may not be important, but what happens to the view and the viewed landscape may be critical.

Documentation may be acceptable for places valued as *remembrances,* for the depressing reason that what we remember is in and of the past. I can't recover The Hill as my personal TCP, but the photograph I have of it on my office wall, gilded in the light of a rising sun, is a piece of documentation that I value. I would value The Hill itself more, of course, and any community would give priority to actually keeping the places that are warm in their memory. But almost inevitably such places must change, as must those who remember them, and documentation becomes, in the end, about all we can do to retain any sort of connection with them.

Considering the attributes that make a place culturally important is not a complete, infallible way to figure out how to mitigate impacts on it, but it's a useful thing to do, at least to give some discipline to one's thoughts. Each TCP is its own unique phenomenon, and understanding what makes it unique—and consulting and getting the opinions of those who have such understanding—is necessary to developing properly tailored mitigation options.

Of course, the fact that a mitigation solution is appropriate to the attributes that make the property important is no guarantee that it will be happily accepted by the community. In a case whose eligibility issues were featured in National Register Bulletin 38,[32] a series of sandbars in the Rio Grande were (and, I hope, still are) used by traditionalists of Sandia Pueblo in rituals that involve immersion in the river's water. The Pueblo entered into Section 106 consultation over the proposal to build a residential development on the opposite bank, which would pump sewage effluent into the river upstream of the sandbars. Obviously this would have an adverse effect on the Pueblo's traditional use of the place—as would the fact that residents of homes close to the riverbank would be able to watch the rituals in progress. The solution eventually agreed to by the federal agency involved, the SHPO, and the Advisory Council addressed these impacts on practice by (1) requiring the development's sewage treatment plant to be upgraded, producing effluent that was a good deal purer than the water already running past the sandbars, and (2) causing the residential development to be redesigned to pull houses away from the riverbank and reduce the opportunities for rubbernecking. The Pueblo, which I feel pretty sure simply wanted the project to go away, would not sign the resulting MOA.[33] One might say that our focus on the attributes that made the sandbars important caused us to adopt a solution that was inadequate in the eyes of the community. Since there probably was no solution that *would* have been adequate in the community's eyes, other than to have canned the project altogether,[34] I don't know what else we could have negotiated. I only hope that the immersion rituals are still being carried out and that no one has gotten sick or been embarrassed as a result of the solution we reached.

Negotiate

Whatever mitigation measures are put in place, they're established through negotiation among the concerned parties—agency, community, SHPO or THPO, sometimes the Advisory Council, sometimes a developer or other change agent. Under the Section 106 regulations, consultation goes on until either an MOA is reached or one of the core players—agency, SHPO or THPO, Advisory Council—pulls the plug. If consultation is terminated, the Advisory Council comments to the agency head, who makes a final decision.

Negotiation can be a long, difficult, painful process, particularly when, as is usually the case with TCPs, the negotiation occurs across cultural boundaries and addresses culturally sensitive issues. There's an extensive literature on how to negotiate[35] and an increasing body of expertise on doing it across cultural divides. A good general guide, I think, is Alan R. Emery's *Integrating Indigenous Knowledge in Project Planning and Implementation,* which is divided into guidelines for project proponents, oversight agencies, and indigenous communities.[36] While not directed toward them, I think it would be useful to nonindigenous communities engaged in TCP negotiations with change agents, too. The bottom line, I think, is that the negotiation process will be a lot less painful than it would otherwise be if all concerned will (1) focus on real issues of concern, not

on nit-picking bureaucratic details, and (2) focus on impacts and their resolution, rather than rehashing (or just hashing) arguments about significance and
eligibility. As Carol Legard of the Advisory Council put it in a recent conversation, "In three of my most contentious projects, . . . so much effort and time
was spent in arguing about eligibility and the boundaries of the TCPs that little
energy—or time—was left to address the effects of the undertakings on the
properties."[37]

A THPO recently contacted me with a question. He was working with an
agency to come up with ways to mitigate the impacts of a mining project on a
pictograph site which he understood to have been used for power questing. The
mine already was in place and apparently had pretty thoroughly trashed the site's
surroundings. The agency's mitigation proposal was to put a fifty-foot buffer
zone around the site and allow mining beyond the buffer zone. The THPO
argued that since the site was used for power questing, the vista and landscape
around it "are a part of the site." For this reason, he was uncomfortable with the
agency's mitigation plan.

I have no idea whether the agency's plan was a good one, but it seems to me
(as I told him) that the question of what was and wasn't "part of the site" (i.e.,
within its boundaries) was beside the point and would only lead to fruitless
argument. The questions to be addressed, it seemed to me, were these: First,
given what's already happened to its surroundings, does anybody continue to
seek spiritual power at the site? If so, then what impact would the expanded
mining have on this use? Finally, if there were impacts, what could be done
about them? These real-world questions, I think, might be answerable and could
be fruitfully discussed. The abstract question of the site's boundaries can certainly be discussed, but I doubt if there's a useful result to be reached.

We'll return to the practice of consultation/negotiation in chapter 11. The
point I want to end this chapter with is this: As illustrated by the preceding
story, and the frustration expressed by Legard, I think that one of the first things
the consulting parties ought to establish is just what they're going to consult
about. And in deciding, the prime question to ask is whether the subject of consultation is a real-world issue whose solution will define whether and how something is actually going to be done. If it's not—if it's merely an argument about
abstractions like boundaries and what is or isn't part of the property—it ought
to be recast into a form whose solution can actually affect the way things are
done on the ground.

Notes

1. This case presented constitutional issues that the Federal Communications Commission probably wouldn't have been able to deal with even if it had gotten over the hur-

dle of figuring out that it needed to comply with Section 106, so the tribes' anger did little besides rattling the windows at the SHPO's office and getting some publicity; the antenna went up.

2. 36 CFR 800.5(a)(2)(i).

3. 36 CFR 800.5(a)(2)(ii). The "Secretary" referred to is the secretary of the interior, and the "standards," with accompanying guidelines for preservation, rehabilitation, restoration, and reconstruction, are published by the National Park Service.

4. In those happy days, the Historic Preservation Fund administered by the National Park Service through the SHPOs included money for "acquisition and development" grants to people who wanted to get and do good things with historic properties.

5. 36 CFR 800.5(a)(2)(iii).

6. 36 CFR 800.5(a)(2)(iv), first clause.

7. Alan Downer, personal communication, 1996, e-mail November 26, 2002. On the other hand, Downer (e-mail, November 26, 2002) reports a case in which a chanter regarded the complete destruction of a medicine source as not an adverse effect, because the plants, having been provided by the Holy Beings, would take care of themselves. As he notes, "the users/traditionalists are the only experts. . . . No defensible decisions can be made without consulting with them. And we have learned that you should never assume you know what they'll tell you."

8. Source: author's personal experience. This adverse effect was avoided when it was found that the chief judge's mother had a PO box in the building, and the court moderated its demand that the Postal Service move out.

9. 36 CFR 800.5(a)(2)(iv), second clause.

10. 36 CFR 800.5(a)(2)(v).

11. This was in fact the Federal Aviation Administration's finding in the case of flight paths into Los Angeles International Airport, which was upheld over tribal objections by the Ninth Circuit Court of Appeals in *Morongo Band of Mission Indians v. Federal Aviation Administration,* 161 F.3d 569 (9th Cir. 1998).

12. 36 CFR 800.5(a)(2)(vi), independent clause.

13. "Save Our Seminary," or SOS. See *National Trust for Historic Preservation v. Blanck,* Civ. Action No. 94-1091 (PLF) (D.D.C. September 13, 1996).

14. 36 CFR 800.5(a)(2)(vi), dependent clause.

15. 36 CFR 800.5(a)(2)(vii).

16. Executed before my time at the Advisory Council, I am happy to say, but I was never able to undo it.

17. Letter of June 22, 2001, EPA assistant regional administrator Max Dodson to BLM Montana State Office.

18. This case has a happy ending; in 2002, the owner of the mineral estate donated its rights to the National Trust for Historic Preservation.

19. 460 U.S. 766, 103 S.Ct. 1556 (1983).

20. Andrew L. Othole and Roger Anyon, A Tribal Perspective on Traditional Cultural Property Consultation, in P. L. Parker (ed.), *Traditional Cultural Properties: What You Do and How We Think*, CRM Special Issue (National Park Service, Washington, D.C., 1993), 45.

21. 40 CFR 1508.20.

22. Lowell J. Bean, Silvia Brakke Vane, and Jerry Schaefer, *Archaeological, Ethnographic, and Ethnohistoric Investigations at Tahquitz Canyon*, 3 vols. (Cultural Systems Research, Inc., Ballena, Ramona, CA, publication anticipated ca. 2004).

23. If there had been any Section 106 review. It's possible that a federal permit of some kind would have been required, triggering Section 106 and NEPA review, but this isn't certain, and even if it happened, the federal "handle" on the project would be much weaker than the handle that NPS could manipulate on the tribe's behalf.

24. As this is written, the current federal administration is considering undoing the deal and awarding the permit previously denied.

25. Patricia L. Parker and Thomas F. King, Intercultural Mediation at Truk International Airport, in R. W. Wulff and S. J. Fiske (eds.), *Anthropological Praxis: Translating Knowledge into Action* (Washington Association of Professional Anthropologists, Westview, Boulder, CO, 1987).

26. Joseph C. Winter, Navajo Sacred Sites and the Transwestern Pipeline Expansion Project, in *Papers from the Third, Fourth, and Sixth Navajo Studies Conferences* (Navajo Nation Historic Preservation Department, Window Rock AZ, 1993); see Alan S. Downer, Alexandra Roberts, Harris Francis, and Klara B. Kelley, Traditional History and Alternative Conceptions of the Past, in Mary Hufford (ed.), *Conserving Culture: A New Discourse on Heritage* (University of Illinois Press, Urbana, 1994), for another account.

27. Winter, Navajo Sacred Sites, 97–98.

28. Brian Reeves, Ninaistàkis—The Nitsatapii's Sacred Mountain: Traditional Native Religious Activities and Land Use/Tourism, in David L. Carmichael, Jane Hubert, Brian Reeves, and Audhild Schanch (eds.), *Sacred Sites, Sacred Places* (Routledge, London, 1994), 290.

29. Winter, Navajo Sacred Sites.

30. Alan Stanfill, Advisory Council on Historic Preservation, personal communication, 1998.

31. Keith H. Basso, *Wisdom Sits in Places: Landscape and Language among the Western Apache* (University of New Mexico Press, Albuquerque, 1996), 98.

32. National Register, *Guidelines for Evaluating and Documenting Traditional Cultural Properties* (National Park Service, Washington, D.C., n.d. [sometimes (accurately) dated 1990]), 38:3.

33. Under the Section 106 regulations, the failure of a tribe to sign an MOA in such a case does not keep the MOA from being finalized and going into effect. The tribe does not have a veto over Section 106 agreements except on its own fee or trust land or, where

a THPO has taken on the role of the SHPO, on all lands within the external boundaries of its reservation.

34. A political impossibility, since the federal "handle" on the case was only a Clean Water Act permit to be issued by EPA, which would be very hard for EPA to deny altogether for an otherwise environmentally sound project.

35. See, for instance, Roger Fisher, William Ury, and Bruce Patton, *Getting to Yes: Negotiating Agreement without Giving In,* 2d ed. (Penguin, New York, 1991); William Ury, *Getting Past No: Negotiating Your Way from Confrontation to Cooperation* (Penguin, New York, 1993).

36. Alan R. Emery and Associates, *Integrating Indigenous Knowledge in Project Planning and Implementation,* Partnership Publication of the International Labour Organization, the World Bank, the Canadian International Development Agency, and KIVU Nature Inc. (Washington D.C., Quebec, and Nepean, Ontario, 2000).

37. Carol Legard, personal communication, 2002.

Chapter Ten

Beyond Bulletin 38

Managing Tcps Themselves

The moment a move is made to conserve a place, a number of alternative political, social, and cultural uses of a location may be eliminated, and the ramifications of all such choices must be carefully examined and evaluated.

—Setha Low (1994:67)

M ANAGING Tcps is much like managing impacts on them. In fact, it often *means* managing impacts on them, but rather than doing it in connection with a single project and its impacts, you're doing it day in and day out, year after year. And you're managing all kinds of impacts, with all kinds of causes.

Federal land management agencies—the Bureau of Land Management, the Forest Service, the National Park Service, the Department of Energy, the military services—manage vast numbers of Tcps just as they manage thousands of archaeological sites and historic buildings. But they're not the only ones; other federal and state agencies may find themselves directly or indirectly responsible for the long-term management of Tcps on land they manage as parts of wildlife refuges, reservoirs, watersheds, campuses, and transportation or utility routes. City governments manage traditional neighborhoods, counties manage rural cultural landscapes. Public utilities manage hydroelectric projects whose lands contain Tcps. If you have land to manage, you may have Tcps to manage.

Virtually everything we've discussed about managing impacts on Tcps applies to managing the places themselves, but long-term management presents some more or less unique challenges and opportunities—including opportunities to waste time and money on dubious strategies. Let's begin by looking at some of these.

Inventory as the Critical First Step

"Without a proper inventory under the direction and control of Native people
. . . it is doubtful that many spiritual sites will survive modern land uses."[1]

Thus says Gordon Mohs in his excellent study of Sto:lo spiritual places. It's
a common assumption, and understandable. If I'm to manage my money, one
of the first things I need to do is figure out how much of it I have and where it
is. Likewise with my household goods, professional papers, and socks. But it's
also misleading, sometimes dangerously so. If you assume that you can't manage
something without knowing where it is and what it's like, then two things follow. One is that you'll have to spend time and money up front doing some kind
of inventory, as Mohs implies. The other is that until that inventory has been
done, you're likely to defer doing actual management.

Is inventory—at least detailed, systematic, all-encompassing inventory—
necessarily the first step toward good management? In a word, no.

Consider socks. My first need in managing my socks is to have two of them,
of approximately the same color, to put on whenever I need to wear shoes.
Beyond this I need to think about making the socks match the shoes and whatever else I'm wearing, making sure they don't have holes, and making sure they're
clean or at least not offensively dirty. How much do I need to know in order to
meet my sock management needs?

I know that I have quite a few brown socks and not as many black or blue
ones. Knowing this much—and no more—gives me a basis for a couple of management decisions: I should give preference to wearing brown shoes and stay out
of my blue suit. Not all of my brown socks quite match, and I have a number
of individual brown socks that don't match any others but that I'm too cheap to
replace. Knowing this—without knowing exactly how many of each kind of
sock I have, or how many orphans, or even the total population of socks of all
colors in my possession—I can make another management decision: Wear mis-
matched brown socks when working at home or in the field, reserving my
matched ones for more formal occasions. Without getting into such detail as to
prompt questions about foot fetishism, my point is just that I need *some* inventory data, but not necessarily *a whole lot*, to manage my socks. It's just the same
with TCPs. There are situations in which you need to know a lot about the
TCPs you're managing, and others in which you can get by with virtually no
information at all. Just as in the review of impacts under Section 106, the wise
manager will pay attention to Sebastian's Dictum.[2]

In 1999, the Sierra and Inyo National Forests were updating their management plans for three federally designated wilderness areas[3] that embrace the crest
of the Sierra Nevada between Yosemite and Sequoia–Kings Canyon National
Parks—the breathtakingly beautiful "Range of Light." Updating the plans

required review under Section 106, and ongoing management had to be responsive to Section 110 of NHPA. The forests' staff knew that several tribes, mostly Mono and Mewuk on the west side, Paiute on the east, were concerned about the area's cultural resources, notably but not exclusively a big complex of sites at Mono Hot Springs. They also knew that there were ancient trails running across the range between California's San Joaquin Valley on the west and the Great Basin on the east. These were important trails to the tribes, who conduct walks across them to honor the ancestors and feel their connections to the land, and to archaeologists interested in prehistoric trade systems.

Some archaeological survey had been done, and the tribes had identified some places, but the information was sparse. There were old line cabins and drift fences and defunct mines, too—which were valued by equestrian groups and the mule-train packers who carried tourists across the mountains, but which were also regarded as human intrusions under the Wilderness Act. The forests' staff were in varying degrees of contention with the packers, the equestrians, the tribes, and the archaeologists about how to manage the resources—as well as with the backpackers who would just as soon nobody but they were allowed on the ground.

What did the forests need to do to manage TCPs, other kinds of historic properties, and other cultural aspects of the environment? I was privileged to help their staff and the other interested parties try to answer this question.

We concluded that *no* inventory was needed. The forest staff, tribes, packers, equestrians, and others knew enough to establish a responsible management program without identifying a single cultural place that wasn't already identified.[4] What the forest staff needed was a set of *processes*. Processes for consulting with the various groups—what would trigger consultation, and how it would be carried out. Processes for managing the woods and ridges and watercourses so as to minimize the likelihood of damage to cultural resources and maximize the potential for enhancement.

The national forests had a couple of reasons for minimizing inventory that are common to land management agencies working with Indian tribes but not relevant to a lot of other management situations (like managing socks). One was that the tribes were reluctant to share information about places that they considered to be spiritually or culturally important—a common "problem" that we'll discuss in the next chapter. The other was that some of the things the tribes thought important weren't easily recognizable as "historic properties," so it wasn't easy to fit them into standard Section 106 review procedures. The tribes are very concerned about water quality, for example, and some elders feel responsible for the Sasquatch[5] population.

But we *could* address such things. Everybody could discuss how to keep the water pure, and the national forests could adopt measures to implement what was agreed on. The forests' staff could agree to protect what the tribes view as Sasquatch habitat, to discourage hunters from shooting any they come upon, and to consult with the tribes about any proposals for research into the existence and lifeways of the Sasquatch. Similarly, we didn't need to know where all the spiritual places were along the trails before developing plans for trail access designed to minimize the likelihood of damaging such places. It was also apparent that the trails were of cultural importance to the packers, who represented a multigeneration community in the mountains; the trails were TCPs for the packers, as well as for the tribes. We could work toward keeping the packing business economically viable, thus maintaining its relationship to the trails, without doing studies of who used which trail and how long they'd done so.

In short, for managing the Range of Light Wildernesses, we could develop strategies for addressing cultural resource issues, including TCPs but without breaking TCPs out as a particular category and without any inventory data.[6] Had we been planning to manage the range as a place to dump radioactive waste or test smart bombs, our inventory needs would have been different. As usual, my suggestion is to think through your management needs as the basis for deciding what (if any) identification you need, rather than jumping to the conclusion that documenting everything out there is a threshold planning requirement.

One reason people give knee-jerk priority to inventory, I suspect, is that they're using city historic landmarks programs—the only kind of ongoing cultural resource management programs that have much time depth in practice—as implicit models.

In the typical city landmarks program (e.g., New York's), once something has been shown through scholarly documentation to be historic, it is protected rather absolutely by some kind of ordinance. This means that compiling an inventory, based on solid documentation, is the key management activity.

When someone with this kind of model in mind sets out to write about management, what he or she winds up writing about is documentation. For example, in a recent World Bank publication[7] that's ostensibly about managing historic landscapes and cities, Activa Benzinberg Stein writes about preserving landscapes almost entirely in terms of documenting them.[8] The article says many true things—for example, that one needs to understand a landscape's hydrology and ecological cycles—but it doesn't really say anything about how to preserve a landscape through management. Once you've documented that the thing is there, what do you do to keep it there or to control the way it evolves?

I suspect that for most mainstream historic preservationists, this is almost a non-question. One preserves places by officially designating them historic—hence the importance of documentation—and imposing governmental controls on them.

Designation as Management

In his excellent 1994 article on the Blackfoot spiritual mountain Ninaistàkis—a fine example of a TCP study, though not billed as such—Brian Reeves's top two recommendations for the mountain are designation as a National Historic Landmark and nomination to the World Heritage List.[9] Why? Reeves doesn't say, probably because he thinks it's self-evident. But outside the context of local historic landmarks programs, designation does not define management. Designating something a National Historic Landmark doesn't do anything but draw attention to it—a not-unmixed blessing for tribal spiritual places—and recognition as a World Heritage List property merely encourages states party to UNESCO's World Heritage Convention to give the place some respect—something that neither the United States nor Canada, which comanage the mountain with the Blackfoot tribe—needs to worry very much about. And both designation procedures take time and money and can deflect attention from real management. They're "feel-good" measures, giving the impression of accomplishing something for a place without actually doing anything.

If pressed, Reeves would probably say that formal designation would make managers in the two national parks[10] that meet near Ninaistàkis pay more attention to it, give its protection greater priority. Perhaps it would, but these two parks *control the area*, for heavens' sake, and they have their own internal planning and management systems. Wouldn't it be more efficient to address the mountain's real management issues in the context of these systems, rather than just hoping that giving the mountain a fancy external designation would encourage managers somehow to take better care of it? The Blackfoot Tribe values the mountain; the U.S. government has a trust relationship with the Blackfoot. What more do we need to know about the place before we give it respect?

And if we're going to make Ninaistàkis a National Historic Landmark, what about Mount Shasta? The San Francisco Peaks? Mount Graham? The trouble with national lists like the National Historic Landmark list, or international ones like the World Heritage list, is that they're meant to be exclusive. Get one "sacred mountain" on, and the next one or two may get listed too, but eyebrows are going to start going up when number four or five comes along. Aren't we getting a few too many sacred mountains on this list, someone will ask, compared with, say, opera houses and shipyards?

If becoming designated does a place any good—hardly a foregone conclusion—then achieving this benefit for Ninaistàkis would decrease the likelihood that another mountain would be able to enjoy it. Is this responsible? I can't think so. And whether it's responsible or not, seeking designation can divert attention away from real management into fruitless fights with distant registration bodies (the National Register, UNESCO) about whether the place is "worthy" of designation or meets specified criteria. Management ought to be focused on actually managing things.

Real Management

After making his recommendations about designation, Reeves goes on to provide concrete recommendations for management. In the case of Ninaistàkis these include hiker control, signage, limiting use of one access road and closing others, and the installation of interpretive exhibits in cooperation with the tribe.[11] I don't know whether these are good recommendations or not; they make sense to me, but I've never been to Ninaistàkis. What's good about them in principle is that they're real; real things to do in response to real issues. This of course does not mean that they'd be appropriate in another context.

Consultative Planning in Land Management

Generally speaking, land managers should try to keep some distance between TCPs and incompatible use. How can we do this without spending a lot of time and money finding out where each TCP is and what it's like?

Consider the hypothetical case illustrated in figure 10.1. We know that the top of Blue Butte is important to the Ebirt Tribe. We know this because they've told us, but we haven't asked them to tell us *why* it's important or what its boundaries are or what tribal members do there (if anything). We *have* asked them what's OK to do in the neighborhood, from their point of view, and what isn't. We've probably had to make our questions rather pointed but hypothetical: would it be OK to cut trees? Would it be OK to build something across the viewshed to the North? South? East? West? What about letting hikers pass through in the summer? Cross-country skiers in the winter?

Probably, being a federal agency, we can't guarantee that we'll do what the tribe tells us to do and not do what they say not to do, but we can guarantee that we'll *try* to respect their wishes, and that we'll talk with them as early and carefully and thoroughly as possible if we have to consider doing something they may not want us to do. We can then build reminders to ourselves into our planning system—maybe as a layer in our Geographic Information System. Try not to cut anything on top of Blue Butte, but if you must, talk with the Ebirt Cultural Committee first, try to figure out how to mitigate the damage. Maybe it's OK, or not so bad, to cut in the winter, but real bad in June. We don't necessarily need to know that, or have that information in our GIS, but we need to be reminded to talk to the right people about the right things when we're planning something.

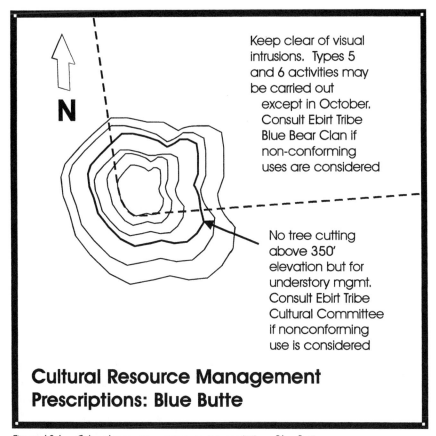

Keep clear of visual intrusions. Types 5 and 6 activities may be carried out except in October. Consult Ebirt Tribe Blue Bear Clan if non-conforming uses are considered

No tree cutting above 350' elevation but for understory mgmt. Consult Ebirt Tribe Cultural Committee if nonconforming use is considered

Cultural Resource Management Prescriptions: Blue Butte

Figure 10.1. Cultural resource management prescriptions: Blue Butte

And we ought to try to keep the northeastern view from the butte clear and natural, though activities of Type 5 (helicopter logging, prescribed burns) and Type 6 (low-impact recreation, nonmechanized military exercises) are OK anytime but October. If we have to consider doing anything contrary to these prescriptions, we need to talk with the Blue Bear Clan. Why? We don't know, and we don't have to. Maybe they do vision quests there; maybe they meditate. Maybe they never go there, but believe that their totem bears watch there for visions in October. It doesn't matter; we try to accommodate their needs as much as we can, based on as little information as we can get away with. If it comes to pass that we really need to log the top of the butte or build a highway across the northeastern viewshed, we may—or may not— have to find out more, but the main thing we'll need to do is talk, try to find a way to do what we need to do with as little impact as possible, or to find an alternative.

Cooperative Management

Beyond consultation, we can engage in active cooperative management. Some tribes and groups, picking up on sometimes-popular jargon in planning circles, like to call this "comanagement," but many agency officials shy away from this term because it implies surrendering some of their managerial control. Such power sharing may not be a problem for the individual manager, but it is sometimes contrary to agency policy or even law,[12] so it's a good term not to use, I think. But there are lots of ways to establish cooperative management schemes.

The Forest Service in California, after the trauma of the GO Road, instituted a vigorous program of consultation and cooperation with tribal governments and elders. In most of California's national forests, notably including the Six Rivers, where the Helkau Historic District and the two stubs of the GO Road are located, consultation with tribes is continuous, aimed not only at ensuring that impacts on specific sites by specific projects are considered, but that tribal land use and resource management concepts are reflected wherever possible in Forest Service management.[13]

Kaho'olawe Island in Hawaii was used for years by the U.S. Navy as a target for gunnery and aerial bombardment exercises, but in the 1970s a group of native Hawaiians and supporters, the Protect Kaho'olawe Ohana, challenged the navy's use and, in their eyes, desecration of the island. They asserted that Kaho'olawe was a traditional holy place, repeatedly occupied the island and were taken off by the navy, publicized their beliefs about the island and their belief that the navy was destroying it, and finally took the navy to court for violation of Section 106, NEPA, and other environmental laws.[14] Eventually a settlement was reached, under which the navy would phase out bombardment of the island and work with native Hawaiian groups to clean it up, identify and preserve cultural sites, and manage routine access by native Hawaiians and their friends for cultural purposes. An MOA was written based on the settlement agreement and providing for survey, nomination to the register (it made sense in this case) and development of a "cultural resource management plan." The island was listed in the register, the plan was developed, and both cleanup and regular Ohana-managed visits to the island are continuing. This cooperative arrangement has been in place for over twenty years, and seems to be working well.[15]

The Bighorn Medicine Wheel in Wyoming is one of the nation's best-known and most photographed tribal spiritual places. A classic example of the medicine wheel form, some say it was used for Sun Dances, but its best documented use in the past and today is for peaceful contemplation in search of spiritual guidance. Used by traditionalists from the Northern Cheyenne, Northern Arapahoe, Eastern Shoshone, Blackfoot, Lakota, and other tribes, the Medicine Wheel was designated a National Historic Landmark back in 1970, as an archaeological site. In the late 1980s, the Bighorn National Forest considered undertaking or allowing several actions in its vicinity—logging, a road, a visitor's center, and a viewing stand for tourists looking at the wheel. The tribes and their supporters objected, and during the course of a lengthy, complicated Section 106 review several related issues came to light.

One was that the tribes weren't thrilled about having the wheel interpreted for the public, particularly so they could ogle it from a viewing stand. A related issue involved the needs of traditional users in practicing their beliefs—what it comes down to is quiet and expansive, uninterrupted views. Unfortunately, the need for expansive views got translated into arguments about where the designated site boundaries should be set. This unnecessarily complicated consultation, in part because it was interpreted by the rather aggressively hostile local community as an Indian land grab. Agreement was eventually reached on a management plan providing for tribal access to the site, routine consultation about anything planned in the vicinity, and mutual care for the site. The viewing stand proposal was abandoned, the timber sale was cancelled, and restrictions were placed on use of roads near the site and in its viewshed.[16]

On the wildernesses of the Range of Light in the Sierra Nevada, the forests' staff and tribes agreed to regular meetings about management issues; they also agreed on how the tribes would be afforded access to the high country for cultural use without opening the area to everybody. The forests' staff agreed to try to hire tribal members to do trail maintenance and other activities that might have cultural implications and to try to apply traditional land management practices like prescribed burning to maintain the health of the wilderness.[17]

As part of World War II's Manhattan Project, the Hanford Site in Washington state was carved out of lands used by the Wanapum, Yakama, and other tribes along the Columbia River. Hanford was a major atomic bomb production facility for decades. In the 1980s, however, its defense uses were dwindling and it became a candidate site for disposal of high-level radioactive waste. The Department of Energy was directed by Congress to consult with potentially affected tribes during planning for the site, and funds were made available to the tribes to support their end of the consultation. The Yakama, Umatilla, and Nez Perce all took part in consultation, and identified a number of places—mostly mountains and buttes—as spiritual sites.

After some fits and starts, a cultural resource management program was initiated at Hanford, with the tribes as active partners. When the Hanford Cultural Resource Management Plan was updated in 1994 the tribes—now organizing their own on-reservation programs—played dominant roles. They insisted on dealing with not only historic properties as the National Register understands them but a wider range of cultural and natural resources, and they insisted on participating in Hanford's CRM program at all levels. Today the Hanford Site coordinates routinely with tribes both on individual actions and on overall management of the cultural environment.[18] The tribes also consult regularly with the U.S. Army's Yakima Training Center and the local public utility—the Grant County Public Utility District, in effect creating a multientity regional cooperative management program. A particularly impressive partnership is one worked out by the Wanapum (a nonrecognized tribe strongly committed to tradition) and the Public Utility District (a remarkably enlightened local agency).[19]

Devil's Tower in the Black Hills of Wyoming presents a well-known case of cooperative management that has had its ups and downs, but seems to be stabilizing. The "tower," a volcanic plug known to the Lakota and others as *Mato Tipi*, or "Bear's Lodge," is a spiritual place at whose base sun dances are carried out and in whose cracks—it's made of columnar basalt—medicine bundles are secreted. It's managed by the National Park Service.

Those cracks are the problem; they attract rock climbers, who use them to ascend to the tower's summit. In the beginning there were only a few hundred climbers annually, but by the mid-1990s, the number exceeded six thousand. NPS consulted with tribes in establishing a management plan that was sensitive to their cultural values. One thing NPS quickly learned from the tribes was that they regarded crack climbing as desecration, particularly when it conflicted with their Sun Dances. So the management challenge in this case was somehow to control climbing. NPS worked with the tribes to develop a climbing plan that would minimize climbing that conflicted with the Sun Dance and other tribal cultural uses of Mato Tipi. Unfortunately, the plan as originally formulated was found to violate the First Amendment to the U.S. Constitution; we'll look at this case in chapter 12. Reworked, however, the plan has passed legal muster and is now in place. It's certainly not perfect from the tribes' point of view (nor from that of at least some of the climbers), but it seems a workable compromise, and it certainly reflects a good-faith effort by NPS to accommodate tribal cultural values within constitutional limits.[20]

The Bureau of Land Management in California has negotiated a number of consultative agreements or "protocols" with tribes both in-state and elsewhere (e.g.,, with the Modoc of Oklahoma). Some other BLM state offices have also developed such protocols, and various national forests, national parks, and military bases have developed similar understandings. Most of these are general, specifying how BLM (or NPS, or the Forest Service, or the military base) will consult with tribes on routine and non-routine land management activities.

A few protocols are property-specific and lay out cooperative management strategies. BLM's memorandum of understanding with the Northern Chumash Bear Clan provides for cooperative management of Painted Rock on central California's Carrizo Plain. The Bear Clan carries out a summer solstice ceremony at Painted Rock, which bears elaborate ancestral Chumash paintings. The bureau and the clan agreed to cooperate in the protection and preservation of the site. The clan agreed to notify BLM at least thirty days before they needed to conduct a ceremony, and BLM agreed to provide the clan with routine access. BLM also agreed to close the Rock to the public during the clan's ceremonial activities there, and the clan agreed to help maintain the rock and its surroundings in a manner sensitive to its plants and animals.[21]

In 1998 Washington Water Power, Inc.,[22] executed a programmatic agreement under Section 106 with the Federal Energy Regulatory Commission, the Advisory Council, the Idaho and Montana SHPOs, and four tribes regarding two reservoirs on Clark Fork, along the Idaho-Montana border. Washington Water Power was going through relicensing by FERC, and had become embroiled in time-consuming arguments over identification of historic properties under Section 106. The company had already formed a working relationship with the area's tribes; the problem was to translate that relationship into a program that would meet muster under FERC's interpretation of Section 106.

The company's proposed solution was to treat the entire Clark Fork as a National Register–eligible TCP, and develop a consultation-based management plan for it, which would be blessed by the programmatic agreement. The management plan[23] ended up being a good deal less creative than I, at least, had hoped it would be, largely because of one SHPO's preoccupation with archaeological site identification, but if you gloss over the survey details, the plan is an interesting example of a consultative system for managing cultural resources of all kinds in the context of an "ethno-habitat"—defined in the plan as "culturally defined places that may be associated with culturally important plant or animal species."[24]

In another northwestern hydropower case, Gail Thompson of Historical Research, Inc., under contract with Puget Sound Power & Light Company, developed a management plan for Snoqualmie Falls east of Seattle. As in the Clark Fork case, the plan was prepared as part of FERC relicensing, but in this case it focused on a single, relatively small but spectacular TCP. A major concern was that the upgraded power plant would reduce flow over the falls, a place of contemplation and worship for the Lummi, Snoqualmie, and Tulalip Tribes. This problem was solved when Puget Sound agreed to refurbish the plant in a way that if anything increased flow, but the question of how to manage the falls remained—particularly since some 1.5 million visitors stop to view the place each year.

The Lummi provided Thompson with their own analysis of the situation, including a list of the four key site qualities that needed to be addressed in management. These were "purity" (protection from human disturbance), "privacy" (protection from observation by outsiders), "isolation" (separation from visual and auditory impacts), and "permanence" (protection from future disturbance).

The Snoqualmie and Tulalip provided more general comments, pointed in the same direction.

Based on these concerns, Thompson developed a set of management prescriptions, which with implementing administrative measures constitute Puget Sound's plan for managing the falls. These prescriptions emphasize maintaining natural views and soundsheds, maintaining flow over the falls, controlling visitor access and discouraging recreational use of the area, and making sure that such controls extend into the future.[25]

The case of the Arlecho Creek basin demonstrates how even—maybe especially—where federal agencies are not involved, cooperative management arrangements may be attainable. In this case, the same Lummi Tribe that helped define a management strategy for Snoqualmie Falls fought private logging interests for years to preserve the basin—a stream valley in the Cascade Mountains with pure water, old-growth forest, and a fine salmon fishery, a spiritual place to the tribe. In the end, the tribe worked out a cooperative arrangement with the Crown Pacific lumber company and the Nature Conservancy to manage the basin in its natural state and eventually take possession of it. To reach this happy conclusion the Lummi first had to fight the lumber industry to a standstill and force completion of a biological inventory demonstrating the presence of the endangered marbled murrulet, *and* negotiate the terms of a discounted sale, *and* organize to meet the purchase price, but it got the job done, and Arlecho Creek is safe from the logging as a result.[26]

On the other hand, managing TCPs in the nonfederal world can be complicated, as illustrated by *Chelhtenem,* on Point Roberts, also in Washington state and involving the Lummi. This case is interesting both for the predictable ways that consultation went off track and for the management measures that the consulting parties envisioned in retrospect, after consultation collapsed.

Chelhtenem is a place of spiritual importance to the Lummi, which was (and I presume still is, if it has not fallen victim to it) threatened by residential and golf resort development. The Lummi and the SHPO sought to work out some way of managing the property to protect its cultural values. Unfortunately, the approach they selected involved nominating the area to the National Register as a first step, and predictably, consultation never got beyond this point. As documented by Ellen Prendergast in her 1998 master's thesis at Western Washington University,[27] discussions with property owners and developers (and their attorneys) quickly bogged down in confrontational nondialogue over boundaries, significance, separation of church and state, and all the other bugaboos that arise when someone tries to nominate a spiritual TCP to the register. After the fact, many of the key players on all sides of the issue, interviewed by Prendergast, came to similar conclusions about what might productively have been done differently.

Procedurally, everyone—the tribe, the SHPO, property owners, the attorney for the developer, preservation experts, the county—seem to have agreed that a more cooperative approach would have been helpful, with more information exchanged up front and more efforts made at building trust. The nomination, of course—particularly when launched as the first step in the planning process, got people's backs up, and destructive confrontation was inevitable.[28] Prendergast's interviews with property owners revealed a willingness to negotiate about actual protective measures like design controls and open-space maintenance, and there seems to have been some interest in preservation easements and similar legal devices.[29] My strong impression is that agreement could have been reached, or at least some accommodation worked out, if the focus of consultation had been on *what to do,* in the real world, about protecting what the Lummi see as important about Chelhtenem, rather than on whether to call the place a National Register property.

Which brings us to the Leon River Medicine Wheel at Fort Hood in Texas. This site is similar to medicine wheels on the northern Plains (e.g., the Bighorn Medicine Wheel). It was found by the army base in one of its training areas, and the first impulse was to determine whether it was *really* a medicine wheel—had it really been built by Indians and used in some kind of ritual? The site was mapped, test excavated, described in detail, and made the subject of interviews with prior landowners and Native American groups. All kinds of studies were done, with inconclusive results. There is some coalescence of opinion that the wheel may have been of pre-contact tribal origin, rebuilt by Native American soldiers in the 1940s or 1950s as a secret ritual location, but really, nobody knows.

While the studies were going on to determine what the thing "really" was, and whether it was eligible for the National Register, the army also began working with tribes and intertribal groups, notably the American Indian Resource and Education Coalition (AIREC), trying to figure out *what to do* with the wheel. AIREC members helped clear and study the site, but ultimately decided that it didn't really matter to them when and by whom the wheel was created; it *felt* like a spiritual place, and that was sufficient.

The army and AIREC reached a remarkable cooperative arrangement. AIREC oversaw rebuilding and reconsecrating the wheel, and the army fenced a good-sized chunk of land around it and literally gave it over to AIREC's management, together with a parcel to use for reburying repatriated ancestors. The army could do this because Fort Hood is very large and the parcel occupied by the Leon River Medicine Wheel and Comanche National Cemetery is pretty small, and because training scenarios at Fort Hood are flexible enough to allow a parcel controlled by someone else to exist in the midst of the installation. Still, though, the case is to my mind a remarkably positive example of an agency and an indigenous group thinking creatively and working together to achieve balanced management of a traditional cultural property. Which may or may not be eligible for the National Register; the army (wisely, I think) seems to have agreed with AIREC that it really doesn't matter.[30]

TCPs Alive: The Purpose of Management

The Leon Medicine Wheel, which was rebuilt and is undoubtedly continually renewed by its users (the site is off-limits to most visitors), raises a question that often arises with cooperatively managed TCPs: What is it acceptable for the cooperating group to do to the place? How we answer this question depends on what we construe to be the purpose of our enterprise. Just why are we trying to manage TCPs?

Rebuilding the medicine wheel evokes echoes of Yi-Fu Tuan's observation that "[a] truly rooted community may have shrines and monuments, but it is unlikely to have museums and societies for the preservation of the past."[31] However much historic preservationists may tout adaptive use, the "preservation ethic" favors retaining historic places as they were during their period of significance. But to many traditionalists in a grounded society, a TCP is not of the past but of the present, and to fossilize it in some past state makes no sense. True (sometimes) the ancestors worshipped or danced or collected medicine or played Parcheesi here, but that doesn't mean we need to keep it just as the ancestors experienced it. The idea is to keep *respecting* the place as the ancestors did, by continuing to *interact* with it as the ancestors did, or as its spirits direct.

Which means, of course, that it's perfectly appropriate to rebuild the eroded Leon River Medicine Wheel, to move rocks around at the Bighorn Medicine Wheel, to rebuild temples on Kaho'olawe and build them anew, and to update and paint over prehistoric rock art. Such practices, of course, can drive preservationists and archaeologists crazy. Johannes Loubser writes that in Australia

> [p]laces with rock imagery have spiritual significance to four broad categories of peoples: indigenous peoples who are the direct descendants of painters and engravers in a particular area; revivalists who want to reestablish broken links with their former cultures and places of habitation; subsistence agriculturalists who supplanted the original gathering and hunting people in a region; and various New Agers who embrace the spiritual and shamanic values of preliterate cultures.[32]

He goes on to discuss painting and repainting by each of these groups—to maintain links with the spiritual, to reestablish such links, to connect with antecedent cultures, and to tap into a spiritual world thought superior to the daily grind around us. He draws special attention to "uprooted Aboriginal communities in southeastern Australia" who see repainting "as a revival of extinct cultural practices."[33] He suggests that

> such cases should be handled with utmost circumspection, and not only because they are so emotionally charged, but also because it may prove beneficial in the long-term. Recognition should be given to the traumatic changes that produced today's southeastern Australian Aboriginal communities and the current aspirations of these communities.[34]

By "beneficial," I presume Loubser means beneficial to the Aboriginal communities, and to the long-term maintenance of cultural identity. Archaeologists may grumble that repainting and rebuilding isn't necessarily very beneficial to the sites where they take place, but this is not necessarily true. Keeping a place in active use, as "a living part of our community life and development,"[35] is surely one of the best ways to preserve it. What such use does *not* benefit is research in fields like archaeology that are based on the study of unchanged old cultural phenomena. This can be a problem, but it's not insurmountable if everyone can work together. Just as archaeologists perform data recovery in advance of destructive modern land use, people can document sites that are going to be reused, provided this isn't abhorrent to the users. Where it is, there may be other options; it all depends on consultation in each case. Whatever the mitigation options, it makes no sense not to let people use places whose very significance lies in their cultural use. Sometimes that use modifies the places; that, I think, is simply something mainstream preservationists and archaeologists have to swallow.

Brand-New TCPs

But if the importance of some TCPs lies more in the present and future than in the past, doesn't it follow that a TCP need not be old at all in order to be significant—that it could be created or recognized for the first time today, or tomorrow, and still be eligible for the National Register? I'd say yes to the overall question and, regretfully, no to the clause about the National Register.

Consider the Cushman Hydroelectric Project, near the city of Tacoma in Washington state. The project, which drowned the North Fork of the Skokomish River, was built by the city in the 1920s and 1930s, under a rather expansive interpretation of its permit to flood 8.8 acres of federal land. In the 1980s, the city and the Federal Energy Regulatory Commission (FERC) began discussing relicensing the project. The Skokomish Tribe, whose homeland, fishing places, and cultural landscape had been inundated by the reservoir, pointed out that "relicensing" was something of a misnomer since the project had never been legally licensed in the first place. The tribe sought to have the project removed, or at least modified to restore the health of the river and its fisheries.

During a lengthy, complicated Section 106 review that featured a programmatic agreement, abrogation of the agreement's terms, termination of consultation, and a harsh negative comment from the Advisory Council (which FERC apparently ignored), several "Traditional Cultural Property Districts" were identified. It was largely over impacts on these districts, particularly as places where the Skokomish could continue or restore their traditional relationships with the river and its salmon, that consultation broke down. At the time the council commented, however, the eligibility of another TCP district remained in dispute. The tribe and SHPO argued that the inundated North Fork and its surroundings should be recognized as eligible for the National Register, because of its continuing cultural importance to the tribe. This cultural importance was expressed in the fact that tribal members carried out subsistence and ceremonial activities in the highlands around the lakeshore that they had in earlier times carried out within the inundated area. In the end, the keeper of the register determined that the district was not eligible because the sites now in use, although used for traditional purposes, had not been used this way for fifty years and more into the past.[36]

In strict National Register terms, the keeper was correct. Under Criteria Consideration G,[37] properties whose significance doesn't extend at least fifty years into the past are ineligible unless they're of "exceptional significance." National Register Bulletin 38 dutifully notes the application of this principle to TCPs. Perhaps an argument could have been made for exceptional significance, in the context of Skokomish culture and history, but it would probably have been greeted at the register with just as much skepticism as the original eligibility proposal. And it is surely demeaning for the Skokomish to have to advance such an argument. They know that the river is central to their identity, that the project threatened to erase that identity, and that they have been doing the best they can to maintain some vestige of their traditional way of life on whatever the project left them. Why should they have to prove "exceptional significance" to some bureaucrat in Washington? And for that matter, why should the length of time something has been done at a particular spot be such a key issue?

The keeper would doubtless respond, with some justification, that we are, after all, working with the National *Historic* Preservation Act, and whatever the Skokomish may be doing up there in the hills, it is probably not what their ancestors did down along the river, and it certainly isn't being done *in the same place.* Therefore, the places where they're doing it aren't historic.

It's hard to disagree with this argument as it applies to National Register eligibility, but the register is not an end in itself. Nor is historic preservation. The purpose of historic preservation, or at least of the National Historic Preservation

Act, surely is—as Congress found and declared in enacting it—to "give a sense of orientation to the . . . people."[38] Do we advance this purpose by declining to consider impacts on traditionally grounded beliefs and practices that are important parts of a community's life, simply because they don't happen to take place in "authentic" historical locations? Or, for that matter, if the beliefs or practices themselves aren't "authentic" in the sense of reflecting unbroken continuity of tradition?

I think the answer lies in the words of James Weiner and Robert Winthrop:

> The enduring and stable in what we call culture and religion is always negotiated and made visible through the contingent and mutable conventions of the present; to the extent that there is never any perfect instauration of law or convention, then every conventional act or belief is . . innovative, or "new," or fabricated.[39]

And

> [T]he objective of cultural resource management policy should not be to ensure the strict perpetuation of earlier practices, or to demand an unbroken continuity of ritual observance. Rather, to the extent feasible federal policy should be directed toward protecting and extending access to those resources and landscapes through which traditions can be adapted and renewed.[40]

What we should be able to do in a case like Cushman is seek agreement with those who ascribe cultural value to the landscape about how that value can be respected. Whether the particular place in which they want to express their values was used for that purpose in the past is irrelevant to the goal of respecting the adaptation and renewal of traditions—which, I think, is fundamental to retaining "the historical and cultural foundations of the Nation" as "a *living* part of our community life."[41]

But we can't attain that goal using the National Register and Section 106 as they're currently interpreted.

Going beyond Historic Preservation

The limited scope of the National Register and Section 106 are, of course, the reasons it's important not to treat the National Historic Preservation Act as the be-all and end-all of cultural resource management. We need, as well, to use all manner of other equally compelling laws and executive orders: the Federal Land Policy and Management Act (FLPMA) if we're in the Bureau of Land Management; the National Forest Management Act (NFMA) if we're in the Forest Service. NEPA if our management program or action requires environmental review; AIRFA if tribal religious concerns may be affected. Executive Order 12898 on Environmental Justice if low-income or minority groups are involved. Non-"cultural" laws like the Endangered Species Act and the Clean Water Act where they're relevant to the places we're trying to manage. State and local planning, zoning, and environmental laws and ordinances where they apply.

Richard Stoffle and his colleagues have made good use of AIRFA to justify addressing tribal environmental and landscape concerns in planning, sometimes emphasizing it, in fact, to the near-exclusion of NHPA.[42] Military bases across the country are developing "Integrated Cultural Resource Management Plans" that are supposed to address all cultural resource legal requirements in coordinated ways.[43] Grass-roots organizations interested in landscape preservation—and landscapes, of course, can be or embrace TCPs—routinely use a wide range of legal tools to promote wise management of the cultural environment.[44]

Many if not most of the cooperative management programs mentioned in this chapter—Hanford, Kaho'olawe, the Range of Light, among others—draw on multiple laws for their authority, and try to address the cultural values of the landscape in comprehensive, flexible ways. But the laws and their institutions do not entirely encourage this. When the Sierra and Inyo National Forests sent up the Programmatic Agreement covering the cooperative program for the Range of Light wildernesses, the Advisory Council declined to sign it, because it feared going beyond its authorities. This problem—of fractionated legal authorities that don't fully address the cultural universe, and unnecessarily complicate good practice—is one we need to address, and that we'll return to in chapter 13.

TCPs in General Land Use and Urban Planning

As usual, this chapter has focused on TCPs in mostly rural, federal land contexts, because that's where most such places have been identified and where most of the hot issues have been raised. But TCPs are found on nonfederal, non-Indian land, of course, in contexts where federal law has no sway. They aren't very commonly identified as TCPs per se, but if Randolph Hester wasn't identifying Manteo's traditional cultural places in defining the town's "Sacred Structure,"[45] I don't know what he *was* defining.

Communities and groups interested in protecting TCPs on nonfederal land have a range of local and regional planning tools with which to work. And the notion that planning, zoning, and other mechanisms for controlling development and design should be sensitive to the character of places and the identity of communities is, as far as I know, universally accepted among city and regional planners, designers, architects and landscape architects.

Kevin Lynch, for example, identifies "sense" as one of the seven dimensions by which the quality of a city or other settlement can be judged. *Sense* in this context is

> the degree to which the settlement can be clearly perceived and mentally differentiated and structured in time and space by its residents and the degree to which that mental structure connects with their values and concepts—the match between environment, our sensory and mental capabilities, and our cultural concepts.[46]

> The simplest form of sense is identity, in the narrow meaning of that common term, "a sense of place." Identity is the extent to which a person can recognize or recall a place as being distinct from other places—as having a vivid, or unique, or at least a particular, character of its own.[47]

But Hester shows how in Manteo, as of the late 1980s, none of the available legal mechanisms afforded protection to Manteo's Sacred Structure:

> Because the Town Board and the Planning Board in Manteo supported the preservation of the Sacred Structure, they used it throughout the planning and design process. Legally, however, there were few precedents for this approach. Of the seventeen most valued places, only five could be protected by existing legal mechanisms (using historic preservation legislation, the Coastal Act, and the local zoning ordinance).[48]

It would be nice to think that things have improved, and not only in Manteo, because of Hester and those he has influenced. Or because Hester's work was one expression of a widespread movement toward greater sensitivity to the cultural environment as communities, not just business leaders and tourists, experience it. Or because Bulletin 38 has widened the range of places that a town like Manteo can squeeze into protected status under North Carolina's definition of "historic preservation." I don't think that's happened, though—at least not as a rule.

The Livable City,[49] a fairly current publication by Partners for Livable Communities, provides a convenient compendium of good models and best practices for local planning and urban revitalization. Many of the examples given are grass-roots projects that clearly involve the community because the community is the project proponent. What I don't find are cases where Hester-style Sacred Structures (by whatever name) are being identified and addressed in planning, zoning, historic district creation, and so on. Nothing in Susan Guyette's *Planning for Balanced Development,*[50] either—an excellent book, I think, aimed at tribes and rural communities and devoted in substantial part to helping communities preserve and revitalize their traditional cultures. Culturally valued places are mentioned,[51] but only in passing, and there's no specific discussion of how a community might deal with them.

Is this because such participatory definition and management of TCP-like places has become so well embedded in local and regional planning that it's no longer anything to write about?

Maybe. A lovely little booklet produced by the Northeastern Regional Office of the National Trust for Historic Preservation, called *Saving Place* and now over ten years old—a citizen's primer on conserving community character—starts out with a worksheet on which readers are supposed to jot down the ten things about their communities that are most important to quality of life[52]—reminiscent of one of the early steps in Hester's Manteo analysis or of a self-administered triage, in Stoffle's terms. Maybe the neighborhood organizations, civic groups, and local planning bodies responsible for models like those described in *The Livable City* are routinely, automatically performing such analyses and making sure that the places that really matter to residents are given their due, so planning guides like Guyette's don't need to address them.

But if that's so, why is it that when a local citizen's group contacts me about invoking Section 106 to save some place the group thinks is important, the local planning documents they send me as background are so often only transcripts of formal public hearings where the people have been suffered to comment, often late in the game of project planning, with every indication that they'll be ignored? I have to conclude that while there may be more Manteos out there, they're not very common, and the idea of addressing a community's or neighborhood's self-defined places of cultural importance has not become entirely integral to many local planning processes.

And it's worth noting that the people of Manteo—a community of only about 1500 souls, according to its website—are necessarily very well connected with their local government; they certainly do not constitute a social, ethnic, or economic minority. The likelihood that an approach like Hester's would be employed in, say, planning airport expansion near Corona, or condominiums on the East Side of Cincinnati, is probably pretty low.

Notes

1. Gordon Mohs, Sto:lo Sacred Ground, in David L. Carmichael, Jane Hubert, Brian Reeves, and Audhild Schanch (eds.), *Sacred Sites and Sacred Places* (Routledge, London, 1994), 206.

2. See chapter 2, n. 42. In this case, collect, or at least document, only such information about TCPs or their uses as is necessary to meet a management need.

3. The Ansel Adams, John Muir, and Dinkey Lakes Wildernesses.

4. In fact, most of the site-specific information we did have wasn't particularly useful.

5. A "mythical" hominid-like animal, known by many names in different American Indian languages and popularly as "Bigfoot;" see Grover Krantz, *Bigfoot Sasquatch: Evidence* (Hancock House, New York, 1999), for discussion.

6. The biggest issues, ironically, were the constraints put on cultural resource management by the Wilderness Act's mythic assumption that "wilderness" must be "untrammeled by Man," and the exploitation of this assumption by a narrow range of ostensible environmentalists to promote the exclusion of all human trammeling but their own, together with all evidence of prior trammeling.

7. Ismail Serageldin, Ephim Shluger, and Joan Martin-Brown (eds.), *Historic Cities and Sacred Sites: Cultural Roots for Urban Futures* (World Bank, Washington, D.C., 2001).

8. Activa Benzinberg Stein, Preserving the Cultural Significance of Landscapes, in Serageldin et al. (eds.), *Historic Cities and Sacred Sites*.

9. Brian Reeves, Ninaistàkis—The Nitsatapii's Sacred Mountain: Traditional Native Religious Activities and Land Use/Tourism, in Carmichael et al. (eds.), *Sacred Sites, Sacred Places*, 288.

10. Glacier National Park in the United States, Waterton Lakes National Park in Canada.

11. Reeves, Ninaistàkis, 289.

12. Notably the Federal Advisory Committees Act (FACA: 5 U.S.C. App. 1), particularly where the group interested in comanagement is not a federally recognized tribe. See Thomas F. King, *Cultural Resource Laws and Practice: An Introductory Guide* (AltaMira, Walnut Creek, CA, 1998a), 110–14, for discussion.

13. Pacific Southwest Region, *Working Together: California Indians and the Forest Service, Accomplishment Report 2000* (Pacific Southwest Region, USDA Forest Service, Vallejo, CA, 2000); see also additional works by Pacific Southwest Region: *Sacred Places*, videotape (Pacific Southwest Region, USDA Forest Service, Vallejo, CA, 1994); *Working Together: Tribal Governments and the Forest Service*, videotape (Pacific Southwest Region, USDA Forest Service, Vallejo, CA, 1995a); and *Perspectives on Working Together*, videotape (Pacific Southwest Region, USDA Forest Service, Vallejo, CA, 1995b). Forest Service, *Forest Service National Resource Book on American Indian and Alaska Native Relations* (USDA Forest Service, State and Private Forestry, Washington, D.C., 1997), and Forest Service, *Report of the National Tribal Relations Program Task Force* (USDA Forest Service, Washington, D.C., 2000), provide consistent national perspectives.

14. *Aluli v. Brown*, Civil # 76-0380, U.S. District Court, District of Hawaii.

15. See www.kahoolawe.org/ohana.html. See also Vincent R. Shigekuni, The Kaho'olawe Use Plan: Non-traditional Planning for Traditional Use, *CRM* 23(7) (2000):36–40, who describes the plan and an alternative view of its legal origins.

16. Consultation on this case was contentious, and implementation of the management plan continues to be. For perspectives, see Andrew Guilliford, *Sacred Objects and Sacred Places: Preserving Tribal Traditions* (University Press of Colorado, Boulder, 2000), 135–44; Nichol Price, Tourism and the Bighorn Medicine Wheel: How Multiple Use Does Not Work for Sacred Land Sites, in Carmichael et al. (eds.), *Sacred Sites, Sacred Places;* Jack F. Trope, Existing Federal Law and the Protection of Sacred Sites: Possibilities and Limitations, *Cultural Survival* 19(4) (1995):30–35; Fred Chapman, The Bighorn Medicine Wheel 1988–1999, *CRM* 22(3) (1999):5–10; and Sandra B. Zellmer, Sustaining Geographies of Hope: Cultural Resources on Public Lands. *University of Colorado Law Review* 73(2) (2002):451. The local community has not entirely embraced the plan, and, as Zellmer notes, local logging interests mounted a legal challenge alleging that the plan inhibits economic opportunities and gives the tribes "veto power" over activities in the area; see Zellmer, Sustaining Geographies, 473. The plaintiffs in *Wyoming Sawmills, Inc. v. United States Forest Service* (No. 99-CV-31J, D. Wyo., February 16, 1999) did not prevail in district court, but they have appealed.

17. Depending on their mood, Native Americans can be offended or amused by the notion of "pristine wilderness." The woodlands and grasslands of North America have been managed for thousands of years, using such techniques as burning to reduce fuel load and keep meadows open for game, and brush clearing to keep springs open. Trying to make a forest into a "pristine wilderness" may be the worst thing that can be done, if one is interested in keeping the place healthy.

18. Darby C. Stapp and Michael S. Burney, *Tribal Cultural Resource Management: The Full Circle to Stewardship* (AltaMira, Walnut Creek, CA, 2002), 125–33.

19. See Julia G. Longnecker, Darby C. Stapp, and Angela M. Buck, The Wanapum of Priest Rapids, Washington, in Tom Greaves (ed.), *Endangered Peoples of North America: Struggles to Survive and Thrive* (Greenwood, Westport, CT, 2002), for details.

20. See Guilliford, *Sacred Objects,* 162–67, for details; and Christopher McLeod (producer/director), *In the Light of Reverence,* videotape, Sacred Lands Film Project (Earth Images Films, La Honda, CA, 2001), for a sensitive cinematic presentation of the controversy from several perspectives.

21. Bureau of Land Management (BLM)/Northern Chumash Bear Clan, Memorandum of Understanding for Summer Solstice Ceremony, Painted Rock (CA-SLO-79). Carrizo Plain, San Luis Obispo County, CA. Bakersfield Field Office, Bakersfield, 1997.

22. Which has now abandoned its solid, honest name in favor of the postmodern nonname "Avista Corporation."

23. Washington Water Power [now Avista], Clark Fork Heritage Resource Program, attachment 1 to Programmatic Agreement Among the Kootenai Tribe of Idaho, Confederated Salish and Kootenai Tribes of the Flathead Reservation, Coeur d'Alene Tribe, Kalispel Tribe, the Federal Energy Regulatory Commission, the Forest Service, Washington Water Power, the Advisory Council on Historic Preservation, Idaho State Historic

Preservation Office and Montana State Historic Preservation Office for the Clark Fork Heritage Resource Program, 1998.

24. Washington Water Power, Clark Fork Heritage Resource Program, 2.

25. Gail Thompson, Cultural Resources Mitigation and Management Plan for Snoqualmie Falls Project, FERC No. 2493 (Historical Research Associates, Inc., for Puget Sound Power and Light Company, Seattle, WA, 1996).

26. Kurt Russo, The Lummi in Washington State, in Greaves (ed.), *Endangered Peoples of North America*.

27. Ellen Prendergast, Perceptions of the National Register Nomination Process: A Case Study at *Chelhtenem*, Point Roberts, Washington, master's thesis, Western Washington University, 1998.

28. Prendergast, Perceptions, 159–60.

29. Prendergast, Perceptions, 160–61.

30. Michael J. Quigg, Charles D. Frederick, and Dorothy Lippert, *Archaeology and Native American Religion at the Leon River Medicine Wheel*, U.S. Army, Fort Hood, Archaeological Resource Management Series Research Report No. 33 (Fort Hood, TX, 1996).

31. Yi-Fu Tuan, *Space and Place: The Perspective of Experience* (University of Minnesota Press, Minneapolis, 1977), 198.

32. Johannes Loubser, Management Planning for Conservation, in David S. Whitley (ed.), *Handbook of Rock Art Research* (AltaMira, Walnut Creek, CA, 2001), 91.

33. Citing Blundell (1982) and Morris and Hamm (1995).

34. Loubser, Management Planning for Conservation, 92.

35. National Historic Preservation Act, Sec. 1(b)(2): "The Congress finds and declares that . . . [t]he historical and cultural foundations of the Nation should be preserved as a living part of our community life and development in order to give a sense of orientation to the American people."

36. See Ed Chaney and Victor Martino, *Estimated Economic Damage to the Skokomish Indian Tribe from Unregulated Construction and Operation of the City of Tacoma's Cushman Hydroelectric Project, 1926–1997* (Chinook Northwest Inc. and Martino and Associates, for Skokomish Indian Tribe, Shelton, WA, 1998), for a general summary of the project, the case, and some of the outcomes, as well as the tribe's estimate of damages resulting from the project.

37. 36 CFR 60.4.

38. National Historic Preservation Act, Section 1(a)(2).

39. James Weiner, Anthropologists, Historians, and the Secret of Social Knowledge, *Anthropology Today* 11(5) (1994):6.

40. Robert H. Winthrop, Tradition, Authenticity, and Dislocation: Some Dilemmas of Traditional Cultural Property Studies, *Practicing Anthropology* 20(3) (1998b):27.

41. National Historic Preservation Act, Section 1(b)(2), emphasis added.

42. See Richard W. Stoffle, Michael J. Evans, M. Nieves Zedeño, Brent W. Stoffle, and Cindy J. Kesel, *American Indians and Fajada Butte: Ethnographic Overview and*

Assessment for Fajada Butte and Traditional (Ethnobotanical) Use Study for Chaco Culture National Historical Park, New Mexico, report to New Mexico State Historic Preservation Officer and Regional Ethnographer, Southwestern Regional Office, National Park Service, by the Bureau of Applied Research in Anthropology (University of Arizona, Tucson, 1994).

43. Department of Defense Instruction 4715.3: Integrated Cultural Resource Management Plans.

44. See Samuel N. Stokes, A. Elizabeth Watson, Genevieve P. Keller, and J. Timothy Keller, *Saving America's Countryside: A Guide to Rural Conservation* (National Trust for Historic Preservation; Johns Hopkins University Press, Baltimore, 1989).

45. Randolph T. Hester, Subconscious Landscapes of the Heart, *Place* 2(3) (1987):10–22; see chap. 4.

46. Kevin Lynch, *A Theory of Good City Form* (MIT Press, Cambridge, 1981; in later editions, *Good City Form*), 118.

47. Lynch, *A Theory of Good City Form*, 131.

48. Hester, Subconscious Landscapes of the Heart, 18.

49. Partners for Livable Communities, *The Livable City: Revitalizing Urban Communities* (McGraw-Hill, New York, 2000).

50. Susan Guyette, *Planning for Balanced Development: A Guide for Native American and Rural Communities* (Clear Light, Santa Fe, NM, 1996).

51. Guyette, *Planning for Balanced Development*, 25, regarding resource assessment.

52. Philip B. Herr, *Saving Place: A Guide and Report Card for Protecting Community Character* (Northeast Regional Office, National Trust for Historic Preservation, Boston, 1991), 18.

Chapter Eleven

Consultation

People don't like change. A lot of neighborhoods tell you, if only they'd been consulted first, they could have worked it out. But in many cases, neighbors are fully obstructionist from the start.

—Rita Bamberger, Holladay Corp., quoted in Fisher (2002:C-1)

T HE words *consult* and *consultation* have appeared scores of times in this book, and they will appear often on the pages to come. Consulting is the most important thing anyone can do to identify and manage TCPs and the things that affect them, so we need a clear understanding of what it means. It's also worth considering what methods are and are not likely to be effective in consulting about TCP-related issues.

What It Means

As with so many words, *consultation* means different things to different people, and that may be the first important thing to know about it. I have seen Indian tribes take umbrage with offers to consult, holding out for "collaboration." Of course, *collaboration* has its downsides as a term for cooperative discourse, too; remember Vichy France. But it's obvious that to some people, *consultation* means only notification, taking comments, and ignoring them.[1] That's not what I mean by consultation, and it's not what the term means in Section 106 review—and hence in the context where consultation most often happens—or is supposed to—with respect to TCPs.

According to the Section 106 regulations:

Consultation means the process of seeking, discussing, and considering the views of other participants, and, where feasible, seeking agreement with them.[2]

Key words: *discussing, considering, seeking agreement.* Consultation requires *discussion*—not always face-to-face, but often so, around a table or over a campfire or on a street corner. It requires *consideration*—honestly thinking about, weighing, paying attention to, people's points of view. And underlying everything, it seeks *agreement.* This is not to say that agreement is always reached, or need always be, but agreement is what we're trying to get.

These features—especially seeking agreement—set consultation apart from other things that agencies and others tend to do under the rubric of "public involvement" or "public participation." Consultation is not just sending out a letter or publishing notice. It's not holding a formal hearing. It's not circulating a document for comment. All those things may of course be *parts* of consultation, but they're not the whole enchilada. Consultation means reasoning together, negotiating, trying to come to a meeting of the minds.[3]

Impediments to Good Consultation

Many things stand in the way of good and effective consultation, particularly where federal, state, and other governmental agencies are concerned, and particularly where things as vaguely defined as TCPs are involved.

Figure 11.1.   Consultation about TCPs and their management is often best carried out in the field. Medicine Lake Highlands, California. Photo by the author.

Mind-set

If one is quite convinced that one knows best—because one is the government, or a scientist, or a professional—or conversely if one is really not convinced at all and needs to keep up a facade to avoid acknowledging lack of conviction—one is likely to have a hard time consulting with people. One is likely, in fact, to have a hard time even *starting*, even asking people to consult or welcoming their requests to do so. Unfortunately, a lot of agency people have this sort of problem, and practice under NEPA, with its strong emphasis on science and weak attention to public participation, almost encourages it. And someone who's convinced that he or she occupies the moral high ground on behalf of the environment, or the ancestors, or truth and beauty, can have an equally hard time acknowledging the rightful existence of contrasting points of view, too.

Few Alternatives/Late Start

If you don't present your consulting partners with a range of alternatives, they're likely to feel that your mind is made up and you're trying to ram something down their throats. The quote that began this chapter is from a developer's representative whose project had run into what the columnist referred to as "a firestorm of NIMBY[4] madness" over a modest townhouse development in a northern Virginia neighborhood. Without implying anything about the project or the neighborhood, or that there was anything TCP-like involved, I wonder what the developer put before the neighborhood for consideration. "We're interested in doing something economically viable and appropriate to the neighborhood. Can we talk?" is a good deal different from "We plan to build twenty-six townhouses on this lot. Whaddya think?" If you want to engage people in a positive, cooperative discussion of a project, you can't start off giving them the impression that you know what you're going to do and are only giving them the opportunity to make cosmetic adjustments.

Of course, presenting a range of alternatives means consulting very early in planning—impossibly early, in some cases. It's unlikely that the developer in the northern Virginia case acquired development rights to the property without a pretty clear idea of what he or she wanted to do with it. But it's also easy to back into consulting too late—to figure that there's really nothing to talk about until you have some concept drawings of the townhouses to show people, or to delay consultation until it's required by law or regulation (assuming it is). The bottom line is: The earlier you can start, and the wider the range of alternatives you can talk about, the more likely you are to have a positive consultation experience.

Lawyers

More and more attorneys are being trained in alternative dispute resolution (ADR)—that is, facilitated negotiation, mediation, arbitration, generally trying to work things out. People with that kind of training, together with a legal background, can be invaluable. Unfortunately, many lawyers are still inculcated in law school with the idea that every interpersonal relationship is an adversarial one. Occasionally, too, you'll run into a lawyer who is hidebound, narrowminded, and supremely impressed with his or her importance. There are lawyers who are excellent participants in consultation, but many who are not. Those who are not are most often those who want to take control of the process, and some agencies let them get away with it.

Agency Procedures

Some agencies have created amazingly inflexible, counterproductive procedures for interacting with parties to a dispute or with the public in general. Quasijudicial regulatory agencies are particularly extreme examples, Gilbert-and-Sullivanesque models of the inaccessible agency. No talking with anyone without talking with everyone; no meetings without court reporters; everything copied in umptuplicate and filed with everyone's counsel.

Perceptions of What's Required

Many people—and not only people in agencies—have very stilted impressions of what's required by law, or regulation, or custom. It's not uncommon to find a project's critics clamoring for a "public hearing," as though such a hearing were going to do them any good. When confronted with the fact that the hearing may be just a rote exercise, where the agency hears what the public has to say and goes off to "decide" to do what it already intended to do, they shrug their shoulders—what else can we do? Public hearings *are* required by some agency procedures, but not by the Section 106 or NEPA regulations; they're not *all* that's required if an authority like Section 106 is in play.

FACA

The Federal Advisory Committees Act and its implementing regulations establish detailed procedures for establishing and managing advisory committees. "Advisory committee" is defined broadly, to include any group "established or utilized by . . . any agency official for the purpose of obtaining advice or recommendations on issues or policies which are within the scope of his or her responsibilities."[5] FACA was enacted in the wake of Watergate to keep special interests from cooking up deals with government officials behind closed doors. Taken literally, however, it can be interpreted virtually to bar consultation-to-agreement with nongovernmental stakeholders, unless those stakeholders are organized as a duly constituted advisory committee. I don't know of an agency that actually interprets it that way, but most don't pay much attention to it at all, and it lurks out there as a possible impediment to consultation. I've argued elsewhere that I don't think FACA really stands in the way of consultation; it just requires that consultation be open both in terms of agenda and in terms of participation.[6] I think that's the smart way to read the law, and consistent with Congress's intent.

Inexperience and Fear

Few people are trained in consultation techniques. Members of the Advisory Council's staff aren't, and neither are the cultural resource staffs of most Federal agencies, SHPOs, tribes, local governments, and "consulting" firms. This can lead to mistakes that derail consultation. And inexperience breeds insecurity, which breeds fear, and fear can cause all kinds of problems. Of course, over years of practice people *get* experience, but it's not always the best experience; it may even be counterproductive. I didn't get training in consultation (actually mediation, but the same principles apply) until after I left the Advisory Council's staff in 1989, and I think I learned more then, in a forty-hour class at Maryland's Center for Alternative Dispute Resolution, than I had in my preceding twenty years of practice. And there was quite a lot of what I'd developed over those twenty years that I had to unlearn. I can't overemphasize how valuable training in dispute resolution can be.[7]

Cross-Cultural Impediments

Consulting across cultural boundaries carries its own burden of impediments to understanding. There may be language barriers, of course, but there are many that are more subtle.

Time

Every non-Euro-American group with which I've ever consulted has had its own "time." "Indian time," "Micronesian time," "Samoan time," "Fijian time," "Hawaiian time." I've never heard anyone refer to "small town time," "rural time," or "ghetto time," but I imagine they exist. Usually this means that things are going to happen at the pace they happen, and you might as well relax and accept it. Trying to force people to meet a tightly constrained schedule is fruitless.

Forms of Discourse

Every culture has its own rules about how polite discourse is carried out, and these norms can conflict. Writing about the Amungme of Papua New Guinea, Carolyn Cook says:

> Amungme traditions are still alive and well in many respects, but tradition can carry mixed blessings. The Amungme begin negotiation speeches with a discourse on how God created the heavens and the earth. They then progress through history and finally they come to the point they want to make. Time-oriented administrators often swear they have heard the same speech a thousand times; they become bored before the Amungme have a chance to make their point.[8]

Anyone who has consulted with an American Indian tribe will nod in recognition; such discursive protocol is not limited to Papuans. And it's not only a matter of opening speeches; there may be many other times in the course of a consultation where cultural norms will require a community's representatives to behave in ways that seem strange to negotiators from "the other side." Often it is inappropriate to agree to something without consulting people who are not at hand—elders back in the hills or an official or unofficial tribal body. But often, too, it's thought polite to tell people what they want to hear, so there can be an appearance of agreement where no agreement exists. On the other hand, it may be necessary, in the context of the local culture, its history, and its internal power relationships, *not* to be seen as agreeing even when one actually does agree, and to be seen as extracting a pound of flesh from the "enemy"—sometimes as prelude to agreement.

Grievances

A variant on the opening discourse described by Cook, often used by American Indian elders (and often by the not-so-elderly) is Aggrieved Indian Speech #1. In this common formula, you're treated to an opening monologue that recites everything the White Man has done to the tribe since 1492; the sermon carries with it the implied question "what are you going to do to make all this right?" And, of course, the implication is that you, the White Man (whatever your race and sex), are lower than the belly of a banana slug, and so are all your ancestors and descendants. It can be *very* irritating, especially if you think you're there to help. But it's often something that simply must be said, and listened to; something that's required by the norms of the society—and, of course, something that's probably justified by history, however little we may now be able to do about it.

Choices of Words

Words mean different things to different people. The choice of a "wrong" one, in all innocence, can be a consultation stopper. Here are a few:

Human remains to refer to the mortal remains of someone's ancestors;
archaeological site to refer to the place where ancestors lived or did things;
tribe, if you're dealing with both recognized and unrecognized tribes and the former object to attention being given the latter;
cultural resource, which can simply cause eyes to glaze over;
archaeologist for the agency's cultural resource expert;
mitigation, widely misunderstood to mean archaeological excavation;
the public, when it's implied that a tribe is part of it, rather than a sovereign nation;
avoidance, which is not usually offensive but may be misunderstood—by one party to mean simply not driving a bulldozer through something, and by another to mean avoiding physical, visual, auditory, and other kinds of effects

Alternative Universes

People in the real world outside the strange universe of cultural resource management often aren't used to thinking in the same terms that practitioners are. This isn't only a matter of not understanding our jargon—though it's important to be alert to your use of jargon and try to minimize it—but a more generally different structure of thinking. I don't know quite how to describe it, but the Yapese case I used in chapter 9 is an example. The idea of having to excavate and do something with the dead and buried had just never entered the mind of anyone in the village; it was an absolutely foreign concept, while to me it was an everyday affair. These perceptual conflicts can arise quite unexpectedly, and they can bring consultation to a screeching halt.

Alan Emery and his associates, in guidelines prepared for the World Council of Indigenous People, the Canadian International Development Agency (CIDA), and Environment Canada, provide a side-by-side comparison of the ways in which many indigenous people and many people raised in the Euro-American scientific tradition tend to think.[9] The contrast helps make it clear why we often have problems communicating. For example:

- Indigenous knowledge is assumed to be true, while scientific knowledge is thought of as a "best approximation." As a result, what a scientist views as healthy skepticism can be insulting to a practitioner of indigenous knowledge.

- Indigenous knowledge is taught through storytelling, while scientific knowledge is didactic. What seems like a long-winded, irrelevant folktale in fact is designed to make a point, perhaps explain why a community feels as it does about something.

- Indigenous knowledge is integrated, based on whole systems, and intuitive, while scientific knowledge is analytical, based on subsets, and tests models and hypotheses. This contrast strikes home with me. I know that I tend to pull things apart, play thought games, posit "if this, then that." This kind of analytical reductionism can be foreign to an indigenous thinker, and I know that sometimes the windows of communication have slammed shut when I've said, "But let's suppose, for the sake of argument . . . ."

- Indigenous knowledge is usefully predictive in local areas, but weakly predictive in a wider sphere, while scientific knowledge is the opposite. Start talking to a local indigenous thinker about how something is done elsewhere, and he's likely to listen politely and then ignore you; the fact that something has worked elsewhere is quite irrelevant to what works *here*.

Obligations

Finally, on a very practical level, people in communities have work to do. They very likely have to earn a living, and they often have important social, cultural, community, family obligations. A tribal member may need to hunt or gather food or medicine for the elders, carry out rituals, fast (which can make for a very cranky negotiator), seek spiritual guidance. A funeral can unexpectedly tie up the whole community for days. Obligatory functions and the events that precipitate them can interfere significantly with the process of consultation.

What to Do?

With all these impediments, how can we possibly consult effectively?

Sometimes, of course, we can't. There may simply be no grounds for reaching agreement, and it's not worth wasting time trying. But such situations are rare, I think. In most cases it's at least worth trying. Even if you fail, even if there's no agreement, the act of trying to get there, of giving the community the respect inherent in seeking its agreement, may pay dividends.

Imagine you're a federal land manager responsible for a chunk of land that the government took from a tribe a couple of hundred years ago. The tribe is still irritated about it. You're directed from much higher in the agency food chain to take an action that you know the tribe is going to find objectionable—putting in a road across a spiritually significant chain of hills, let's say. You may not reach agreement with the tribe about how to build the road, but if you approach them early in planning, explain your problem honestly and discuss it with them at least long enough and deeply enough to be able to document why agreement *can't* be reached, you will have built a better administrative record than you'd otherwise have, and you may be able to preserve *your* relationship with the tribe, however they may feel about your agency and its political leadership. And of course, it's just possible that by participating in Section 106 review the upper echelons of your agency will be persuaded that the road is a bad idea.

There are also things you can do—and I'm thinking here that "you" are someone working for a change agent of some kind, as a consultant or employee—to increase the likelihood of agreement. Emery and his associates offer some advice in another publication for CIDA about indigenous people in planning:[10]

- Learn about customs and etiquette. In other words, prepare to do as the Romans do, or at least understand why they do it.

- Build community and individual capacities. In other words, make sure your team has the expertise needed to include people from the community, and do what you can to help the community develop *its* capacity.

Figure 11.2. Consultation in Chuuk, carried out in Chuukese language observing appropriate cultural norms. Photo by Patricia Luce Chapman, Micronesia Institute.

- Include the community in estimating project impacts. It makes no sense to figure out what *you* think the impacts are and *then* go talk to the people, but surprisingly that's what some people do.

- Play it straight. Be honest and straightforward. As Emery and associates point out, if a relationship of trust with the community is damaged, "it is very difficult to repair it."

- Adjust the way you communicate to suit the community. Again, do as the Romans do, or at least be prepared to speak Latin.

- Respect intellectual and traditional resource rights. Recognize that what people tell you is *worth* something. Maybe in money, maybe not, but it's valuable, and it's perfectly reasonable for the community to want something in return—at the very least, a meaningful say in the outcome of the consultation.

- Work with community experts as equals. For purposes of calculating in-kind match on a federal grant, I was once called on to establish the dollar value of the expertise contributed by traditional elders. I argued—successfully, to my surprise—that an elder's time is worth the same as that of a Ph.D. specialist in archaeology, anthropology, or history. This seems only fair; I still stand rather in awe of elders, even now when they want me to go the head of the line for food at powwows. Their knowledge is prodigious, and they deserve more respect than we can usually give them.

- Negotiate based on trust, equity, empowerment, and respect. Emery and associates have a certain leaning toward ethereal concepts, but at base they're right. However you do it, you need to trust the community to mean what it says, and try to maintain their trust. You need to treat them as equals, and do what you can to help them build and sustain their dignity and power in the negotiating process. All this adds up to respect.

- The community will need lots of information. Supply it, and "[m]ake sure it is in a form they can easily comprehend." Giving a community a twenty-volume environmental impact statement to wade through may be a bad idea if they don't have people who can make sense of it. Translate, summarize, interpret.

- Respect people's daily routines. As discussed earlier, they have their own jobs, their own obligations. Accept it; live with it; work with it. If you can work around your boss's summer vacation, you can work around a community's schedule of work or ritual.

- Try self-examination. If things begin to break down, back off, think about what you may be doing wrong or how you can do better. Remember that you can't control anyone but yourself, so only your part of the consultation is under your control, more or less. "If the situation continues to feel irretrievable," Emery et al. go on, "ask for an intermediary to mediate between the two sides."

Such official U.S. government guidance as there is echoes the Canadian recommendations. The U.S. Environmental Protection Agency (EPA) has published guidelines for consultation with tribes and tribal members that make sense when consulting with any "self-defined" community.[11] They can be summarized as follows:

- Know the group. Make every effort to identify all those you're going to need to consult, and learn what you can about them.

- Build ongoing relationships. Consultation on individual proposed actions will be more constructive if it's done in the context of an ongoing relationship. Try to establish such a relationship before you have a particular project or problem to discuss.

- Institutionalize procedures. Consult about how to consult; establish methods. Enshrine these in a written agreement if possible.

- Contact the group early in planning; provide time for consultation to take place. Recognize that the group may not be able to respond in what seems to an agency like a timely manner. If they don't respond, follow up. Recognize that the group may not trust the agency's motives, that they "may well enter consultation questioning whether their participation will be meaningful."

- Train staff. Make sure that those doing the consulting understand agency policy and procedures, and principles of effective consultation.[12]

- Maintain honesty and integrity. This "includes being candid and open with all available information," making sure that "concerns are acknowledged" and that responses are timely and complete.

- Don't view consultation as simply "a procedural requirement." View it as an opportunity for creative problem solving.[13]

But how do we actually consult? What do we do when we sit down at the table? In an earlier book[14] I suggested some guidelines, which are mostly derived from the work of Roger Fisher and William Ury.[15] There isn't space, or need, to reiterate all this here, but there are a few points worth emphasizing.

- *Be patient.* Let Aggrieved Indian Speech #1 wash over you, listen to it, and see whether you can find something to build on. Let the speaker finish; don't interrupt, correct, or argue. Ask him or her to finish. Then try to use what he or she has said; don't just let it drop. "I hear what you say about how the government interpreted the treaty of 1882 and took your land. We don't want our great-grandchildren and yours saying we did the same thing this year. What can we do to avoid repeating the mistakes of the past?"

- *Listen actively.* Too often, we're so busy figuring out what we're going to say next that we neglect to listen to what the other person is saying. Listen carefully, actively; ask questions, seek clarification, and rephrase to make sure you understand. Look for points you can agree with and build on.

- *Don't articulate positions; formulate issues.* This is very important and a surprisingly effective technique. We tend to want to walk into a meeting with our positions formulated. "Let's caucus before the meeting to make sure we all understand our position." This probably can't be avoided to some extent, but it's death in consultation. Positions are to be defended and assaulted; issues are to be discussed and resolved. Take Enola Hill (chapter 6) as an example. Consider the difference between saying, "We propose to log Enola Hill to save it from root-rot," and saying, "We have a lot of sick trees on Enola Hill. We need to do something about it. We think maybe we should log out the sick trees. What do you think?" The first is a statement of position; it doesn't imply any flexibility, and it invites assault. The second states an issue, a problem, and invites reasoning together to solve it.

- *Try to understand the issues behind their positions.* When Rip Lone Wolf told the Forest Service that Enola Hill was sacred, and therefore they couldn't log it (a statement of position), what would have happened if the Forest Service had asked "Why not?" instead of disputing the hill's sacredness? What was the issue behind Mr. Lone Wolf's position? Probably that he thought logging would destroy his ability to connect with the spirit world, or violate the spiritual sanctity of the hill itself. Either one is an issue that can be discussed. How can we avoid interfering with your worship, Mr. Lone Wolf, and still save the forest? How can we respect the spiritual character of the hill and still save the forest?

- *Look for solutions that represent mutual gain.* Arguably, Rip Lone Wolf gained from the selective logging on Enola Hill, because it maintained the health of the forest in which he practiced his religion. Since logging also benefited the Forest Service by allowing it to do its job, there could have been mutual gain. Persuading Mr. Lone Wolf that he would gain from the project might have been possible if the consultation had gotten off on the right foot, but once it was going wrong, the possibility of turning it around was almost nil.

Another kind of mutual gain is sometimes referred to as "dovetailing." The gains for both parties may not be the same, or arise from the same action, but they dovetail in such a way that everybody gains something. I once worked on a case involving a tribe that wanted and needed to expand its land base. My client, the project proponent, wanted to use land long ago ceded by the tribe but still within its aboriginal territory. The tribe was concerned about impacts on TCPs. As one mitigation measure we proposed that the proponent would buy land adjacent to the reservation and turn it over to the tribe; as another element we proposed that the proponent purchase a nearby farm that was up for sale and contained one of the tribe's ancestral villages, and turn *it* over. Dovetailing is mutual gain; the tribe gets something it wants, the project proponent does, too. The problem with this kind of solution, of course, is to avoid making it look like a pay-off. Arguably, I suppose, it *is* a pay-off, but if everyone is satisfied, what's the problem?

How Broadly Must We Cast the Net?

Since you have to talk with people to find out about TCPs, and since everybody's time and money are limited, it's reasonable to ask how hard one has to beat the bushes to find people to talk with. As usual, there's no hard and fast rule, but I think we can establish some general boundaries and guidelines.

One boundary is represented by what the Cibola National Forest did in the case of Las Huertas Canyon. *Pueblo of Sandia v. United States*[16] tells us that it's not sufficient to send out letters asking people to cough up information on TCPs.

Where the opposite boundary may lie—the limit beyond which an agency need not go to find and engage consulting parties—is another matter. As the court in *Pueblo of Sandia* suggested, the agency has to use all the information available to it to decide what constitutes a reasonable and good-faith effort to identify historic properties. This includes all the information available to it about who to consult, and how.

In the case of Okmulgee Old Fields, FHWA and the Georgia DOT knew that the Creek had been marched off along the Trail of Tears back in the 1830s, so their descendants living in Oklahoma and Alabama might have interests in the site. So they contacted the tribal governments, engaged them in consultation, and assisted them financially to make site visits. This seems reasonable and responsible to me.[17] GSA did something similar in the Boulder Medicine Wheel case, but with a whole group of tribes that had possible connections to the area. FHWA didn't ask the Cheyenne whether they'd like to consult about Okmulgee, and GSA didn't query the Creek. In each case, the agency looked at what it knew about tribal use of the area, and the history of the tribes that might have connections, contacted the tribes that it thought might be interested, and helped them participate. This is consistent with the *Sandia* court's direction.

When the action is a broad-scale one without location-specific effects, it's harder to engage interested groups. I've been working recently on some nationwide programmatic agreements, and unsatisfying as it is, I've found no better way to engage tribes than to have letters sent to all the tribal governments and THPOs in the country, explaining what we're about and asking if they'd like to consult. If they all said, "Yes, and we'd like you to pay our plane fares to monthly meetings in Washington till we finish," I'm not quite sure what I'd suggest, but I don't think that's likely to happen. Tribal government officials, THPOs, and elders are all busy people, and they're not likely to demand extensive, expensive, time-consuming meetings if they don't think they're really needed.

Paying for Participation

In chapter 8, we talked about the need not to overburden the community and not to expect them to do the agency's work. Does it follow, then, that when they *do* participate, they ought to be paid for it?

Some agency officials (among others) bristle at the notion. "They're being asked to consult about places that are important to *them*. Why should *we* pay them to talk?"

Graybeards like me can recall the days when archaeologists were treated that way. "You want us not to blow away the archaeo sites? Fine, tell us where they are and we'll think about it." And then: "*Pay* you to find them? Why in the world would we do that? It's *you* who thinks they're important."

"But *you're* the ones who are going to muck them up," we replied, "and you're the ones who'll benefit from doing so. As far as we're concerned, they can lie out there till hell freezes over; we're happy for them just to be there. If you want our help figuring out how to deal with them and build your project under these squeaky new environmental laws, you'll bloody well pay us to do it."

We made that argument stick; while there's still plenty of no-pay archaeological work to do, it's rare for any of us to volunteer to do it for a federal agency or well-heeled corporation. There's no reason for a tribe or local group to volunteer, either.

But wait a minute, I imagine the reader musing, if you carry *that* premise to its logical conclusion, there's no reason for anyone to volunteer their thoughts about a project's impacts. *Everybody* ought to be paid.

That's carrying the premise too far, but as is often the case, it's not altogether easy to draw a line separating "too far" from "far enough." Stapp and Burney, in their study of tribal CRM, write a lot about money.[18] It costs money to run a program. It costs money to consult. Someone has to receive those letters from agencies, and respond to them. Talk to the elders; see whether they have problems with a project. Attend meetings, often a long way from the reservation. Someone has to get the training needed to translate the tribe's interests into the language of Section 106, NEPA, and other legalities that agencies can understand.

On the other hand, the Advisory Council accurately advises agencies that neither Section 106 nor its regulations "requires Federal agencies to pay for any aspect of tribal nor other consulting party participation in the Section 106 process."[19]

But on the third hand, what about the Council on Environmental Quality's guidance that under Executive Order 12898, agencies should "encourage the members of the communities that may suffer a disproportionately high and adverse human health or environmental effect from a proposed agency action to help develop and comment on possible alternatives to the proposed agency action"?[20] Surely if an affected community enjoys low income or is made up of minorities, environmental justice suggests that an agency help the community participate in planning. Covering costs is a pretty basic form of encouragement. Where Indian tribes are involved, what about Executive Order 13175's prohibition on promulgating regulations with "tribal implications" unless "the funds necessary to pay the direct costs incurred by the Indian tribal government or the tribe in complying with the regulation are provided by the Federal Government"?[21] Doesn't this suggest that tribes should be compensated when they assist in agency planning?

There's a fourth hand, too, based on intellectual property rights. The information, after all, belongs to the community. Aren't they entitled to some compensation for it? Alan Emery advises indigenous communities to "use your traditional knowledge; don't give it away."[22]

And to add a fifth hand for creative asymmetry, many who have worked in California CRM—including some tribes and intertribal groups—have come to recognize how the routine practice of hiring "Native American monitors" has come to corrupt relationships among tribes, archaeologists, and change agents. Tribal monitors are widely perceived as little more than extortionists, paid off to keep the tribes quiet. Whether or not the perception is correct, it doesn't encourage effective tribal involvement.

What to do? I think the Advisory Council is on the right track when it suggests:

> If an agency or applicant attempts to consult with an Indian tribe and the tribe demands payment, the agency or applicant may refuse and move forward.
>
> If, on the other hand, the agency or applicant seeks information or documentation that it would normally obtain from a professional contractor or consultant, they should expect to pay for the work product.[23]

In other words, if the tribe (or other group) is simply providing its opinion about something, there's no need to pay, but if it's actually producing information for the agency's use, then it ought to get paid for it.

Even that simple distinction masks some complexity, however, and doesn't solve the problem of fundamentally inadequate resources that Stapp and Burney emphasize. Nor does it solve the problem presented by a case like Okmulgee, where the tribe was relocated away against its will and now necessarily will incur costs if it even visits the site to consult about it.

I don't know of a solution besides sitting down in each case with the tribe or group and trying to figure out what they should be paid for, what they can do for free, and what ought to be done by somebody else. The bottom line is that it's the change agent's responsibility, or that of the overseeing regulatory agency, to determine the project's environmental impacts; it's not the public's responsibility. The agency shouldn't accede to extortion, but it bears the burden of getting the information it needs and shouldn't transfer that burden to others without compensation.

Collaboration Again

One way to solve the problem of whether you're going to pay for a group's participation is to engage the group in an agreed-on program of ongoing collaboration. Sometimes a group will welcome this and sometimes they won't. As noted earlier, in some contexts *collaboration* is a pretty dirty word. A contract may be viewed with particular suspicion—"you're trying to buy us." But contracts aren't the only solution. There are several ways an agency can reimburse a group for the costs it incurs in helping the agency make its decisions.

A creative example of such an arrangement and its advantages is given from Australia by Ciaran O'Faircheallaigh, who analyzed social impact assessments

(SIAs) conducted on the Cape York Peninsula. He found that typically, indigenous groups had not been able to participate in assessments at all, or at best found themselves "powerless to influence its outcome." This caused "cynicism and even hostility. "It also resulted in the systematic marginalization of aboriginal "nonscientific" views, and (interestingly though not surprisingly) in a tendency to view projects in isolation, ignoring cumulative impacts.[24] O'Faircheallaigh suggests that SIA ought to be iterative, extend over the life of the project whose impacts are at issue, and involve affected indigenous groups as partners. As an example of such an improved system, he discusses the Cape Flattery Silica Mines on Cape York. Here, rather than doing an external SIA, the mining interests negotiated an agreement with the village of Hope Vale, which commissioned its own studies to identify potentially affected cultural sites and groups. The village also commissioned studies of the mining company's "culture," leading to negotiations about changes to the royalty system to reduce negative impacts on and improve benefits for the village. The negotiation was done in accordance with the village's customs, and a final written agreement was executed. By bringing the community into planning as an actor rather than a party acted upon, the mining interests created a more positive atmosphere than would otherwise have existed, and probably wound up with faster project approval.

Cape York seems to have been an unusual example of organic collaboration. It may have been easier to pull off in Australia than anything similar would be in the United States. But it *is* possible in this country (sometimes) to involve affected communities in a collaborative process, and it can save everyone a lot of trouble and angst. The Grand Canyon Monitoring and Research Center, National Park Service, and Bureau of Reclamation have tried to do this with the several tribes affected by water releases from Glen Canyon Dam through the Grand Canyon. One element of this collaboration has involved funding the tribes' own TCP and ethnobotanical studies. Similar examples include ongoing collaboration between the Grant County Public Utilities District and the Wanapum Tribe in Washington state and between the Hanford Nuclear Reservation and a number of Columbia River tribes. On the Department of Energy's Nevada Test Site and elsewhere in the Southwest, the University of Arizona's Bureau of Applied Research in Anthropology has worked with tribes to set up representative working groups to oversee studies providing cultural resource input to NEPA analyses.

Confidentiality

In planning for expansion of Chuuk International Airport in 1978, the U.S. Navy held a public hearing. A fairly silly thing to do, since such hearings were utterly alien to Chuukese tradition, but it was a hoop the navy thought it had to jump through. Through the hearing its representatives sought information on what they should consider in NEPA review of the project. A group of Chuukese elders sat in the back of the room, stony-faced; they didn't say a word. After the hearing, acting on Parker's advice (the elders included her adoptive Chuukese father and others she consulted), I told the navy representative that the project would affect the "sacred" Mount Tonaachaw.

"So why didn't they speak up?" he asked me, irritated. "It can't really be very important."

In fact, they didn't speak up because it was *so* important that to do so, to talk about the mountain's spiritually charged character, would tempt supernatural retribution. In fact, one person—a member of the island legislature though he was from another island—did speak up, and being a supporter of the airport insisted that the mountain had lost its significance when the Japanese military tore up the summit during World War II to fortify it. He shortly suffered a stroke, I was later told, and lost the power of speech.

Particularly where a place is thought to have spiritual power, the community may feel strongly that information about it must be kept confidential. As Darby Stapp of the Hanford Site in Washington state said in a recent e-mail about tribes in the area where he works, such information is "just not to be shared outside the family unless absolutely necessary, and even then it might be better to let the resource go than to violate their own laws about divulging information." Or as someone directly concerned put it, "You have to be careful with what you tell others, especially things which should not be written about. This is spiritual knowledge and not meant to be taken away. You take anything away from the Great Spirit and you're going to suffer for it."[25]

This can be frustrating to managers and CRM consultants. In preparing this book, I polled the American Cultural Resource Association's ACRA-L Internet discussion group about problems its participants see in dealing with TCPs. One respondent asked how to protect himself and his clients "against 'instant' sacredness—situations where no one knew about the sacredness of a location until a project was proposed near that location?"

It may be, of course, that in some cases people make sacred sites up at the last minute; there's nothing to keep that from happening, and if it does it's a problem. However, recognizing that hesitancy to reveal anything about spiritual places is quite common among indigenous people—and it is—puts "instant sacredness" in a different light. People often haven't talked about these places to outsiders in the past because it was dangerous or just plain inappropriate to do so, and there was no reason to do so. Now, all of a sudden, maybe there's a reason; the place is in danger. As Jane Hubert has said:

> It may be difficult to define what is meant by "sacred" among different peoples and in varying contexts, but when the land comes under threat then the sacred

sites, sacred places, and sites of special significance become identifiable, even to outsiders, by the extent to which the communities concerned will fight to preserve and protect them from disturbance, interference, or destruction.[26]

Or, unfortunately, maybe they don't become identifiable, because on balance the people would rather let the site go than reveal its powers.

This is one of the best reasons I know for asking people to reveal as little as possible about TCPs—for not following the preferences of the National Register for lots and lots of documentation, for adhering to Sebastian's Dictum[27] and collecting only what's absolutely necessary for the decision that has to be made.

Incidentally, keeping the lid on special places like TCPs until some threat looms isn't something that only indigenous people do and isn't done only in order to avoid spiritual injury. Randolph Hester writes that the people of Manteo, North Carolina, ordinarily took their community's special places for granted and that they only "loomed large in the minds of locals" once "the places were threatened. . . . The dramatic scope of the proposed plans to alter the town forced people to think about the social institutions and the environments that mattered most to them."[28]

If you do have to collect detailed information that people are reluctant to share, there are various ways to try to keep it confidential. Probably the most foolproof is to return it to the community—collect it, use it in decision making, don't copy it, and deliver the original notes back to the community. If you then wind up in court, though, or with your decision challenged in some other arena, you don't have much of an administrative record to show as a basis for the decision.

Some agencies, and some consultants, blithely put their faith in what they think is an authority granted them by NHPA, and put something like the following on the cover pages of their reports: "Information on specific resource locations is presented in a separate, confidential appendix that is withheld from public disclosure pursuant to Section 304 of the National Historic Preservation Act."

Anyone who had actually read Section 304 would not use such language unless they had carefully met some preconditions. Section 304 is in fact not a blanket authorization to withhold information from public scrutiny. It authorizes and directs maintaining confidentiality only when the agency determines that releasing information could risk a significant invasion of privacy, risk harm to a historic place, or impede the use of a traditional religious site by religious practitioners. The agency can do this only "after consultation with the Secretary" of the interior—which means, given the secretary's delegation system, the keeper of the National Register. And under Section 304(b), the keeper—not the agency, and certainly not its consultant—gets to decide who can have access to the information.[29]

Agencies would be well advised, I think, to consult programmatically with the keeper and establish the circumstances under which they will keep information confidential, and how and to whom it will be released. They certainly shouldn't rely on the sort of wild misinterpretation of law that's represented by standard "no public disclosure" language on the flyleaves of survey reports.

The need for confidentiality is a tricky problem with no simple solution. I can only suggest:

1. request and collect no more information than you really need;
2. get as much of it back to the community and out of your hands as possible;
3. establish internal systems for maintaining confidentiality that are demonstrably legal; and
4. don't promise what you can't deliver. In other words, don't tell people that you can keep information confidential if you're not sure you can.

Sometimes, then, people may decide that they'd prefer to remain silent and let the TCP fend for itself. That's their call; when it happens, I suppose all one can do is document what you think the situation is and let it go at that.

Notes

1. One tribal representative described this to me as "the Three-I model of consultation—Inform, seek Input, and Ignore."

2. 36 CFR 800.16(f).

3. C. Timothy McKeown, The Meaning of Consultation, *Common Ground* 2(3/4) (1997):16–21, provides a good overview of consultation principles.

4. "Not in my back yard," a term of disapprobation for people opposed to change in their neighborhoods. I wonder, though, how many readers of chapter 1 identified back yards as their special places.

5. 41 CFR 101-6.1003.

6. Thomas F. King, *Federal Planning and Historic Places: The Section 106 Process* (AltaMira, Walnut Creek, CA, 2001), 110–14.

7. Training in dispute resolution is available from a variety of institutions and organizations. A good general source of information is the Association for Conflict Resolution, www.acresolution.org/.

8. Carolyn D. Cook, Papuan Gold: A Blessing or a Curse? The Case of the Amungme, *Cultural Survival Quarterly* 25(1) (2001):44.

9. Alan R. Emery and Associates, *Guidelines for Environmental Assessments and Traditional Knowledge,* report from the Centre for Traditional Knowledge to the World Council of Indigenous People, Funded by the Canadian International Development Agency and Environment Canada (1997), 7.

10. Alan R. Emery and Associates, *Integrating Indigenous Knowledge in Project Planning and Implementation,* (Partnership Publication of the International Labour Organization, the World Bank, the Canadian International Development Agency, and KIVU Nature Inc., Washington D.C., Quebec, and Nepean, Ontario, 2000), 83–84.

11. EPA, *Guide on Consultation and Collaboration with Indian Tribal Governments and the Public Participation of Indigenous Groups and Tribal Members in Environmental Decision Making,* EPA/300-R-00-009, November 2000 (Environmental and Compliance Assurance Division [2201A], Washington, D.C., 2000).

12. See n. 7. Don't assume that anybody who can speak English can carry on a successful consultation.

13. EPA, *Guide on Consultation,* 16–17.

14. Thomas F. King, *Cultural Resource Laws and Practice: An Introductory Guide* (AltaMira, Walnut Creek, CA, 1998a), 120–24.

15. Roger Fisher, William Ury, and Bruce Patton, *Getting to Yes: Negotiating Agreement Without Giving In,* 2d ed. (Penguin, New York, 1991); William Ury, *Getting Past No: Negotiating Your Way from Confrontation to Cooperation* (Penguin, New York, 1993).

16. *Pueblo of Sandia v. United States,* 50 F.3d 856 (10th Cir. 1995).

17. Not all the tribes, or other project opponents, are satisfied, however.

18. Darby C. Stapp and Michael S. Burney, *Tribal Cultural Resource Management: The Full Circle to Stewardship* (AltaMira, Walnut Creek, CA, 2002), especially chap. 6.

19. Advisory Council on Historic Preservation (ACHP), Fees in the Section 106 Review Process, Information Sheet (ACHP, Washington, D.C., 2001).

20. Council on Environmental Quality (CEQ), *Environmental Justice Guidance under the National Environmental Policy Act* (CEQ, Executive Office of the President, Washington, D.C., 1997), 15.

21. Executive Order 13175, Section 5(b)(1).

22. Emery and Associates, *Guidelines for Environmental Assessments,* 30. Of course, he went on, realistically, to say that the community should "be prepared to encounter resistance or outright rejection by the [project proponent] of your demand that it pay for knowledge." Thus the indigenous group should consider "what is your bottom line— how far do you intend to push the [proponent]?"

23. ACHP, Fees in the Section 106 Review Process.

24. Ciaran O'Faircheallaigh, *Making Social Impact Assessment Count: A Negotiation-based Approach for Indigenous Peoples,* Aboriginal Politics and Public Sector Management Research Paper No. 3 (Centre for Australian Public Sector Management, Griffith University, Brisbane, 1996), 2-4.

25. Sto:lo consultant A.C., quoted by Mohs (1994:184).

26. Jane Hubert, Sacred Beliefs and Beliefs of Sacredness, in David L. Carmichael, Jane Hubert, Brian Reeves, and Audhild Schanch (eds.), *Sacred Sites, Sacred Places* (Routledge, London, 1994), 18.

27. See chap. 2, n. 42.

28. Randolph T. Hester, Subconscious Landscapes of the Heart, *Place* 2(3) (1987):15.

29. 16 U.S.C. 470w-3. The keeper's involvement is an artifact of an effort by the Hawaii Department of Transportation to misuse an earlier iteration of Section 304 to keep information out of the hands of a project's opponents. This led to an amendment requiring consultation with the Advisory Council, to which Interior objected as the amendment moved through committee; as a result, consultation with Interior was substituted. The keeper has never quite figured out what to do with this authority.

Chapter Twelve

Some TCP Issues

The River is our lifeblood. Anything that happens to it is a concern to us.

—Sto:lo consultant "AP," quoted in Mohs (1994:189)

I N the preceding chapters we've touched on a number of issues that tend to trouble TCP practice. We've touched some of them pretty lightly, though, and there are others we've not addressed at all, because they don't relate very neatly to the chapter topics. In this chapter we'll explore a potpourri of these issues.

Why No Nonindigenous TCPs?

This question is kind of a straw man, because in fact nonindigenous communities *do* recognize TCPs by other names (e.g., "Sacred Structure," in Randolph Hester's terms). And they're beginning to call them TCPs and use the National Register. The residents of The Aldens, in Delaware, a complex of three linked communities that trace their shared philosophy back to the Single Tax and Arts and Crafts movements of the late nineteenth and early twentieth century, have been working since 1997 to nominate their communities to the register as a TCP district,[1] partly to influence local planning. Ronald May in San Diego has been successful in getting the DeWitt C. Mitchell American Legion Post 201[2] placed on a local landmarks list as a TCP.

But when Bulletin 38 was written, a bigger crisis existed—or at least was perceived—with indigenous sites than with others. Poletown notwithstanding, few people saw the loss of architecturally undistinguished but culturally impor- tant neighborhoods as being much of a problem, or if they did, they didn't look to historic preservation for a fix. And historic preservation, at least at the national level, wasn't looking for them. Tribes and native Hawaiian groups, on the other hand, had a problem, knew they had a problem, and some of us in historic preservation were prepared to try to help solve it.

Finally, Bulletin 38 was written by a cultural anthropologist and an archaeologist. It probably simply speaks to indigenous communities and their friends more readily than it does to people whose main concern is the built environment.

That said, I expect to see more nonindigenous TCPs making news in the future. As I argued in chapter 2, respecting the identities of traditional communities is what historic preservation is all about—or at least *was* all about when the national program started, forty years ago. I think we'll see that program evolve back toward its roots. At least, I hope so.

Do They Have to Know It's There?

There's been an ongoing debate in the southwestern United States about whether a group needs to know a place exists in order to claim it as a TCP. Lynne Sebastian,[3] Richard Hart,[4] and representatives of the Hopi and Zuni tribes[5] offer divergent views on the subject in Parker's 1993 special issue of *CRM*, and there is a good deal more treatment of it in the gray literature—the question can stimulate heated discussion among CRM practitioners and tribal representatives. The contrasting views can be summarized as follows.

On the one hand: "For a place to be traditional and cultural, it has to figure in traditional culture. That means that those who practice the culture need to know about it to some extent; it has to be more or less specifically mentioned in traditions."[6]

On the other: "You don't have to know a particular place exists in order to know there's a *type* of place out there that has traditional cultural significance. Just as an archaeologist can know that there are likely to be ancient village sites around springs without knowing about a specific site or a specific spring, so a tribal elder can know that spiritual power is likely to concentrate in big rocks, without having a particular rock in mind."

I'm persuaded by the latter argument. The Hopi and Zuni know that in their traditions the ancestors traveled widely over the Southwest and left signs of their passage. Knowledgeable people can recognize those signs. Why is a legend that "the ancestors lived for a time at a place called X" or "the ancestors fought a monster in a box canyon at the foot of Mount Y" more persuasive than an elder's recognition, based on observation, that a found place must have been one of the places the ancestors stopped?

The premise that a place can be recognized as culturally significant without foreknowledge of its presence has particular resonance, I think, when it's advanced by people—like many Indian tribes—who have been forcibly separated from a place for generations. It hardly seems fair to drive people away from their ancestral lands and keep them away so long that it's virtually impossible for them to remember specific locations, and then ignore their interest in any location not specifically recalled.

A vivid example of the meaningfulness of places one may know nothing about, but recognize from tradition as types, comes from southern Australia. Howard Morphy describes walking in the Snowy Mountains on the border of New South Wales and Victoria with Narritjin, a Yolnga from Arnhem Land, which lies on the north side of the continent. Narritjin tells him that they're walking through land of the Dhuwa moiety, connected with the ancestral woman Ganydjalala.

> I asked Narritjin how he knew it was *Dhuwa* moiety country since neither of us had ever been there before. Moreover, little was known of the mythology of the people who had once lived in the area, before their lives had been so rudely interrupted by European colonization in the middle of the last century. Narritjin pointed to the sharp pebbles that lay beside the stream that were *Ganydjalala*'s stone spears, and he pointed out the trees that were similar to those in the forests through which *Ganydjalala* hunted, and finally he reminded me of how the lake she created was represented in paintings on the *djuwany* posts made for the *Djungguwan* ceremony by his brother Bokarra, and how its shape resembled the shape of the lake by which we were sitting. . . . Yes, we were in *Dhuwa* moiety country.[7]

I'm also puzzled by why people are so anxious not to acknowledge "nonremembered but recognized" places. So, Eldred Elder says that all pointy rock outcrops on the Whiffenpoof Plateau are TCPs associated with his tribal ancestors. This doesn't mean that all pointy rock outcrops have to be preserved, or that no project affecting pointy rocks can go forward; it simply means that Eldred or his tribe has a seat at the consultation table to discuss what should happen to pointy rocks when they're in the way of development. Is that so terrible? If we have to err in one direction or another, isn't it best to err on the side of inclusion and respect for what communities tell us?

If we came to the point at which a go/no-go decision about an action depended on the cultural importance of pointy rocks—teetered on their fulcrum, as it were—then I'd want to have something other than Eldred's unverified word that pointy rocks were important to the tribe, but even in this case I don't think the question would be whether its culture-bearers revere specific pointy rocks. If they say, "Oh, sure, the ancestors got visions around pointy rocks," that should be enough to verify that pointy rocks are important to them, whether or not they can identify specific rocks.

Can All Archaeological Sites Be TCPs?

A variant on the question of nonremembered but significant places is that of whether a group can legitimately identify all "archaeological sites" in an area as TCPs. As one respondent to my ACRA-L poll reported:

> An issue of concern here is that the indigenous tribal group has decided that every archaeological site, regardless of data potential (or some other unmet criterion) is a TCP by virtue of a sacred nature. Doesn't matter how sparse, disturbed, eroded, whatever. The very suggestion of asking for the Keeper's opinion damn near created a riot.

It follows from what I've said that I think, sure, everything that archaeologists recognize as the leavings of a past culture can legitimately be claimed by a living group as the leavings of their ancestors. In fact, it seems their claim would be a better one than if they were claiming, say, pointy rocks. We know our ancestors were here; this looks like an ancestral site to us; the archaeologists say people lived here in the past. Ergo . . . .

As to "data potential," I think my respondent is mixing apples and oranges. Why should "data potential" be relevant to someone who values a TCP? Does it matter to you whether anyone could learn anything from your special place? And the fact that it's "sparse" or "eroded" doesn't make it any less a place associated with the ancestors.

I hear someone ask, "But what if it's a site dating to long before the group's ancestors ever got here?" What if it's a Kennewick Man site, nine thousand years old, and the tribe's been in the area only since the fourteenth century?" I don't think it matters, for at least two reasons.

First, while it may be that the tribe, *qua* tribe, has been here only since the fourteenth century, we can't begin to say how long all its forebears have been here. Maybe the tribe's language is one that linguists are sure arrived in North America only a few centuries ago; that doesn't mean that some of the tribe's genetic ancestors didn't speak a language that's been around longer, and that was spoken by the people who created the site. Second, a wise Apache woman once told me, "We're responsible for *everybody's* ancestors."[8] To a group that's closely attached to an area, everybody who's walked the land in the past may be an ancestor, just as all the animals and plants and rocks may be ancestors.

And again, I wonder what the problem is with recognizing a tribal interest in "archaeological sites." I suspect that it's this: Archaeologists are quite responsibly accustomed to advising clients that if sites are too beat up to provide much information, they're not worth worrying about—and hence can be destroyed without muss and fuss. The tribe, on the other hand, may feel that every single place the ancestors did anything is not only terribly important, but ought to be preserved. That's a conflict, no question about it. It's very unlikely that the modern world can permit the preservation of every single place associated with a tribe's ancestors. People are going to have to work that problem out, and the only way they'll do it is to get everybody to the table to discuss it. You don't get everybody to the table by claiming that one party doesn't have the authority to sit there unless another party verifies their credentials.

The Problem of Religion

The separation of church and state is a fundamental premise of our democracy. Where a TCP is a spiritual place, any approach to its management by a government agency has to confront that separation. To some, even identifying such places and dealing with them in project planning can raise constitutional questions. As a result, it's no surprise that some of the most high-profile, contentious litigation surrounding TCPs has involved contentions of church–state entanglement.[9]

The core legal base for these contentions lies in the First Amendment to the Constitution. The First Amendment has a number of clauses in which the government commits itself not to abridge the rights of citizens. Two of these clauses deal with religion; they are referred to as the Establishment Clause and the Free Exercise Clause. The Establishment Clause says:

Congress shall make no law respecting the establishment of religion—

and the Free Exercise Clause goes on:

—nor prohibiting the free exercise thereof.

Many bookshelves of court findings and learned analyses have interpreted these two clauses. The only thing that may be worth my saying about all this interpretation, by way of clarification by one nonlawyer for others to whom it may not be obvious—is that the First Amendment doesn't control only the Congress; it controls all of government. No agency of the U.S. government, or any state, can take action that "establishes" a religion, nor can it restrict any citizen in his or her exercise of religion.

But what if one's religion involves human sacrifice? Or polygamy? And is it "establishment" for a local government to put a crèche on the city hall lawn at Christmastime? What about Christmas vacation, for that matter? Government has had to make decisions about such questions, with the help of the courts. Hence the huge body of First Amendment case law.

When we wrote National Register Bulletin 38, since TCPs like the San Francisco Peaks had obvious religious connotations, we had to be careful not to imply that the National Register promoted support for tribal religions—this would have risked violating the Establishment Clause. But we did feel that we could encourage use of procedures to accommodate religious practice—we should, after all, help agencies avoid inadvertent violations of the Free Exercise Clause. Our task was complicated by an earlier effort to address the issue; the drafters of the National Register Criteria had included the so-called religious exclusion, providing that "properties owned by religious institutions or used for religious purposes" are not ordinarily eligible for the Register.[10]

After consultation with the drafters of the criteria, we made the following argument in the bulletin:

Many traditional societies don't distinguish rigidly between "religion and the rest of culture."

Hence TCPs are "regularly discussed by those who value them in terms that have religious connotations," but this doesn't deprive them of their cultural significance. Applying the religious exclusion to find a place not eligible simply because a group tends to express a place's significance "in terms that to the Euro-American observer appear to be 'religious' is ethnocentric in the extreme" and, more important, "can result in discriminating against the group by effectively denying the legitimacy of its cultural heritage."[11]

In other words, we implied that a narrow-minded application of the religious exclusion could violate a group's civil rights in contravention of the Fourteenth Amendment and threaten a violation of the Free Exercise Clause. We couldn't be more explicit without a great deal of frustrating consultation with NPS solicitors, but we wanted to do everything we could to discourage overzealous (and self-serving) use of the religious exclusion.

Perhaps because of the persuasiveness of our prose, but more likely because people aren't as ethnocentric as we feared, the religious exclusion hasn't been a huge impediment to recognizing spiritual places as eligible for the National Register. But if church–state questions haven't stood in the way of *recognizing* spiritual TCPs, they've certainly had an impact on how such places, and impacts on such places, are managed.

It was on First Amendment grounds that the tribes in the GO Road case stopped the road at the District and Appeals Court levels. The Forest Service had complied with NEPA, had complied with Section 106, had complied with AIRFA by consulting with the tribes, but it had, the courts ruled, abridged the tribes' free exercise of religion—or rather, would do so if it completed the road through the Helkau Historic District.

The government appealed to the Supreme Court, which reversed. In essence, the Court said that the government's compelling interest in opening up the timber resources of the interior might justify infringing on the religion of the tribes, but that in any event there was no infringement because the government was not intentionally restricting the tribes' right to free exercise. The tribes could practice their religion; they'd just have to dodge some logging trucks.

Far more astute legal minds than mine have analyzed the decision in *Lyng v. Northwest Indian Cemetery Association*.[12] I'll only say that like it or not, it gives us an idea of what government can do without being held in violation of the Free Exercise Clause. As long as the action doesn't actually *prohibit* people from practicing their religion, and as long as it's not *intended* to do so, it's probably permissible. Maybe not wise, maybe not good government, certainly not *required* by the Constitution but constitutionally permissible.

The *Lyng* decision included a caveat of sorts, noting with approval the "many ameliorative measures" the Forest Service had adopted, and insisting that "nothing in our opinion should be read to encourage governmental insensitivity for the religious needs of any citizen."[13] Considering how ridiculous the Forest Service's proffered "ameliorative measures" were, this language provides pretty cold comfort, but it does indicate court approval for agency efforts to accommodate religious practice, and to its credit the Forest Service, at least in California where the case had the most impact, has since *Lyng* bent over backward to be accommodating.[14]

On the Establishment Clause side, the pertinent case law is thinner, but it's there. Without addressing establishment except by implication—but pretty strong implication—the Supreme Court in *Lyng* expressed concern that in seeking to protect their religious use of the Helkau Historic District, the tribes might "seek to exclude all human activity but their own from sacred areas of the public lands." The justices went on to say that while "[n]o disrespect for these practices is implied," "one notes that such beliefs could easily require *de facto* beneficial ownership of some rather spacious tracts of public property." Such a "subsidy of the Indian religion," they said, "would in this case be far from trivial."[15]

In *Badoni v. Higginson*,[16] the Tenth Circuit Court of Appeals found that NPS regulations excluding tourists from Rainbow Bridge National Monument in order to accommodate Navajo religious ceremonies "would seem a clear violation of the Establishment Clause." The test to be applied, the court said, was that to "withstand the strictures of the Establishment Clause there must be a secular legislative purpose and a primary effect that neither advances nor inhibits religion." It went on to note that "the exercise of First Amendment freedoms [*sic*: under the Free Exercise Clause] may not be asserted to deprive the public of its normal use of an area."

In *Bear Lodge Multiple Use Association v. Babbitt*, the District Court of Wyoming found similarly with regard to NPS management of Devil's Tower.

This case is particularly interesting because of the way NPS eventually finessed the decision.

As discussed in chapter 10, at Devil's Tower, or Mato Tipi, the National Park Service tried to resolve the conflict between the volcanic plug's religious significance and its popularity with "crack climbers"[17] by adopting a "climbing management plan." The plan called on climbers to refrain voluntarily from climbing during June—when Sun Dances are performed—out of respect for tribal religion. It went on to provide that NPS would refrain from issuing permits to commercial climbing guides during the same month. And it said that if the voluntary "no climb" policy was not successful—meaning little or no climbing out of respect for tribal religion—a mandatory closure would be considered.

The District Court, on being petitioned by a climbing guide and his supporters, found that the climbing plan violated the Establishment Clause. The voluntary no-climb policy was all right, but the threat of mandatory closure, and the refusal to issue licenses, coerced the public's respect for tribal religion.[18]

NPS modified the climbing plan, removing the prohibition on licenses, and reissued it. The climbing guide and his advocates were not satisfied, and the case went to the Tenth Circuit Court of Appeals (the same venue as *Badoni*), which found that the plaintiffs didn't have standing because implementing the plan would not substantially injure them. Hence the plan was allowed to stand, but the constitutional question raised by the plaintiffs was never reached.[19]

What this tells me is that we operate within a narrow window[20] between free exercise and establishment in managing TCPs of a spiritual nature and in addressing impacts on them. Although agencies should accommodate religious practice, if they do so to the point of seeming to coerce others into supporting it, they risk violating the Establishment Clause. And while accommodation is encouraged, an agency will not likely be found to have violated the Free Exercise Clause unless it has deliberately prohibited a religious practice without good cause. Tribes would like it to be otherwise, and efforts are constantly afoot to draft legislation to make it otherwise, but laws have to comport with the Constitution. As long as the Constitution is interpreted as it was in *Lyng*, there will be no absolute protection for "sacred sites" other than those—like Taos Blue Lake—that are owned and controlled by those who value them.

On the other hand, there is little evidence that courts will support the premise that paying any attention at all to spiritual places—trying in any way to accommodate people's belief in them—violates the Establishment Clause. In *Attakai v. United States*,[21] the District Court for the District of Arizona, while rejecting the First Amendment claims of individual Navajo plaintiffs in a case involving alleged impacts on spiritual places, held that under the Section 106 regulations the plaintiffs were entitled to participate as consulting parties in Section 106 review. There was no suggestion that such entitlement might raise

Establishment Clause questions. The District Court for the District of Columbia in 2001 rejected the claim that the Advisory Council's Section 106 regulations violated the Establishment Clause in requiring consultation with tribes about religious and cultural interests in historic properties.[22]

A district court in Michigan was even more dismissive when a logging organization brought suit claiming that the Forest Service had allowed itself to be used by environmentalists to promote the religion of "deep ecology"—according to a newspaper account, an "earth-centered philosophy similar to American Indian spirituality." The loggers argued that by allowing environmentalists to challenge logging projects using arguments based on "deep ecology," the Forest Service violated the Establishment Clause. The District Court not only dismissed the case, but did so "with prejudice," noting that environmentalists have the same constitutional rights as anyone else, and further commenting that "many of the parties involved in social and political advocacy in this country have been motivated and inspired, at least in part, by religious views."[23]

TCPs and Natural Stuff

As we've repeatedly seen, many TCPs are natural places—mountains, springs, lakes, groves of trees. But CRM practitioners still have trouble, sometimes, apprehending the notion that what makes up or operates within natural places—plants, animals, water, air—can contribute to a place's cultural significance, so that adverse effects on them are adverse effects on the place itself. One hears, for example, that "water quality (or air quality, or the health of ecosystems, fisheries, or bison herds) isn't a preservation issue," or "ought to be dealt with under NEPA, not Section 106."

Well, of course they should be dealt with under NEPA, like all other environmental impacts, but that doesn't mean they *shouldn't* be dealt with under Section 106, if they're related to the qualities that make a place eligible for the National Register. And often in the case of TCPs, they're absolutely fundamental.

At Zuni Salt Lake, for example, since it's the lake that's the core eligible property, and the lake is made up of water (and salt), it's pretty obvious that water levels in the aquifer that feeds the lake are closely related to what makes the place significant. Without water the lake would not be a lake. And from the Zuni perspective, if the waters of Salt Woman become tainted with unnatural pollutants, that's a problem too.

Effects on the natural environment are or have been issues in many TCP cases. In its comment on the Cushman Hydroelectric Project in Washington State, the Advisory Council quite accurately pointed out that dewatering the North Fork Skokomish River and thus depleting the salmon fishery "had a profound effect on the traditional use of the TCP districts" along the river.[24] One important cultural concern about Crandon Mine in Wisconsin is that it would pollute the subsurface water—now pure enough to be used in water ceremonies—that flows into Mushgigagamongsebe—"Little River of Medicine," part of a TCP district that's central to the identity of Sokaogan Ojibwe Community.[25] There are other cases, current and pending, that involve the complex interactions among the natural environment, the traditional cultural environment, and things that affect one by changing the other.

TCPs and "Intangibles"

As discussed in chapter 2, in 1980 Congress directed NPS and the American Folklife Center to "submit a report to the President and Congress on preserving and conserving the *intangible* elements of our cultural heritage such as arts, skills, folklife, and folkways."[26] This initiative, in which Parker and I played minor roles, coincided with development of Bulletin 38, and had some influence on our thinking.[27] This does not mean, however—as is sometimes suggested—that Bulletin 38 somehow made "intangible cultural resources" eligible for the National Register. In fact, the bulletin quite explicitly points out that to be eligible for the National Register, a TCP has to be a "place," a piece of tangible, physical property.[28] Even if the National Reg-

Figure 12.1.   First Amendment problem? National Park Service sign in Hawaii. Photo by the author.

ister were not involved, it would make no sense for a traditional cultural *property,* or *place,* not to have a tangible property referent.

But that doesn't mean that TCPs don't have significant "intangible" qualities, that can be affected to the detriment (or compliment) of their cultural character. It is no more correct to say, for instance, that socioeconomic effects on a TCP should be dealt with under NEPA and not Section 106 than it is to say such a thing about effects on the natural environment.

The spiritual beliefs and practices of the Hualapai, for example, are by their nature "intangible," but it is they that give significance to the landscape over which air tours operate. The only effect such tours can have on the cultural value of the landscape is via their effects on the intangibilities of perception and practice. If Hualapai perceptions of the landscape weren't affected by the overflights, there would be no effect on the landscape as a cultural resource. Since such perceptions *can* be affected, there *is* an effect.

At base, *all* cultural values are "intangible," in that they exist in our heads. Whether it's an appreciation for a battlefield's association with the Civil War or the interests of archaeologists in a research topic, the values we attach to places are "intangible." While an intangible cultural value without a property referent can't be considered under Section 106 (but could and should be under NEPA), it does not follow that an impact on a place's intangible cultural, or social, or economic qualities is not an impact on the place. If a federal agency were going to assist in the gentrification of the East End of Cincinnati, and the East End were found to be eligible for the National Register as a TCP, the socioeconomic and sociocultural impacts of gentrification would certainly need to be considered under Section 106, as well as under NEPA.

TCPs and Environmental Justice

Environmental justice, or EJ, involves efforts to avoid or eliminate disproportionate adverse environmental impact on low-income groups and minority communities. In the United States, its centerpiece is Executive Order 12898, issued by President Bill Clinton in 1994. The executive order and an accompanying presidential memorandum on NEPA review direct agencies to do what they can, under NEPA and other environmental authorities, to make sure that disproportionate adverse effects don't result from government actions.

The EJ "movement" originated in activism by minority (usually African American) groups over the government's tendency to favor placement of toxic, hazardous, polluting facilities in their neighborhoods. As a result, it's often thought of as relating only to things like air and water pollution. However, guidance from the Council on Environmental Quality and other oversight agencies indicates that all kinds of environmental impacts must be examined under EJ's lens.[29] So, in simplest terms, in carrying out review of impacts on the cultural environment under NEPA, Section 106, and other authorities, agencies have to give special attention to impacts on resources important to low-income and minority communities. TCPs, *whether eligible for the National Register or not,* are clearly among such resources.

A case that illustrates the application of Executive Order 12898 to TCPs is the South Lawrence Trafficway in Douglas County, Kansas.

The proposed South Lawrence project is a fourteen-mile four-lane divided road bypassing the city of Lawrence. Several of the alternative routes run through wetlands on and adjacent to the campus of the Haskell Indian Nations University—a former Indian boarding school now run by American Indians themselves as an institution of higher learning.

During the university's bad old days as a boarding school—when inmates were aggressively separated from their families and culture—the wetlands are said to have provided sanctuary. There students could speak their own languages among themselves, sometimes meet with relatives, and recall the religious and cultural practices of their tribes. It's not quite clear where in the extensive wetlands all this happened, but the site of a standing sweat lodge lay near the path of the proposed trafficway.

The South Lawrence project is currently in Section 106 review, and the eligibility of the wetlands for the National Register has become an issue. Originally, however, the recent character of the sweat lodge—it had been built just a few years earlier by teachers and students—led project planners to conclude that there were no historic properties involved, and hence no Section 106 trigger. What there was, however, was environmental justice. The university quickly let it be known that its students and faculty—members of a minority group, of course, and mostly of low income—had very serious cultural-environmental concerns about impacts on the sweat lodge site and the surrounding wetlands in general. It was on this legal basis that the State Department of Transportation and Federal Highway Administration first began looking at how cultural resources might be affected by the project.[30] The U.S. Environmental Protection Agency uses South Lawrence in Environmental Justice training as an example of how Executive Order 12898 can figure into federal planning under NEPA.[31]

In review of the proposed King William Reservoir in Virginia—a local project falling under NEPA and Section 106 because it needs a permit from the Corps of Engineers—the Mattaponi, Pamunkey, and Upper Mattaponi tribes have successfully asserted their special status under Executive Order 12898. EPA has taken part in the Section 106 process as well, to make sure the tribes are properly treated. The tribes are not federally recognized (though they are state recognized, based on colonial-era treaties with the British Crown). Partly as a result of environmental justice concerns, the project proponent[32] and the Corps of Engineers agreed to treat the Mattaponi and Pamunkey Rivers as National Register–eligible TCPs and to treat the project's potential impacts on the natural and cultural environments as an integrated whole, rather than trying to tease them apart. Invoking EJ can be useful in promoting this sort of integrated analysis. It can also be helpful in getting agencies and project proponents to flex their procedures to overcome cultural, linguistic, and economic barriers to consultation, because the executive order directs that such flexibility be exercised.

Use of Executive Order 12898 in review of impacts on cultural resources is complicated, however, by guidelines from the Council on Environmental Quality and EPA that emphasize quantitative measures like percentage of officially classified low-income people in a given census tract.[33] If you're dealing, say, with a tribe whose reservation is in Green County but whose deeply significant TCP is in Blue County, a standard sort of EJ analysis may not reveal that a project in Blue County will have disproportionate adverse effects on the tribe over in Green. When confronted with this sort of issue, I've found that EJ practitioners will fairly readily adjust their procedures to take the effects into account, but it's not something they'll necessarily do without persuasion, and it won't happen automatically.

TCPs and "Cultural Triage"

Richard Stoffle and his colleagues at the University of Arizona's Bureau of Applied Research in Anthropology (BARA) have pioneered the idea of "cultural triage" as a means of making decisions about whether and how to manage impacts on TCP-like places.[34] Stoffle, his students and colleagues, and tribes with which they work seem to have made good use of the method, but others bristle at the term.

Triage, of course, is a medical technique, wherein patients are screened to determine in what priority they should be treated, and how. Implicitly it involves life and death decisions—who is worth trying to save, and who is not. So "cultural triage" is "defined as a forced choice situation in which an ethnic group is faced with the decision to rank in importance cultural resources that could be impacted by a proposed development project."[35]

Brutal as it sounds, the notion of cultural triage arises naturally from a much gentler concept that Stoffle and his student Michael Evans, in their introductory article on the subject,[36] call "holistic conservation." They describe holistic conservation as the traditional approach to the environment taken by tribal people who see themselves as "a functional and essential part of the natural elements in their traditionally occupied lands."[37]

The philosophy of holistic conservation often leads a tribe, when confronted by a development project proposal, to respond in a manner familiar to all CRM practitioners and Federal land managers: "This land is ours, leave it alone."[38] However, Stoffle and Evans note that tribes sometimes do not feel conflict with their own development projects, because they know how to carry such projects out in ways that aren't injurious to the life force of the land. As a result, they say, technological change can succeed on culturally significant land if the tribe and its members are "brought into its planning and executing, and feel it to be their own."[39]

From this comes the idea of cultural triage. Stoffle and Evans note that medical people doing triage "accept the principle that all human life is valuable" but do not find this incompatible with the practical need for triage. Similarly, they say, "Indian cultural experts . . . who triage cultural resources accept the principal that all traditional cultural resources are of equal importance."[40] They don't quite say it, but apparently a triage practitioner thinks: "Everything's equally important, but some things *can* be saved and others can't, so let's distinguish between them and try to make sure that the ones lost are the ones we can afford to lose." A triage-based document typically articulates the position that all resources should be preserved, then goes on to say that if some *must* be lost, the following should definitely not be among those sacrificed.

Cultural triage methodology involves initial consultation with a tribal government, leading to the establishment of an official tribal contact representative (OTCR). All OTCRs are trained and then work with anthropologists to consult tribal cultural experts, do background research, and carry out on-site visits. Mail surveys of a sample of tribal members are used on large projects, carried out in ways that facilitate quantitative analysis. Numeric scores resulting from such surveys are compared with cultural expert opinions, leading to draft findings, review by OTCRs, revisions, and finally recommendations submitted to tribal governments. Stoffle and Evans report that when they "agree with the judgment of tribal elders, tribal governments have been confident in passing mitigation resolutions regarding how to triage cultural resources."[41] They don't say what happens when the tribal government and elders *don't* agree.

The BARA researchers and their tribal colleagues, particularly in Nevada and Arizona, have developed, refined, and elaborated the holistic conservation/cultural triage model in a number of large scale studies.[42] It seems to work for them, and they insist that "holistic conservation is strengthened, not compromised, by cultural triage."[43]

Others are not so sure. Stoffle and Evans themselves quote the museum director for the Colorado River Indian Tribes as saying that cultural triage is "like lining up my children and asking which ones I want you not to shoot."[44] I've heard tribal people say the same, often with considerable vigor.[45] Stoffle and Evans say that often tribal representatives will initially take the abstract position that everything is equal and must be saved but, particularly upon going into the field, will acknowledge that some resources or areas are more important than others, and that "we have to choose."[46] I don't doubt it, but I have to wonder whether this realistic process is helped or hindered by making it explicit as a named methodology.

I also have to wonder what internal stresses it puts on a tribe and its members when individual OTCRs are called on to make decisions broadly affecting the cultural values of the whole group, including people who may be entirely unrelated to the OTCR. In the not entirely different New Zealand context, Harini Matunga has said of Maori spiritual places that *"waahi tapu* cannot be forced into preconceived categories of importance, and one group cannot determine what is *waahi tapu* to another."[47]

Few other CRM practitioners are quite as up-front as are Stoffle and his colleagues about cultural triage, but it's a difficult thing *not* to do when addressing the management needs of a big project or large land area, whether one calls it "triage" or not. Since things can't be held in stasis, decisions have to be made about what can be changed and what cannot or about what can be *easily* changed and what requires more effort. Still, explicit efforts to rank the relative significance of TCPs are not common. Most people, I think, if they rank TCPs at all do so implicitly. Explicit ranking systems have been essayed in planning things like the partition of the Navajo–Hopi joint use area. John Wood and Walter Vannette developed a ranking system for Navajo "sacred sites" at Big Mountain in 1979;[48] Vannette and Alison Feary offered modifications to the scheme with reference to several Southwestern National Forests in 1981,[49] and Kelley and Francis cited both efforts with cautious approval and suggested refinements in 1994.[50] These systems are interesting within the context to which they apply—Navajo spiritual places—but applying them more broadly would be a very chancy undertaking.

What's attractive—to me at least—in the BARA approach is its clear engagement of the tribe as an up-front partner in the planning process. It seems to me, though, that it would be better, where possible, for this to be done without shaking and tooting all the methodological bells and whistles that formal cultural triage seems to entail, and without forcing people to confront the fact that they are, in fact, making triage decisions.

How Much Does a "TCP Study" Cost?

Finally, there's the very practical issue of money. Dealing with TCPs requires making some effort to find them, evaluate them, and consider how to manage effects on them. This costs money.

As the alert reader will have noticed, I promote soft, flexible approaches to the identification and management of impacts on TCPs. Such approaches should keep costs down by minimizing unnecessary descriptive and evaluative studies. Ideally, I don't think there should be a need for specific "TCP studies"—separate projects aimed at identifying, evaluating, and determining effects on TCPs. The consultation needed to address impacts on places of cultural value should be an integral part of the project review process, not a stand-alone element separated from everything else. But "TCP studies" are done, and it's not unreasonable for people—especially those who must establish their scopes and budget for them—to wonder what they're likely to cost.

Unfortunately, while lots of people talk about doing "TCP studies" or "TCP surveys," there's no real agreement on what such a creature is. Most would probably say that what they mean when they talk of such a thing is a study to identify and evaluate possible TCPs per National Register Bulletin 38. However, people interpret Bulletin 38 in different ways, particularly as it relates to other guidance like Bulletin 15. A TCP study based on the assumption that you've got to document the bejeebers out of each place, following the kind of direction you get from the National Register in Bulletin 15, is going to be a lot more expensive than the more flexible kind of survey/study I prefer.

I also prefer a study that looks simultaneously at the eligibility of properties and at project effects. This is because the level of detail one needs to develop about the character of potentially affected properties depends in part on the kinds of effects you're dealing with. Where you're dealing with visual effects on a neighborhood, say, or effects on water quality in a medicine swamp, you may need a lot less place-specific data than where you're dealing with direct physical destruction.

All that said, in 1999 I conducted an informal poll, via the Internet, to see what "TCP studies" were costing. The great bulk of responses I got were from the Southwest; indeed, the only cost figures I got from anyplace else were one very early and unfulfilled estimate from Alaska, and my own figures from Wisconsin.

At the low end of the cost spectrum, a study along a proposed pipeline through parts of New Mexico, Colorado, and Utah cost $13,000. My study of Chequemegan Bay cost $20,000. Another project on which no details were provided cost $22,000. A highway-related survey in Arizona cost $44,000.

At the high end, one study in New Mexico cost $279,000 and another—I suppose I can acknowledge that it was the infamous Fence Lake Mine near Zuni Salt Lake—was estimated at $250,000 by one expert, while an even more authoritative source put it at $500,000. At what may be the absolute high end of the spectrum, a native group in Alaska is said to have offered to identify TCPs for $10,000 per hour, their justification for the high price being that once they released the information they would never again be able to sell it. Of course, it's possible that it would have taken them only a few hours to download the data, but on the other hand, maybe not.

Two respondents from the Southwest compared the costs of TCP studies with the costs of archaeological surveys on the same projects. Two TCP studies costing $40,000 to $50,000 and $70,000 to $100,000 were estimated to be about half as costly as archaeological surveys done on the same areas of potential effects. Another estimate was that TCP work on a hypothetical twenty-mile road with five tribes involved and lots of archaeological sites might cost $20,000 to $30,000 per tribe ($100,000 to $150,000 total), while the archaeology on the same project might cost up to $2 million. I think my respondent in this case was probably including data recovery costs in his archaeological estimate.

I suspect that this wide range of costs reflects widely differing scopes of work. The pipeline through New Mexico, Colorado, and Utah can't have been a very short one, but it cost very little to study. On the other hand, it probably had limited effects beyond the immediate pipeline corridor, which may have been in old, disturbed right-of-way; there may not have been much to consult local communities about. Fence Lake, on the other hand, involves a tremendously large area and has been extremely contentious. Contention tends to make prices ratchet up. I also suspect that the pricier studies were relatively "pure" identification and evaluation efforts—whose scopes of work called for a lot of detailed property documentation uninformed by the potential effects of the projects that motivated them.

Notes

1. Draft nomination package provided to the author for review March 27, 2001, by Robin Bodo, National Register Coordinator, Delaware SHPO.

2. Ron May, personal communication, 2002.

3. Lynne Sebastian, Protecting Traditional Cultural Properties through the Section 106 Process, in P. L. Parker (ed.), *Traditional Cultural Properties: What You Do and How We Think, CRM* Special Issue (National Park Service, Washington, D.C., 1993), 26.

4. E. Richard Hart, The Fence Lake Mine Project: Archaeology as Traditional Cultural Property, in Parker (ed.), *Traditional Cultural Properties,* 38–41.

5. T. J. Ferguson, Kurt Dongoske, Leigh Jenkins, Mike Yeatts, and Eric Polingyouma, Working Together: The Roles of Archaeology and Ethnohistory in Hopi Cultural Preservation, in Parker (ed.), *Traditional Cultural Properties,* 27–37; Andrew L. Othole and Roger Anyon, A Tribal Perspective on Traditional Cultural Property Consultation, in Parker (ed.), *Traditional Cultural Properties,* 42–45.

6. Some argue that the specific location has to be known. Lynne Sebastian, who I think frames this side of the argument more reasonably, simply wants the place to figure somehow in tradition, even if its actual location is not remembered.

7. Howard Morphy, Landscape and the Reproduction of the Ancestral Past, in E. Hirsch and M. O'Hanlon (eds.), *The Anthropology of Landscape: Perspectives on Place and Space* (Clarendon, Oxford, 1999), 184.

8. Thomas F. King, Stupid TCP Tricks, in *Thinking about Cultural Resource Management: Essays from the Edge* (AltaMira, Walnut Creek, CA, 2002), 105–6.

9. For a detailed discussion of most of the relevant case law, see Sandra B. Zellmer, Sustaining Geographies of Hope: Cultural Resources on Public Lands, *University of Colorado Law Review* 73(2) (2002):413–519.

10. 36 CFR 60.4, sometimes referred to as "Consideration (a)," though the relevant (a)-labeled subparagraph of the rather clumsily written regulatory provision actually refers to *exceptions* to the consideration.

11. National Register, *Guidelines for Evaluating and Documenting Traditional Cultural Properties* (National Park Service, Washington, D.C., n.d. [sometimes (accurately) dated 1990]), 38:12–13.

12. See Lydia T. Grimm, Sacred Lands and the Establishment Clause: Indian Religious Practices on Federal Lands, *Natural Resources and Environment* 12(1)(1997):19–24; 78 (American Bar Association of Natural Resources, Energy, and Environmental Law); Zellmer, Sustaining Geographies of Hope.

13. *Lyng v. Northwest Indian Cemetery Protective Association*, 485 U.S. 439, 455 (1987).

14. It's also worth noting that by the time the Supreme Court's decision came down, the mills that needed the timber had mostly gone belly-up and the forest in the interior had been put in protected wilderness status. Congress then prohibited the Forest Service from using appropriated funds to complete the road, and today its two stubs serve Forest Service administrative purposes and facilitate access to the Helkau District by tribal religious practitioners.

15. *Lyng* at 452–53.

16. *Badoni v. Higginson,* 638 F.2d 172, 179 (10th Cir. 1980).

17. People who climb the cracks in columnar basalt outcrops, not people who climb on recreational drugs.

18. *Bear Lodge Multiple Use Association, et al. v. Bruce Babbitt, Secretary of the Interior, et al.,* No. 96-CV-063-D (D. Wyo. 1996).

19. *Bear Lodge Multiple Use Association, et al. v. Bruce Babbitt, Secretary of the Interior, et al.,* 175 F.3d, 814 (10th Cir. 1999).

20. Or, as Craig Alexander puts it (Protection of Indian Sacred Places and the Religious Accommodation Doctrine, in the proceedings of *Sovereignty Symposium X: Circles of Life* (sponsored by the Oklahoma Supreme Court, the Oklahoma Indian Affairs Commission, and the Sovereignty Symposium, Inc., Tulsa, June 9–11, 1997), a "sphere of religious autonomy" (93). He goes on to argue, however, that the window is a pretty wide one. Suggesting that the district court "erred" in its *Bear Lodge* decision, he asserts that at least where federally recognized tribes are involved, a broad range of "sacred sites" protections "fall within the permissible zone of the standard religious accommodation

doctrine" or "are not religious accommodations at all, but constitute permissible aspects of the government-to-government relationship" (99, 103). Maybe.

21. 746 F.Supp. 1395 (D. Ariz. 1990).

22. *National Mining Association v. Slater,* 167 F.Supp. 2d 265, 296 (2001). As this is written, however, a number of new cases have been filed specifically charging Establishment Clause violations in Section 106 reviews of impacts on tribal spiritual TCPs. The last dog is by no means hung.

23. Tom Meersman, Judge Dismisses Logging Group's Suit Alleging Religious Bias, *Minneapolis Star Tribune,* 2000.

24. ACHP comment to FERC, April 7, 1998, quoted in Ed Chaney and Victor Martino, *Estimated Economic Damage to the Skokomish Indian Tribe from Unregulated Construction and Operation of the City of Tacoma's Cushman Hydroelectric Project, 1926–1997* (Chinook Northwest Inc. and Martino and Associates, for Skokomish Indian Tribe, Shelton, WA, 1998), 3–56.

25. See Larry Nesper, Anna Willow, and Thomas F. King, *The Mushgigagamongsebe District: A Traditional Cultural Landscape of the Sokaogon Ojibwe Community,* report submitted to the Corps of Engineers, St. Paul District, by the Mole Lake Sokaogon Community of Great Lakes Chippewa Indians (Crandon, WI, 2002).

26. Codified as Section 502 of NHPA, 16 U.S.C. 470a note; emphasis added.

27. The report, *Cultural Conservation* (discussed in chap. 2), among other things ended up recommending that it be made clear that NHPA, NEPA, and other such laws extended protection to "the full range of cultural resources," including "historic properties, folklife, and related lifeways" (Ormond H. Loomis, *Cultural Conservation: The Protection of Cultural Heritage in the United States* [American Folklife Center, Library of Congress, Washington, D.C., 1983], 74). Needless to say, the change in national administrations that took place in 1980 doomed this recommendation to oblivion.

28. "There is naturally a dynamic relationship between tangible and intangible cultural resources, and the beliefs associated with a traditional cultural property are of central importance in defining its significance. However, it should be clearly recognized . . . that the National Register does not include intangible resources themselves." National Register n.d. 38:9.

29. See Council on Environmental Quality (CEQ), *Environmental Justice Guidance under the National Environmental Policy Act* (CEQ, Executive Office of the President, Washington, D.C., 1997).

30. Charles E. Haines, The South Lawrence Trafficway: Environmental Justice Guidance for Native Americans, in Robert D. Bullard and Glenn S. Johnson (eds.), *Just Transportation* (New Society, Gabriola Island, British Columbia, Canada, 1997). Also see *Thomasine Ross, et al. v. Geiger et al.,* 972 F.Supp. 552, (D. Kan. 1997).

31. Environmental Protection Agency (EPA), "Mission Possible," South Lawrence Trafficway: A National Environmental Policy Act Case Study, EPA Region 8, Environmental Justice Workshop (Denver, 1999).

32. The city of Newport News, Virginia, for which I consult on the case.

33. CEQ, *Environmental Justice Guidance*, 14: "Agencies may use demographic data available from the Bureau of the Census (BOC) to identify the composition of the potentially affected population." However, CEQ goes on, on the same page, to note that "impacts . . . may be different from impacts on the general population due to a community's distinct cultural practices. For example, data on different patterns of living, such as subsistence fish, vegetation, or wildlife consumption and the use of well water in rural communities may be relevant to the analysis."

34. Stoffle seems to interpret Bulletin 38 to demand that TCPs be small and bounded things, and hence prefers to talk about "cultural landscapes." At the same time, he seems (understandably) to dislike referring to the National Register at all and hence invokes AIRFA as the primary authority under which places of cultural importance to tribes must be considered in planning.

35. Richard W. Stoffle and Michael J. Evans, Holistic Conservation and Cultural Triage: American Indian Perspectives on Cultural Resources, *Human Organization* 49(2) (1990):95.

36. Published coincidentally with Bulletin 38, though without relationship other than that Stoffle, Evans, Parker, and I had communicated and crossed paths. Evans and Parker would later work together on Micronesian projects, and Evans is now an NPS ethnographer.

37. Stoffle and Evans, Holistic Conservation and Cultural Triage, 92. Examples of the approach include Richard W. Stoffle, David B. Halmo, John E. Olmsted, and Michael J. Evans, *Native American Cultural Resource Studies at Yucca Mountain, Nevada* (Institute for Social Research, University of Michigan, Ann Arbor, 1990); and Richard W. Stoffle, David B. Halmo, Michael J. Evans, and Diane E. Austin, *Piapaxa 'Uipi (Big River Canyon): Ethnographic Resource Inventory and Assessment for Colorado River Corridor, Glen Canyon National Recreation Area, Utah and Arizona, and Grand Canyon National Park, Arizona* (Bureau of Applied Research in Anthropology, University of Arizona, Tucson, 1993).

38. Stoffle and Evans, Holistic Conservation and Cultural Triage, 93.

39. Stoffle and Evans, Holistic Conservation and Cultural Triage, 94, quoting Dobyns (1951:31).

40. Stoffle and Evans, Holistic Conservation and Cultural Triage, 95.

41. Stoffle and Evans, Holistic Conservation and Cultural Triage, 97.

42. See Stoffle et al., *Native American Cultural Resource Studies;* Stoffle et al., *Piapaxa 'Uipi (Big River Canyon);* David B. Halmo, David B., Richard W. Stoffle, and Michael J. Evans, Paitu Nanasuagaindu Pahonupi (Three Sacred Valleys): Cultural Significance of Gosiute, Paiute, and Ute Plants, *Human Organization* 52(2) (1998): 142–50.

43. Stoffle and Evans, Holistic Conservation and Cultural Triage, 98.

44. Stoffle and Evans, Holistic Conservation and Cultural Triage, 95.

45. See T. J. Ferguson, Kurt Dongoske, Leigh Jenkins, Mike Yeatts, and Eric Polingyouma, Working Together: The Roles of Archaeology and Ethnohistory in Hopi

Cultural Preservation, in Parker (ed.), *Traditional Cultural Properties*, 36: "Cultural triage . . . is a non-Hopi concept."

46. Stoffle and Evans, Holistic Conservation and Cultural Triage, 95.

47. Hirini Matunga, Waahi Tapu: Maori Sacred Sites, in David L. Carmichael, Jane Hubert, Brian Reeves, and Audhild Schanch (eds.), *Sacred Sites, Sacred Places* (Routledge, London, 1994), 221.

48. John J. Wood and Walter M. Vannette, A Preliminary Assessment of the Significance of Navajo Sacred Places in the Vicinity of Big Mountain, Arizona, ms., Bureau of Indian Affairs (Navajo Area Office, Window Rock, AZ, 1979).

49. Walter Vannette and Alison Feary, Navajo Sacred Places and Resource Use in and near the Coconino, Kaibab, and Apache Sitgreaves National Forests, confidential ms. on file (Coconino National Forest, Flagstaff AZ, 1981).

50. Klara B. Kelley and Harris Francis, *Navajo Sacred Places* (Indiana University Press, Bloomington, 1994), 92–94.

Chapter Thirteen

A View from the Hill

The cave has power
Whirlwind dances
On the valley floor
Sometimes people
Come to watch.
Not all of them can see.

—Wintu poet Tauhindali (1979:24),
quoted in Theodoratus and LaPena (1994:24)

Losing Special Places and Living in the Present

MY sunny, horehound-fragrant hillside in Northern California has become landscaping for the million-dollar homes of cyberexecutives and their lawyers and accountants. Is this a bad thing? I don't suppose so, but I do feel some regret, and I think my feelings aren't entirely selfish. I wish every dreaming adolescent such a hillside, or island, lake, rock, grove, or urban rooftop, and every such place that's lost diminishes us all.

And if losing my hillside is diminishing, how much worse is the loss of a place held dear by a whole community, through generations?

Lots worse, of course. Lots worse to lose Woodruff Butte, the Hopi shrine site blasted and bulldozed into oblivion for gravel.[1] Lots worse for giant telescopes and their accoutrements to be built on land scraped off the top of Mount Graham over the objections of Apache spiritual people—even in the service of space exploration.[2] Lots worse when the people of Poletown were dragged out of their neighborhood as it was leveled for an auto plant. Lots worse, if it happens, for the Quechan Trail of Dreams landscape to be torn up by the Glamis Mine.

But speaking of mines, not long ago I was privileged to sit in on a conference of indigenous fighters of mines—the kind one digs, not the kind that blow people up, though I imagine the conferees felt pretty negative about that kind, too. I work with a couple of Indian tribes that are trying to stop mines that will do violence to their TCPs; I was, and am, entirely sympathetic to the overall goals of the conference. But as I sat and watched the participants discuss strategies for increasing public support for, and influencing decision makers toward, "our side," which was defined as "the *no mining*" position, I found myself feeling uneasy. I couldn't help but ponder the pickups parked around the powwow ground—every one, ultimately, dug out of a mine. And I couldn't help thinking that if we want pickups, we can't *not* want mines.

I imagine that after some quibbling, the conferees would acknowledge this fact. I imagine that having done so they'd refocus their discussion. We aren't necessarily opposed to all mines, they'd say, but indigenous people need to fight *this* particular mine or *that* mine, or the other mine, and we're trying to help each other develop the tools to do so.

Fair enough, I think, and I'm happy to try to help. But to the extent each group is successful, doesn't this simply shift the burden to others? Ultimately doesn't it mean that we—we antimining North American indigenes and friends—are foisting mines and all their impacts off on our brethren in Africa or Brazil or Siberia, who aren't in as good a legal or social or economic position as we to fight them off? Is *that* right?

Hardly an original problem, and I'm sure the organizers of the conference—smart, wise, dedicated people—would be impatient with me for bringing it up. But it's an unresolved problem, and one that we who work on the identification and management of special places like TCPs have to wrestle with all the time. Or, more often, elect *not* to wrestle with, either adopting a simple position pro or con, or deciding that our clients' interests, whatever they are, are our own.

As usual, my own approach to the problem, such as it is, is equivocating. There are, I think, some mines (and roads, and telescopes, and power plants) that simply can't be put in place without doing such violence to the valued cultural landscape that they shouldn't be allowed. The two that my clients are fighting are among these, which I must admit raises even *my* eyebrow. But we've got to have things like mines somewhere, and while it's nice to have the luxury to be simply antimining (or anti–any kind of development) without having to be troubled by the practical consequences, in general we in CRM are in the business of seeking compromises. We seek middle ways that permit and even facilitate the work of the present and future while respecting . . . .

Well, respecting what? Not respecting *the past,* as the tired old formula of historic preservation would have it, because the past doesn't give a damn whether it's respected or not.[3]

Respecting what people in the present value about the past, certainly. Or what they value about their cultures and traditions, which are rooted in the past but actually operate in the present and find their meaning in the future. Respecting their attachment to places, and maybe respecting the places themselves, for their intrinsic power where they're thought to have it, and for their power to influence people's lives wherever that power resides.

Respecting Place Attachment

How can we—and by "we" I mean we CRM practitioners, the agencies and change agents for which we typically work, and our elected representatives—respect people's attachment to places? The answer that threads its way through this book is "by interpreting the laws and regulations we work with, notably Section 106, to require and facilitate such respect."

But the language of the laws, the structure of the systems set up as results of the laws, and the character of those—we—who practice under the laws don't necessarily do this. The laws and regulations were written from inside mainstream culture, not by "natives" either in the strict sense of indigenes or in Mary Hufford's sense of someone whose culture is "most endangered because it is hard to see except when cast into relief by cultural change."[4] It's easiest to interpret them from the same perspective, especially when one is oneself a product of mainstream culture, as most CRM practitioners are.

It's easy for those of us who don't have well-emplaced roots, who are sufficiently separated from our ancestors to have lost touch with the places they treasured, to be impatient with more rooted communities and particularly with groups that are trying to reestablish roots across historical and cultural gulfs.

It's tempting to impose our mainstream expertise on them—to bore holes in the sacred grove's trees and show that they couldn't have been standing when the ancestors were doing scaffold burials, to demonstrate that the skeleton's DNA isn't consistent with its being the tribe's ancestor, to discredit the story that Murrieta robbed stagecoaches at The Rocks.

And if a community continues to insist that despite our solid, well-founded evidence and logic, the place is really significant, that we just don't understand, one can be tempted to fall in with Haley and Wilcoxon, and the critics of the women of Hindmarsh Island—accusing the stubborn people of making it all up and causing us all a lot of trouble just to feed their fantasies.

But then, what is fantasy? If the Western Gate and the place of women's business on Hindmarsh Island are fantasies, Marshall Sahlins would have us understand that similar fantasies lie at the core of Western intellectual history.

[I]t happens that in the fifteenth and sixteenth centuries a bunch of indigenous intellectuals and artists in Europe got together and began inventing their traditions and themselves by attempting to revive the learning of an ancient culture which they claimed to be the achievement of their ancestors. . . . All this came to be called the Renaissance in European history, because it gave birth to "modern civilization." What else can one say about it, except that some people have all the historical luck? When Europeans invent their traditions . . . it is a genuine cultural rebirth, the beginnings of a progressive future. When other peoples do it, it is a sign of cultural decadence, a facetious recuperation, which can only bring forth the simulacra of a dead past.[5]

We CRM practitioners—descendants of those lucky Renaissance inventers—are in an odd position. Our business is to apply our intellectual traditions of science and the humanities to conflicts that are often between those very values and the interests of "natives" in retaining and reinventing their traditional cultures.

Surely it is *not* our business to decide whether a given group's attachment to place is part of a fruitful renaissance or merely a facetious recuperation—to determine that, say, Hopi TCPs are valid and Cincinnati's East Enders' are not. Nor, I believe, is it our business to apply our scientific skills to validating or invalidating traditions like those that identify Point Conception as the Western Gate.

So, what *is* our job?

I think it's essentially a job of translation—trying to understand clearly what the "natives" are saying (and sometimes not saying) about the places that matter to them and recasting what they say in terms that resonate with the mainstream legal system and that make some modicum of sense to managers and politicians. At the same time, it's trying to find ways in which the conflicting values can be harmonized. How can we have our telescopes and Mount Graham too? To put it another way, we're trying to make sure that the cultural interests of traditional communities are understood and given fair consideration in planning and decision making, on a par with the way everyone else's cultural interests are considered.

Has Bulletin 38 Helped?

If our purpose is to respect the cultural values and aspirations of traditional communities by making sure they're addressed fairly in planning and decision making, have we advanced that purpose by writing and implementing National Register Bulletin 38?

There are really two parts to this question. First, has Bulletin 38 actually encouraged better consideration of TCPs by federal agencies and other change agents?

I think the answer to this one is yes, though it's hard to point to a lot of really obvious cases. At this writing the Glamis gold mine has not been permitted by BLM, and I have to think that the attention it got via Section 106 review has something to do with that. True, the Glamis case has been reopened by the Bush administration, and the permit may yet be issued, but no decision-making system I know of is immune to the influences of politics and money. At Mount Graham, a rather belated decision by the Keeper of the National Register that the mountain is in fact eligible makes it very likely—for better or worse for those of us who support both preservation and space science—that future astronomical observatory development there will be curtailed. Section 106 and Bulletin 38 provided the basis for doing something about the power substation next to the Matachines Dance Site at El Rancho and for getting the Forest Service to pay closer attention to tribal cultural concerns in Las Huertas Canyon. Section 106 and Bulletin 38 were deployed in the fight to save the Valley of the Chiefs in Wyoming—certainly along with other weapons—and the valley has been saved.

On the other hand, some of the celebrated cases in which Section 106 review has *not* protected TCPs are instructive—in many ways exceptions that prove the rule.

At Mount Graham, for example, before the keeper's determination, observatory and road construction was permitted by the Forest Service despite the mountain's well-documented cultural significance to the Apache, but this was a case in which the Section 106 process was bollixed by all sides. The Forest Service Regional Office had a long history of aggressive ignorance toward both tribal issues and Section 106 review, and interpreted its responsibilities accordingly. The tribe raised its objections much later in the review process than it should have, after allowing a record to be created that suggested no particular concern about the project. And the case is one that has been in train since before Bulletin 38 hit the streets; some learning time has to be expected.

At Woodruff Butte, where Hopi shrines were destroyed by a private rock quarry, the federal "handle" on the destruction—use of some of the rock on a federally assisted highway project—was a very slender one, made more so by a bizarre Federal Highway Administration policy excluding certain kinds of materials sources from Section 106 review. This policy had nothing to do with TCPs or Bulletin 38 per se, and has been undermined (as it were) by the district court's decision[6] in the Woodruff Butte case.

At Mount Shasta, though the eligibility determination process was badly mishandled, the ultimate result was a decision not to permit the ski resort, and a great increase in overall understanding and coordination between the Forest Service and the tribes.

Enola Hill was logged only through an extraordinary act of Congress and was hardly devastated to the extent its protectors predicted.

Less visibly, I think that Bulletin 38 has given tribes, communities, and caring people in agencies and SHPO offices and the Advisory Council staff something to hang their hats on in negotiations with change agents, and it's certainly given a number of plaintiffs something to use in court. All this, I think, has resulted in a lot of low-visibility cooperation, coordination, consultation, and through it all a lot of low-visibility preservation of places and landscapes that matter to people. Where it doesn't result in actual "preservation" in a physical sense, I think it's often helped achieve compromises that respect, and avoid great damage to, community interests in maintaining and renewing traditional culture. This sort of day-to-day achievement doesn't get a lot of attention, but it happens.

But of course, it might have happened anyway. Richard Stoffle uses AIRFA and NEPA more than NHPA as bases for coordination between land management agencies and tribes. A great deal can be said for the growing tribal willingness and ability to use the tools that treaties, the Constitution, NEPA, and Justice John Marshall[7] gave them. The people of Manteo protected their town's "sacred structure" without using the National Register. The fact that Bulletin 38 has not been much seized upon by non-Indian communities may be evidence that by itself it's not good for much; it's only riding on the coattails of more powerful laws and social forces.

And then there's the second part of the question. Even assuming that Bulletin 38 has done some good, has it had negative effects that overbalance its contributions?

There is no question that the application of Section 106, and NHPA in general, to TCPs as a result of Bulletin 38—or at least to indigenous TCPs—has a serious downside for the very communities whose interests the bulletin was designed to help protect. In response to an internet query about problems with Bulletin 38, Lynne Sebastian wrote:

> TCPs fit very, very badly into the Section 106 process because it is a negotiated process and there is almost always no room for negotiation with TCPs. Usually there is no possible mitigation, the only valid outcome from the perspective of the tribe is "Don't build the project." And so if you do build the project, they see it as an egregious act of bad faith. So most of the time we end up going through a frequently painful process of identification of properties that we already know we aren't going to be able to protect. It becomes a very hollow and unsatisfying process for both sides.[8]

So the question can't be avoided:

Was Bulletin 38 a Mistake?

Sebastian's comment suggests that it was—that by writing and publishing the bulletin, Parker and I raised expectations that could only be crushed by the cold weight of reality. She also emphasizes, correctly I think, the "painful process of identification" that the bulletin imposes on efforts to protect TCPs.

Moreover, the focus of Bulletin 38 on places eligible for the National Register—which of course creates Sebastian's "painful process"—clashes with the very cultural values for which the bulletin was intended to encourage respect, and hence can itself have the effect of distorting and damaging those values. As Alan Downer and Alexa Roberts dryly commented back in 1993, "Not surprisingly, Navajos (and undoubtedly many other American Indians) have great difficulty in dividing up the physical world in a way that is most comfortable and convenient for cultural resource managers."[9]

Pat Parker was a bit gentler in commenting on the disconnect between the world of mainstream historic preservation and the values of traditional tribal communities, but she made essentially the same point, in the year Bulletin 38 was published:

Historic properties important for the "retention and preservation of the American Indian way of life" include not only the places where significant events happen or have happened, but also whole classes of natural elements: plants, animals, fish, birds, rocks, mountains. These natural elements are incorporated into tribal tradition and help form the matrix of spiritual, ceremonial, political, social, and economic life.[10]

One of the participants in Parker's "Keepers of the Treasures" conferences was more blunt: "I'm not really sure that [historic preservation]'s the way we want to look at these things at all. In our way of thinking, everything is a significant event, and the past is as real to us as being here right now. We are all connected to the things that happened at the beginning of our existence. And those things live on as they are handed down to us."[11]

Examples could be proliferated, but Robert Winthrop has summed up the problem nicely, I think: "[T]he policy and practice of cultural resource management (including the study of 'traditional cultural properties') are not well grounded in culture theory. Any public policy framework for protecting places of cultural value to contemporary communities should start by emphasizing communities rather than places, and the interrelation of tradition and change rather than cultural stasis."[12]

I'm very much attracted to Winthrop's conclusion about policy and practice—indeed, I agree with it entirely. If I were king of the world, I'd certainly make policy start where he suggests. But I'm not, so I can't. Nor was I, or Pat Parker, in the mid-1980s when the idea for Bulletin 38 began to filter through our heads. We were both mid-level federal bureaucrats in the national historic preservation program. That program is built around the National Register and Section 106.

In these roles, in that program, we saw segments of the American public being deprived of the opportunity to get agencies to pay attention to places they held dear. That seemed wrong. We also saw cultural resource management becoming more and more a narrow, esoteric sort of thing, of interest only to archaeologists and architectural historians. That seemed dangerous.[13] We wrote Bulletin 38 to help get CRM focused back on what mattered to real people, in real communities. I don't think that was a wrong thing to do.

So no, I don't think Bulletin 38 was a mistake; it's just not perfect, not the be-all and end-all. And as with anything else in life, we have to be alert to its unintended side-effects, and try to make adjustments to keep them under control.

Sebastian suggests that the bulletin and the involvement of TCPs in Section 106 review have raised people's expectations only to dash them. I don't disagree, but I think that anybody who expects a federal guideline to guarantee the permanent protection of his special places must be living in an alternative universe. At the very least, the nature of the Section 106 process must not have been explained very well to him. Traditional tribal religious practitioners, and many others who value various types of TCPs, would like very much for the law to provide permanent and absolute protection to the places they hold dear, but it simply doesn't. Section 106 doesn't, and neither does any other law. We couldn't change that with a National Register bulletin, even if we'd wanted to.

And speaking strictly for myself, I'll say that I didn't want to. That is, I didn't want, and don't want, to see the protection of TCPs elevated above everything else in public policy. Not only is this a completely unrealistic thing to wish for, I can't even believe that it would be a good thing. I respect and support the protection of Apache traditional culture, but I also think it's important to probe the depths of the universe, and that requires telescopes on high places. Should such things be built without consulting the Apache and looking for ways to build them without injury to the tribe and their special places? Absolutely not, but in the final analysis, after due consideration, if there's no feasible compromise some public official is going to have to make a decision. I don't think the decision maker should be precluded from making a decision that comes down on the side of probing the universe, even if it does injury to the tribe's cultural values, if he or she concludes that that's where the public interest lies.

That said, however, I'll also acknowledge that we're a long, long way from making sure the Apache, or any other group outside the central line of descent from Sahlins' bunch of European revivalists, gets a fair shake in environmental and land use planning. Bulletin 38 was designed to help force that fair shake, but it's by no means enough by itself, even in the small world of CRM. And it's by no means without its warts.

So What Now?

So in our small world of CRM, if it wasn't enough to issue Bulletin 38, if it's not enough to try to practice well under its guidance, what else should be done?

Self-Flagellation

One of the least useful things for cultural resource managers to do, I think, is to bemoan our failures. Anthropologists and archaeologists often do this, ascribing to themselves a level of responsibility for poor management that ironically may let managers themselves go on ignoring the problem. Gordon Mohs decries the fact that "[d]amage to spiritual sites has gone largely unnoticed by non-Indians" and goes on to attribute this, in Canada, to "a general lack of interaction between Indians and archaeologists and a failure on the part of archaeologists to incorporate native research interests and/or religious concerns into their project designs."[14] The same can certainly be said about the failure of historic preservation professionals of all stripes to relate effectively with the communities in and with which they work.

With respect, however, I think that Mohs gives himself and his colleagues more (dis)credit than is due, and in doing so, indulges in something of a cop-out. However self-absorbed archaeologists have been, in Canada and elsewhere, and however thoughtlessly we have appropriated the pasts and cultures of other people without their consent or participation, archaeologists are not the ones who manage the land or control the projects. In a way, blaming ourselves is itself an example of our self-absorption; it's easier to berate oneself for insensitivity than to try actually to work with managers and decision makers to improve the situation. I may be doing Mohs a great disservice here, and I stress that I have no axe to grind with him personally or professionally. But indigenous people and others outside the mainstream of political power have far bigger fish than archaeologists and anthropologists to fry, and we're not going to help them by filling the pan with our own flapping filets.

Stronger Protective Legislation

If self-blame doesn't help, what about legislation? Should we toughen up our laws to give absolute protection to TCPs or to some subset of TCPs like "sacred sites?"

Absolutely not, for at least two reasons.[15]

The biggest reason is that such a law, like lots of other protective laws—the Endangered Species Act, for instance—would be a Band-Aid applied to a gushing belly wound. Spiritual places and treasured neighborhoods and sun-dappled hillsides don't have a chance of survival as long as we persist in our quaint belief that Growth is Good, as long as we continue to define ourselves as "consumers," and as long as we fail to control our penchant for procreation. Huffing and puffing about protecting this, that, and the other specific kind of thing from the depredations of the modern world are exercises in futility if we can't or won't address the basic factors that make the modern world predatory.

A less cosmic reason to eschew draconian preservation laws is the one I touched on in chapter 1: It must follow as the night the day that the more stringent the protections given a thing, the more narrowly the thing will come to be defined, and the more the thing and its protections will become matters for lawyerly hairsplitting. Give absolute protection to TCPs—or historic properties in general, or endangered species, or "sacred sites"—and you will soon find yourself locked in mortal combat over whether or not this thing or that is a protected thing, and the criteria for recognizing a protected thing will become more and more crabbed and lawyerly. While Rome burns, you'll be fighting over how to recognize a fiddle.

So What's the Alternative?

Legislation may be needed to do a better job by TCPs—it probably is, and I'll suggest a possibility shortly. But something might also be done with the laws already on the books. Admittedly, by themselves these laws don't protect much, but they provide ways for concerned people to engage the political process in ways that *do* achieve protections, of various kinds, at various levels. And these protections bear some crude relationship to the level of importance of the thing for which protection is sought. A hillside valued by one aging adolescent gets no protection; a Trail of Dreams or a Helkau Historic District gets a lot more.

What's on the books? Let's begin with the National Environmental Policy Act. The *policy* established by NEPA, as opposed to the law's procedural elements, favors careful attention in everything the government does to the quality of the human environment, including "cultural . . . aspects of our national heritage."[16] That's a powerful policy, a profound policy, but little real attention is paid to it. NEPA is thought of as strictly a procedural law; all the focus is on whether to do an EIS or an EA, or whether a given project can be squeezed into a category that's excluded from review. If agencies were motivated to really consider the environment, including its cultural aspects, when they formulate policy or make recommendations to Congress, and for that matter if Congress and the president could be encouraged to hold themselves to such a standard, it could make some difference.

More specifically, we could try to take hold of NEPA's regulatory language and do something with it. The regulations say that in establishing the significance of impacts, agencies must consider "historic and cultural resources."[17] NEPA analysts tend to interpret both words to mean "places eligible for or included in the National Register," but clearly that's not what *cultural* means, or it wouldn't have been set apart from *historic*. Somebody like the Council on Environmental Quality could develop guidance about what cultural resources really are, and what ought to be done about them when planning something that might affect them. This could be the basis for giving more, better, earlier, consultative attention to TCPs without having to worry about whether they're eligible for the register—and for addressing impacts on less material aspects of culture as well.

Then there's the American Indian Religious Freedom Act. Lawyers tend to scorn AIRFA because it's "just policy." It doesn't tell anybody to do anything specific. The same lawyers, and the agencies they work for, also complain about "micromanagement" if Congress gives them very specific direction. AIRFA articulates sound policy; what's needed is for agencies to apply it when they set up their operating procedures—when they design the systems by which environmental impacts will be considered under NEPA, for example, and when they carry out Section 106 review. The same goes for the Religious Freedom Restoration Act and Executive Order 12898 on Environmental Justice. There's room for agency and interagency initiative in developing such systems, and for executive direction to agencies from the White House, if anyone there were so inclined. There's also room for some suasion by outside organizations, notably such culture-oriented organizations as the American Anthropological Association.

And, of course, there's Section 106. I've argued elsewhere that the best thing to do with Section 106 is to uncouple it from the National Register.[18] I think such an uncoupling would make for better historic preservation, and it would make the process of dealing with TCPs (among other things) a lot easier and less silly. But that's not going to happen without legislation.

What could be done with Section 106 without legislation is to rethink the regulations by which it's implemented, improving coordination with NEPA, AIRFA, and the rest. This would be good for a lot more than just the management of impacts on TCPs—one of the biggest problems we face in cultural resource management in this country is the plethora of uncoordinated culturally related laws and regulations.[19] But it could help TCPs specifically by focusing impact review on those impacts that are important to communities.

What should we try to get from such a coordination of regulations? Clear, unequivocal direction to agencies that in planning things—whether specific things like timber sales and low-income housing construction or general things like assistance to farmers; they need to consult with communities about what's culturally important to them that might be affected and work with communities to keep the effects under control.

Why would better and earlier consultation help? Because many of the conflicts we face over impacts on TCPs arise as a result of agency failure to consult well enough, or to do it early enough, to catch problems before they become intractable. The conflict over Mount Graham in Arizona is largely the product of very poor consultation with tribes by the Forest Service early in planning the observatories on the mountain. The fight over the Valley of the Chiefs (Weatherman Draw) in Montana was the product of a bizarre Bureau of Land Management policy that defers environmental review of—and hence consultation about—mineral leases until the lessee is ready to start drilling holes in the ground. The same policy is at the base of the conflict over geothermal development on the Medicine Lake Highlands in California. Failure to consult with the community, and seriously address its cultural concerns, certainly lay at the base of the conflicts in Corona[20] and in Cincinnati's East End.[21] Early and full community participation in planning, focusing on the cultural values that turned a conglomeration of ordinary places into a "sacred structure," was what made Randolph Hester's Manteo plan[22] a model.

Getting agencies to take their environmental planning responsibilities more seriously and to exercise those responsibilities in a more consultative, open way would go far toward preserving all kinds of environmental values, including cultural values.

Note: *cultural values*, not just TCPs, and certainly not just National Register–eligible TCPs. Not just small plots of land that some outside authority certifies are special. In planning changes to the world we ought to be looking broadly at, and consulting about impacts on, the cultural, spiritual, human values that people ascribe to rocks and trees, animals and water, boat docks and parking lots and street corners, and to such "intangible" cultural institutions as stories, social institutions, music, art, and property rights. In a system with this sort of scope, TCPs would get plenty of consideration without our having to tease them apart from the human contexts that make them worth considering.

Every annual meeting of the National Association of Environmental Professionals has sessions on "public participation." There are good models of consultation about environmental matters out in the world. But there's no overall, authoritative direction to agencies to do such consultation, to use such models, so on the whole it doesn't happen. On the whole, agencies continue to hold public hearings and think they've done the job of consulting the interested public. A lot could be done by prevailing on such agencies as the Council on Environmental Quality and the Environmental Protection Agency to put out not just guidelines but regulations calling for real consultation about matters of community concern.

But CEQ and EPA are unlikely to undertake such rule making—they're certainly not going to do so without some clear articulation of need, powerfully argued from within the agency or pressed on it from outside. Neither seems very likely in the foreseeable future, so we come back to the idea of legislation.

A Legislative Fix

Charles E. Little has advanced a proposal that I think has merit in his article, "Toward a Sacred Lands Policy Initiative"[23]—though in the end, it, like other highly protective legislative proposals fails to control for protection's unforeseen (but foreseeable) implications.

Little puts considerable emphasis on appropriating funds to purchase "sacred sites." He would create a federally funded foundation to make grants to nonprofit groups, charge the Bureau of Indian Affairs with acquiring sites and bringing them into trust status, and amend the Land and Water Conservation Fund Act to provide acquisition grants to tribes. I think these and perhaps other ways of funding outright fee-simple or less-than-fee acquisition (easements, etc.) are worth a great deal of attention. The only way a group can be really sure of protecting its spiritual places is to get possession of them.

When it comes to regulating the activities of federal agencies, Little proposes amendments to NHPA and AIFRA requiring "the explicit application of a 'three-part test' regarding management decisions on public lands, namely, 'If a government action imposes a burden on religion, then the action must be justified by a compelling government interest that cannot be met through less restrictive means.'" In other words, Little would up the ante in the Section 106 process, in concert with AIRFA, where impacts on a "sacred site" or the practice of traditional religion is involved. As a means of protecting spiritual places and practices (but not, obviously, all kinds of TCPs), this approach makes sense, but it could be improved. For one thing, of course, since Section 106 applies to all kinds of Federal actions, not just those on "public lands," that should be the scope of the proposed amendment as well. An agency should have to apply the three-part test to any decision it makes, whether the decision is about actions on land it controls, or about granting a permit or assistance. I also think there might be some alternatives to the "three-part test" that could be explored—for example, the "no prudent and feasible alternative" standard used in Section 4(f) of the Department of Transportation Act.

But in using NHPA as a major vehicle for deciding whether and how "sacred sites" should be protected from impact by government actions, Little falls into the same trap as has everyone else who's set out to ratchet up the

protection given "sacred sites." NHPA is built around the National Register—a list of places documented to be significant, to the satisfaction of the
Keeper. And while it is possible for an agency, tribe, and others to agree that
a place will be "considered eligible" without a lot of study and documentation, it's also possible for an agency, the Park Service, or others to insist on a
lot of proof that the place really meets the National Register's criteria. If this
happened—as it inevitably would if Little's "three-part test" became a
requirement of law—then those seeking to protect a "sacred site" would find
themselves humbly petitioning the keeper for her indulgences, submitting a
great deal of information and hoping that the keeper would find it convinc-
ing enough to "certify" that their spiritual places were "really sacred." The
politics and litigation that would inevitably come to surround the identification and management of "sacred sites" would create a world in which very
few sites would be protected from a very small range of impacts.

And, of course, Little's approach wouldn't do anything for TCPs that aren't
American Indian "sacred sites."

The strength of Little's model lies in its proposals for land acquisition and
in its reliance on consultation and resolution of conflicts rather than on absolute
prohibitions. I think that something very useful could be made of legislation
that,

- following Little's direction, established vehicles for acquiring threatened
  TCPs, or high-profile charismatic TCP-like places, and for their management by concerned communities; and

- established a general requirement for consultation and conflict resolution, like Section 106 but better, without links to the National Register—to resolve culture/development conflicts of all kinds.

How might this work? Imagine a change agent—call him Joe—who wants
federal assistance to put in a llama farm. Suppose that under our hypothetical
new law the assistance agency required Joe to consult early in planning his project with whoever might be concerned about any cultural impact of his project,
and to try to reach accommodation with them. So Joe contacts everybody in the
neighborhood and learns, let's say, that there's a rocky hillock on the property
that a local Indian tribe is very concerned about, though they don't want to tell
him why.

I think there's an excellent chance that accommodation could be reached
between Joe and the concerned tribe, because it may well be that the llama farm
can be built and operated without doing damage to the hillock—which let's say
is important to the tribe because of the medicinal plants that grow there. Joe

might very easily and happily be able to fence the hillock and agree to perpetual tribal access to it—if everybody sits down and talks about the potential conflict early, in a congenial, problem-solving way. And if they reach agreement, there's no need to release a lot of information about the hillock and its plants and what the tribal medicine people do there. The conflict gets resolved without violating the cultural values of the tribe, and without embroiling Joe and everybody else in a lot of esoteric arguments about the significance of plant gathering areas.

But suppose the hillock isn't just an important medicine place but the tribe's traditional origin site—a very, very important spiritual place that's supposed to be kept very, very secret. And suppose it's right in the middle of the only place Joe can put his llama barn. Suppose, then, that consultation reaches an impasse.

At this point, our legislation might have the tribe and Joe go to the assistance agency and make their cases. Joe's case would have to be that his llama operation was more important than whatever it was the tribe thought was so important about the hillock, or that he could make the farm work without damaging it—whatever it is. The tribe's job would be to show that there are ways to protect the site without unduly encumbering other public interests. In making this showing, the tribe would decide how much special information about the site it wanted to put on the table; it wouldn't be forced to reveal more than it thought strategically necessary.

The task of the assistance agency then would be to try to find a solution and make a decision in the public interest. Would the decision always be in favor of the tribe? No, of course not. Would it *often* be in favor of the tribe, or whatever group values the place? That depends substantially on how the process is set up—how well consultation articulates with planning, how the review takes place, by whom the decision is made, what constraints are placed on the decision. It would also depend on what options—like buyouts by government, the tribe, a non-profit foundation, or whatever—are available.

What is certain is that a consultation-centered process wouldn't automatically create conflicts. It also wouldn't require tribes to reveal all their spiritual areas and what makes them special, and to defend their beliefs in public. And unlike "sacred sites" legislation, it wouldn't result in—at best—protecting just a few places from just a few kinds of impacts. It could be a means of causing all kinds of TCPs, and other culturally valued aspects of the environment, to be better treated in planning for land use and development.

The Future of TCPs

It's been about fifteen years since Pat Parker and I first began kicking around the idea of writing about what eventually came to be called TCPs. My hope is that in another fifteen years the idea of giving sensitive consideration to places that communities think are important will be such a basic part of environmental and land use planning that nobody needs to talk about "TCPs" anymore.

Bob Garvey used to say that our job at the Advisory Council was to work our way out of our jobs, by making historic preservation such an automatic part of the federal government's business that the Council's oversight and advice were no longer needed. I'd like to think the same thing about TCPs.

TCPs are places of powerful attachment for living communities, that don't fit very well into the traditional paradigms of historic preservation; environmental impact assessment; and land use, regional, and urban planning.[24] I'd like to think that getting agencies and planners to give explicit attention to this kind of property is a step on the road to a more sophisticated, culturally sound way of planning. One that, in Rob Winthrop's words, emphasizes "communities rather than places, and the interrelation of tradition and change rather than cultural stasis."[25]

If we ever get such a system, we won't have to talk about TCPs anymore. Instead; we'll simply ascertain, through thoughtful and effective consultation, what a community's concerns are about its environment, and seek as best we can to avoid treading on those concerns.

I recently had occasion to visit Mount Shasta, and to walk in Panther Meadow. It was a beautiful, clear, blue-skied day, and the great stone-gray and snow-white bowl where the ski resort had been planned hung above us, unmarred by lifts and lodges. The whole meadow gurgled with snowmelt and spring water running through the tufted grasses and sedges. There were only a few people—one woman doing a charcoal sketch, a man with long blonde hair meditating on a rock, in the lotus position, another woman just sitting quietly.

What most impressed me was how the meadow—this unquestioned TCP, this obvious cultural resource—was being truly managed. We walked along meandering paths, mostly without markers or borders, that led us gently and without damage through the lush alpine vegetation. Where a pathway had gotten overused, it was closed with a low-key marker—a stake little bigger than a large tongue depressor, marked with a struck-out shoe sole symbol. These closures were being respected; the vegetation was growing back.

Where the trails began, near a campsite and parking lot a discrete distance from the meadows, there was a modest interpretive exhibit—just a big signboard, really—with rules posted for using the area. But not just a list of "thou shalt nots." There was a simply written explanation of *why* one should respect the meadow both because of its ecological fragility and to respect its cultural and religious importance. There was a specific discussion of what the meadow means to the tribes and how tribal representatives had worked with the Forest Service to develop the rules that visitors were asked to follow. Very happily, considering past conflicts between tribal traditionalists and New Age practitioners over the latter's use of the meadows, there was a simple, clear explanation that such activities as drumming and putting things (like crystals) in the springs are considered disrespectful. Maybe it's different at other times, but I heard no drumming, and saw nothing in the springs other than plants, insects, and clean water.

Down in Mount Shasta City, we picked up a little brochure, a *Sacred Sites Pocket Directory*[26] written to guide visitors on a tour of twelve New Age "sacred sites" on and around the mountain. Straight-facedly reporting on the water spirits, Lemurians, and "unusual inner-earth energies" to be encountered at the various sites, the *Directory* routinely and quietly encouraged respectful treatment of spirits and sites alike. "Please respect the sacred grounds," the *Directory* says of Pluto Caves; for example, "keep to the marked paths and carry out everything that you carry in." We visited Pluto Caves and found the lava tubes there unmarred by anything but very old graffiti.

Later, dining with the inimitable Michelle Berditschevsky, spokesperson for coalitions to save Mount Shasta and the Medicine Lake Highlands, long a formidable fighter against the Forest Service, we learned that she and her colleagues, tribal and Anglo alike, had worked with the Forest Service to develop the management approach and interpretive signs at Panther Meadows, and with the publishers of the *Directory* to make sure that visiting New Agers (and touring CRM practitioners) were properly sensitized to how the area's spiritual sites should be respected. The adversaries who had fought one another tooth and claw over where to establish the boundary of Mount Shasta as a National Register eligible TCP are quietly working together, and with others, to manage the place.

It reminded me of a story I heard a few years ago about a forest fire that had swept through the Six Rivers National Forest and approached the Helkau Historic District—pivot point in the GO Road case. The Forest Service deployed its firefighters, the story went, and the tribes deployed their elders—up the GO Road to the site, where they prayed and invoked the spirits. And the fire turned around and went back down into the canyons.

Maybe the story's apocryphal, but it *ought* to be true, because it is the case that the Forest Service and the tribes in California have emerged from contention over TCPs into a better place, where they often—not always, but often—are able to talk, to respect one another's views, and more often than not to cooperate in the management of the National Forests' special places.

I'd like to think that Panther Meadow and the Helkau Historic District represent the future of TCPs everywhere. Quietly, cooperatively managed by government and communities in a spirit of mutual respect, without concern for proofs of historicity, or designation, or boundaries. Available to the people who value them to use and experience, but not shut away from respectful use by others.

On Mount Shasta and the Six Rivers, though, before the contenders could become cooperators, they had to beat on one another for awhile. It's too bad, and perhaps it's largely an artifact of our planning and decision-making system, but this sort of pummeling seems almost always to be a necessary prelude to cooperative management. If National Register Bulletin 38 has helped equalize this contention a bit, given communities a stick to use in getting government's attention, then it has served its purpose.

But the day may yet come when we don't have to talk about TCPs and the National Register and can just respect one another and the places that each community counts as special. I don't expect to live to see such a day, but it's something to aspire to.

Notes

1. Woodruff Butte, site of a privately owned and operated rock quarry, was also the site of important Hopi shrines. It was effectively destroyed in 1999. See Christopher McLeod (producer/director), *In the Light of Reverence*, videotape, Sacred Lands Film Project (Earth Image Films, La Honda, CA, 2000).

2. Development of observatories on the mountain, by the University of Arizona and a number of cooperating institutions (including the Vatican) has been permitted by the Forest Service after long-running Section 106 litigation.

3. At least, I don't think it does. People who say they've been told by spirits that some ancient place shouldn't be disturbed—a not uncommon phenomenon among indigenous groups—would not, I think, say that such spirits are "of the past," but that they're timeless, beyond time.

4. Mary Hufford (ed.), *Conserving Culture: A New Discourse on Heritage*, published for the American Folklife Center, Library of Congress (University of Illinois Press, Urbana, 1994), 7.

5. Marshall Sahlins, *Waiting for Foucault* (Prickly Pear Press, Fort Worth, TX, 1993), 6–7.

6. *Hopi Tribe v. Federal Highway Administration*, Civ-98-1061-PCT-EHC, (D. Ariz. 1998).

7. Chief Justice John Marshall's Supreme Court articulated the "Marshall Trilogy" of findings on tribal sovereignty, the relationships between tribes and the U.S. government, and the interpretation of treaties that have been fundamental to the development of Indian law.

8. Lynne Sebastian, e-mail to the author, April 6, 2002.

9. Alan S. Downer and Alexandra Roberts, Traditional Cultural Properties, Cultural Resources Management, and Environmental Planning, in P. L. Parker (ed.), *Traditional Cultural Properties: What You Do and How We Think, CRM* Special Issue (National Park Service, Washington, D.C., 1993), 12.

10. Patricia Parker, *Keepers of the Treasures: Protecting Historic Properties and Cultural Traditions on Indian Lands,* a report on tribal preservation funding needs, submitted to Congress by the National Park Service (1990), 7.

11. Parris Butler, Fort Mohave, quoted in Parker, *Keepers of the Treasures,* 5.

12. Robert H. Winthrop, Contribution to Erlandson et al. 1998, *Current Anthropology* 39(4)(1998a):499.

13. To say nothing of boring.

14. Gordon Mohs, Sto:lo Sacred Ground, in David L. Carmichael, Jane Hubert, Brian Reeves, and Audhild Schanch (eds.), *Sacred Sites and Sacred Places* (Routledge, London, 1994), 202.

15. For details, as of late 2002, see www.wishtoyo.org/pdf/sacred-sites.pdf or www.sacredland.org/thomas_king.html (accessed April 15, 2003).

16. NEPA, Sec. 101(b)(4).

17. 40 CFR 1508.27(b)(3).

18. Thomas F. King, *Thinking about Cultural Resource Management: Essays from the Edge* (AltaMira, Walnut Creek, CA, 2002), 24–25, 60–62, 176–77.

19. The problem is not widely recognized, however, because most of the laws are simply ignored.

20. Steven Gregory, *Black Corona: Race and the Politics of Place in an Urban Community* (Princeton University Press, Princeton, NJ, 1999).

21. Rhoda H. Halperin, *Practicing Community: Class Culture and Power in an Urban Neighborhood* (University of Texas Press, Austin, 1998).

22. Randolph T. Hester, *Planning Neighbourhood Space with People,* 2nd ed. (Van Nostrand Reinhold, New York, 1997).

23. In Jake Page (ed.), *Sacred Lands of Indian America* (Abrams, New York, 2001).

24. Though see Jack D. Elliott Jr., Drinking from the Well of the Past: Historic Preservation and the "Sacred," *Historic Preservation Forum* 13(3) (1994):26–35; and Jack D. Elliott Jr., Toward a New and More Ancient Paradigm, 2002, available at www.radicalpreservation.com/ancientparadigm.htm (accessed April 24, 2003).

25. Winthrop, Contribution to Erlandson et al. 1998, 499.

26. No author, *Sacred Sites Pocket Directory, Mt. Shasta Area* (2002), Sacred Sites Directory, (530) 926–1678.

Bibliography

Abee, Albert
1982   Forest Management Plan, Umatilla Indian Reservation, Oregon. Ms.,
       Bureau of Indian Affairs, Umatilla Indian Agency, Mission, OR.

Abungu, George H. Okello
1994   Islam on the Kenyan Coast: An Overview of Kenyan Coastal Sacred Sites.
       In David L. Carmichael, Jane Hubert, Brian Reeves, and Audhild Schanch
       (eds.), *Sacred Sites and Sacred Places.* Routledge, London.

Advisory Council on Historic Preservation (ACHP)
1999   Comment to Secretary of the Interior Bruce Babbitt, pursuant to Section
       106 of the National Historic Preservation Act, regarding the impacts of the
       proposed Glamis Imperial Mine, Imperial County, California. Letter dated
       October 19, 1999. ACHP, Washington, D.C.
2001   Fees in the Section 106 Review Process. Information sheet. ACHP, Wash-
       ington, D.C.
2002   New Mexico and Arizona: Construction of Fence Lake Mine. Spring 2002
       Case Digest on ACHP website, www.achp.gov/casearchive/casesspg02NM-AZ.html.
       ACHP, Washington, D.C.

Alexander, Christopher
1979   *The Timeless Way of Building.* Oxford University Press, New York.

Alexander, Craig
1997   Protection of Indian Sacred Places and the Religious Accommodation Doc-
       trine. In the proceedings of *Sovereignty Symposium X: Circles of Life,* sponsored
       by the Oklahoma Supreme Court, the Oklahoma Indian Affairs Commission,
       and the Sovereignty Symposium, Inc., Tulsa, June 9–11, 1997, 92–103.

Altman, Irwin, and Setha M. Low (eds.)
1992   *Place Attachment.* Plenum, New York.

Anderson, Eugene N.
1996   *Ecologies of the Heart: Emotion, Belief, and the Environment.* Oxford Univer-
       sity Press, New York.

Anfinson, John
1997   Lake Superior Sunken Log Permits: Interviews with Red Cliff and Bad
       River Chippewa Bands. Memorandum for CEMVP-CO-R, U.S. Army Corps of
       Engineers, St. Paul District, July 16, 1997.

Anfinson, Scott
2002 National Register of Historic Places nomination for *Maka Yusota* ("Boiling Springs"), Savage, Minnesota. Minnesota Historical Society, St. Paul.

Anyinam, Charles
1999 Ethnomedicine, Sacred Spaces, and Ecosystem Preservation and Conservation in Africa. In Ezekiel Kalipeni and Paul T. Zeleza (eds.), *Sacred Spaces and Public Quarrels: African Cultural and Economic Landscapes*. Africa World Press, Asmara, 127–46.

Archibald, Robert A.
1999 *A Place to Remember: Using History to Build Community*. AltaMira, Walnut Creek, CA.

Bachelard, Gaston
1994 *The Poetics of Space*. Translated by Maria Jolas. Beacon, Uckfield, UK.

Barbeau, M.
1960 *Indian Days on the Western Prairies*. National Museum of Canada Bulletin 163.

Barrett, J.
1989 Time and Traditions: The Rituals of Everyday Life. In H. A. and A. Knape (eds.), *Bronze Age Studies*. Statens Historika Museum, Stockholm, 113–26.

Basso, Keith H.
1996 *Wisdom Sits in Places: Landscape and Language among the Western Apache*. University of New Mexico Press, Albuquerque.

Bean, Lowell J., Silvia Brakke Vane, and Jerry Schaefer
Forthcoming *Archaeological, Ethnographic, and Ethnohistoric Investigations at Tahquitz Canyon*. 3 vols. Cultural Systems Research, Inc., Ballena, Ramona, CA, publication anticipated ca. 2004.

Beebe, James
1995 Basic Concepts and Techniques of Rapid Appraisal. *Human Organization* 54:42–51.

Bestor, Theodore C.
1989 *Neighborhood Tokyo*. Stanford University Press, Palo Alto, CA.
1993 Rediscovering Shitamachi: Subculture, Class, and Tokyo's "Traditional" Urbanism. In Robert Rotenberg and Gary McDonogh (eds.), *The Cultural Meaning of Urban Space*. Bergin & Garvey, Westport, CT, 47–60.

Bloch, Maurice
1995 People into Places: Zafimiry Concepts of Clarity. In. E. Hirsch and M. O'Hanlon (eds.), *The Anthropology of Landscape*. Clarendon, Oxford, 63–77.

Bloomer, Kent C., and Charles W. Moore
1977 *Body, Memory, and Architecture*. Yale University Press, New Haven, CT.

Blundell, G.
1996 The Politics of Public Rock Art: A Comparative Critique of Rock Art Sites Open to the Public in South Africa and the United States of America. Master's thesis, University of the Witwatersrand, Johannesburg.

Bridgewater, Peter, and Theo Hooey
1995 Outstanding Cultural Landscapes in Australia, New Zealand, and the Pacific: The Footprint of Man in the Wilderness. In B. von Droste, H. Plachter, and M. Rössler (eds.), *Cultural Landscapes of Universal Value— Components of a Global Strategy.* Fischer, Jena, Germany, 162–69.

Brockington and Associates, Inc., and Ethnoscience, Inc.
1999 National Register of Historic Places Determination of Eligibility (Draft), Ocmulgee Old Fields Traditional Cultural Property. Ms., Georgia Department of Transportation, Atlanta.

Brodie, Fawn
1971 *No Man Knows My History: The Life of Joseph Smith.* Random House, New York.

Buggey, Susan
1999 *Approach to Aboriginal Cultural Landscapes.* Historic Sites and Monuments Board of Canada, Parks Canada, Ottawa.

Bureau of Land Management (BLM)/Northern Chumash Bear Clan
1997 Memorandum of Understanding for Summer Solstice Ceremony, Painted Rock (CA-SLO-79). Carrizo Plain, San Luis Obispo County, CA. Bakersfield Field Office, Bakersfield.

Burney, Michael S., Jeff Van Pelt, and Paul L. Minthorn
2002 Palàyniwaash: A Traditional Cultural Property of the Imatalamláma, Weyíiletpuu, Walúulapam, and Niimíipuu of the Southern Columbia Plateau of the Pacific Northwest. In M. S. Burney and Jeff Van Pelt (eds.), *It's about Time, It's about Them, It's about Us, Journal of Northwest Anthropology,* Memoir No. 6, Moscow, Idaho, pp. 44–47 (original 1993).

California Department of Transportation (Caltrans)
1999 Negative Declaration and Finding of No Significant Impact: Realignment of Route 101 Southbound Lanes Near Pinedate Rocks. Author, Sacramento.

Carmean, Kelli
2002 *Spider Woman Walks This Land: Traditional Cultural Properties and the Navajo Nation.* AltaMira, Walnut Creek, CA.

Carmichael, David L.
1994 Places of Power: Mescalero Apache Sacred Sites and Sensitive Areas. In David L. Carmichael, Jane Hubert, Brian Reeves, and Audhild Schanch (eds.), *Sacred Sites, Sacred Places.* Routledge, London.

Carmichael, David L., Jane Hubert, Brian Reeves, and Audhild Schanch (eds.)
1994 *Sacred Sites, Sacred Places.* World Archaeological Congress. Routledge, London.

Carroll, Charles
1993 Administering Federal Laws and Regulations Relating to Native Americans: Practical Processes and Paradoxes. In P. L. Parker (ed.), *Traditional Cultural Properties: What You Do and How We Think, CRM* Special Issue. National Park Service, Washington, D.C., 16–21.

Carsten, Janet, and Stephen Hugh-Jones (eds.)
 1995   *About the House: Lévi-Strauss and Beyond.* Cambridge University Press,
    Cambridge.

Carter, Thomas, and Carl Fleischhauer
 1988   *The Grouse Creek Cultural Study: Integrating Folklife and Historic Preservation
    Field Research.* American Folklife Center, Library of Congress, Washington, D.C.

Casey, Edward S.
 1996   *The Fate of Place: A Philosophical History.* University of California Press,
    Berkeley.
 1997   How to Get from Space to Place in a Fairly Short Stretch of Time: "Phe-
    nomenological Prolegomena." In Steven Field and Keith H. Basso (eds.), *Senses
    of Place.* School of American Research, Santa Fe, NM.

Chambers, R.
 1994   The Origins and Practice of Participatory Rural Appraisal. *World Develop-
    ment* 22(7):953–69.

Chaney, Ed, and Victor Martino
 1998   *Estimated Economic Damage to the Skokomish Indian Tribe from Unregulated
    Construction and Operation of the City of Tacoma's Cushman Hydroelectric Project,
    1926–1997.* Chinook Northwest Inc. and Martino and Associates, for
    Skokomish Indian Tribe, Shelton, WA.

Chapman, Fred
 1999   The Bighorn Medicine Wheel 1988–1999. *CRM* 22(3):5–10.

Chawla, Louise
 1992   Childhood Place Attachments. In Irwin Altman and Setha M. Low (eds.),
    Place Attachment. Plenum, New York, 63–86.

Cook, Carolyn D.
 2001   Papuan Gold: a Blessing or a Curse? The Case of the Amungme. *Cultural
    Survival Quarterly* 25(1):44–45.

Cooney, Gabriel
 1994   Sacred and Secular Neolithic Landscapes in Ireland. In David L.
    Carmichael, Jane Hubert, Brian Reeves, and Audhild Schanch (eds.), *Sacred
    Sites, Sacred Places.* Routledge, London.

Council on Environmental Quality
 1997   *Environmental Justice Guidance under the National Environmental Policy Act.*
    Council on Environmental Quality, Executive Office of the President, Washing-
    ton, D.C.

Creamer, Howard
 1983   Contacting Aboriginal Communities. In Graham Connah (ed.), *Australian
    Field Archaeology: A Guide to Techniques.* Australian Institute of Aboriginal Stud-
    ies, Canberra, chap. 2.

Cushman, David W.
 1993   When Worlds Collide: Indians, Archaeologists, and the Preservation of

Traditional Cultural Properties. In P. L. Parker (ed.), *Traditional Cultural Properties: What You Do and How We Think*, *CRM* Special Issue. National Park Service, Washington, D.C., 49–54.

Daniels, S. E., G. B. Walker, M. S. Carroll, and K. Blatner
1996   Collaborative Learning and Fire Recovery Planning. *Journal of Forestry* 94(4):4–9.

Dauenhauer, Nora M., and Richard Dauenhauer
1990   The Battle of Sitka, 1802 and 1804, from Tlingit, Russian, and Other Points of View. In R. A. Pierce (ed.), *Russia in North America: Proceedings of the 2nd International Conference on Russian America*. Limestone Press, Fairbanks, AK.

DeMunn, Michael, and Noah Buchanan (illustrator)
1997   *Places of Power*. Dawn, Nevada City, CA.

DeNatale, Douglas
1994   Federal and Neighborhood Notions of Place: Conflicts of Interest in Lowell, Massachusetts. In Mary Hufford (ed.), *Conserving Culture: A New Discourse on Heritage*. Published for the American Folklife Center, Library of Congress, by the University of Illinois Press, Urbana, 56–65.

Devereux, Paul
1990 *Places of Power: Measuring the Secret Energy of Ancient Sites*. Blandford, London.

Dobyns, H. F.
1951   Blunders with Bolsas. *Human Organization* 10:25–32.

Downer, Alan S.
1989   Anthropology, Historic Preservation and the Navajo: A Case Study in Cultural Resource Management on Indian Lands. Ph.D. diss. University of Missouri–Columbia.

Downer, Alan S., and Alexandra Roberts
1993   Traditional Cultural Properties, Cultural Resources Management, and Environmental Planning. In P. L. Parker (ed.), *Traditional Cultural Properties: What You Do and How We Think*, *CRM* Special Issue. National Park Service, Washington, D.C., 12–15.

Downer, Alan S., Alexandra Roberts, Harris Francis, and Klara B. Kelley
1994   Traditional History and Alternative Conceptions of the Past. In Mary Hufford (ed.), *Conserving Culture: A New Discourse on Heritage*. Published for the American Folklife Center, Library of Congress, by the University of Illinois Press, Urbana, 39–55.

Elliott, Jack D., Jr.
1994   Drinking from the Well of the Past: Historic Preservation and the "Sacred." *Historic Preservation Forum* 13(3):26–35. National Trust for Historic Preservation, Washington D.C.
2002   Toward a New and More Ancient Paradigm. Available at www. radicalpreservation.com/ancientparadigm.htm (accessed April 15, 2003).

Emery, Alan R., and Associates
1997   *Guidelines for Environmental Assessments and Traditional Knowledge.* Report from the Centre for Traditional Knowledge to the World Council of Indigenous People, Funded by the Canadian International Development Agency and Environment Canada.
2000   *Integrating Indigenous Knowledge in Project Planning and Implementation.* Partnership Publication of the International Labour Organization, the World Bank, the Canadian International Development Agency, and KIVU Nature Inc., Washington D.C., Quebec, and Nepean, Ontario.

Environmental Protection Agency (EPA)
1999   "Mission Possible." South Lawrence Trafficway: A National Environmental Policy Act Case Study. EPA Region 8, Environmental Justice Workshop, Denver.
2000   *Guide on Consultation and Collaboration with Indian Tribal Governments and the Public Participation of Indigenous Groups and Tribal Members in Environmental Decision Making.* EPA/300-R-00-009, November 2000, Environmental and Compliance Assurance Division (2201A), Washington, D.C.

Epperson, Terrence W.
1997   The Politics of "Race" and Cultural Identity at the African Burial Ground Excavations, New York City. *World Archaeological Bulletin* 7:108–17.

Erlandson, Jon M., and others
1998   The Making of Chumash Tradition: Replies to Haley and Wilcoxon. *Current Anthropology* 39(4):477–501.

European Union
1993   *Treaty on European Union* (The Maastricht Treaty) as amended.

Fatunmbi, Awo Fa'lokun
1996   Kekere Kan Ati Ase Ayie: The Ifa Concept of Work and the Power of the Earth. In J. Swan and R. Swan (eds.), *Dialogues with the Living Earth.* Quest, Madras, 62–74.

Feiss, Carl
1966   Our Lost Inheritance. In *With Heritage So Rich.* Report of a Special Committee on Historic Preservation under the auspices of the United States Conference of Mayors. Random House, New York, 129–38.

Ferguson, T. J., Kurt Dongoske, Leigh Jenkins, Mike Yeatts, and Eric Polingyouma
1993   Working Together: The Roles of Archaeology and Ethnohistory in Hopi Cultural Preservation. In P. L. Parker (ed.), *Traditional Cultural Properties: What You Do and How We Think, CRM* Special Issue. National Park Service, Washington, D.C., 27–37.

Field, Steven
1996   Waterfalls of Song: An Acoustemology of Place Resounding in Basavi, Papua New Guinea. In Steven Field and Keith H. Basso (eds.), *Senses of Place.* School of American Research Press, Santa Fe, NM.

Field, Steven, and Keith H. Basso (eds.)
1997   *Senses of Place*. School of American Research Press, Santa Fe, NM.

Fisher, Marc.
2002   "Smart Growth Meets Unthinking Resistance." *Washington Post*, August 4, C-1.

Fisher, Roger, William Ury, and Bruce Patton
1991   *Getting to Yes: Negotiating Agreement without Giving In*. 2nd ed. Penguin, New York.

Forest Service, USDA
1997   *Forest Service National Resource Book on American Indian and Alaska Native Relations*. USDA Forest Service, State and Private Forestry, Washington, D.C.
2000   *Report of the National Tribal Relations Program Task Force*. USDA Forest Service, Washington, D.C.

Fowler, Don D., and Marion W. Salter
Forthcoming   Archaeological Ethics in Context and Practice. In Christopher Chippendale and Herbert Maschner (eds.), *Handbook of Archaeological Theories*. AltaMira, Walnut Creek, CA.

Franklin, Robert, and Pamela Bunte
1994   When Sacred Land Is Sacred to Three Tribes: San Juan Paiute Sacred Sites and the Hopi-Navajo-Paiute Suit to Partition the Arizona Navajo Reservation. In David L. Carmichael, Jane Hubert, Brian Reeves, and Audhild Schanch (eds.), *Sacred Sites, Sacred Places*. Routledge, London.

Fredrickson, Vera-Mae, and David W. Peri
1984   *Mihilakawna and Makahmo Pomo: People of Lake Sonoma*. U.S. Army Corps of Engineers, Sacramento, CA.

Gallagher, Winifred
1994   *The Power of Place: How Our Surroundings Shape Our Thoughts, Emotions, and Actions*. HarperCollins, New York.

General Services Administration
1995   Memorandum of Agreement between the U.S. Department of Commerce, the U.S. General Services Administration, and the Southern Ute, the Ute Mountain Ute, the Northern Ute, the Jicarilla Apache, the Apache of Oklahoma, the Kowa of Oklahoma, the Comanche of Oklahoma, the Cheyenne and Arapaho of Oklahoma, the Pawnee of Oklahoma, the Eastern Shoshone, the Northern Arapah, the Northern Cheyenne, the Oglala Sioux, and the Rosebud Sioux, regarding The Department of Commerce Campus, Boulder, Colorado. GSA, Denver, November 21, 1995.

Gesler, Wilbert
1999   The Construction of Therapeutic Spaces. In Ezekiel Kalipeni and Paul T. Zeleza (eds.), *Sacred Spaces and Public Quarrels: African Cultural and Economic Landscapes*. Africa World Press, Asmara, 111–25.

Giles-Vernick, Tamara
 1996   Na lege ti guiriri (On the Road of History): Mapping Out the Past and Present in M'Bres Region, Central African Republic. *Ethnohistory* 43:2, 244–75.

Gough, Austin
 1995   Hindmarsh Island and the Politics of the Future. *Adelaide Review* (June 1995):8–9.

Greaves, Tom
 2002   The Amish of Lancaster County, Pennsylvania. In Tom Greaves (ed.), *Endangered Peoples of North America: Struggles to Survive and Thrive.* Greenwood, Westport, CT, chap. 10.

Greaves, Tom (ed.)
 2002   *Endangered Peoples of North America: Struggles to Survive and Thrive.* Greenwood, Westport, CT.

Gregory, Steven
 1998   *Black Corona: Race and the Politics of Place in an Urban Community.* Princeton University Press, Princeton, NJ.

Greiser, Sally T., and T. Weber Greiser
 1993   Two Views of the World. In P. L. Parker (ed.), *Traditional Cultural Properties: What You Do and How We Think,* CRM Special Issue. National Park Service, Washington, D.C., 9–11.

Grimm, Lydia T.
 1997   Sacred Lands and the Establishment Clause: Indian Religious Practices on Federal Lands. *Natural Resources and Environment* 12(1):19–24; 78. American Bar Association of Natural Resources, Energy, and Environmental Law.

Groth, Paul, and Todd W. Bressi (eds.)
 1997   *Understanding Ordinary Landscapes.* Yale University Press, New Haven, CT.

Guilliford, Andrew
 2000   *Sacred Objects and Sacred Places: Preserving Tribal Traditions.* University Press of Colorado, Boulder.

Guyette, Susan
 1996   *Planning for Balanced Development: A Guide for Native American and Rural Communities.* Clear Light, Santa Fe, NM.

Hadley, Judy Brunson
 1993   Traditional Cultural Properties: Pros, Cons, and Reality. In P. L. Parker (ed.), *Traditional Cultural Properties: What You Do and How We Think,* CRM Special Issue. National Park Service, Washington, D.C., 46–48.

Haines, Charles E.
 1997   The South Lawrence Trafficway: Environmental Justice Guidance for Native Americans. In Robert D. Bullard and Glenn S. Johnson (eds.), *Just Transportation.* New Society, Gabriola Island, British Columbia, Canada.

Haley, Brian, and Larry Wilcoxon
1997 The Making of Chumash Tradition. *Current Anthropology* 38(5):761–94.
1998 Reply. *Current Anthropology* 39(4):501–8.

Halmo, David B., Richard W. Stoffle, and Michael J. Evans
1998 Paitu Nanasuagaindu Pahonupi (Three Sacred Valleys): Cultural Significance of Gosiute, Paiute, and Ute Plants. *Human Organization* 52(2):142–50.

Halperin, Rhoda H.
1998 *Practicing Community: Class Culture and Power in an Urban Neighborhood.*
University of Texas Press, Austin.

Hannerz, Ulf
1969 *Soulside: Inquiries into Ghetto Culture and Community.* Almqvist & Wiksell,
Stockholm.

Hart, E. Richard
1993 The Fence Lake Mine Project: Archaeology as Traditional Cultural Property.
In P. L. Parker (ed.), *Traditional Cultural Properties: What You Do and How We
Think,* CRM Special Issue. National Park Service, Washington, D.C., 38–41.

Hayden, Dolores
1995 *The Power of Place: Urban Landscapes as Public History.* MIT Press, Cambridge.
1997 Urban Landscape History: The Sense of Place and the Politics of Space. In
P. Groth and T. Bressi (eds.), *Understanding Ordinary Landscapes.* Yale University Press, New Haven, CT.

Herr, Philip B.
1991 *Saving Place: A Guide and Report Card for Protecting Community Character.* Northeast Regional Office, National Trust for Historic Preservation,
Boston.

Hester, Randolph T.
1987 Subconscious Landscapes of the Heart. *Place* 2(3):10–22.
1997 *Planning Neighbourhood Space with People.* 2nd ed. Van Nostrand Reinhold,
New York.

Hill, Jonathan
1993 *Keepers of the Sacred Chants: The Poetics of Ritual Power in an Amazonian
Society.* University of Arizona Press, Tucson.

Hirsch, Eric, and Michael O'Hanlon (eds.)
1995 *The Anthropology of Landscape: Perspectives on Place and Space.* Clarendon,
Oxford.

Hiss, Tony
1991 *The Experience of Place.* Random House, New York.

Hockenberry, John
2002 *A River Out of Eden.* Anchor, New York.

Hostetler, John A.
1993 *Amish Society.* 4th ed. Johns Hopkins University Press, Baltimore.

Hubert, Jane
1994 Sacred Beliefs and Beliefs of Sacredness. In David L. Carmichael, Jane Hubert, Brian Reeves, and Audhild Schanch (eds.), *Sacred Sites, Sacred Places.* Routledge, London, chap. 1, 9–19.

Hufford, Mary
1986 *One Space, Many Places: Folklife and Land Use in New Jersey's Pinelands National Reserve.* American Folklife Center, Library of Congress, Washington, D.C.

Hufford, Mary (ed.)
1994 *Conserving Culture: A New Discourse on Heritage.* Published for the American Folklife Center, Library of Congress, by the University of Illinois Press, Urbana.

Humphrey, Caroline
1995 Chiefly and Shamanist Landscapes in Mongolia. In. E. Hirsch and M. O'Hanlon (eds.), *The Anthropology of Landscape.* Clarendon, Oxford, 135–62.

Interorganizational Committee on Guidelines and Principles for Social Impact Assessment
1993 Guidelines and Principles for Social Impact Assessment. *Environmental Impact Assessment Review* 15(1):11–43.

Jabbour, Alan
1996 The American Folklife Center: The First Twenty Years. *Folklife Center News* XVIII:1/2. Library of Congress, Washington, D.C.

Jackson, John Brinckerhoff
1994 *A Sense of Place, a Sense of Time.* Yale University Press, New Haven, CT.

Joseph, Frank (ed.)
1997 *Sacred Sites of the West: A Guide to Mystical Centers.* Hancock House, Surrey, B.C.

Kahn, Kenneth
1993 *Comrades and Chicken Farmers: The Story of a California Jewish Community.* Cornell University Press, Ithaca, NY.

Kalipeni, Ezekiel, and Paul T. Zeleza (eds.)
1999 *Sacred Spaces and Public Quarrels: African Cultural and Economic Landscapes.* Africa World Press, Asmara.

Kearns, Robin
1991 Place of Health in the Health of Place: The Case of the Hokianga Special Medical Area. *Social Science and Medicine* 33:519–30.

Kelley, Klara B., and Harris Francis
1994 *Navajo Sacred Places.* Indiana University Press, Bloomington.

King, Thomas F.
1993 Beyond Bulletin 38: Comments on the Traditional Cultural Properties Symposium. In P. L. Parker (ed.), *Traditional Cultural Properties: What You Do and How We Think*, CRM Special Issue. National Park Service, Washington, D.C., 60–64.
1994 Comments on Studies of Enola Hill. Ms. Supplied to Michael V. Nixon, attorney for plaintiffs in *Native Americans for Enola et al. v. U.S. Forest Service* CV 92-1534-JF, District of Oregon, Portland.
1998a *Cultural Resource Laws and Practice: An Introductory Guide*. AltaMira, Walnut Creek, CA.
1998b How the Archaeologists Stole Culture: A Gap in American Environmental Impact Assessment and What to Do about It. *Environmental Impact Assessment Review* 18(2):117–34.
1999a In the Light of the Megis: The Chequamegon Bay Area as a Traditional Cultural Property. Report to the Bad River and Red Cliff Bands of Lake Superior Tribe of Chippewa, Bad River and Bayfield, Wisconsin.
1999b Letter to Bruce Babbitt, Secretary of the Interior, regarding Glamis Imperial Mine and impacts on Quechan Trail of Dreams landscape, March 29.
2001 *Federal Planning and Historic Places: The Section 106 Process*. AltaMira, Walnut Creek, CA.
2002 *Thinking about Cultural Resource Management: Essays from the Edge*. AltaMira, Walnut Creek, CA.

King, T. F., R. Jacobson, K. R. Burns, and K. Spading
2001 *Amelia Earhart's Shoes: Is the Mystery Solved?* AltaMira, Walnut Creek, CA.

King, Thomas F., and Patricia L. Parker
1985 *Pisekin Nóómw Nóón Tonaachaw: Archaeology in the Tonaachaw Historic District, Moen Island*. Micronesian Archaeological Survey Report No. 18, Southern Illinois University at Carbondale Center for Archaeological Investigations Occasional Paper No. 3, Carbondale.

King, Thomas F., and Samuel Struelson
2002 Historic Preservation Laws. In *Encyclopedia of Life Support Systems*. EOLSS Publishers for UNESCO, Geneva.

Krantz, Grover
1999 *Bigfoot Sasquatch: Evidence*. Hancock House, New York.

Lattimore, Owen
1942 *Mongol Journeys*. Travel Book Club, London.

Layton, Robert
1995 Relating to the Country in the Western Desert. In E. Hirsch and M. O'Hanlon (eds.), *The Anthropology of Landscape: Perspectives on Place and Space*. Clarendon Press, Oxford, 210–31.
2001 Ethnographic Study and Symbolic Analysis. In David S. Whitley (ed.), *Handbook of Rock Art Research*. AltaMira, Walnut Creek, CA, 312–31.

Layton, Robert (ed.)
1989 *Who Needs the Past? Indigenous Values and Archaeology.* World Archaeological Congress, Routledge, London.

Layton, Robert, and Sarah Titchen
1995 Uluru: An Outstanding Australian Aboriginal Cultural Landscape. In B. von Droste, H. Plachter, and M. Rössler (eds.), *Cultural Landscapes of Universal Value—Components of a Global Strategy.* Fischer, Jena, Germany, 174–81.

Levine, Frances, and Thomas W. Marlan
1993 Documenting Traditional Cultural Properties in Non-Indian Communities. In P. L. Parker (ed.), *Traditional Cultural Properties: What You Do and How We Think, CRM* Special Issue. National Park Service, Washington, D.C., 55–64.

Lévi-Strauss, Claude
1983 *The Way of the Mask.* Trans. S. Modelski. Cape, London.

Liebow, Elliot
1967 *Tally's Corner: A Study of Negro Street Corner Men.* Little, Brown, New York.

Lin, Jan
1998 *Reconstructing Chinatown: Ethnic Enclave, Global Change.* University of Minnesota Press, Minneapolis.

Linklater, Joe, and Faith Gemmill
2001 Sacred Place Where Life Begins. *Washington Post,* January 17.

Little, Charles E.
2001 Postscript: Toward a Sacred Lands Policy Initiative. In Jake Page (ed.), *Sacred Lands of Indian America.* Abrams, New York, 131–35.

Longnecker, Julia G., Darby C. Stapp, and Angela M. Buck
2002 The Wanapum of Priest Rapids, Washington. In Tom Greaves (ed.), *Endangered Peoples of North America: Struggles to Survive and Thrive.* Greenwood, Westport, CT, chap. 8.

Loomis, Ormond H.
1983 *Cultural Conservation: The Protection of Cultural Heritage in the United States.* American Folklife Center, Library of Congress, Washington, D.C.

Loubser, Johannes
2001 Management Planning for Conservation. In David S. Whitley (ed.), *Handbook of Rock Art Research.* AltaMira, Walnut Creek, CA, 80–115.

Low, Setha
1994 Cultural Conservation of Place. In Mary Hufford (ed.), *Conserving Culture: A New Discourse on Heritage.* Published for the American Folklife Center, Library of Congress, by the University of Illinois Press, Urbana, 66–77.

Lynch, Kevin
1960 *The Image of the City.* MIT Press, Cambridge.
1981 *A Theory of Good City Form.* MIT Press, Cambridge (in later editions, *Good City Form*).

MacDonald, R. H.
1994   *The Language of Empire: Myths and Metaphors of Popular Imperialism 1880–1918*. Manchester University Press, Manchester.

Marcus, Clare Cooper
1992   Environmental Memories. In Irwin Altman and Setha M. Low (eds.), *Place Attachment*. Plenum, New York, 87–112.

Masse, W. Bruce, Laura A. Carter, and Gary F. Somers
1991   Waha'ula Heiau: The Regional and Symbolic Context of Hawai'i Island's "Red Mouth" Temple. *Asian Perspectives* 30(1):19–56.

Matunga, Hirini
1994   Waahi Tapu: Maori Sacred Sites. In David L. Carmichael, Jane Hubert, Brian Reeves, and Audhild Schanch (eds.), *Sacred Sites, Sacred Places*. Routledge, London.

McKeown, C. Timothy
1997   The Meaning of Consultation. *Common Ground* 2(3/4):16–21.

McLeod, Christopher (producer/director)
2001   *In the Light of Reverence*. Videotape. Sacred Lands Film Project, Earth Image Films, La Honda, CA.

Meersman, Tom
2000   Judge Dismisses Logging Group's Suit Alleging Religious Bias. *Minneapolis Star Tribune*.

Milnes, Gerald
1999   *Play of a Fiddle: Traditional Music, Dance, and Folklore in West Virginia*. University Press of Kentucky, Lexington.

Mohs, Gordon
1994   Sto:lo Sacred Ground. In David L. Carmichael, Jane Hubert, Brian Reeves, and Audhild Schanch (eds.), *Sacred Sites and Sacred Places*. Routledge, London.

Morphy, Howard
1995   Landscape and the Reproduction of the Ancestral Past. In E. Hirsch and M. O'Hanlon (eds.), *The Anthropology of Landscape: Perspectives on Place and Space*. Clarendon, Oxford, 184–209.

Morris, G., and G. Hamm
1992   Aboriginal Use of Traditional Rock Painting and Engraving sites as a Means of Cultural Revival. In G. K. Ward and L. A. Ward (eds.) *Management of Rock Imagery*. Occasional AURA Publication 9, Melbourne, 63–70.

Mulk, Inga-Marie
1994   Sacrificial Places and Their Meaning in Saami Society. In David L. Carmichael, Jane Hubert, Brian Reeves, and Audhild Schanch (eds.), *Sacred Sites, Sacred Places*. Routledge, London.

Mumah, Mary Maimo
1994   Sacred Sites in the Bamenda Grassfields of Cameroon: A Study of Sacred
    Sites in the *Nso Fondom*. In David L. Carmichael, Jane Hubert, Brian Reeves,
    and Audhild Schanch (eds.), *Sacred Sites, Sacred Places*. Routledge, London.

Mutoro, H. W.
1994   The Mijikenda Kaya as a Sacred Site. In David L. Carmichael, Jane
    Hubert, Brian Reeves, and Audhild Schanch (eds.), *Sacred Sites, Sacred Places*.
    Routledge, London.

Myers, Fred
1991   *Pintupi Country, Pintupi Self: Sentiment, Place, and Politics Among Western
    Desert Aborigines*. University of California Press, Berkeley.

National Register of Historic Places[1]
    n.d. 15   *How to Apply the National Register Criteria for Evaluation*. National Park
        Service, Washington, D.C.
    n.d. 16A   *How to Complete the National Register of Historic Places Registration
        Form*. National Park Service, Washington, D.C.
    n.d. 16B   *How to Complete the National Register of Historic Places Multiple Prop-
        erty Documentation Form*. National Park Service, Washington, D.C.
    n.d. 30   *Guidelines for Evaluating and Documenting Rural Historic
        Landscapes*. National Park Service, Washington, D.C. (published *after*
        Bulletin 38).
    n.d. 38   *Guidelines for Evaluating and Documenting Traditional Cultural Properties*.
        National Park Service, Washington, D.C. (sometimes [accurately] dated 1990).
    n.d. 42   *Guidelines for Identifying, Evaluating, and Registering Historic Mining
        Properties*. National Park Service, Washington, D.C. (dated 1992).
    1995   *Through the Generations: Identifying and Protecting Traditional Cultural Places*.
        Videotape, National Park Service, in collaboration with the Natural Resources Con-
        servation Service and Advisory Council on Historic Preservation, Washington, D.C.

Nesper, Larry, Anna Willow, and Thomas F. King
2002   *The Mushgigagamongsebe District: A Traditional Cultural Landscape of the
    Sokaogon Ojibwe Community*. Report submitted to the Corps of Engineers, St.
    Paul District, by the Mole Lake Sokaogon Community of Great Lakes
    Chippewa Indians, Crandon, WI.

Neumann, Thomas W., and Robert M. Sanford
2001   *Practicing Archaeology: A Training Manual for Cultural Resources Archaeology*.
    AltaMira, Walnut Creek, CA.

No Author
2002   *Sacred Sites Pocket Directory, Mt. Shasta Area*. Sacred Sites Directory, (530)
    926-1678.

Occhipinti, Frank D.
2002   American Indian Sacred Sites and the National Historic Preservation Act:
    The Enola Hill Case. *Journal of Northwest Anthropology* 36(1):3–50.

O'Faircheallaigh, Ciaran
1995   *Making Social Impact Assessment Count: A Negotiation-based Approach for Indigenous Peoples.* Aboriginal Politics and Public Sector Management Research Paper No. 3, Centre for Australian Public Sector Management, Griffith University, Brisbane.

O'Reilly, Sean, James O'Reilly, and Tim O'Reilly (eds.)
2002   *The Road Within: True Stories of Transformation and the Soul.* Travellers' Tales, San Francisco.

Organization of African Unity
1981   African Charter on Human and Peoples' Rights. www.umn.edu/humanrts/instree/zlafchar.html

Othole, Andrew L., and Roger Anyon
1993   A Tribal Perspective on Traditional Cultural Property Consultation. In P. L. Parker (ed.), *Traditional Cultural Properties: What You Do and How We Think,* CRM Special Issue. National Park Service, Washington, D.C., 42–45.

Ovsyannikov, O. V., and N. M. Terebikhin
1994   Sacred Space in the Culture of the Arctic Regions. In David L. Carmichael, Jane Hubert, Brian Reeves, and Audhild Schanch (eds.), *Sacred Sites, Sacred Places.* Routledge, London.

Pacific Southwest Region, USDA Forest Service
1994   *Sacred Places.* Videotape, Pacific Southwest Region, USDA Forest Service, Vallejo, CA.
1995a   *Working Together: Tribal Governments and the Forest Service.* Videotape, Pacific Southwest Region, USDA Forest Service, Vallejo, CA.
1995b   *Perspectives on Working Together.* Videotape, Pacific Southwest Region, USDA Forest Service, Vallejo, CA.
2000   *Working Together: California Indians and the Forest Service. Accomplishment Report 2000.* Pacific Southwest Region, USDA Forest Service, Vallejo, CA.

Page, Jake (ed.)
2001   *Sacred Lands of Indian America.* Abrams, New York.

Parker, Patricia
1990   *Keepers of the Treasures: Protecting Historic Properties and Cultural Traditions on Indian Lands.* A Report on Tribal Preservation Funding Needs, submitted to Congress by the National Park Service.

Parker, Patricia (ed.)
1993   *Traditional Cultural Properties: What You Do and How We Think,* CRM Special Issue. National Park Service, Washington, D.C.

Parker, Patricia, and Thomas F. King
1987   Intercultural Mediation at Truk International Airport. In *Anthropological Praxis: Translating Knowledge into Action.* R. W. Wulff and S. J. Fiske (eds.) Washington Association of Professional Anthropologists, Westview, Boulder, CO.

Partners for Livable Communities
2000   *The Livable City: Revitalizing Urban Communities.* McGraw-Hill, New York.

Pellow, Deborah
1992   Spaces That Teach: Attachment to the African Compound. In R. Altman and S. Low (eds.), *Place Attachment.* Plenum, New York, 187–210.

Pettis, Chuck
1999   *Secrets of Sacred Space.* Llewellyn, St. Paul, MN.

Pigniolo, Andrew R., Jackson Underwood, and James H. Cleland
1996   *Where Trails Cross: Cultural Resources Inventory and Evaluation for the Imperial Project, Imperial County, California.* Environmental Management Associates, Inc. Appendix L to Draft Environmental Impact Statement/Environmental Impact Report, Imperial Project, Imperial County, CA; U.S. Department of the Interior Bureau of Land Management and County of Imperial Planning/Building Department, El Centro, CA.

Prendergast, Ellen
1998   Perceptions of the National Register Nomination Process: A Case Study at *Chelhtenem,* Point Roberts, Washington. Master's thesis, Western Washington University.

Price, Nichol
1994   Tourism and the Bighorn Medicine Wheel: How Multiple Use Does Not Work for Sacred Land Sites. In David L. Carmichael, Jane Hubert, Brian Reeves, and Audhild Schanch (eds.), *Sacred Sites, Sacred Places.* Routledge, London.

Quigg, Michael J., Charles D. Frederick, and Dorothy Lippert
1996   *Archaeology and Native American Religion at the Leon River Medicine Wheel.* U.S. Army, Fort Hood, Archaeological Resource Management Series Research Report No. 33, Fort Hood, TX.

Rapoport, Amos
1982   *The Meaning of the Built Environment: A Nonverbal Communication Approach.* Sage, Beverly Hills.

Rappaport, Joanne
1989   Geography and Historical Understanding in Indigenous Colombia. In R. Layton (ed.), *Who Needs the Past? Indigenous Values and Archaeology.* Routledge, London, 84–94.

Reap, James
2000   Information for Ghana Project. Request for advice, with proposed project description, forwarded to ACRA-L by Sue Henry Renaud, National Park Service, November 15, 2000.

Reeves, Brian
1994   Ninaistàkis—The Nitsatapii's Sacred Mountain: Traditional Native Religious Activities and Land Use/Tourism. In David L. Carmichael, Jane Hubert, Brian Reeves, and Audhild Schanch (eds.), *Sacred Sites, Sacred Places.* Routledge, London, 265–95.

Ritchie, David
1994 Principles and Practice of Site Protection Laws in Australia. In David L. Carmichael, Jane Hubert, Brian Reeves, and Audhild Schanch (eds.), *Sacred Sites, Sacred Places.* Routledge, London.

Rodman, Margaret
1993 Beyond Built Form and Culture in the Anthropological Study of Residential Community Spaces. In R. Rotenberg and G. McDonogh (eds.), *The Cultural Meaning of Urban Space.* Bergin & Garvey, Westport, CT.

Rosengarten, Dale
1994 "Sweetgrass Is Gold": Natural Resources, Conservation Policy, and African-American Basketry. In Mary Hufford (ed.), *Conserving Culture: A New Discourse on Heritage.* Published for the American Folklife Center, Library of Congress, by the University of Illinois Press, Urbana, 152–166.

Rotenberg, Robert, and Gary McDonogh (eds.)
1991 *The Cultural Meaning of Urban Space.* Bergin & Garvey, Westport, CT.

Russell, J. C., C. M. Woods, and J. Underwood
2002 *Imperial Sand Dunes as a Native American Cultural Landscape.* EDAW, Inc. for Bureau of Land Management California State Office, Sacramento.

Russo, Kurt
2002 The Lummi in Washington State. In Tom Greaves (ed.), *Endangered Peoples of North America: Struggles to Survive and Thrive.* Greenwood, Westport, CT, chap. 6.

Sahlins, Marshall
1993 *Waiting for Foucault.* Prickly Pear Press, Fort Worth, TX.

Santos-Granero, Fernando
1998 Writing History into the Landscape: Space, Myth, and Ritual in Contemporary Amazonia. *American Ethnologist* 25(2):128–48, American Anthropological Association, Washington, D.C.

Schensul, Stephen L., Jean J. Schensul, and Margaret D. LeCompte
1999 *Essential Ethnographic Methods.* Vol. 2 of the Ethnographer's Toolkit. AltaMira, Walnut Creek, CA.

Sebastian, Lynne
1993 Protecting Traditional Cultural Properties through the Section 106 Process. In P. L. Parker (ed.), *Traditional Cultural Properties: What You Do and How We Think, CRM* Special Issue. National Park Service, Washington, D.C., 22–26.

Seltz, Ruth H.
1991 *Amish Ways.* RB Books, Harrisburg, PA.

Selwyn, Tom
1995 Landscapes of Liberation and Imprisonment: Towards an Anthropology of the Israeli Landscape. In. E. Hirsch and M. O'Hanlon (eds.), *The Anthropology of Landscape.* Clarendon, Oxford, 114–34.

Serageldin, Ismail, Ephim Shluger, and Joan Martin-Brown (eds.)
2001   *Historic Cities and Sacred Sites: Cultural Roots for Urban Futures.* World Bank, Washington, D.C.

Shigekuni, Vincent R.
2000   The Kaho'olawe Use Plan: Non-traditional Planning for Traditional Use. *CRM* 23(7):36–40.

Sole, T., and K. Woods
1993   Protection of Indigenous Sacred Sites: The New Zealand Thesis. In J. Birckhead, T. de Lacy, and L. Smith (eds.), *Aboriginal Involvement in Parks and Protected Areas.* Aboriginal Studies Press, Canberra.

Sommers, Lauri K., Yvonne R. Lockwood, Marsha MacDowell, and Richard W. Stoffle
1994   Folklife Assessment in the Michigan Low-Level Radioactive Waste Siting Process. In Mary Hufford (ed.), *Conserving Culture: A New Discourse on Heritage.* Published for the American Folklife Center, Library of Congress, by the University of Illinois Press, Urbana, 198–214.

Stapp, Darby C., and Michael S. Burney
2002   *Tribal Cultural Resource Management: The Full Circle to Stewardship.* AltaMira, Walnut Creek, CA.

Staub, Shalom
1994   Cultural Conservation and Economic Recovery Planning: The Pennsylvania Heritage Parks Program. In Mary Hufford (ed.), *Conserving Culture: A New Discourse on Heritage.* Published for the American Folklife Center, Library of Congress, by the University of Illinois Press, Urbana, 229–44.

Stein, Activa Benzinberg
2001   Preserving the Cultural Significance of Landscapes. In Ismail Serageldin, Ephim Shluger, and Joan Martin-Brown (eds.), *Historic Cities and Sacred Sites: Cultural Roots for Urban Futures.* World Bank, Washington, D.C., 261–66.

Stoffle, Richard W. (ed.)
1990   *Cultural and Paleontological Effects of Siting a Low-Level Radioactive Waste Facility in Michigan, Candidate Area Analysis.* Institute for Social Research, University of Michigan, Ann Arbor.

Stoffle, Richard W., and Michael J. Evans
1990   Holistic Conservation and Cultural Triage: American Indian Perspectives on Cultural Resources. *Human Organization* 49(2): 91–99.

Stoffle, Richard W., David B. Halmo, John E. Olmsted, and Michael J. Evans
1990   *Native American Cultural Resource Studies at Yucca Mountain, Nevada.* Institute for Social Research, University of Michigan, Ann Arbor.

Stoffle, Richard W., David B. Halmo, Michael J. Evans, and Diane E. Austin
1993   *Piapaxa 'Uipi (Big River Canyon): Ethnographic Resource Inventory and Assessment for Colorado River Corridor, Glen Canyon National Recreation*

Area, Utah and Arizona, and Grand Canyon National Park, Arizona. Bureau of Applied Research in Anthropology, University of Arizona, Tucson.

Stoffle, Richard W., Michael J. Evans, M. Nieves Zedeño, Brent W. Stoffle, and Cindy J. Kesel
1994   *American Indians and Fajada Butte: Ethnographic Overview and Assessment for Fajada Butte and Traditional (Ethnobotanical) Use Study for Chaco Culture National Historical Park, New Mexico.* Report to New Mexico State Historic Preservation Officer and Regional Ethnographer, Southwestern Regional Office, National Park Service, by the Bureau of Applied Research in Anthropology, University of Arizona, Tucson.

Stokes, Samuel N., A. Elizabeth Watson, Genevieve P. Keller, and J. Timothy Keller
1989   *Saving America's Countryside: A Guide to Rural Conservation.* National Trust for Historic Preservation, Johns Hopkins University Press, Baltimore.

Sullivan, Sharon
1995   *Cultural Conservation: Towards a National Approach.* Special Australian Heritage Publication Series Number 9, Australian Heritage Commission, Australian Government Publishing Service, Canberra.

Swan, James
1996   Working with the Spirit of Place. In James Swan and Roberta Swan (eds.), *Dialogues with the Living Earth.* Quest Books; Theosophical Publishing House, Wheaton, IL.

Swan, James, and Roberta Swan (eds.)
1996   *Dialogues With the Living Earth.* Quest Books; Theosophical Publishing House, Wheaton, IL.

Taplin, D. H., S. Scheld, and S. M. Low
2000   Rapid Ethnographic Assessment in Urban Parks: A Case Study of Independence National Historical Park. *Human Organization* 61:80–93.

Tatar, Magdelena
1984   Nature-Protecting Taboos of the Mongols. In E. Ligeti (ed.), *Tibetan and Buddhist Studies Commemorating the 200th Anniversary of the Birth of Alexander Csoma de Koros.* Akademia Kiado, Budapest.

Tauhindali
1979   *Sanusa Stopped the Rain.* Charlatien, Charmichael, CA.

Theodoratus, Dorothea, and Frank LaPena
1994   Wintu Sacred Geography of Northern California. In David L. Carmichael, Jane Hubert, Brian Reeves, and Audhild Schanch (eds.), *Sacred Sites, Sacred Places.* Routledge, London.

Thomas, Stephen D.
1987   *The Last Navigator.* Ballantine, New York.

Thompson, Gail
1996 Cultural Resources Mitigation and Management Plan for Snoqualmie Falls Project, FERC No. 2493. Historical Research Associates, Inc., for Puget Sound Power and Light Company. Seattle, WA.

Tonetti, Al
1998 Civil War Battlefields as TCPs. E-mail to author, November 12.

Toren, Christina
1995 Seeing the Ancestral Sites: Transformations in Fijian Notions of the Land. In E. Hirsch and M. O'Hanlon (eds.), *The Anthropology of Landscape*. Clarendon, Oxford, 163–83.

Toussaint, Sandy (ed.)
2001 Practicing Anthropology in Australia. *Practicing Anthropology* 23:1, Society for Applied Anthropology.

Trope, Jack F.
1995 Existing Federal Law and the Protection of Sacred Sites: Possibilities and Limitations. *Cultural Survival* 19(4):30–35.

Tuan, Yi-Fu
1977 *Space and Place: The Perspective of Experience*. University of Minnesota Press, Minneapolis.

Tunnard, Christopher
1966 Landmarks of Beauty and History. In *With Heritage So Rich*. Report of a Special Committee on Historic Preservation under the auspices of the United States Conference of Mayors. Random House, New York, 29–34.

United Nations Educational, Scientific, and Cultural Organization (UNESCO)
1962 *Recommendation Concerning the Safeguarding of the Beauty and Character of Landscapes and Sites*. Adopted by the General Conference at its twelfth session, Paris, December 11, 1962.
1972 *Recommendation Concerning the Protection, at National Level, of the Cultural and Natural Heritage*. Adopted by the General Conference at its seventeenth session, Paris, November 16, 1972.
1976 *Recommendation Concerning the Safeguarding and Contemporary Role of Historic Areas*. Adopted by the General Conference, November 26, 1976.
1996 *World Heritage Convention Operational Guidelines*. UNESCO, Paris.
1998 *First Framework Programme in Support of Culture (2000–2004)*, Commission of the European Communities, Brussels.

Ury, William
1993 *Getting Past No: Negotiating Your Way from Confrontation to Cooperation*. Penguin, New York.

U.S. Army Corps of Engineers
1989 *The Environment and the Engineers at Lake Sonoma*. Videotape, San Francisco District, Corps of Engineers. Interface Video Services, Washington, D.C.

U.S. Conference of Mayors
1966 *With Heritage So Rich.* Report of a Special Committee on Historic Preservation under the auspices of the United States Conference of Mayors. Random
House, New York.

van Binsbergen, W. H. J.
1978 Explorations into the History and Sociology of Territorial Cults in Zambia.
In J. M. Schoffeleers (ed.), *Guardians of the Land: Essays on Central African
Territorial Cults.* Mambo, Gwelo, 47–88.

Vanclay, Frank
2002 Conceptualizing Social Impacts. *Environmental Impact Assessment Review*
22:183–211.

Vannette, Walter, and Alison Feary
1981 Navajo Sacred Places and Resource Use in and near the Coconino, Kaibab,
and Apache Sitgreaves National Forests. Confidential ms. on file, Coconino
National Forest, Flagstaff AZ.

von Droste, B., H. Plachter, and M. Rössler (eds.)
1995 *Cultural Landscapes of Universal Value—Components of a Global Strategy.*
Fischer, Jena, Germany.

Walter, E. V.
1988 *Placeways: A Theory of the Human Environment.* University of North Carolina Press, Chapel Hill.

Walton, Beth E.
1992 Enola Hill Project Area Cultural Resources. Ms., Mount Hood National
Forest, Gresham, OR.

Wandibba, Simiyu
1994 Bukusu Sacred Places. In David L. Carmichael, Jane Hubert, Brian Reeves,
and Audhild Schanch (eds.), *Sacred Sites, Sacred Places.* Routledge, London.

Washington Water Power [now Avista Corp.]
1998 Clark Fork Heritage Resource Program. Attachment 1 to
Programmatic Agreement Among the Kootenai Tribe of Idaho, Confederated
Salish and Kootenai Tribes of the Flathead Reservation, Coeur d'Alene
Tribe, Kalispel Tribe, the Federal Energy Regulatory Commission, the
Forest Service, Washington Water Power, the Advisory Council on Historic
Preservation, Idaho State Historic Preservation Office and Montana State
Historic Preservation Office for the Clark Fork Heritage Resource Program.

Weiner, James
1991 *The Empty Place: Poetry, Space, and Being among the Foi of Papua New
Guinea.* University of Indiana Press, Bloomington.
1994 Anthropologists, Historians, and the Secret of Social Knowledge. *Anthropology Today* 11(5):3–7.

Wharton, Roger
1996 But You, O Bethlehem of Ephrathah: Bethlehem as a Sacred Place. In James Swan and Roberta Swan (eds.), *Dialogues with the Living Earth*. Quest Books; Theosophical Publishing House, Wheaton, IL.

Whitehill, Walter Muir
1966 The Right of Cities to Be Beautiful. In *With Heritage So Rich*. Report of a Special Committee on Historic Preservation under the auspices of the United States Conference of Mayors. Random House, New York, 45–56.

Wilkinson, Charles F.
1988 *American Indians, Time, and the Law: Native Societies in a Modern Constitutional Democracy*. Yale University Press, New Haven, CT.

Williams, Nancy M., and Daymbalipu Mununggurr
1989 Understanding Yolngu Signs of the Past. In R. Layton (ed.), *Who Needs the Past? Indigenous Values and Archaeology*. Routledge, London, 70–82.

Winter, Joseph C.
1993 Navajo Sacred Sites and the Transwestern Pipeline Expansion Project. In *Papers from the Third, Fourth, and Sixth Navajo Studies Conferences*. Navajo Nation Historic Preservation Department, Window Rock, AZ, 65–109.

Winthrop, Robert H.
1991 Enola Hill Ethnographic Reconnaissance. Ms., Mount Hood National Forest, Gresham, OR.
1998a Contribution to Erlandson et al. 1998. *Current Anthropology* 39(4):496–99.
1998b Tradition, Authenticity, and Dislocation: Some Dilemmas of Traditional Cultural Property Studies. *Practicing Anthropology* 20(3):25–27.

Wood, John J., and Walter M. Vannette
1979 A Preliminary Assessment of the Significance of Navajo Sacred Places in the Vicinity of Big Mountain, Arizona. Ms., Bureau of Indian Affairs, Navajo Area Office, Window Rock, AZ.

World Bank
2000 Policies, procedures, and operational directions for environmental assessment. Available at http://lnweb18.worldbank.org/ESSD/essdext.nsf/47ByDocName/EnvironmentalAssessment (accessed April 15, 2003).

Zellmer, Sandra B.
2002 Sustaining Geographies of Hope: Cultural Resources on Public Lands. *University of Colorado Law Review* 73(2):413–519.

Zuidema, R. Tom
1989 Reyes y Guerreros. *Ensayos de Cultura Andina*. Fomciencis, Lima.

Judicial Opinions Cited

Aluli v. Brown, 437 F.Supp. 602 (D. Haw. 1977)

Apache Survival Coalition v. United States, 21 F.3d 895 (9th Cir. 1994)

Apache Survival Coalition v. United States (Apache Survival II), 118 F.3d 663 (9th Cir. 1997)

Attakai v. United States, 746 F.Supp. 1395 (D. Ariz. 1990)

Badoni v. Higginson, 638 F.2d, 172 (10th Cir. 1980)

Bear Lodge Multiple Use Association v. Bruce Babbitt, et al., No. 96-CV-063-D (D. Wyo. 1996).

Bear Lodge Multiple Use Association v. Bruce Babbitt, et al., 175 F.3d, 814 (10th Cir. 1999)

Colorado River Indian Tribes v. Marsh, 605 F.Supp. 1425 (C.D. Cal. 1985)

El Rancho La Comunidad v. United States, No. 90-113 (D.N.M. May 21, 1991)

Hoonah Indian Association v. Morrison, 170 F.3D 1223 (9th Cir. 1994)

Hopi Tribe v. Federal Highway Administration, Civ-98-1061-PCT-EHC, D. Ariz. (1998)

Lyng v. Northwest Indian Cemetery Protective Association. 485 U.S. 439, 455 (1987)

Mabo and Ors v. the State of Queensland, 175 CLR1, Australia (1992)

Metropolitan Edison Co. v. People Against Nuclear Energy. 460 U.S. 766, 103 S.Ct. 1556 (1983)

Morongo Band of Mission Indians v. Federal Aviation Administration, 161 F.3d 569 (9th Cir. 1998)

Muckleshoot Indian Tribe v. United States Forest Service, 177 F.3d 800 (9th Cir. 1999)

National Mining Association v. Slater, 167 F.Supp. 2d 265, 296 (2001)

National Trust for Historic Preservation v. Blanck, Civ. Action No. 94-1091 (PLF) (D.D.C. Sep 13, 1996)

Native Americans for Enola v. United States Forest Service, 832 F.Supp. 297 (D. Or. 1993)

Northwest Indian Cemetery Protective Assn. v. Peterson, 565 F.Supp. 586 (N.D. Cal 1983); 764 F.2^d 581 (9th Cir. 1985)

Pueblo of Sandia v. United States, 50 F.3d 856 (10th Cir. 1995)

Thomasine Ross, et al v. Geiger et al, 972 F.Supp. 552, (D. Kan. 1997)

Warm Springs Dam Task Force v. Gribble, 378 F.Supp. 240 (N.D. Cal 1974)

Wilson v. Block, 708 F.2d 735 (D.C. Cir.)

Wyoming Sawmills, Inc. v. United States Forest Service (Complaint), No. 99-CV-31J (D. Wyo., Feb. 16, 1999)

Laws and Executive Orders Cited

American Folklife Preservation Act, 20 U.S.C. 2101-07

American Indian Religious Freedom Act (AIRFA), aka *American Indian Freedom of Religion Act,* 42 U.S.C. 1996

Federal Advisory Committees Act (FACA), 5 U.S.C. App. 1

Indian Self Determination and Education Act, 42 U.S.C. 450-458

National Environmental Policy Act (NEPA), 42 U.S.C. 4321-47

National Historic Preservation Act (NHPA), 16 U.S.C. 470

Native American Graves Protection and Repatriation Act (NAGPRA), 25 U.S.C. 3001-13

Native Title Act 1993, No. 110–1993 as amended (Australia)

Executive Order 11593: *Protection and Enhancement of the Cultural Environment.* May 15, 1971

Executive Order 12898: *Federal Actions to Address Environmental Justice in Minority Populations and Low-Income Populations.* February 11, 1994

Executive Order 13007: *Indian Sacred Sites.* May 26, 1996

Executive Order 13175: *Consultation and Coordination with Indian Tribal Governments.* November 9, 2000

Regulations Cited

36 CFR 60: *National Register of Historic Places.* National Park Service

36 CFR 800: *Preservation of Historic Properties.* Advisory Council on Historic Preservation

40 CFR 1500-1508: *Implementing the Procedural Provisions of the National Environmental Policy Act.* Council on Environmental Quality

41 CFR 101-6.10: *Federal Advisory Committee Management.* General Services Administration.

Note

1. The National Register does not routinely put dates on its publications, so as a convention I use "n.d." followed by the bulletin number. Unfortunately, the register no longer very consistently gives its bulletins numbers, either.

Index

About the Author

TOM King holds a Ph.D. in anthropology from the University of California, Riverside, and has worked as a university archeologist and private contractor in California, as an archaeologist with the U.S. National Park Service, as consultant in archaeology and historic preservation to the High Commissioner of the Trust Territory of the Pacific Islands, and as an executive with the U.S. Advisory Council on Historic Preservation. He left government in 1989 and now consults in cultural resource management (CRM), historic preservation, and environmental dispute resolution. He teaches short courses in CRM and historic preservation for the National Preservation Institute (www.npi.org) and writes extensively on CRM topics.

King is the author of three textbooks published by AltaMira Press—*Cultural Resource Laws and Practice: An Introductory Guide* (1998), *Federal Planning and Historic Places: The Section 106 Process* (2001), and *Thinking about Cultural Resource Management: Essays from the Edge* (2002)—as well as an award-winning book coauthored with R. Jacobson, K. R. Burns, and K. Spading titled *Amelia Earhart's Shoes: Is the Mystery Solved?* (AltaMira, 2001) on the archaeological pursuit of Amelia Earhart—his recreational activity with The International Group for Historic Aircraft Recovery (TIGHAR; see www.tighar.org). He has conducted projects to identify and manage traditional cultural properties in California, Micronesia, and Wisconsin.

King welcomes comments on his books and other writings (as well as consulting business and teaching or speaking opportunities); he can be contacted at tfking106@aol.com.